AF713061

SECURITY SECTOR REFORM IN CONSTITUTIONAL TRANSITIONS

Security Sector Reform in Constitutional Transitions

Edited by

ZOLTAN BARANY, SUMIT BISARYA,
SUJIT CHOUDHRY,
AND
RICHARD STACEY

OXFORD
UNIVERSITY PRESS

OXFORD
UNIVERSITY PRESS

Great Clarendon Street, Oxford, OX2 6DP,
United Kingdom

Oxford University Press is a department of the University of Oxford.
It furthers the University's objective of excellence in research, scholarship,
and education by publishing worldwide. Oxford is a registered trade mark of
Oxford University Press in the UK and in certain other countries

© The several contributors 2019

The moral rights of the authors have been asserted

First Edition published in 2019

All rights reserved. No part of this publication may be reproduced, stored in a retrieval system, or transmitted, in any form or by any means, without the prior permission in writing of Oxford University Press, or as expressly permitted by law, by licence or under terms agreed with the appropriate reprographics rights organization. Enquiries concerning reproduction outside the scope of the above should be sent to the Rights Department, Oxford University Press, at the address above

You must not circulate this work in any other form
and you must impose this same condition on any acquirer

Crown copyright material is reproduced under Class Licence
Number C01P0000148 with the permission of OPSI
and the Queen's Printer for Scotland

Published in the United States of America by Oxford University Press
198 Madison Avenue, New York, NY 10016, United States of America

British Library Cataloguing in Publication Data
Data available

Library of Congress Control Number: 2019946251

ISBN 978–0–19–884894–3

Links to third party websites are provided by Oxford in good faith and
for information only. Oxford disclaims any responsibility for the materials
contained in any third party website referenced in this work.

Acknowledgements

We have accumulated many debts in the preparation of this volume.

The origins of this project extend back to November 2011 when Sujit Choudhry travelled to the Arab region to identify topics where democratization processes could benefit from comparative knowledge, as part of the preparatory work for the launch of the Center for Constitutional Transitions. The relationship between security sector reform and constitutional transitions emerged as an important theme across the region. Sumit Bisarya had also identified the relationship between security sector reform and constitutional transitions to be of great interest at International IDEA, because the issue had arisen in many of the processes it was engaged in. We joined forces and recruited Zoltan Barany and Richard Stacey to our team.

This project arises from a close partnership between the worlds of scholarship and practice. It furthers an important research agenda at the intersection of law and political science, captures the knowledge of leading experts with first-hand experiences of addressing security sector reform in the context of constitutional transitions in many countries, and abstracts general lessons from those experiences that have practical relevance.

We were fortunate to recruit to this project leading international experts on security sector reform and constitutional transitions: Zaid al-Ali, Kwesi Aning, Philippe Droz-Vincent, Sandra Elena, Andrew Ellis, Ernest Lartey, Christina Murray, Lawrence Gitonga Mwongera, Gonzalo García Pino, Julia Pomares, Narcís Serra, and Agus Widjojo. We learned much from them, both during our meeting, and also during the lengthy editorial process.

The Embassy of Canada in The Hague generously hosted our meeting of project authors in April 2014. Ambassador James Lambert and Ann Flanagan-Whalen deserve our deepest thanks for making this event possible.

During the 2017–18 academic year, Sujit Choudhry was in residence at the Center for Global Constitutionalism at the WZB Social Science Center, where its vibrant and interdisciplinary intellectual life provided an ideal environment for working on this project. He thanks Mattias Kumm for his generous hospitality. Carlos Herrera Vacaflor provided valuable research assistance and helped the editors navigate key Spanish-language sources in Argentina and Chile.

As we reached the final stages of the project, we could not have completed this manuscript without the superb support of Jem Langworthy, who led the copyediting process. Finally, we would like to thank Jamie Berezin, Alex Flach, and John Louth at Oxford University Press for agreeing to enter into a unique arrangement whereby pre-publication versions of the chapters are available online to ensure their availability to as broad a global audience as possible.

A policy manual based on the completed project will be published in 2020, jointly by the Center for Constitutional Transitions and International IDEA, and will be made available online.

Contents

PART III POST-AUTHORITARIAN REFORM: RUPTURES, CONFLICT, AND MANAGED TRANSITIONS

Table of Cases

INTERNATIONAL CASES

List of Contributors

Zaid Al-Ali is the senior adviser for constitution building in the Arab region for International IDEA. From 2015 to 2016, he was a Law and Public Affairs Fellow at Princeton University.

Kwesi Aning is Director, Faculty of Academic Affairs and Research (FAAR), Kofi Annan International Peacekeeping Training Centre. He specializes in peacekeeping economies, hybrid security/political orders, and organized crime.

Philippe Droz-Vincent is Professor of Political Science and international relations, Sciences-Po/University of Grenoble, France, and associative delegate (head of the Syrian mission) of the NGO Médecins du Monde (Doctors of the World), France.

Sandra Elena, LLM in International Legal Studies, is Director of the Justice Programme at CIPPEC.

Andrew Ellis is a senior consultant adviser on constitutional and electoral frameworks. He was previously Director for Asia and the Pacific for International IDEA. He acted as Senior Adviser in Indonesia for the National Democratic Institute (NDI) from 1999 to 2003 throughout the constitutional amendment process.

Ernest Ansah Lartey is a researcher and head of peace and security studies (PSS) programme at the Kofi Annan International Peacekeeping Training Centre (KAIPTC) in Accra, Ghana. His research interests include security sector reform, peacekeeping, peace building, and election security. He has published several papers in these research interests.

Christina Murray is Senior Adviser on Constitutions and Process Design, Mediation Standby Team, Mediation Support Unit, Department of Political Affairs, United Nations; and Emeritus Professor of Constitutional and Human Rights Law, University of Cape Town.

Gonzalo García Pino is a Justice of the Constitutional Court of Chile (from 2011 to 2022). He was previously Undersecretary of War (2006–2010) and Undersecretary of Navy (2005). He is a Professor of Constitutional Law of the Faculties of Law of the Alberto Hurtado University and Catholic University of Chile.

Julia Pomares, PhD in Political Science, is the Executive Director of the Center for the Implementation of Public Policies for Equity and Growth (CIPPEC).

Kent Roach, CM, FRSC, is Professor of Law and Prichard Wilson Chair in Law and Public Policy at the University of Toronto. He served on the research advisory committee of Canada's inquiry on the rendition of Maher Arar and as director of research for its Air India inquiry.

Narcís Serra has been the president of IBEI (Institut Barcelona d'Estudis Internacionals) since its foundation in 2004, encouraging its efforts to turn Barcelona into a reference city for international studies. He is a former Mayor of Barcelona, Spanish Minister of Defence and Vice-president of the Spanish government. He has a BA in Economics from the University of Barcelona and a PhD by the Autonomous University of Barcelona.

Richard Stacey is Associate Professor of Law at the University of Toronto. He has advised on constitutional transition processes in Kenya, Tunisia, and Egypt, and was a law clerk at the Constitutional Court of South Africa. His publications include academic work on questions of sovereignty, economic and social rights and legal theory, as well as practitioner-focused studies of semi-presidentialism, constitutional consolidation, and constitutional design.

Lt. Gen. (Ret) Agus Widjojo graduated from Indonesian Military Academy in 1970. His tenure as Commandant of the Joint Command and General Staff College and Chief of Staff for Territorial Affairs provided him the role of policy-making and implementation to the TNI reform in 1998–2004. He was appointed as Governor of the National Resilience Institute in April 2016. He holds a Masters Degree in Military Art and Science, National Security Strategy and Public Administration.

Introduction

Leverage, Sequencing, Design, and Separation—Considerations in Security Sector Reform during Constitutional Transition

Zoltan Barany, Sumit Bisarya, Sujit Choudhry, and Richard Stacey

In late 2010 and 2011, the 'Arab Spring' promised an end to authoritarian government in the Middle East and North Africa. Protests led to the fall of long-serving presidents in Tunisia and Egypt. Five years later, an elected constituent assembly has enacted a new constitution in Tunisia; a military-appointed committee has adopted a new constitution in Egypt and the leader of the military's 2013 coup is now the president; constitutional negotiations have made only sporadic progress amid militia-driven conflict in Libya; and civil war rages in Syria and Yemen, made all the more destructive with the involvement of outside powers. The Arab Spring may initially have been viewed as a 'fourth wave' of democratization following the third-wave transitions in Southern and Eastern Europe, Latin America, and sub-Saharan Africa,[1] but the strong reaction of the military and security forces has, for the most part, proved an obstacle to widespread or deep-seated constitutional transition and democratization across the region.

This volume is born of the experience of post-authoritarian democratization across the world, with the Middle East and North Africa just one set of recent examples of a far more widespread twentieth-century phenomenon. Although negotiating the new constitution is a primary element of a political transition to constitutional democracy, security sector reform (SSR) is critical to the success of any political transition. This is especially so when the outgoing regime has relied on the security services to consolidate and maintain its grip on power, and has created a strong and politicized security sector in order to undermine and suppress opposition to its rule. Indeed, SSR itself has the explicitly democratizing objective of ensuring security and justice are provided in a manner consistent with democratic norms, human rights, and the rule of law. SSR must ensure that security services are subject to civilian control, and that their activities are controlled through

[1] Samuel Huntington, *The Third Wave: Democratization in the Late Twentieth Century* (University of Oklahoma Press, 1991); Larry Diamond, 'A Fourth Wave or a False Start?' *Foreign Affairs*, 22 May 2011, <https://www.foreignaffairs.com/articles/middle-east/2011-05-22/fourth-wave-or-false-start>.

democratic processes that minimize opportunities for partisan or politically motivated abuse at the hands of civilian government officials.

It is not surprising that civilian control of the security sector within a constitutional framework has long been recognized as fundamental to democracy—reflected in its inclusion as a key democratic standard in regional and international instruments. The United Nations High Commissioner for Refugees (UNHCR) Resolution 2000/47, the Community of Democracies' Warsaw Declaration (2000), the Council of Europe's Recommendation 1402 (1992), the Summit of the Americas' Quebec Plan of Action (2001), and the African Union Policy Framework (2013) provide examples of instruments enshrining this principle. In this light, democratic and civilian control over the security sector has now emerged as a critical issue for constitutional negotiators in post-conflict settings and in states under transition from authoritarian regimes. A failure to attend to the democratization of the security sector during the process of constitutional transition may prove fatal to the entire project of constitutional transition, allowing the security forces to interfere with civilian politics after the transition and lubricate the return of an authoritarian government supported by the state security apparatus. At the same time, the security services that emerge from a constitutional transition must remain effective, efficient, and capable of performing their primary functions of maintaining internal security and responding to external threats.

The danger of ignoring this imperative is perhaps nowhere more apparent than in Iraq in 2014/15, as virtually unopposed Islamic State militants expanded the area under their influence. Zaid al-Ali's chapter in this volume describes in great detail the dangers of ill-conceived SSR during a constitutional transition. The twofold objective of SSR is thus to ensure an effective and competent security sector while facilitating democratic and civilian control and oversight of the security forces. While the focus of much of the literature and of the people and organizations involved in the institutional design of new democracies has been the second objective, it is nevertheless important to recognize that the design choices that promote civilian control and oversight of the security sector will be influenced by the need to ensure that the security sector institutions are capable of fulfilling their primary mission. Institutional arrangements for oversight and civilian control must be sensitive to the imperatives of competence and efficiency.

Issues of SSR and constitutional reform are relevant in one form or another to currently ongoing political transitions or SSR processes in states ranging from those affected by the Arab Spring—Egypt, Tunisia, Yemen, and Libya—to nearby countries such as Turkey and Syria as well as countries further afield such as Fiji, Burma/Myanmar, and South Sudan. They are persistent issues of global relevance, bounded by neither geography nor time. This volume is intended to bring together a handful of cases of SSR during constitutional transitions and to offer a sketch of what works, what fails, and what reformers and constitutional negotiators should bear in mind as they approach the project of SSR.

The Processes of Constitutional Transition

Processes of constitutional transition and democratic reform inevitably create winners and losers as they challenge vested interests and existing power relationships.[2] Constitutional negotiations and, indeed, the issues on the agenda for negotiation demand careful attention from the parties involved in constitutional transitions. Open dialogue between negotiating parties is crucial to the success of constitution-building processes in general, and is of paramount importance in the context of negotiations between civilian and security sector actors both because mutual understanding may be low and because the costs of failure are high. Understanding may be low not only because civilian actors and security sector officials may have vastly differing backgrounds, perceptions of each other's importance in governance, and visions of democracy, but also because in many cases where SSR is necessary, national security issues have been kept out of the realm of political debate and placed beyond the reach of civilian oversight. Costs are high because a failure to manage the process can result in a stillborn democratic transition where the military retains control over politics and the economy, where new governments lack the support of the security forces posing risks of violence, insecurity, and coup, or where the institutional capture of the security forces by the governing political party allows abuse of the security forces for partisan political gain.

At moments of constitutional transition, decision-makers and civil society groups often know what they want to achieve: more accountable and transparent government, popular sovereignty, the rule of law, and protection for human rights. These are no longer new or unfamiliar ideas for any society, but while there exists a large literature on democratization, and a similarly large literature on SSR generally, there is a notable lack of study of SSR during the process of constitutional transition. Constitutional drafters and their advisors face a dearth of knowledge and policy guidance on how to select mechanisms, structures, and processes to ensure the democratization of the security sector.

This volume aims to fill this gap by generating a body of knowledge from comparative analysis of global experiences of SSR during constitutional transitions. Our hope is that the book will not only prove valuable to students of the constitutional and security sector transitions that have already occurred but will also

[2] Organisation for Economic Co-operation and Development (OECD), *The OECD DAC Handbook on Security System Reform: Supporting Security and Justice* (OECD Publishing, 2008), 28.

provide a valuable addition to the resources available to those wishing to further their understanding of how SSR works in practice during times of democratic transition.

Structured Comparative Case Study

No two journeys to democracy are alike. Each is characterized by unique challenges, outcomes, obstacles, and causes that can only be explained with a detailed knowledge and deep understanding of that country's historical, socio-economic, geopolitical, and cultural context. Understanding the context in which a particular transition takes place is crucial to understanding each country's experience of SSR in a way that those lessons can be applied more widely. This volume therefore presents detailed studies of several cases of SSR in the context of constitutional transitions from authors intimately familiar with each country's context, relying on a methodology of structured comparative case study. Eight of the case studies examine countries that have undergone a transition from an authoritarian state to constitutional democracy. Moreover, in each of these eight countries the security services played an important role in maintaining an authoritarian state structure before the transition, making the establishment of civilian control and oversight over the security sector a key element of the constitutional transition. The ninth case study traces developments in the Middle East and North Africa (MENA) region. Since the region is in transition at the time of writing, this contribution takes the form of a snapshot of transition in progress rather than a case study of a completed transition.

All nine chapters, however, address a specific set of questions regarding SSR processes in each country. These questions concern three broad aspects of the legal foundations of the security sector: (i) the institutional structure of the security services, particularly the position of civilian officials in the chain of command, and the separation of powers and functions between the three branches of the security sector; (ii) mechanisms and institutions for external oversight by civilian institutions such as the legislature, judiciary, other independent oversight bodies, or civil society and processes for internal oversight by the security services themselves; (iii) questions of constitutional design including whether the constitution, ordinary law, or organic law governs the security sector and how detailed these legal instruments are, and questions of process including the sequencing of security sector and constitutional reform.

By keeping in view the changes from pre-transitional, authoritarian contexts to the (purportedly) democratic post-authoritarian system, the case studies provide an insight into how the process of constitutional transition engages with these questions of structure, oversight, and design, and in particular how constitutional changes to these three aspects of the security sector affect the role of the security services and the state's capacity for civilian oversight over the security services, before and after the transition.

Scope

There are four broad parameters that limit the scope of this volume. First, it is necessary to distinguish between different segments of the security sector. While some overarching principles are similar and apply to all branches of the security sector, there are discrete sets of issues and problems raised by reform of the armed forces, police, and intelligence agencies, respectively. The case studies discuss these distinct issues as necessary. Moreover, this volume is limited to study of only these three institutions: reform of constitutional rules governing civilian militias or specialized security forces such as border guards is beyond our scope. Our focus is on the overarching issues of security sector strategy as they are relevant to matters of constitutional transition, very few of which arise outside the walls of these three branches of the security sector.

Second, the timing of reform is also important. Issues of SSR may arise at very different stages in a constitution-building process, ranging from peace-making in a conflict situation to the implementation of a new constitution following its enactment. The point along this range at which SSR occurs depends on the circumstances of each state; consequently, the case studies cover instances of challenges at all stages, such as agreement on principles and process before the constitutional negotiations, the constitutional negotiations themselves, and the implementation of reform after the constitution itself has been enacted.

Third, constitutional reform processes can range from wholesale replacements of the constitution to single, stand-alone amendments to the text of an existing constitution. Interim constitutional arrangements are also a not infrequent steppingstone to new, 'permanent' constitutional frameworks. This volume deals with all reform processes where alterations to the constitutional framework were part of a major democratic transition. The case of Indonesia, where the nature of the state was radically changed through four democratizing constitutional amendments, is as relevant as Kenya where the 1963 Constitution was entirely replaced in 2010.

Fourth, the case studies in this volume include democratic transitions after conflicts such as foreign invasion (Iraq) or civil uprising or revolution (the countries affected by the Arab Spring), and mostly peaceful and bloodless transitions from authoritarian regimes (Chile, Spain). Transitions in South Africa and Kenya avoided all-out civil war, but political violence in both countries nevertheless claimed many lives before and during those transitions. While the challenges presented by a transition that follows immediately from conflict are different to those faced during a transition in a more stable environment, and the experiences and lessons of each case are unique to each particular set of circumstances, this volume aims to draw out common experiences across the case studies.

Inferential Learning: Lessons from Common Experiences

The case studies collected in this volume serve two broad purposes. The first is to present a narrative of SSR in the context of each country's transition to constitutional democracy. Each chapter stands on its own as an account of security reform during that country's transition to democracy, highlighting both the importance of SSR to democratization and how the commitment to democratization influenced and informed SSR. Each country's experience of SSR is different. For instance, the relationship between military and civilian institutions required careful management in the reform processes in Latin America in the 1980s (e.g. in Chile and Argentina), while in South Africa the reform process in the early 1990s grappled with the questions of demilitarizing a 'securocratic' state structure and integrating a liberation army into the existing national security services. The constitutional transition in Ghana in 1992 focused largely on establishing civilian control over a military that had itself been heavily involved in government. The close links between the military and a government led by a military official posed unique challenges in post-Suharto Indonesia from 1999 to 2002 and post-Francoist Spain from 1975 to the early 1980s. In Kenya, the process of enacting a new constitution in 2010 involved dismantling the police state that had supported a nepotistic and patrimonial state structure for decades. Iraq and the countries included in the chapter on the MENA region—Egypt, Libya, Tunisia, and Yemen—face ongoing challenges of political instability or democracy shortfalls, related in different ways to the success or failure of SSR.

Taken together, the collection of case studies provides a sample of the global experience of SSR during constitutional transition. By taking a cross-section of this sample, this volume looks beyond the distinctiveness of each case study and, while acknowledging that the unique context of each transition influences the outcomes of both SSR and constitutional transition, identifies common themes that emerge from comparative analysis of all the cases. In making these comparisons, the volume groups the case studies into three sections according to the broad commonalities they display in the nature of their pre-democratic political organization; the role of the security forces before, during, and after the transition; and the process of constitutional transition. It is perhaps not entirely coincidental when we consider the effects and impact of shared historical and cultural trajectories that our grouping of case studies displays some geographic and cultural-linguistic commonality as well.

Our first group includes countries with experiences of rule by a military junta or dictator with military ties: Spain, Chile, Argentina, and Indonesia. The objective of SSR in these countries was to remove the military from positions of political leadership; that is, to demilitarize government. In each of these countries, the military was able to manage or influence the terms of its withdrawal from government to a different extent, with important implications for how long it took to establish effective civilian oversight of the military—if at all.

The second group includes the sub-Saharan African countries of Kenya, Ghana, and South Africa which, before their constitutional transitions, relied heavily on a secret police and state security structure to harass and suppress political opposition. The primary focus of SSR in this second group of cases has been to depoliticize the security services, ensure they are not—and cannot be—used to further the partisan objectives of political actors, and establish civilian oversight mechanisms capable of preventing such abuse in the future.

Our final group considers the experience of countries in transition from authoritarian regimes where the ruling elite enjoyed close links to a sympathetic and supportive military. This group includes the fluid and dynamic cases of Iraq and four countries in the MENA region (Egypt, Libya, Tunisia, and Yemen). In the decidedly transitional contexts in the MENA region, merely establishing basic security and order in the face of insurgents or militias, civil war, or terrorist attacks was an urgent goal. The inability to do that effectively, however, has compromised the success of these transitions.

Despite the differences in the nature of pre-transitional regimes and the consequently different objectives of SSR in each of these three broad groupings of cases, there are several dominant themes of SSR that emerge as critical to the broader success of constitutional transition. The case studies highlight how decisions and approaches within each of these themes have shaped the trajectory of transition in each case, while the concluding synthetic chapter describes the analytical coherence of these themes across the case studies. The fact that cross-cutting themes emerge from, and common experiences are shared across the range of case studies, is precisely what allows us to describe a set of principles for effective SSR during constitutional transition. A major contribution of the volume, in this light, is to offer the following cross-cutting themes as a lens through which to read the case studies' accounts of SSR and constitutional transition.

Leverage: the influence of security services in the transition

The shape of post-authoritarian democracy depends to a large extent on who is involved in shaping it. Where agents of the old regime are able to keep a hand in the process of transition and to exert an influence over the substance of negotiations about the new constitutional order, they may be able to secure benefits for themselves or for the institutions they represent in that new order. As a general rule, the degree of leverage that agents of the security services hold in the transition process depends on the nature of the transition itself. In cases of complete regime replacement such as a revolution, civil war, or foreign invasion, the previous leadership is unlikely to have any impact on the shape of the post-transitional state. In Iraq, for example, all vestiges of the Ba'athist leadership were eliminated leaving the United States with a virtually free hand to define transitional political arrangements. The constitution-drafting process that followed was similarly shielded from the influence of the previous regime. The groundswell of opposition that carried the junta from power in Argentina and prevented a resurgence of Francoist leadership in Spain had much the same impact, effectively excluding those influences from the transition process. In Chile, Indonesia, and South Africa, on the other hand, the outgoing authoritarian leadership was able to manage its own exit from power, maintaining a hand in the design of the new constitutional order. While the apartheid government in South African was not a military regime of the kind in power in pre-transition Chile and Indonesia, the relationship between the apartheid security sector and the apartheid government was such that the former was able to protect its interests in much the same way as the military governments in Chile and Indonesia.

In this light, the objective of political reform becomes relevant. In cases where the transition is intended to establish civilian government in place of military government (Argentina, Chile, Indonesia, Spain), the primary objective is, bluntly, to get the military out of politics. Where the military government has been defeated (Argentina), it is more likely that the separation of security and government will be clearer than in cases where the military government is able to stage-manage the transition (Chile, Indonesia). But where the objective is primarily to establish civilian oversight of the security sector to ensure that political actors are not able to co-opt the security services to their own ends, the security sector is less likely to have political objectives of its own (Ghana, South Africa, Kenya, Tunisia, Iraq).

Drawing a distinction between a military government and a security sector that has been used to prop up an authoritarian civilian government adverts to the importance of distinguishing between the influence on transitional politics that the security sector can exert on one hand, and that the leadership of the pre-transitional authoritarian regime can exert on the other. The objectives of these actors are different. The outgoing military junta in Chile was able to enact a battery of laws as it left power that guaranteed the pensions of military officers and ensured that the military budgets under the new order would not be entirely in the hands of civilian politicians. In Egypt, the military coup-makers who ushered a nominally civilian government into power after the ousting of Mohamed Morsi were able to see to it that Egypt's 2014 Constitution retained a political role for the military in cabinet, and limited legislative oversight of the defence budget. In Tunisia, while early drafts of the constitution would have entrenched similar powers for military and security leaders, the final version of the 2014 Constitution does not do so.

In South Africa and Kenya, the process of reforming the internal structures of the security sector occurred in parallel to, but separate from, the negotiations about the constitutional and political transition. The members of the security establishment had a significant influence on the character and identity of the security services after the transition, but were for the most part neither concerned with nor involved in the engineering of a post-authoritarian political system. It is important, however, to distinguish between three broad categories of reform: internal security sector structural reforms, purely political reforms, and new arrangements for civilian oversight. South Africa's case provides a useful illustration. The apartheid military leadership prided itself on its professionalism and non-partisanship, insisting that it would continue to fulfil its national defence mandate under whatever new government was established after the transition. Both the military and the police force in South Africa distanced themselves from the process of designing the institutional structures of a post-apartheid South Africa. The security sector was largely uninvolved with the political arrangements for the new constitutional democracy.

However, the military's primary concern was with ensuring that the integration of the liberation armies into a new national defence force would proceed in a way that did not cause too much disruption to settled hierarchies and vested interests. The apartheid military and the armed wings of the liberation movements (the African National Congress and the Pan Africanist Congress) played a significant role in negotiating how the integration of these formerly opposed forces would proceed, and thus had a heavy hand in designing the internal structures of the new military.

Finally, in making arrangements for civilian control and oversight of the security sector after the transition, civilian negotiators relied on the advice and input of the security sector. Although the security sector did not take an active role in this aspect of transition, their views were influential in the outcome.

Agents of military regimes, security services under civilian authoritarian regimes, and civilian authoritarian leaders alike may have equally compelling desires to limit their exposure to retribution or punishment for crimes committed in the service of maintaining power. In South Africa, the security sector held its capacity to provide stability during the transition as a bargaining chip, eliciting assurances from the political negotiators that some form of amnesty would be extended to security agents and civilian leadership. Indeed, an agreement in principle that amnesties would be a feature of the transition was easy to reach, as the armed wings of South Africa's liberation movements enthusiastically supported amnesty. Provisions for amnesty were ultimately included in South Africa's transitional interim Constitution.

In Argentina, where the junta left power without being able to manage its own exit, a much harder line was taken. Members of the junta were prosecuted in ordinary courts for crimes committed between 1976 and 1983. In Chile, the junta initially escaped prosecution through the laws it had itself passed, but was subsequently held to a morally significant truth and reconciliation process that attributed accountability for the junta's wrongs and awarded reparations for wrongs suffered. The Indonesian government has been able to shield itself from prosecution for its crimes, but has been strategically cunning in allowing a truth and reconciliation commission to go ahead in respect of East Timor.

Another determinant of the influence of the security services on post-authoritarian constitutional design is the extent of the security sector's involvement in the economy. In Indonesia as well as in Egypt and Chile, the security sector's economic interests have brought it significant independence and autonomy as an actor in the economy. The military's control of the arms industry in each of these countries meant that significant economic consequences would have followed an attempt to limit its control after the transition. The security sector's commercial interests meant that it could not be ignored as a player in its own right in the economy, and that its views had to be considered in the discussion of how to manage the economy after the transition. On the other hand, in Argentina the junta's mismanagement of the economy—including a costly war with the United Kingdom over the Malvinas (Falkland Islands)—meant that there was relatively little at stake in divesting the military of its economic and commercial enterprises and erecting a separation between the security sector and the economy.

Separating the functions of security agencies

The case studies reveal that the mission and scope of operation of the security services are commonly poorly defined under authoritarian conditions. Under democratic conditions the military's scope of operation is confined to safeguarding the state against threats from foreign and external threats, while the police force is mandated to secure internal law and order in the face of only domestic threats. Intelligence-gathering is performed by dedicated intelligence agencies, sometimes divided into domestic intelligence and foreign intelligence services. Authoritarian regimes by contrast show a definite trend towards a permeable boundary between these functions. The South African Defence Force was frequently called on to suppress mass protests against the apartheid government while special branches of the police force pursued political targets outside the country; under the military juntas in Argentina and Chile the military was a central actor in domestic governance and policing; and in Tunisia, Kenya, and Ghana secret police forces engaged in widespread intelligence-gathering.

In just about all the case studies included in this volume, the mandate and scope of operation of the intelligence agencies were not clearly delineated in legislation, nor was it entirely clear to the political leadership in many cases what the intelligence agencies were up to. Indeed, both the police and the military in authoritarian contexts ran their own intelligence operations alongside formally recognized intelligence agencies, leading to a duplication of functions as well as conflict between the rapidly proliferating special branches and more-or-less secret divisions of the security services.

A key process of SSR in all these cases has been the separation of the powers and functions of the security services and the establishment of clearer and more formalized boundaries between the branches of the security sector. The importance of this separation is not limited to cases of transition from either military regimes or civilian regimes in which the security sector had been co-opted for partisan purposes. Where the objective of reform has been to establish civilian rather than military government, it has been important to limit the ability of the military to engage in operations inside the country in order to influence politics or protect its vested interests after the transition. Where the objective has been to establish effective oversight over civilian government to limit or eradicate the partisan abuse of the security services, it has been equally important to ensure, for example, that the police's intelligence role is limited to crime prevention rather than to a political role, and that the military cannot be deployed domestically to protect partisan political interests. Of course, the extent to which the military, police, and intelligence agencies are subject to political partisan abuse cannot be controlled merely by a separation of security functions into matters of internal and external security. A central objective of this volume, which we introduce later, is to compare the various mechanisms that have been established in post-authoritarian democracies for the civilian oversight of the security services.

While comparative analysis of the case studies suggests that separating security functions is a determinant of successful reform, it suggests just as strongly that there is no one, correct way to separate these functions. Post-authoritarian democracies have diverged both in the mechanisms by which they distinguish between security functions and when they do it. In Argentina, the military was confined to dealing with external threats by ordinary laws passed after the Junta was forced from power but before constitutional reform in 1994, while in Chile and Spain the restriction of the military's role was effected in statutes passed only after the constitutional transition had occurred. In South Africa, Kenya, Egypt, and Tunisia where constitutional reform and political transition happened at roughly the same historical moment, the separation of functions is contained in the text of the constitutions of those countries—although the actual extent of separation varies in these cases. In Ghana, the adoption of a new Constitution in 1992 and the fall of the 'hybrid' military/civilian dictatorship were followed only several years later by reforms establishing divisions between the functions of the security services. Some of the reforms in Ghana were, notably, initiated by the security services themselves rather than by legislation or regulation.

In Kenya, however, the constitutional separation of the powers and functions of the security services has been significantly undermined by the proliferation of specialized police forces. The constitutional reform process was unsuccessful in fully merging the colonial administrative police with the new national police service, allowing competition and tension to grow between two services responsible for essentially similar functions. In response to increasing threats of terrorism in East

Africa, the Anti-Terror Police Unit (ATPU) was established. It operates with broad powers and through layers of administration and an obtuse chain of command that makes holding this unit to account for its actions difficult. Along with the police's paramilitary General Service Unit, the ATPU has been accused of numerous human rights abuses in Kenya, including torture and extra-judicial killings.

In Indonesia, in similar fashion, there is no legal instrument at all that confines the military to an external role. The military is frequently called on to respond to internal instability, opening the door to the suppression of legitimate political or civil society activity under the machinery of the military. In Argentina, there are frequent suggestions that the military should be used to deal with internal threats to law and order, prompting debates about the repeal of legislation limiting the military's role. In Chile, the military has been deployed to provide internal stability and humanitarian assistance following the declaration of a state of 'catastrophe', such as in the aftermath of the 2010 and 2014 earthquakes. While law limits the scope of operation of the military, the declaration of exceptional circumstances is provided for in the Chilean Constitution and effectively suspends the operation of these statutory limits. In Kenya, on the other hand, neither statute nor the Constitution goes far enough in establishing clear lines of separation between the police and the intelligence services, with the result that the intelligence operations of the police remain beyond the effective reach of civilian oversight institutions.

Timing security sector reform

One of the central observations to be drawn from the case studies is that SSR often proceeds along a timeline that has less in common with the milestones of political transition than might seem to be the case at first glance. Especially in cases of transition from military regimes, the intuition may be that SSR will happen at the same time as the transition to civilian government. However, in Chile, Spain, and Ghana the process of SSR, especially of the military, was not completed until after—in some cases, many years after—the adoption of a new constitutional framework and the establishment of civilian government. That approach is partly inverted in the Argentinian case, where constitutional reform followed some years after an initial removal of the military from government and the election of a civilian administration. Changes to the statutory foundations and controls over the military continued to be made in Argentina after constitutional revision in 1994, however.

The timing of SSR, in relation to constitutional reform, is a product of the leverage that the security services hold. In Argentina, the military had little credibility after its disastrous attempt to claim the Malvinas, and was unable to guard its position in the ensuing change in government. SSR consequently happened soon after the junta left power, but democratic reform waited for another ten years. The military junta in Chile, by contrast, was able to hold onto power for several months after it lost a referendum on its future, ensuring enough time for Pinochet and his comrades to protect the privilege of the security sector after a democratically elected government took power. Democratic change happened quickly, but comprehensive SSR was put on hold for two decades.

The mechanisms by which reform is achieved is also relevant to the timing of these changes. There is a danger of entrenching rules and principles governing the security sector in the constitution prematurely, eliminating the capacity to adapt to the rapidly changing political, institutional, and social conditions of transitional societies. Indonesia and Egypt provide examples of cases in which the military has been able to influence the direction of constitutional negotiations to protect its interests and position in the terms of the constitution. While a moment of constitutional transition opens up the space for the fundamental political and institutional reform, it is often difficult to make fundamental change once the constitutional moment has passed. Setting the institutional rules for the security sector in the provisions of the constitution at these exceptional constitutional moments may close doors to fine-tuning those arrangements as evolving circumstances require, since constitutional amendments are usually more difficult, procedurally and politically, than statutory changes.

South Africa's two-stage transition offers one way of managing this difficulty. Even though the rules for the security sector are set out in the 1996 Constitution, the initial political transition and SSR was governed by the 1993 interim Constitution. The 'sunset' provisions of the negotiated interim Constitution provided that a new Constitution would have to be adopted by an elected constituent assembly. The interim period thus provided an opportunity for learning, while the deliberations of the constituent assembly provided an opportunity for fine-tuning the provisions of the new constitutional order, including those governing the security sector. In Kenya, the impetus for constitutional reform in 2010 was the violence and abuse committed in part by security services after the disputed 2007 elections. In this case it made sense that the new Constitution would contain provisions governing the security sector.

Oversight mechanisms

The experience of the cases collected in this volume affirms that the familiar mechanisms of legislative oversight—such as legislative standing committees, ad hoc investigative committees, or parliamentary questions to cabinet members—are important in establishing an independent and accountable security sector. In this light, the case studies are representative of both successful and less effective mechanisms of legislative oversight. Indonesia illustrates the challenges to oversight posed by a lack of experience and expertise in a newly constituted legislature, while Chile and South Africa offer contrasting examples of how investigatory committees or specially constituted commissions of inquiry can be effective in some cases but that their effectiveness can be undermined by partisan manipulation in other cases.

The case studies drive home that the legislature is not the only institution through which the independence and accountability of the security sector can be maintained. Three areas of alternative oversight emerge. First, how the chain of command is constructed may work to minimize or facilitate partisan abuse of the security services. Second, independent complaints directorates or oversight institutions dedicated to each security service allow the initiation of investigations into misconduct or abuse by the public rather than by political elites alone. Third, civil society and independent watchdog institutions can help to expose impropriety in the relationship between the government and the security sector.

The imprecision of the chain of command has had an impact in Iraq, where the Prime Minister was able to exploit the ambiguity of the 2005 Constitution's provision regarding the chain of command and assume more or less unimpeded control of the military. Similarly, the close relationship between the civilian government and the military in Indonesia, combined with weak institutional and legal definition of the chain of command, has allowed the President to maintain a largely open line to the military's top brass. In South Africa, by contrast, the cabinet member responsible for each of the security services intervenes in the chain of command between the top brass and the President as the commander-in-chief. The requirement of a civilian secretariat responsible for all non-operational administrative matters promotes transparency in the management of the security services, reducing the likelihood that security officers will be subjected to partisan manipulation or follow their own political agenda.

Even where the chain of command is clearly set out, the account of some countries' 'whole-of-government' approach to security sector management reveals an unexpected tension between oversight and efficiency. In Kenya and Ghana, a single national security council (NSC) has been established to exercise supervisory control over the entire security sector. The membership of these NSCs includes the chief executive and cabinet ministers alongside top-ranking officials in the security services. The sharing of information and the collaboration in the setting of national security policy that a single NSC facilitates may streamline and rationalize security sector management, but there is a cost to this benefit. In the first place, these arrangements may allow the chief executive to circumvent the chain of command by consulting directly with security leadership rather than through the conduit of the cabinet. Secondly, the whole-of-government approach may make it more difficult for both legislative oversight committees and internal complaints directorates to scrutinize the conduct of each security service discretely.

Finally, while civil society can play an important role in exposing partisan abuse or security sector impropriety (as in Argentina, Chile, and Indonesia), in other cases those institutions must work hard both at building the trust of the public and at solidifying their position as truly independent bodies.

Conclusion

The lessons that this volume delivers are gathered from a sample of constitutional transitions around the world, where SSR was an important element of that transition. There is a great deal of variation in these cases, however, in the pre-transitional circumstances each country faced, the process by which transition occurred, and the outcome of the transition. A key observation is that SSR, if it is to be effective in establishing civilian control over the security services and ensuring that security actors have no influence on politics, must be tailored to the circumstances and conditions of each case. The case studies in this volume identify at least three themes across which these variations occur, and to which reformers, political actors, and activists agitating for SSR must be aware.

The first of these themes is the leverage or power that the security sector wields, and the concessions that it may be able to extract from civilian reformers in exchange for providing stability for the transition itself. Second, it may be necessary to separate the transition from military or authoritarian government from the institutional reform of the security sector. In some cases, these two processes will flow naturally together, but in others there may be compelling reasons to focus on just one change first. Third, and relatedly, not all SSR has to happen at the constitutional level. Entrenching the institutional architecture of the relationship between the civilian government and the security sector may have benefits in some cases, but may ultimately undermine democratic reform in other cases. Reformers should be sensitive to whether constitutionalizing SSR achieves a desirable outcome immediately, sets the agenda and provides guidelines for doing so later, or closes the door to future reform.

Finally, although it is crucial to remain sensitive to the variance and variability between cases, and to remain flexible enough to adapt each project of SSR to a specific country's circumstances, the one lesson that emerges from all cases is that democratization is difficult without separating the functions of the different services within the security sector. Political abuse of the security sector is far easier when the military, police, and intelligence services can all be deployed in pursuit of the same set of internal and external partisan goals.

Our intention is that the insights this structured comparative case study provides will be useful to both practitioners and scholars as they think about what SSR might look like in a particular context. If there is one thing this volume aims to drive home forcefully it is that no project of SSR need design the process in a vacuum. History and global experience provide valuable lessons for what might succeed, fail, expedite, or delay SSR. Which lesson is relevant to a particular country in transition, however, depends on careful attention to the circumstances, context, history, and experience of that country itself. Context matters.

PART I
MILITARY DICTATORSHIPS

The countries studied in Part I all experienced a transition to democracy following a period of military government or dictatorship. Argentina and Chile were ruled by a cabal of elite military officers, each assigned various portfolios of government alongside their ordinary security functions. These military governing councils were known as the *Junta*, and although the Spanish and Portuguese word translates literally as committee or council, to the English-speaking world the term has come to refer to authoritarian military government. In Francoist Spain, the government was tightly controlled by Franco's highly personalized dictatorship, and depended crucially on his connections to the army. After Franco's death the army's political strength allowed it to maintain some continuity in the political system, although it was unable to fully determine the country's political direction. In Indonesia, more to the point, the military was able to remain largely in control of the process of reform by itself initiating the transition to democracy. The result has been the depoliticization of the security services, but on the military's own terms.

In all four cases, the government itself was in direct control of a disciplined military which it was able to deploy to support the regime and neutralize opposition. The key to a successful democratic transition in each country, in consequence, was the removal of soldiers from government and the restoration of a professional and non-partisan fighting force subject to civilian control. In language that has become common in security sector reform, the objective was to ensure that the military returned to and remained in the barracks. The four case studies present important lessons for how this objective can be achieved.

1
Security Sector Reform in Post-Franco Spain

Narcís Serra

Background

Character of the Spanish transition to democracy

The transition to democracy in Spain began after the Franco regime, a few months after the dictator died on 20 November 1975. The Franco regime, which was established after the Civil War (1936–39) which followed the military coup on 18 July 1936, was an authoritarian regime under the terminology defined by Linz and Stepan,[1] in which although the Head of State was a military official, it cannot be said that the military governed the country. It tolerated a minimum of political plurality, especially in its final years, in which the Communist Party increased its activity, parties which had existed in the Republic were re-established—among them the *Partido Socialista Obrero Español* (PSOE: Spanish Worker's Party)—and other new parties were created. These together with the trade unions—*Comisiones Obreras* (Workers' Committees) and *Unión General de Trabajadores* (UGT: General Union of Workers)—played an important mobilizing role and were in dialogue during the political transition.

The Franco regime was based on three large institutions.[2] One of them was the National Movement, a type of single party created by Franco based on different political forces that supported him in the Civil War. Another was the Catholic Church, which gave legitimacy to his coup and which Franco controlled through his participation in the appointment of bishops. The third was the Army, the ultimate guarantor of survival of the regime. In order to play this role, the Army had all the instruments required to maintain order.

The first pillar progressively lost influence and cohesion with the passage of time, especially beginning with the first technocratic government in 1957 and the success of the subsequent Stabilization Plan (1959–62), which broke the autarky of the Spanish economy and prepared the field for economic growth in the 1970s.

[1] See Juan J. Linz and Alfred Stepan, *Problems of Democratic Transition and Consolidation* (Johns Hopkins University Press, 1996), chapters 3 and 6.

[2] See Santos Juliá Diaz, 'La política militar del presidente Suárez', <http://www.santosjulia.com/Santos_Julia/2010-13_files/Poli%CC%81tica%20militar%20de%20Sua%CC%81rez.pdf>.

After Franco, this pillar was split between '*continuistas*' (those for continuing the regime) and 'reformers', and important political figures in the dictatorship, such as Fraga Iribarne, Adolfo Suárez, or Martin Villa, played an essential role as reformers during the transition.

The relationships with the Church also deteriorated with the passage of time. In 1961, *Ecclesia*, the Spanish episcopal body, requested that the right to strike be granted and regulated and in 1968 Pope Paul VI asked Franco, unsuccessfully, to waive the privilege of appointing bishops. Confrontations with Catalan and Basque clerics were frequent and Cardinal Vicente Enrique y Tarancón, Archbishop of Madrid in the transition and a clear supporter of democracy, was vilified by the extremists in the regime. Adolfo Suárez placed relations with the Church back on track a few weeks after forming a government, waiving the power to appoint bishops.

For these reasons, when the dictator died, only the military was maintained as a pillar of the regime and the guarantor of the continuity of its institutions. They did not have the ability to determine the political direction of the country, or a recognized leader that could lead them, but they could prevent or veto any change they considered contrary to the rules and institutions of the previous regime. In fact, immediately after the death of Franco, it appeared that continuity was ensured. Juan Carlos I, who was appointed as his successor by the dictator, was crowned King and maintained the last President of the Government appointed by Franco.

The experience of the first government of the monarchy was disastrous and the increasing popular pressure in favour of civil liberties demonstrated that the 'opening up' that the continuist government was disposed to was not viable. Thus, half-way through 1976, the King decided to appoint Adolfo Suárez as President of the Government, who would be responsible for proposing and implementing the political reforms that led to the democratic transition. Two factors which would be essential in the process were present from the beginning: on one hand, the monarchy, which supported the initial decisions of the transition, preventing its veto by the military; and on the other hand, Spanish society, which due to economic growth in the 1970s had a solid middle class that aspired for Spain to adopt the European model as the ideal of civil liberties and well-being.

The transition under Adolfo Suárez had the benefit of two very specific characteristics, which were relevant to the arguments against military interventionism in the initial phases of the transition. The first was that democratic reform started from within institutions of the Franco regime. The *Cortes* (the pseudo-parliament created by the dictatorship) approved the Law for Political Reform which, after it was voted for massively in a referendum, opened the way to democracy. This enabled Admiral Pita da Veiga, Minister of the Navy and a prominent Francoist military official, to assert that 'my conscience is calm, because the democratic reform will be based on the legality of the Franco regime'.[3]

[3] See Felipe Agüero, *Militares, civiles y democracia* (Alianza, 1995), 139.

The second characteristic was the consensus reached at three key points in the transition: (i) the Moncloa covenants in 1977, which were agreements between the government and the Opposition, as well as with employer organizations and trade unions, which addressed everything from the economic policy to address the crisis at that time to aspects of military justice reform, including the prohibition on civilians being tried by military courts; (ii) the creation of the Constitution by an authority that represented the parliamentary spectrum and nationalist Catalan party in 1978; and (iii) the approval in 1979 of the Basque and Catalan Autonomy Statutes. It is obvious that the unity of the democratic political forces on such relevant issues, as well as the major support for reforms at the voting booth, contributed to reducing the probability that a military reaction might occur, although they did not prevent the ability of the armed forces to place conditions on—and, in some cases, to veto—decisions.[4]

The Army before the transition

The Spanish armed forces, especially the Army, were, around the mid-1970s, in a situation of limited operational capacity, due to various factors. One of the most important was over-expansion, especially among high-ranking officers and generals of whom there were so many that they could barely be in control of units for a few months in order to allow a good ratio of them to have command of a regiment. One of the causes of this excess was the integration into the armed forces of officer roles improvised during the civil war, those referred to as provisional second lieutenants. In this manner, the number of army officers in 1945 was twice the number that existed in 1935.[5]

The deployment around Spain, concentrating the majority of units in military barracks called *Brigadas de Defensa Operativa del Territorio* (BDOT—Brigades for Operational Defence of the Territory) which were in the urban centre of provincial capitals, was another factor that contributed to the units being poorly trained. Until 1953 when the first agreement was signed with the United States, there was a serious lack of resources (in 1945 the cost of coal used by the Army for the heating of headquarters was four times the cost of fuel used in the Army's vehicles[6]). The agreements with the United States alleviated this situation with the delivery of excess equipment that came from the Korean War and even the

[4] Recent thoughts about the process and the importance of the covenants can be found in Richard Gunther, 'The Spanish Model Revisited' in Gregorio Alonso and Diego Muro (eds), *The Politics and Memory of Democratic Transition: The Spanish Model* (Routledge, 201[illegible]).

[5] Fernando Puell de la Villa provides the figures of 10,417 officers in 1935 and 22,081 in 1945. See 'El devenir del ejército de tierra' in Fernando Puell de la Villa and Sonia Alda Majías (eds), *Los ejércitos del Franquismo* (Instituto Universitario Gutiérrez Mellado, 2010), 69.

[6] Ibid., 66 et seq.

Second World War, but they also contributed to a change in the thinking of many senior officials regarding the role of the military as they took courses in North American schools. Beginning in the early 1960s, the economic growth of the country allowed for budgets for the armed forces that were a bit more generous. Despite this, the wages received by those in the military continued to be very low and pushed many in the military to do two jobs, in other words to look for a second job to occupy the afternoons and thus combine two salaries. Second jobs among the military were tolerated by the authorities but were hidden from society. The consequences on the ability to operate units were very serious, up to the point that one of the initiatives of the Ministry of the Army at the beginning of the transition was to conduct an investigation intended to determine the magnitude of the problem. This established that 27.2 per cent of officers had another job in the afternoons.[7] Other evaluations conclude that second jobs in Madrid extended to over 65 per cent of officers and over 30 per cent in the rest of Spain.

This scenario became even more problematic if it is also considered that Spanish armed forces had officers who had an average age higher than that of any other of the Western armed forces: until 1981 the retirement age of a lieutenant general was seventy years, and of a colonel, sixty-four years. One consequence of this was that the transition was carried out in Spain with the Higher Councils of the three armed forces made up of lieutenant generals who had fought in the 1936–39 Civil War.

As for the ideological position of those in the military, it is difficult to provide specific information, but it can be argued that the ideological features—the mentality, to use the expression preferred by Juan Linz—which have been attributed to the Franco regime (a non-specific sum of religiosity, anti-democratic conservatism, nationalism, and anti-communism) are also those which the commanders of the armed forces had during the transitional years.

It is not surprising that at the time of Franco's death the Spanish armed forces were in a situation of isolation from Spanish society, which, in turn, had gone through a deep process of transformation and modernization over the previous fifteen years, a process which did not in any way affect those in the military.[8] International isolation (the Spanish Army maintained more or less close relationships with the Latin American dictatorships, with Korea, Taiwan, and only a few other countries) also contributed to the rigidity of the mentality of the Spanish military.

[7] Julio Busquets commented on the results of the investigation in *El militar de carrera en España* (Ariel, 1984), 229.

[8] General Jorge Ortega Martin in his work *La transformación de los ejércitos españoles* (UNED, 2008), 38, includes a confession which is indicative of the isolation of the armed forces in the training of new officers: 'in the almost five years of his career, he did not recall having read even one single newspaper in detail or listening to one entire radio news programme'.

Cross-cutting Themes

Before analysing the changes that the transition process and specifically the Constitution caused in the Spanish security sector, it should be clarified that the transition in the military field began in Spain with the appointment, in September 1976, of General Gutiérrez Mellado as Vice President for security matters, succeeding General de Santiago, who had resigned from the post because he did not agree with the legalization of trade unions, in a demonstration of military resistance to the democratization measures at the beginning of the transition.

The dynamics of the transition as well as military reforms caused continuous conflicts with the armed forces, the most dangerous of which was the reaction to the legalization of the Communist Party in March 1977. That led to acts of indiscipline and insubordination against General Gutiérrez Mellado, in his visits to various barracks, as well as at the time of the funerals of ETA victims, culminating in a failed *coup d'état* on 23 February 1981.

The opposition of the military to the reforms was focused on General Gutiérrez Mellado to such an extent that Adolfo Suárez, in the overhaul of his government in March 1979, without removing the general from his position of Vice President of the Government, appointed the first civilian Minister of Defence, Agustín Rodríguez Sahagún. The objectives of this new phase were the same as before: to prevent military intervention in politics and to continue reform. But the exhausting nature of governmental work, the growing disunity in the rank and file of the *Unión del Centro Democrático* (UCD—Union of the Democratic Centre), after the Constitution was approved, and the fact of going from a politics of consensus to a politics of debate and confrontation among the different political options debilitated the Adolfo Suárez Government and also slowed down the rhythm of military reform. Nevertheless, in 1980 two important laws were approved: the law on the national defence organization and the law that initiated the reform of the military criminal code.

Adolfo Suárez resigned in early 1981 and it was at the inauguration session of the person who would be his successor, Leopoldo Calvo Sotelo, that the attempted *coup d'état* occurred, resulting in the kidnapping of the Government and Parliament during the entire afternoon and night of 23 February. Alberto Oliart was the next civilian minister who had the difficult task of controlling the armed forces and preventing new insubordination while the trial of the participants in the coup took place. In parallel, the Government agreed to the entry of Spain into NATO (North Atlantic Treaty Organization) immediately before the new elections in October 1982.

Felipe Agüero previously stated in his important study of the Spanish case that 'democratization does not only involve excluding the military from political matters and eliminating military disputes; it also involves asserting the prerogatives of civilian governors in military matters and defence'.[9] Following this line of thinking,

[9] Agüero (n. 3), 33.

I have proposed dividing the democratic reform of the Spanish armed forces into two periods: (i) the period of the transition properly speaking and (ii) the period of the consolidation. In the first, the objective was to prevent military interference in politics, generally at the cost of increased conflict between the military and the civilian government, and also an increase in military autonomy. In the second, the objective was that the Government should create the country's defence and military policy, provide for its application, and direct the actions of the armed forces.[10]

The transition period was 1976–82. The period of consolidation commenced when the Socialist Party obtained a broad electoral victory in October 1982.

Institutional structure of security services and separation of powers and functions

The Spanish armed forces, the maintenance of public order, and segregation in the security sector

The armed forces, and especially the Army, guaranteed the continued existence of the Franco regime through strict control of all leverage in the maintenance of order. This was achieved through its deployment in the largest urban centres and the location of the most powerful unit, the armoured division, in the vicinity of Madrid.

To this, the management of all police forces, the Armed Police (which later, now in a democracy, would be called *Policía Nacional*—National Police), as well as the *Guardia Civil* (Civil Guard), had to be added, as these were commanded by generals in the Army, assisted by numerous infantry and cavalry officers, who were transferred to these police bodies in part because the pay was somewhat higher and in part due to the fact that the Government was aware of the over-staffing of officers in the Army and encouraged the transfer of officers to civilian agencies.

Military officers were made responsible for repressing political activities through various different legal provisions. First, the legal state of war was maintained until 1948, nine years after the end of the conflict. From this date, different laws, including the 'repression of freemasonry and communism' made political actions (meetings for political purposes, strikes, publications, etc.) equivalent to the crime of military rebellion, making the military court responsible for applying those laws. Although in 1963 a Public Order Court was established within the framework of the ordinary courts, in 1968 the equivalence of political crimes and military rebellion was re-established and, two months before the death of General Franco, five death sentences ordered by War Councils were carried out.[11]

The intelligence services were also almost totally controlled by the military. With the exception of the Social Investigation Brigade which, from the Ministry of the

[10] Narcís Serra, *The Military Transition* (Cambridge University Press, 2010), 28.

[11] Manuel Ballbé, *Orden público y militarismo en la España constitucional* (Alianza Universidad, 1983).

Interior, worked on prosecution of activities opposed to the regime, the three remaining intelligence services were managed by military officials: that of the Army; the Higher Chiefs of Staff, connected to the President of the Government; and the *Centro Superior de Información de la Defensa* (SECED—Higher Centre of Defence Information), a service created by Admiral Carrero Blanco to penetrate university and neighbourhood movements and other activities in favour of the democratization of the country.

This description of the four areas of control of the internal order defines the role of the Army in the Franco regime. Even if it did not govern the country—although, out of 114 Franco ministers, 40 were military officers[12]—it is clear that Franco assigned to it the task of maintaining public order and gave it all the necessary instruments. This was a role readily accepted by the armed forces.

The democratization of the security sector required, first, segregation of the armed forces and police forces and this segregation was spelt out in the text of the Constitution. The Joint Chiefs of Staff as well as the *Alianza Popular* (Popular Alliance), the most conservative party represented on the constitutional committee, defended the integration of the police and *Guardia Civil* into the category of armed forces, although in the final debates only the continuity of the *Guardia Civil* was requested. On this issue, they were in conflict with the other parties and their proposals were rejected. This is one of the issues clearly resolved by the 1978 Constitution.

A law from the same year changed the name of the police, adopting the title *Policía Nacional* (National Police) as opposed to the previous title of *Policía Armada* (Armed Police), but it was not until the 1986 *Ley Orgánica de Fuerzas y Cuerpos de Seguridad* (LOFCS—Organic Law of the Security Forces and Corps) that the demilitarization of the *Policía Nacional* was completed. Two events that were relevant for the demilitarization of the police had occurred previously: the creation of a police force for the Basque Country, the '*Ertzaintza*', based on its statutory authorities in 1982; and the creation of another autonomous police force, the Catalonian police, called '*mossos d'esquadra*', based on a 1983 law of the Catalonian parliament.

As for the military-controlled intelligence services, in 1977, General Gutiérrez Mellado had already integrated them into a new organization, the *Centro Superior de Inteligencia de la Defensa* (CESID—Higher Centre for Intelligence and Defence). However, effective control by the Government did not occur until after the attempted *coup d'état* on 23 February 1981. From this date, and reporting to the Ministry of Defence, it became an effective service for combating regression and possible anti-democracy movements within the armed forces. With the progress of the democratization process in the armed forces, the CESID aimed, at the end of the 1980s, at fighting terrorism. Until 1995, it was regulated by ministerial orders and by decree. The first regulation ranking as a law occurred in 1995 and

[12] Robert Graham, *Spain: Change of a Nation* (Michael Joseph Ltd, 1984), 195.

another law, of 6 May 2002, transformed the CESID into the *Centro Nacional de Inteligencia* (CNI—National Intelligence Centre), locating it under the direct authority of the President of the Government. On the same date, another organic law established the form of judicial control to which some of the actions of the CNI were subjected.

The change of orientation of the armed forces missions

The fight against the internal enemy was a priority mission of the Army during the regime of General Franco, to the extent that it established a deployment in its own national territory that was similar to that of an occupying army, with garrisons in the centre of the provincial capitals. This characteristic, which was also typical of many Latin American countries in those years, was boosted by anti-communism and also by the feeling cultivated in the armed forces that they had some values which were superior to those shared by the civil society and that it was the mission and responsibility of the armed forces to disseminate those superior values in society as a whole. The democratization of the armed forces could be limited to the loss of the prerogatives of the authoritarian period, or the transformation of structures of the sector adapting them to a democratic system. It had to consist of a professional transformation and mentality for the change to be stable. The clearest way that a government (and society) can indicate this professional change is by defining the missions that democracy requires from the armed forces. This issue was not addressed when the Constitution was drafted, but already in the transition period through the separation of the armed forces from political activities as well as the request to enter NATO in 1981 which both indicated the new direction.

During the consolidation period, this change in the orientation of the missions of the armed forces was completed. The first definition of security policy debated in the parliament consisted of the ten points presented by Felipe González before holding the referendum on Spain continuing as a member of NATO.[13]

[13] The ten points were:

1. Spain should stay in the Atlantic Alliance.
2. Spain should not join NATO's integrated military structure.
3. The ban on installing, storing, or bringing nuclear arms into the territory of Spain should be continued.
4. There should be a new bilateral agreement reducing US military presence in Spain.
5. The Treaty Banning Nuclear Tests should be ratified, not excluding the signing of the Treaty on the Non-Proliferation of Nuclear Arms.
6. Spain should participate in the Western European Union.
7. Spain should continue demanding the sovereignty of Gibraltar.
8. Spain should maintain of an active presence in the European Conference of Disarmament and in the United Nations.
9. Spain should continue developing bilateral agreements in terms of defence cooperation with other European countries.
10. Spain should include the Joint Strategic Plan as an element in the dialogue to achieve a consensus in the area of defence policy.

In the National Defence Directive, signed by the President of the Government after the referendum in the autumn of 1986, the three missions assigned to the armed forces were:

- to contribute to the maintenance of peace between nations and to the security and defence of the Western world to which Spain belongs, especially in relation to the nation's immediate strategic concerns;
- to develop an effective military capacity to deter foreseeable threats;
- to develop an effective civil defence system able to act in any situation.

None of them could be related to the 'enemy within'. However, drafting documents or instructions is not sufficient to change minds. A period of practical action is necessary to continue to assimilate new concepts. In the Spanish case, three factors supported this new direction. First was the decision of all democratic governments to not assign to the armed forces the mission to fight terrorism in the Basque country, reserving the fight against domestic terrorism to the police and intelligence services. Second, NATO membership was finally granted in 1988, which familiarized the Spanish armed forces with the professional characteristics of Western armed forces. Third, beginning in 1987, Spain cooperated in various peace missions. The entry into NATO and the new international mission (the first were in Angola, Namibia, Nicaragua, and the first Gulf War) were relevant facts not only in the change of the mentality of the Spanish military but also in the acceptance and assessment of the armed forces by Spanish society.

The structure of the defence and the chain of command

Despite the immobility of the military leadership, in the 1960s an internal movement for debate and analysis arose within the *Centro de Estudios Superiores de la Defensa* (CESEDEN—Higher Defence Studies Centre) by military officials led by General Díez-Alegría, who were aware of the need to bring the Spanish military structure to approximate those of neighbouring countries. In 1974, they produced a bill which was blocked by those in favour of immobility in the *Cortes* after the assassination of Admiral Carrero Blanco, who had supported it.

The most important aspects in the thinking of the CESEDEN were the provisions ensuring the autonomy of the armed forces in a future without Franco, which was most certainly looming on the horizon. The proposal consisted of distinguishing two parallel lines in the defence structure: the chain of command and the political-administrative branch. The chain of command had a higher body which was the Joint Chiefs of Staff (it could not be the President of the Joint Chiefs of Staff since no armed force was willing to accept as chief a member of either of the other two forces), and the *Junta de Jefes de Estado Mayor* (JUJEM—Joint Chiefs of Staff) was directly responsible to the head of state. The political-administrative line that the Ministry was based on (either civilian or military) took care of the support and connections with the rest of the Government but did not interfere in the chain of command. Finally, the armed forces were not considered as a part of the state administration but rather as an autonomous institution that was in dialogue with the other political institutions.

As in the case of other transitions, the Spanish armed forces tended to reinforce their reserve of control when they were losing the ability to intervene in politics. The non-inclusion of armed forces in the structure of the Ministry as well as the establishment of a chain of command directly connected to the King and not to the Government were fundamental parts of its autonomy plan.

Early on, Gutiérrez Mellado started a process of democratic reform and modernization of military structures following the guidelines provided in the work by the CESEDEN, on which he had collaborated. Before the end of 1976, the position of the Chief of Staff in the Army had already been created and in early February it was replicated in the Air Force. On the same day, 8 February 1977, the Decree-Law creating the JUJEM as a 'superior collegial body of the military chain of command of the armed forces' was published. The idea of collegial command is inconsistent with both military idiosyncrasy and the necessities of discipline and effectiveness of the armed forces, which require that the steps of the chain of command must be limited to one person. However, this formulation was possible for some armed forces accustomed to having their own ministry and not used to joint activities, much less to accepting command by a member of another armed force.

The problems which arose from this formula were aggravated by other points of the Decree-Law. First, in its statement of reasons appeared the 'superior body of joint military command' under the 'supreme command of His Majesty the King'. Second, it indicated that the JUJEM was 'under the political authority of the President of the Government'. These texts established the proposal that the subordination to the Government was not total subordination but rather was only political, while on military command issues the subordination was direct subordination to the King. This Decree-Law is the first legal establishment of the two parallel lines of management of the armed forces, that of the military command and the line called political-administrative, in which governmental authority was limited.

Gutiérrez Mellado was aware of the two problems this formulation created, up to the point, as we will see, of preventing it from being included in the new Constitution. Based on one of its most far-reaching decisions, the elimination of the three military ministries, and the creation of the Ministry of Defence in June 1977, successive decrees reinforced the role of the Ministry and integrated the JUJEM into its structure. Thus, in the law on basic national defence criteria of 1 July 1980, it was already stated that the JUJEM was organically within the Ministry of Defence and that 'it is responsible to the President of the Government, who exercises his authority through the Ministry of Defence, except on those matters which are expressly reserved for the President'. It is no longer said that the office is only political, and the word 'authority' is used, which is the closest to command which could be used at that time.

The JUJEM, in direct contact with the committee that drafted the Constitution, attempted to include in the text of the Constitution the character of collegial command and the connection to the King. Gutiérrez Mellado indicated to the drafting committee that this issue was not a constitutional issue and that it had to be implemented, if applicable, by law. In this manner, it became possible to complete the military reform in the democratic consolidation period, since otherwise Law 1/1984, which formed the JUJEM as an advisory body to the President of the Government and the Ministry of Defence and unified the two parallel lines of management of the armed forces, would not have been possible without a prior change to the Constitution. In addition, the modification of the first articles of the Spanish Constitution is almost impossible, since it requires the dissolution of the parliament and a popular referendum. Obviously, the inclusion of the military demand in the Constitution would have prevented the decisive and necessary step which, six years later, led to Law 1/1984, to complete the military reform and to clarify the subordination of the armed forces to the government.

In fact, this law clarified two essential issues. First, it regulated the JUJEM as a collegial body to advise the President of the Government and the Ministry of Defence organically and functionally within the Ministry of Defence. Second, it assigned to the President of the Government effective command, since he would be responsible for the management of defence policy and in addition 'he exercises authority to order, coordinate and direct the actions of the armed forces'.

Civilian and social oversight

The basic supervisory instrument and driver of the democratizing process of the armed forces is the Ministry of Defence, so much so that its structure and capacities constitute the simplest way to measure the level of democratization achieved. In the Franco regime, there were three military ministries, one for each armed force. Gutiérrez Mellado decided to established the Ministry of Defence during the establishment of the government which arose from the elections of 15 June 1977.

Many conditions were placed on the establishment of the Ministry of Defence by the military leadership, to the point that the decree which organized the Ministry required that all the high positions in the Ministry had to be occupied by generals or other officers of the three armed forces. In any case, during its first six years of existence, it was very difficult to feed the Ministry with officers from the three armed forces, due to their reluctance to provide staff, and also the fact that the Ministry did not have its own building.

Specifically, the key to the consolidation once the legal reforms had been carried out resided in giving the Ministry of Defence the civilian and military resources necessary to perform its mission of directing defence policy and effectively overseeing the actions of the armed forces. Thus, the defence planning initiative came from the Government and was carried out under its control. The same occurred with the budget for the armed forces, with the armament and equipment procurement policy, continuing later with the personnel policy and reform of education in academies and schools.

The control of the parliament played an important role in the process of reform of the armed forces. Especially in the phases of the transition, the parliament acted as a demonstration of the agreement between the democratic parties on the need for—and direction of—reform. From the first moment, a Defence Committee was established to debate before the plenary sessions on issues related to this area and also to receive information on the reform process and other actions directly from the Minister or from other high positions in the Ministry.

In the early years, its work was limited due to lack of preparation of the members of parliament in the area of security and defence. The same occurred with professionals working in the communications media. There were also no university professors or think-tanks specializing in these issues. In fact, the first large debate in Spanish society on the subject of security occurred at the time of the 1986 referendum on NATO membership. However, these failures were being resolved with the passage of time and a proactive policy from the Ministry of Defence itself, so that they could reasonably be considered resolved at the end of the consolidation period at the end of the 1980s. The defence ministry in a country in transition can contribute to raising awareness of security issues, organizing courses for journalists, mixed courses of civilians (members of parliament, officials of other ministries, professors, etc.) and military officers, opening the military academies to universities, and fighting the secrecy that is inherent to armed forces in every case and even more so in authoritarian regimes.

Constitutional and legal issues

Design and choice of law

The design of military reform in Spain was gradual. When it started, the first steps were very clear, but the complete process was far from being so. In the transitional period two areas marked the process: the segregation of the armed forces from politics and the work of a group of modernizing officers in the armed forces who were, at the same time, defending its autonomy. In the consolidation period, the goal of reform consisted in reducing the levels of autonomy of the armed forces at the same time as the Government was reinforcing its role of defining, managing, and overseeing defence policy.

The most important issues were modified by law, but for the fundamental issues the Constitution required them to be regulated by organic law, which requires a broad majority. The laws on basic rules of national defence of 1980 and 1984 were organic laws, as were those reforming military justice. In many cases, the executive promulgated a decree-law, which is a regulation with legal effect issued by the executive authority for reasons of urgency. It was used especially in the first years of the transition and, later, in some specific cases such as in the case of the incorporation of women into the armed forces (Decree-Law 1/1988) in order for women to be able to apply as candidates for new courses in military academies. The gradual empowerment of the Ministry of Defence occurred by means of decrees, which are regulations approved by the Council of Ministers. Finally, issues more related to immediate management were regulated by ministerial orders, signed by the Minister. In a reform process, however, regulations with a lower scope or, simply, decisions by the Minister can be highly significant. A good example of this is the reform of military education. In 1985 and before the process of preparing a law on military education was considered, a ministerial order (OM 66/1985) provided that the maximum term of appointment of an official as a professor in a military academy was six years. It caused a substantial change in the professorial ranks of academies and the renewal of professorships was an indispensable condition in military education reform.

The drafting of the Constitution and reform of the security sector

The new Constitution assumed a fundamental step in the transition process, especially due to the form in which it was agreed at the parliamentary level as well as at the popular level when it was put to a referendum in December 1978. It had to be a new Constitution; the last democratic Constitution of the Second Republic of 1931 could not be restored because too many years had passed and, especially, because the Republic was not a possible option and the new regime to be created was that of a constitutional monarchy.

In order to prepare it, the constitutional Congress elected a seven-member panel that represented the various positions in the parliament, except for the Basque Country. The fact that one of them had been a minister in the governments of the dictatorship (Fraga Iribarne), another was a member of the Communist Party (Solé Tura), and a third was from the nationalist Catalonian Party (Roca Junyent) gives an idea of the diversity of its members. The panel was completed by a socialist member and three centrists from the party of Adolfo Suárez.

The preparation process was relatively quick, but it allowed broad debates to occur at every level. The panel prepared the draft Constitution after five months of work. The draft was published in 1978, following which a period for suggested amendments saw more than 3,000 proposals submitted to the lower house of parliament. Parliamentary debate commenced from April, with twenty-four sessions of the Committee on Constitutional Issues and twelve plenary sessions of the parliament.

The Bill then went to the Senate. Since the Senate amended the Bill, it had to establish a Joint Committee of Members of the Lower House and Senators whose agreement on the text was published on 28 October. This is the text that was voted on in both chambers on the same day, 31 October. In the Lower House, out of 345 votes, the bill obtained 325 in favour, 6 against, and 14 abstentions. In the Senate, out of 239 in attendance, 226 voted in favour, 5 against, and 8 abstained. The referendum for popular approval was scheduled for 6 December: 87.78 per cent of voters approved it.

The drafting of the Constitution faced enormous problems. Key among these was the fact that all parties had to give up proposals they had fiercely defended until that time as absolutely essential. The Communist Party and the socialists conceded on the republican structure of the state and the Right agreed not to maintain the centralized state, accepting autonomy, to cite only two examples. Clearly, the greatest difficulty was raised by the territorial model and the return to the Autonomous Communities of the Second Republic, or in other words, acceptance of self-government of specified regions which consider themselves to be nations due to their history and because they have their own language. This problem was increased by the intervention of the armed forces, which felt that they were depositories of the defence of the principles and structures of the Franco regime, in other words, the guarantee of its continuity.

Finally, the use of the word 'nationality' instead of using the word 'nation' applied to the historically autonomous areas (Catalonia, Basque Country, Galicia) made it possible to approve the second article of the Constitution which 'guarantees the right to autonomy of nationalities and regions' which are a part of the Spanish nation.

This issue, like many others, demonstrates that the 1978 Constitution was a real break in relation to the characteristics of the previous regime. The start of the transition was presided over by a struggle between those for continuing the old regime, basically representing ex-leaders of the old regime and the armed forces, and the reformist ex-leaders represented by Adolfo Suárez and the party he created, the *Unión del Centro democrático* (Union of the Democratic Centre). Examples of this conflict with the armed forces were the previously cited resignation of the Vice President of the Government, General de Santiago, when the trade unions were legalized; the resignation of Admiral Pita da Veiga as Navy Minister, when in March 1977 the Communist Party was legalized so it could run in the first democratic elections; and the resignation of the Chief of Staff of the Army in March 1978 because he refused to accept the authority of the Minister. The creation of the Constitution was thus a debate between reformers and parties from the democratic opposition to Francoism, which desired a total break in relation the former situation, and those who wished to preserve as much as possible from the old regime.

The final broad agreement, has been defined as an 'agreed break-up' since it laid the groundwork for a totally democratic regime, but it occurred through consensus of the political forces at that time.

In the transition process, there was a large debate related to an amnesty, although this was resolved—except for the military officers that constituted the *Unión Militar Democrática* (UMD—Democratic Military Union)—before the preparation of the Constitution. The amnesty was requested by the democratic opposition, especially by the parties on the left, as a way to release and extinguish the liabilities of those convicted by the Franco regime of political crimes.

The Government of Adolfo Suárez responded to this request with an amnesty Decree-Law of 30 July 1976, but this provision did not appear sufficient to the democratic opposition which, after the 1977 constitutional elections, led the Lower House to approve the Amnesty Law of 15 October 1977 by a large majority (296 votes in favour, 2 against, and 18 abstentions).

However, the amnesty could not be applied completely to the UMD military officers, who were sentenced to severe penalties in 1976. Twice, in 1977 and 1980, the high military command would not allow these officers to return to the Army, and the parliament ended up accepting their refusal. Almost six more years were required to defeat it. In 1986, after the referendum on NATO and after some new legislative elections were held, the Ministry of Defence prepared a draft law approved by the parliament on 24 December 1986.

Later—in the twenty-first century—the Amnesty Law would show that it is a double-edged sword because it is used to prevent the investigation of crimes perpetrated by the Franco regime during the Civil War. However, there is no doubt that in 1977, the parliament was aware that the law had these consequences, but it opted for this step, which was necessary for reconciliation before drafting the Constitution.

The Constitution and the Armed Forces

As stated previously, when the constitutional authority had started its drafting work, it received a document send directly by the JUJEM with various requests or indications relating to the text of the future Constitution. Apparently, the document was delivered without the prior knowledge of the Vice President for defence matters, in one more example of the actions of the JUJEM as an organization to defend military corporate interests as well as resistance to the role and decisions of the Minister.

The numerous requests by the JUJEM can be summarized as three, which involved serious risks for the democratic character of the Constitution which was being drafted. The first of these was the placing of any article which defined the armed forces and its missions among the first articles of the Constitution dedicated to the Institutions of the State and in direct connection with the Crown. The second was keeping the police and *Guardia Civil* as a part of the armed forces. The third was including in the Constitution the differentiation of military and political-administrative lines of command, which have already been described. The committee rejected the second proposal, namely the integration of the police and *Guardia Civil* into the armed forces.

In relation to the first request, the article referring to the armed forces, Article 8, was included, specifically in the Preliminary Title, with the following text:

> 8.1 The Armed Forces, made up of the Army, the Navy and the Air Force, have the mission of ensuring the sovereignty and independence of Spain, to defend its territorial integrity and the constitutional order.
>
> 8.2 An Organic Law shall regulate the basic structure of military organization in accordance with the principles of this Constitution.

The final text of this article contained two important differences with respect to the requests of the JUJEM. The first, in the first paragraph, was the elimination of the expression 'ensure the unity of Spain' and the replacement of the word 'unity' with the word 'sovereignty'. The second, which I have previously discussed, was the total elimination of the paragraph that made the JUJEM constitutionally a higher collegial body of the military chain of command.

The balance of the drafting of this part of the Constitution in relation to the democratization of the armed forces was, for these reasons, complex. On one hand, it was decided to demilitarize the police and not to integrate the *Guardia Civil* into the armed forces. Although these decisions were very significant, on the other hand, the armed forces were located in the Preliminary Title together with the monarchic form of the state and the recognitions of the autonomy of nationalities and Spanish regions. It maintained the hopes of some military officers who considered the armed forces as an institution which could be in dialogue with other state institutions. In any case it must be accepted that, despite the lack of clarity in the Constitution, its drafting made possible the culmination of a military reform process that today we have to consider complete with respect to the insertion of armed forces into the structure of a democratic state. Given the military pressure, and the weight of that pressure in the years immediately after the death of General Franco, it must concluded that, with respect to these issues, the imperfect drafting of the Constitution was very close to the best that was possible at that time.

Some Contentious Issues with the Armed Forces in the Creation of the Constitution

The most contentious issue with regards to the military's position, and the most dangerous in relation to its possible reaction, was the issue of the territorial organization of the state. Eventually, as previously stated, the expression 'nationality' to refer to Catalonia and the Basque Country instead of the word 'nation' made it possible to avoid open conflict, although the military pressure against the process of recognition of autonomous governments, a process that the military considered the disintegration of the Spanish state, was very strong.

I now consider other problematic issues which were subject to conflict with the armed forces in the drafting of the text of the Constitution, although some of them have been discussed previously.

Death penalty

Although favoured by the political parties, the military was against the total elimination of the death penalty in the Constitution. In the end, Article 15 was approved as follows: 'The death penalty is abolished, except as provided by military criminal law in times of war.' In the 1985 Military Criminal Code, the death penalty could only be applied in times of war, but it was not in any case the only punishment applicable to a crime, so that it was impossible that a military court would be obligated to impose it. Later, in 1995, the death penalty was totally abolished.

Honour courts

Honour courts were previously used to investigate matters of honour and dignity, in terms of whether the individual merited continued membership of the body to which he/she belonged. Under the previous regime, these courts extended beyond the military to public administration and professional associations as well. Due to military pressure, Article 26 of the Constitution was revised as follows: 'Honour courts are prohibited in the scope of the Civil Administration and professional organizations.' In the period of the consolidation of military reform and specifically with the reform of military justice initiated in 1985, military Honour courts were abolished.

Conscientious objection to military service

This was regulated in Article 30 of the Constitution: 'The law shall set forth the military obligations of Spanish citizens and shall regulate, with due guarantees, conscientious objection, as well as other causes of exemption from mandatory military service, and social service may be required, as may be applicable, as a substitute.' This article recognized the right to conscientious objection, but it could not be implemented during the transition period. The regulatory law of this constitutional mandate was Law 48 of 1984, which established the 'substitute social service' or social service compatible with the reasons for the conscientious objection. This issue was finally resolved with the abolition of military service on 31 December 2001.

Independence of military justice

During the Franco regime, the military built a judicial authority of its own with a Supreme Council of Military Justice which was independent of the civil judicial authority, therefore violating the democratic principle of unity of judicial authority. Naturally, they requested the continuation of those prerogatives and obtained a Constitutional provision permitting them, although only to a limited extent:

> Article 117.5 The principle of jurisdictional unity is the basis of the organization and functioning of Courts. The law will regulate the exercise of military jurisdiction in the strictly military context and in cases of a state of siege, in accordance with the principles of the Constitution.

In fact, the issue of military justice had been discussed previously, in October 1977, when the Moncloa Agreements were signed, which included an agreement to prevent the military justice system from being able to try civilians.

Thus, in 1980, in the transition period, the Military Justice System had already been reformed with two very relevant changes: the first, to prevent public order crimes from being tried and, generally, to prevent civilians from being tried. The second change provided for appeals of military sentences before the national Supreme Court. However, it could not make more progress in a period in which, in addition, the military justice system had to try the participants in the coup of 23 February 1981.

The rigorous interpretation of the constitutional mandate was applied with the reform of military justice initiated in 1985. The independence of military judicial authority was eliminated, creating a Military Chamber in the Supreme Court and integrating both courts. This reform was completed approximately ten years after the approval of the Constitution.

The armed forces as an institution

It is significant that this was one of the most debated issues in the parliamentary discussion of the military aspects of the Constitution. Alianza Popular (Popular Alliance), the most conservative party in the parliament, defended the position that the armed forces were much more than a department of the administration or a section of a ministry. It was previously indicated that the great danger of this position was that it boosted military autonomy with respect to the Government by the military being considered an institution with a supreme collegial command (the JUJEM) connected to the King, to whom Article 62 of the Constitution granted the supreme command of the armed forces. The Constitution did not stop this danger since finally the armed forces article was not placed in the Title on the Government and the Administration, but in the Preliminary Title, as previously indicated.

Some Thoughts on the Spanish Constitutional Process and Military Reform

First, we must mention that the process of military transition to democracy was longer in the case of the armed forces than in strictly political matters, which many analysts considered completed in 1979 with the approval of the statutes of Catalonia and the Basque Country. The division between transition and consolidation is more diffuse in the general political case than in the military case, where the objectives are more clearly distinguished.

The Spanish experience also shows that the Constitution cannot be the final response to questions that are being debated within society. However, the most important aspect is that the Constitution should not block solutions from emerging due to the progress of the debate within society after promulgation. Many issues which were blocked when the Constitution was drafted could be resolved gradually in subsequent years. The Constitution, in addition to resolving all the existing problems, has to allow for the future resolution of problems, which will be gradual in many cases. Democratization processes are long, and it is appropriate that a new Constitution should open windows to the future instead of determining possible solutions at a given time, making it difficult to change them at a later date.

The state of civilian–military relations at the time of drafting and approving the Constitution was in Spain—and also in many other cases of transition to democracy—a conditioning factor for its content. If we consider the seven levels of reduction of military autonomy that I have analysed elsewhere,[14] the opportunities to influence constitutional drafting by some armed forces acting to protect what they consider to be the national essence are much higher than in the case of armed forces that now accept civilian supremacy. However, it usually happens that a Constitution is drafted in the first phases of the transition, which are still a long way from seeing the democratization of the military.

[14] Serra (n. 10), 43–9.

The Constitution must contain the broad outlines of the institutions that are to configure coexistence within the nation, the definition of guaranteed civil liberties, agreements between majorities and minorities, etc. However, it cannot develop and specify these issues such as, for example, the insertion of the armed forces in the democratic structure of the state. The Spanish experience shows that there are issues that must be left to be resolved by law and in a gradual manner. The real guarantee of the culmination of a transitional process resides in the continuity of social will and the political impulse until democracy is consolidated.

The Spanish Constitution allowed specified reforms, but did not require or encourage them. Military reform was carried out by formally invoking the Constitution, but the truth is that the new Constitution was not the engine of this reform. That was achieved above all by the political will to mirror the situation of neighbouring countries and to join Europe. The military reform laws were based on the comparative policies of European democracies and on common sense, all moderated by a sense of prudence and of incremental change.

This does not mean that a Constitution accepted by a very broad majority, as was the case of the 1978 Spanish Constitution, does not assume broad support for any subsequent reform process. Because it is an unequivocal sign of transition and democratic consolidation, the Spanish Constitution constituted an essential element of acceptance of the new situation by the military. Here it must be remembered that there is no form of stable and long-term control of the military if it is not accepted by the military themselves. The military has to believe that subordination to civilian authority is the best, if not the only way to be accepted and valued by society. In this regard, the influence that a broadly debated Constitution, agreed to by the political forces and accepted by a large majority of citizens may have cannot be underestimated. The Spanish transition is a good example of this.

2

The Slow Change in Chile

Long-term Security Sector Reform Alongside Constitutional Transition

Gonzalo García Pino

Introduction

In September 1973 General Augusto Pinochet's military coup ended a period of democratic government uninterrupted in Chile since 1830, ushering in a period of military rule that lasted until 1990. In these seventeen years, the ruling military oligarchy made significant changes that increased the authority of the military and police (collectively the 'security services'), removed mechanisms for civilian oversight of the military and police, and expanded the executive powers of the President. Central to these changes was the introduction of a new Constitution in 1980. The story of Chile's restoration of democracy is in many ways the story of incrementally drawing back the powers granted to the President and the security services by the 1980 Constitution, through constitutional amendments in 1989, 2005, and 2011, and statutory changes made as recently as 2015. The processes of democratic transition and security sector reform (SSR) thus occurred in parallel in Chile: both were slow and methodical and have gradually reintroduced accountability and civilian oversight into a security service that was, for the seventeen years of the Junta, above the Constitution. This chapter recounts this story, expounding the benefits of a gradual process of SSR while remaining alive to the challenges that this brings, aiming to draw from Chile's experience general lessons about SSR during constitutional transition.

Background and Context: From Democracy to Dictatorship and Back

The constitution of military authoritarianism

After deposing President Salvador Allende and dissolving Chile's democratically elected legislature (Congress), Pinochet's military government promised to establish a new democratic system and protect it from both external and internal enemies: the Soviet Union and international forces of communism on one hand, and domestic communists on the other. This 'protected democracy' would require the expansion of the authority and powers of the military and police and, moreover, an entirely new political structure or 'institutionality'.[1] The first step in establishing this new institutionality was for the armed forces to assume the 'supreme command of the nation' as the Junta *de Gobierno*, a ruling council composed of the Commanders-in-Chief of the Army, the Navy, Air Force, and the Director General of the *Carabineros*, the national police force. The Junta was the only institution of government in Chile, exercising both legislative and executive functions without any recognition of the principle of separation of powers. The Junta exercised legislative power by enacting decree-laws, while performing executive functions through supreme decrees and resolutions.

The second step in establishing Chile's protected democracy was to enact a new Constitution to replace the 1925 Constitution. Days after the 1973 coup, the Junta appointed a nine-member constitution-drafting committee under the chairmanship of Enrique Ortuzar Escobar, a former Minister of Justice and Foreign Affairs during Jorge Allesandri's presidency from 1958–64. The Ortuzar Commission published a draft Constitution in 1978, which was in turn approved by plebiscite in September 1980. While the 1980 Constitution was unsurprisingly partial towards the military regime, it is important to highlight a handful of institutional mechanisms that centralized power in the hands of the security services and undermined civilian and political oversight of the activities of the security services.

First, the 1980 Constitution rested on a set of principles catalogued in its opening provisions as the 'bases of institutionality'. Although many of these principles were innocuous and would not be out of place in a constitutional democracy today—including statements committing to individual equality before the law and the family as the foundation of society—others spoke to the Junta's authoritarian character. Article 8, for example, provided that any action by individuals or groups that advocate a conception of society based on 'class warfare' was illegal (para. 1), that any organizations advocating these conceptions of society were unconstitutional (para. 2), and that any persons found to have advocated any such conception of society would be precluded for ten years from holding public office or leadership positions in political, educational, professional, entrepreneurial, or labour organizations (para. 4).

[1] Augusto Pinochet, *Visión futura de Chile* (División Nacional Comunicación Social, 1979), 32. See also Wendy Hunter, *State and Soldier in Latin America: Redefining the Military's Role in Argentina, Brazil, and Chile* (US Institute of Peace, Peaceworks Series, 1996), 30–1, noting that the notion of 'protected democracy' coincided with an alliance between armed forces and conservative or right-wing political parties.

Second, the 'bases of institutionality' provided a constitutional toehold for the expansion of the military's political influence throughout the 1980 Constitution. While Article 1 paragraph 5 provided that 'it is the duty of the State to safeguard national security', Article 90 paragraph 2 declared that the military and the *Carabineros* were essential to national security and emphasized that it was their function to 'guarantee the institutional order of the Republic'. The security services' centrality to the civilian political structure was thus constitutionally entrenched.

A key element of the security services' political role lay in the composition, functions, and operations of the *Consejo de Seguridad Nacional* (COSENA—National Security Council). The Council was to be headed by the President and composed of the President of the Senate, the President of the Supreme Court, the three Commanders-in-Chief of the armed forces, and the Director General of the *Carabineros*.[2] The Council's functions included advising the President on matters linked to national security upon his request, and expressing its opinion to any organ of the state about a 'fact, action, or matter' which in its judgement threatened the 'bases of institutionality or which might affect the national security' of Chile.[3] The Ministers for the Interior, Foreign Relations, National Defence, Economy, and Finance held the right to participate as members of the Council, but without a right to vote.[4] COSENA could be convoked by the President or by two of its members, and a majority of its members was required for a quorum,[5] but the constitutionally prescribed membership of COSENA ensured that the Junta held a majority on COSENA: four of its seven members were the Commanders-in-Chief of the security forces, with the President, and the presidents of the Senate and the Supreme Court the only civilian members. Indeed, even though the President was nominally a civilian position, Pinochet remained Commander-in-Chief of the Army throughout his term as President. This arrangement, as well as COSENA's power to identify threats to the bases of institutionality, which the security services were obliged to eliminate, conferred a great deal of power on the security sector to steer the course of government business.[6]

Third, although the 1980 Constitution provided for the establishment, election, and functioning of a bicameral legislature composed of the Senate and the Chamber of Deputies,[7] the 'transitory provisions' appended to the Constitution

[2] Constitución Política de la República de Chile, 1980 (CP), Art. 95 para. 1.
[3] Ibid., Art. 96(b).
[4] Ibid., Art. 95 para. 2.
[5] Ibid., Art. 95 para. 3.
[6] See also Robert Barros, *Constitutionalism and Dictatorship: Pinochet, the Junta, and the 1980 Constitution* (Cambridge University Press, 2002), 240–4.
[7] CP, Chapter 5.

ensured that Congress would be suspended for at least eight years after 1980. During this period, the Junta itself would operate as the legislature.[8] The Junta thus remained the only legislative organ in Chile even after the adoption of the new Constitution in 1980, until it was forced from power in 1989. Looking beyond this eight-year transition period, the 1980 Constitution sought to prolong the security sector's influence in Congress in other ways: one of each of the former Commanders-in-Chief of the Army, Air Force, and Navy, and a former Director General of the *Carabineros* would hold a seat in the upper chamber of Congress, and these four senators would be appointed by COSENA.[9] COSENA would also appoint two of the seven members of the Constitutional Tribunal.[10]

Alongside legislative supremacy, the 1980 Constitution sought to ensure ongoing executive power for Pinochet. Although Article 25 provided that the President would hold office for eight years and could not be re-elected for a consecutive term, the Fourteenth Transitory Provision provided that Pinochet—identified by name

[8] Ibid., Eighteenth Transitory Provision:

> During the period to which the Thirteenth Transitory Provision refers, the Junta of Government will exercise, by the unanimity of its Members, the following exclusive attributions:
> A. To exercise the Constituent Power, always subject to plebiscitary approval, which will be held in conformity with the rules that the law specifies;
> B. To exercise the Legislative Power;
> C. To issue [*dictar*] the interpretative laws of the Constitution, which may be necessary;
> D. To approve or reject international treaties, prior to the presidential ratification;
> E. To grant its agreement to the President of the Republic in the cases specified in Letter B of the Fifteenth Transitory Provision;
> F. To grant its agreement to the President of the Republic in order to decree the states of assembly and of siege, as the case may be;
> G. To permit the entry of foreign troops into the territory of the Republic, as well as to authorize the departure of national troops from it;
> H. To take cognizance of the conflicts of competence that arise between the political or administrative authorities and the superior tribunals of justice;
> I. To grant the recovery of citizenship, in the cases to which Article 17, Numeral 2 of this Constitution refers [*aludir*];
> J. To declare, in the case of the resignation of the President of the Republic or the Commanders-in-Chief of the Armed Forces and of the Director General of the Carabineros, if the reasons which cause it are well-founded or not, and, consequently, accept it or reject it; and
> K. Other powers conferred thereupon by other transitory provisions of this Constitution.

The Thirteenth Transitory Provision provided:

> The presidential term which shall commence when this Constitution enters in force shall last the time prescribed for in Article 25 [i.e. eight years].

The Fourteenth Transitory Provision then provided:

> During the term stated in the preceding provision, the current President, General of the Army, Augusto Pinochet Ugarte, shall continue being the President, and shall remain in office until the end of said term.

[9] Ibid., Art. 45 para. 3(d).
[10] Ibid., Art. 81 para. 1(c).

in the text of the provision—would continue to hold the office of President for the eight-year term after the 1980 Constitution came into force.

Finally, the obverse to the security sector's involvement in politics was the absence of civilian or political oversight of the activities of the security sector. The 1980 Constitution was again instrumental here, providing that the Commanders-in-Chief of each of the branches of the military and the Director General of the *Carabineros* would be appointed for non-renewable four-year terms 'and shall not be subject to removal'.[11] The only official empowered to question the performance of the leadership of the security services was the President, who could 'in qualified cases' call the Commanders-in-Chief and the Director General of the *Carabineros* to early retirement.[12] Such a call had to be confirmed by COSENA, however, a majority of whose membership was of course constituted by the Commanders-in-Chief and the Director General of the *Carabineros*.

The seeds of transition

Despite the authoritarian flavour of the 1980 Constitution, it was ultimately the Constitution which held the key to the return to democracy in the 1990s. The Twenty-Seventh Transitory Provision, the Thirteenth Transitory Provision, and Article 25 of the 1980 Constitution provided that after Pinochet's eight-year presidential term, the Commanders-in-Chief of the armed forces and the Director General of the *Carabineros* would nominate a candidate to assume the presidency after Pinochet, to be approved by referendum. The provision went on to note that the prohibitions on serving consecutive terms would not apply to this candidate, clearing the way for the Junta to nominate Pinochet as the candidate.

Although resistance to the Pinochet regime had been prevalent before 1988, for example in protest actions and general strikes led by opposition movements, it was the referendum that provided the leverage the opposition and the people of Chile needed to bring about change. The centre-left alliance *Concertación de Partidos por la Democracia* (or *Concertación*—Coalition of Pro-Democracy Parties) mounted a concerted effort to secure a 'no' vote against Pinochet's continued presidency. *Concertación* spearheaded the largest mobilization of voters in Chile's history ahead of the plebiscite: almost 8 million citizens were registered as voters during 1987 and 1988. Electoral volunteers were deployed throughout the country, and *Concertación* advocates took advantage of free television time to speak for fifteen minutes a day for the last thirty days of the campaign, in support of the 'No to Pinochet' campaign.

[11] Ibid., Art. 93 para. 1.
[12] Ibid., Art. 93 para. 2.

The referendum took place in October 1988. Pinochet's candidacy was defeated by a margin of 56 per cent voting against to 44 per cent in favour. The Twenty-Ninth Transitory Provision of the 1980 Constitution provided that in this circumstance, Pinochet's term as President would be extended by one year and elections for a new President and Congress would have to be held ninety days before the end of this term. During this period, the 1980 Constitution was revised, with fifty-four amendments being made by law and approved at referendum by 85 per cent of voters in July 1989.[13] Presidential and parliamentary elections were held as required in December 1989, with Patricio Aylwin assuming the presidency in March 1990 for an exceptional, non-renewable four-year period.[14]

It is worth asking how a well-established military regime, with a grip on the institutions of power secured by the provisions of the Constitution, managed to lose a referendum on its own political future. There are a number of factors that help to explain the Junta's defeat, and while some of these factors have to do with exogenous economic, ideological, and international forces, at least one of them is internal to Chile's the legal institutional arrangements. In September 1985, the Chilean Constitutional Tribunal struck down as unconstitutional a rule in the organic law governing the independent electoral oversight body, the *Tribunal Calificador de Elecciones* (TRICEL), providing that the 1988 presidential referendum would be overseen by an ad hoc electoral court rather than by TRICEL. The court held that the referendum would be constitutional only if overseen by TRICEL,[15] making it more difficult for the Junta to manipulate the results of the referendum to its advantage.

Of course, a majority of the people still had to vote against Pinochet's continued presidency in the referendum. There was a range of diverse factors that help to explain why the people were disenchanted with the Junta government and were reluctant to see Pinochet enjoy another eight years as President. To start with, the Junta oversaw significant reforms to the economy between 1973 and 1990, which left unemployment rates at about 30 per cent at its worst in 1981–82, and near 20 per cent for the rest of this period.[16] The promised benefits of a *laissez-faire* free-market economy, managed by a group of Chicago University-educated neoliberal economists appointed by the Junta—the so-called Chicago Boys—never materialized, doubling the amount of Chileans living below the poverty line between 1973

[13] Law No. 18,825, 17 August 1989, Diario Oficial (DO) (Chile). See further section on 'Constitutional changes during the transition'.

[14] CP (as amended in 1989), Twenty-Ninth Transitory Provision.

[15] Barros (n. 6), 27. Constitutional Tribunal Case Number 33–85.

[16] See e.g. J. Esteban Montes and Tomás Vidal, *The Role of Constitution-Building Processes in Democratization: Case Study Chile* (IDEA & Democracy Building & Conflict Management, 2005), <https://anayasa.tbmm.gov.tr/docs/CBP-Chile.pdf> (an account of the social mobilization and protests brought up by the strong increase in the unemployment rate).

and 1987.[17] The worsening economic conditions fuelled antipathy against the regime which, combined with ongoing court cases alleging human rights violations perpetrated by the security services, led to the cementing of an opposition alliance between socialist parties and church organizations.

Outside Chile, two international trends undermined the basis of the Junta's military regime. First, the thaw in relations between the United States and the Soviet Union, leading eventually to the fall of the Berlin Wall in 1989 and the democratization of the republics of the former Soviet Union, made it difficult for the Junta to rely on the threat of international communism as a justification for its protected democracy. Second, the fall of military dictatorships in Argentina in 1983, Uruguay in 1984, and Brazil in 1988 fostered opposition to the very idea of military rule in the region, and further stoked mobilization for change.

Constitutional changes during the transition

After Pinochet's candidacy for the presidency was defeated in the 1988 referendum, formal negotiations between the military government, right-wing parties, and opposition parties led to the 1989 constitutional reforms. *Concertación* and the National Renovation Party (RN), a conservative party that supported the military government, appointed a joint committee of ten constitutional experts mandated to reach compromise between the wide-ranging changes demanded by *Concertación* and the more moderate changes the government was prepared to accept.[18] Some of the important changes are summarized here.

The bases of institutionality

Article 8 of the 1980 Constitution included the prohibition of activities promoting 'class warfare' and allowing the exclusion of people found to have engaged in these activities from political, social, and economic life. The article was a bulwark against communism and a key tool in the hands of the Government to suppress opposition, but was repealed in its entirety in 1989.

Article 8 also contained prohibitions of advocacy for totalitarianism and political violence. The 1989 amendments retained prohibitions on this form of political activity, but in more moderated form. The prohibitions were removed from the 'bases of institutionality' and included as internal limitations on the right to form and join political parties in Article 19(15) paragraph 5. The prohibitions thus

[17] Ricardo Ffrench-Davis, *Economic Reforms in Chile: From Dictatorship to Democracy* (University of Michigan Press, 2002).

[18] See also Carlos Andrade Geywitz, *Reforma de la Constitución Política de la República de Chile de 1980*, 2nd edn (Editorial Jurídica de Chile, 2002); Esteban Montes and Vidal (n. 16), 15–16.

operate only as a negative 'clawback' of rights of political freedom already granted to persons, rather than as an affirmative statement of one of the foundational principles of the constitutional order.

Further, persons found by the Constitutional Tribunal to have engaged in prohibited activities would be excluded from only political activities for the following ten years, rather than from leadership positions in commercial, professional, and labour organizations as well.

COSENA and the military

Article 94 of the 1980 Constitution provided that the appointment, promotion, and retirement of the officers of the armed forces and the *Carabineros* would be made by supreme decree (i.e. by the Junta). The 1989 amendments changed this rule slightly by requiring that while appointments, promotions, and retirements would still be made by supreme decree, the substance of any such decree would have to be consistent with 'the applicable organic law, which will determine the respective basic norms, as well as those basic norms concerning the professional career, enlisting in their ranks, security, seniority, command, command succession and budget of the armed forces and *Carabineros*'.

The composition of COSENA was expanded to include the Comptroller General of the Republic by amendments to Article 95. The decision rule for COSENA was also changed to require an absolute majority of voting members rather than a majority of members present, which had the effect of reducing the security services' influence over the Council.[19]

These changes began the process of transition to democracy and to restoring civilian oversight of a powerful security sector. Although a good beginning, it was the structural and institutional reforms to the security services themselves in the years since the fall of the Junta regime, in the context of these broader constitutional changes, that brought the oversight and control of the security forces into line with other constitutional democracies around the world. The remainder of this chapter describes these changes in detail.

The Subject of Reform: Changes to Institutional Structure 1980–2015

Tracing the institutional and structural changes to the security services from the Junta regime into Chile's post-authoritarian democracy involves comparing Chile's national defence organization across three different periods: the military regime

[19] Wendy Hunter, 'Continuity or Change? Civil–Military Relations in Democratic Argentina, Chile, and Peru' (1997) 12 *Political Science Quarterly* 453, 457.

from 1980 to 1989; the transitional period under a democratic government between 1990 and 2010; and the period of established democracy after 2010. In the next section of this chapter, we compare at a high level the chain of command, structural organization, and the mission and mandate of the security services for these three different periods, explaining how civilian oversight was either undermined or facilitated by contrasting arrangements. Under the heading 'The military reacts: reasons for, and the value of, slow reform', we recount the armed forces' reaction to the changes, noting that resistance to change both explains the slow pace of SSR in Chile and arguing that this slow pace of reform was valuable in allowing the armed forces to come around to, and eventually accept, increased civilian scrutiny of their functions. Finally, under the heading 'Changes to the structure of the police and intelligence agencies', we describe changes to the institutional structure of the police and intelligence services from 1990 onwards.

Civilian oversight: the effect of institutional structure

Constitutional guarantees of security sector influence and autonomy, 1980–89

There are two broad mechanisms by which the 1980 Constitution ensured the security sector's central role in politics. The first involved embedding the leadership of the armed forces and the *Carabineros* firmly in the institutions of government and shielding the security service from any form of oversight or political accountability. Under the military regime there was little, if any, institutional distinction between the security services and political institutions. The Junta not only exercised legislative power in terms of the Eighteenth Transitory Provisions of the 1980 Constitution, but also exercised 'constituent power . . . subject to approval by plebiscite' and could issue laws 'concerning the interpretation of the Constitution, whenever necessary'.[20] Whatever constraints the 1980 Constitution did place on the power of the Junta was thus subject to its wide power to either amend the Constitution directly, subject to plebiscitary approval, or to massage the meaning of the Constitution by 'interpreting' it in favourable ways through ordinary legislation. The Eighteenth Transitory Provision conferred significant executive powers on the Junta as well, such as the exclusive authority to deploy troops abroad or allow the entry of foreign troops into Chile, and to approve or reject international treaties.[21]

A very small concession to the separation of executive and legislative power, as well as to the separation of civilian and military leadership, existed in the

[20] CP, Eighteenth Transitory Provision, para. 1(A) and (C).
[21] Ibid., para. 1(D) and (G).

Fourteenth Transitory Provision. While Pinochet would continue to act as both Commander-in-Chief of the Army and President, he would not sit on the Junta while President. Instead, his position on the Junta would be filled by the Officer General of Arms of the Army, the second-highest ranking officer in the Army's chain of command.[22] However, the President retained the power to remove the Officer General of the Arms of the Army from the Junta and replace him or her with the next-highest ranking officer in the Army.[23] With regard to the other members of the Junta, the 1980 Constitution confirmed that it would remain constituted by the Commanders-in-Chief of the armed forces (subject to Pinochet's replacement by the Officer General of Arms of the Army) and the Director General of the *Carabineros*.[24] The only way that a member of the Junta other than the Officer General of Arms could be replaced was if he or she was dismissed from his or her position as Commander-in-Chief or Director General. Since Article 93 provided that the President could only call a Commander-in-Chief or the Director General to early retirement with the consent of a majority of the members of COSENA—the majority of which was itself constituted by the Commanders-in-Chief and the Director General—this effectively insulated the members of the Junta from dismissal even by Pinochet himself.

The perverse result of this small concession to separation of powers was that the Junta and the leaders of the security services were subject to no political oversight, even from the President. While the 1980 Constitution established the presidency as an executive institution separate from the Junta, the Constitution nevertheless ensured that the leadership of the security services was not formally accountable to the President and remained largely autonomous and free from political control.[25]

The second mechanism for concentrating political influence in the hands of the security forces was to subordinate the civilian bureaucracy and the government ministries responsible for security matters to the Junta. A Junta decree-law in 1974 removed the domestic police forces from the purview of the Ministry of the Interior and placed them under the control of the Ministry of Defence, along with the external armed forces.[26] In addition, although the Constitution did distinguish between the armed forces as the institutions responsible for national security and the police as the 'forces of order and public security', it nevertheless provided that the *Carabineros* would be 'integrated with the armed forces in the mission to guarantee the institutional order of the Republic'.[27] There was little institutional distinction between the domestic police force focused on internal order, and the armed

[22] Ibid., Fourteenth Transitory Provision.
[23] Ibid., para. 3.
[24] Ibid., para. 2.
[25] See also Barros (n. 6), 245–9 (on an interpretation of the effects and foundations of this constitutional provision limiting the power of the President.)
[26] Decree-Law No. 646, 17 September 1974 (Chile).
[27] Ibid., Art. 90 paras 1 and 2.

forces focused on external security. The concentration of responsibility for all the security services under a single ministry facilitated Junta control of administrative and bureaucratic matters in the security forces, as well as operational matters. The Ministry of the Interior was relegated to regulatory and coordinating functions.[28] For instance, during the 1973–89 period, the Ministry of the Interior had to coordinate with the different regions within Chile on emergency and preventive planning in natural disaster cases.[29] Similarly, the Ministry of the Interior was the executive agency in charge of the drafting of the constitutional organic law of the TRICEL.[30]

The internal structure of the Ministry of Defence further facilitated Junta control. The Ministry was made up of five secretariats, one for each of the four branches of the security services—Army, Navy, Air Force, *Carabineros*—and a fifth for the *Policía de Investigaciones*, a police force focused on criminal investigation and prosecution rather than public order. Between 1980 and 1989, the positions of the Minister of Defence and the five Secretaries were filled by former high-ranking officers in the security services. These men were contemporaries of the officers who staged the 1973 *coup d'état* and later became members of the Junta, and maintained close personal relationships with members of the Junta, permitting it informal influence in the business of the Ministry.[31]

Moreover, the Assistant Secretary of each of the secretariats was an active-duty colonel in the respective security service. Each Assistant Secretary was under the direct command of the Commander-in-Chief of the respective branch of the armed forces or the Director General of the *Carabineros*. The civilian Ministry of Defence was thus brought under the purview of the leadership of the security services, while the Minister and at least four of the five Secretaries were effectively excluded from the chain of command in each of the branches of the security services. In practical terms, there was no civilian official at the head of the military or internal security forces. The *Estado Mayor de la Defensa Nacional* (Defence Chief of Staff), for example, was established to coordinate the functions of the three armed forces, but had no input into strategic or policy matters.[32] The security services

[28] See Felipe Agüero, 'Autonomía de las FFAA en el autoritarismo y la democracia en Chile' in Augusto Varas (ed.), *La autonomía militar en América Latina* (Nueva Sociedad, 1988), 180–1, arguing that the transfer of bureaucratic responsibility for the *Carabineros* and the *Policia de Ivestigaciones* from the Ministry of the Interior to the Ministry of Defence strengthened military influence over Chile's public security policy.

[29] Decree-Law No. 369, 18 March 1974 (Chile); Supreme Decree No. 509, 11 November 1983 (Chile).

[30] Law No. 18,460, 15 November 1985, DO (Chile).

[31] For instance, Carlos Forestier Haengsen, who was Minister of National Defense of Chile between 1980 and 1982 was also Commander of Division Six of the Army and later appointed Chief of Emergency State Zone by Pinochet after the 1973 coup. Washington Carrasco Fernandez was Vice Commander-in-Chief of the Army previous to the coup and was considered a key actor of the coup leadership. Carrasco Fernandez was later appointed as Minister of Defence for the 1982 period. Lastly, Patricio Carvajal Prado was Vice Admiral of the Navy and became Chief of the Estado Mayor de la Defensa Nacional. After the coup, Carvajal Prado was appointed Minister of Defence for the 1973–74 period. After leaving that office, Carvajal Prado was appointed as Minister of Foreign Relations.

[32] Decree-Law No. 181, 5 April 1960 (Chile).

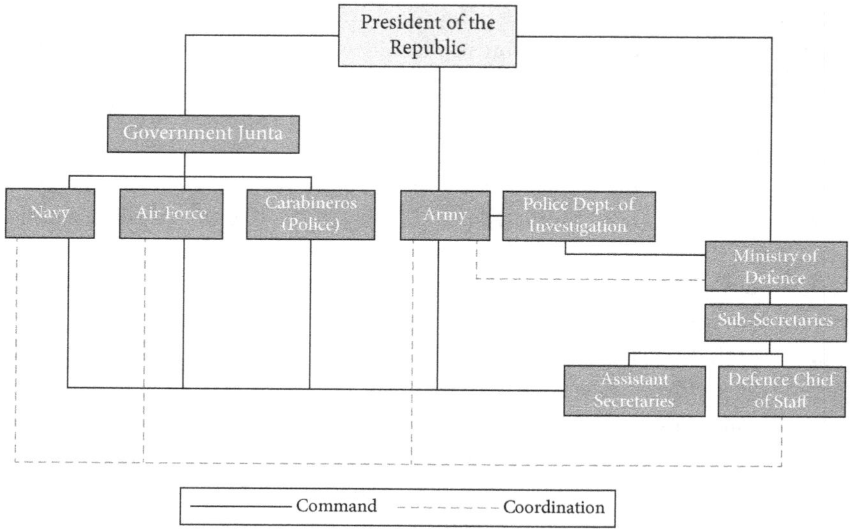

Figure 2.1: Chain of command under the military regime 1980–89.

were thus strong and independent institutions capable of operating without any need for approval or authorization from the civilian Ministry of Defence. The chain of command set out in Figure 2.1 indicates the minimal civilian authority over the security services.

Re-establishing accountability and civilian oversight: 1990–2010

With the rejection of Pinochet's candidacy for President in the 1988 referendum, the path was cleared for a return to a civilian government. It is worth bearing in mind that the 1980 Constitution itself anticipated the demise of the Junta, in the sense that after Pinochet's initial eight-year presidential terms, whatever the result of the 1988 referendum, the Junta would be dissolved and legislative functions would be resumed by the Congress elected in terms of the Eighteenth or Nineteenth Transitory Provision. After Patricio Aylwin assumed the presidency in March 1990, the Commanders-in-Chief of the armed forces and the Director General of the *Carabineros* remained in their offices at the head of each of the security forces, even though they no longer had any formal role in government as the Junta.

It was unlikely, in these circumstances, that the security sector's political influence and autonomy would simply fade away with the Junta. The 1989 constitutional amendments, including the 'civilianization' of COSENA described earlier under the heading 'Constitutional changes during the transition', comprised only a first step on the path to restoring civilian control and oversight of the security sector. Indeed, the security sector did not acquiesce without murmur to the changes. In the first three years of Aylwin's presidency the Army mounted a series of challenges to presidential and ministerial authority: in September 1990 the General of the Santiago Garrison did not request the traditional presidential permit to carry out the Military Parade, which was carried out regardless; in 1993, the 'Boinazo' movement expressed the Army's dissatisfaction with judicial investigations into their activities, including investigations of General Pinochet's son; and in 1994 the Director General of the *Carabineros*, Rodolfo Stange Oelckers, refused to resign after the President's request that he do so and continued to occupy his position. At the same time, retaliatory attacks against members of the security services occurred: the early 1990s saw the assassinations of a former member of the military regime and a former Senator of the Republic, attacks against military personnel believed to have been responsible for human rights abuses during the dictatorship, and other threats of terrorism.

The democratic government had to show both that it had effective command of the security services, and that the police were capable of dealing with internal instability and crime. Aylwin therefore made moves to reduce the autonomy of the armed forces while reducing the armed forces' influence over the police. He was able to move administrative control over the police force to the Ministry of the Interior, by executive decree,[33] although operational control remained with the Ministry of Defence. Further, he created the *Dirección de Seguridad Pública e Informaciones* (Directorate of Public Security and Information) in 1993, an agency within the Ministry of the Interior responsible for coordinating the functions of the *Carabineros* and the *Policía de Investigaciones*.[34] The Directorate was accountable to the Comptroller General on operational and budgetary matters.[35] Shortly thereafter, the Government established by executive decree the *Consejo Coordinador de Seguridad Pública* (Public Security Coordinating Council), empowered to share information between the *Carabineros* and the *Policía de Investigaciones* in anti-terrorism actions.[36]

This institutional reform represents partial success in distinguishing between the internal and external focus of the police and armed forces respectively,[37] but several proposed statutes that would have reasserted the Ministry of the Interior's full operational control over the police forces failed to generate the support of Congress between 1991 and 2001. It was not until 2005 that this change could be made by law.[38] Figure 2.2 illustrates the organizational structure of the security sector in the period 1990–2010.

33 Supreme Decree No. 412, 3 January 1992, DO (Chile.)

34 Law No. 19,212, 30 April 1993, DO (Chile).

35 Ibid., Arts 24 and 27.

36 Supreme Decree No. 363, 18 April 1991, DO (Chile).

37 Hunter (n. 1), 32. See also Lucía Dammert, *Fear and Crime in Latin America: Redefining State–Society Relations* (Routledge, 2012), 67.

38 Azun Candina, 'The Institutional Identity of the Carabineros de Chile' in John Bailey and Lucía Dammert (eds), *Public Security and Police Reform in the Americas* (University of Pittsburgh Press, 2006), 86.

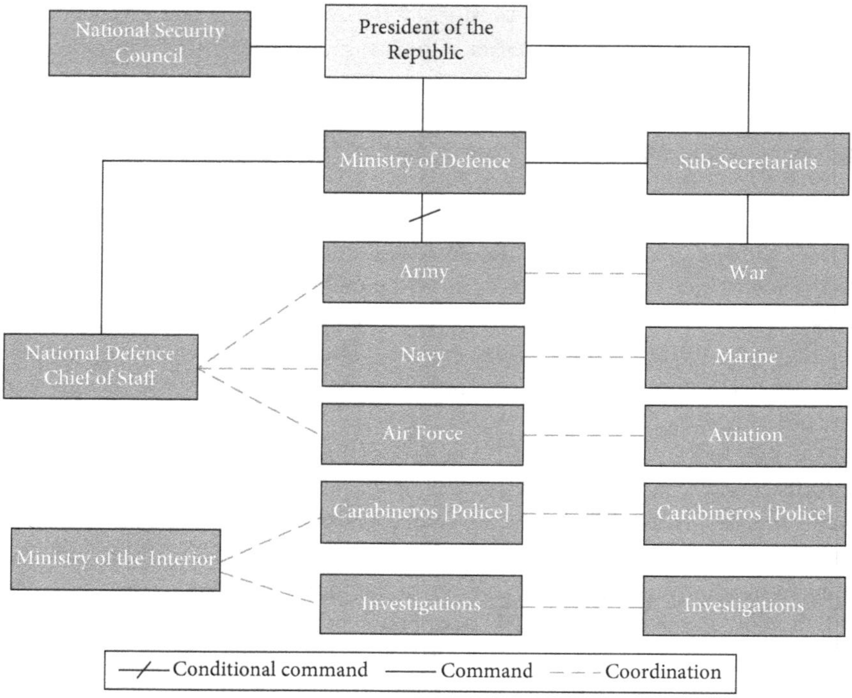

Figure 2.2: Chain of command under the democratic regime, 1990–2010.

Although these structural changes to the organization of the security sector were important, establishing effective civilian oversight of the security service in Chile would require the expansion of the powers and mandate of Congress. To this end, three specialized standing committees were established in Congress.

First, the *Comisión Especial de Inteligencia en la Cámara de Diputados* (CEICD—Special Intelligence Committee in the Chamber of Deputies) was established by Law No. 19,974 in 2004.[39] The CEICD oversees the intelligence activity of the *Agencia Nacional de Inteligencia* (ANI—National Intelligence Agency), a joint body constituted by the armed forces and police intelligence services and mandated to coordinate the intelligence functions of the armed forces and police.

[39] Law No. 19,974, 27 September 2004, DO, Art. 37 (Chile). This article states:

> The Chamber of Deputies, in the scope of its investigative faculties, shall constitute, in accordance with its Regulations, a Special Committee which shall be authorized to take notice of reports and background facts related to the activities of the department and entities that form the Intelligence System of the State. The Director of the National Intelligence Agency shall submit annually to the said Special Committee a secret report on the work performed by the Agency and with respect to the operation of the System. The Committee shall be informed of the reports and background information referred to in the preceding sub-paragraphs at sessions which shall be secret.

The ANI falls under the portfolio of the Ministry of the Interior, although it reports directly to the President of the Republic.[40] Since 2004, a civilian has always held the position of Director of the National Intelligence Agency.

Second, there is a standing committee for national defence in each of the chambers of Congress: the Chamber of Deputies Defence Committee and the Senate Defence Committee. The Chamber of Deputies Defence Committee reviews all draft laws in the defence sector before they are tabled in Congress, and the executive's strategic defence plans must be submitted to the Committee for its general information. Specific procurement plans, however, are not required to be brought to the Committee's attention.[41] The Senate Defence Committee plays a key role in the deployment of the armed forces abroad. While the deployment of Chile's troops abroad was a decision in the hands of the Junta in terms of the 1980 Constitution,[42] Articles 63(13) and 32(17) of the Constitution as amended provide that the President may deploy the armed forces abroad, in accordance with an organic law setting out the norms for foreign deployment. This law was passed in 1991, and it provides that a presidential order to deploy troops abroad must be approved by the Senate.[43] The Senate Defence Committee reviews such orders and proposes whether the Senate should approve or reject the deployment of Chilean troops abroad. Chile's participation in the UN's peacekeeping and humanitarian missions to Haiti in 2004 (MINUSTAH) is an example of the foreign deployment of Chile's troops in accordance with these provisions.[44]

Both Committees can order officials to appear before them to explain the technical details of defence decisions, or appoint experts to serve in an advisory capacity on issues being discussed in Congress.[45] In addition, although the defence sector budget is not approved or supervised by these Committees, they coordinate with the Finance Committee of Congress on defence budgetary matters.[46] Finally, the Committees have a right to access information as well as a right to hold meetings in secret.[47]

[40] Ibid., Art. 7. This article establishes:

> The National Intelligence Agency shall be established, being a centralized public department, with a technical and specialized character, which shall be subordinate to the President of the Republic through the Ministry of the Interior, which shall have the purpose of producing intelligence to advise the President of the Republic and various higher levels of leadership of the State, in accordance with current law.

[41] See Reglamento de la Cámara de Diputados de Chile, March 2010 (Chile), Arts 213–218.

[42] CP, Eighteenth Transitory Provision para. 1(G).

[43] Law No 19.067, 1 July 1991 DO (Chile), Art. 4.

[44] Eduardo Aludante, *Backpacks Full of Hope* (Wilfred Laurier University Press, 2010).

[45] Francisco Rojas Aravena, 'Chile' in Ravinder Pal Singh (ed.), *Arms Procurement Decision Making, Vol. II: Chile, Greece, Malaysia, Poland, South Africa, and Taiwan* (Oxford University Press, 2000), 32–3.

[46] Jaime Baeza Freer, Andrés Dockendorff Valdéz, and Natalia Vargas Palacios, 'El rol de la Comisión de Defensa de la Cámara de diputados en la formulación de la política de defensa' (2010) 2 *Revista Chilena de Derecho y Ciencia Política* 67, 78.

[47] Ibid.

In addition to the standing committees, ad hoc investigative committees may be established by a decision of the plenary session of either Chamber. The law which established the ANI was initiated by an ad hoc Investigative Committee mandated to review whether the scope of activity enjoyed by military intelligence had facilitated the improper surveillance of politicians by the Army in the early 1990s. The Committee found that the absence of civilian executive control was a weakness that had to be overcome in order to refocus military intelligence away from internal political matters and onto external security matters.

These gradual piecemeal changes to the constitutional bases and institutional structure of the security sector culminated in a significant package of reforms in 2005. The 2005 constitutional amendment was the result of long political negotiations since the 2000s between all political parties, the executive, and legislative branches of government. The gestation of this constitutional reform came from the party *Alianza por Chile*, who advocated for the end of the transitional politics period, and the *Concertación de Partidos por la Democracia*, who sought a higher democratization of the Constitution.[48] Furthermore, the political sector of the opposition could no longer afford to veto constitutional reform attempts at Congress in light of the detention of Pinochet in London and the secret bank accounts associated to him that surfaced.[49] These events caused a rupture between the political parties of the right and the military. Consequently, the *Alianza por Chile* realized that it was time to end the powers granted to the military in the 1980 Constitution as these were affected by democratic deficits and were no longer useful for political matters.[50] The constitutional amendment passed in 2005 made five important changes:[51]

1. In a significant change that finally drew a distinction between the civilian bureaucratic institutions responsible for external security on one hand and internal security on the other, the police (*Carabineros* and *Policía de Investigaciones*) were separated from the armed forces and brought under the authority of the ministry responsible for public security, while the armed forces remained under the authority of the ministry responsible for national defence.[52] In addition to the institutional separation, the amendment also separated the functions of the armed forces and police. The Army, Navy, and Air Force are 'essential for national security' and must 'guarantee the institutional order of the Republic', while the *Carabineros* and *Policía de Investigaciones* must implement the law and 'guarantee the public order and

[48] Javier Couso and Alberto Coddou, 'Las asignaturas pendientes de la reforma constitucional chilena' in Claudio Fuente (ed.), *En el nombre del pueblo: debate sobre el cambio constitucional en Chile* (Heinrich Boll Stiftung/ICSO, 2010), 194.
[49] Ibid., 195.
[50] Ibid.
[51] Law No. 20,050, 26 August 2005, DO (Chile).
[52] CP (as amended in 2005), Art. 101 paras 1 and 2.

the public internal security' of the Republic: the *Carabineros* no longer assist the armed forces 'in the mission to guarantee the institutional order of the Republic'. However, it is worth noting that the Constitution as amended in 2005 now requires all organs of state, and not just the armed forces, to 'guarantee the institutional order of the Republic'.[53]

2. The lack of accountability inherent in the immunity from removal previously enjoyed by the Commanders-in-Chief of the armed forces and the Director General of the *Carabineros* was addressed. The President now enjoys the discretion to appoint and remove the Commanders-in-Chief of the armed forces and the Director General of the *Carabineros* by supreme decree. The exercise of this discretion must be 'substantiated' against the organic law setting out the basic norms of the security forces, and the Chamber of Representatives and the Senate must be informed.[54] The top-ranking official in each branch of the security sector is ultimately accountable to the civilian President.
3. The influence and role of COSENA was reduced in a number of ways: it no longer nominates judges to the Constitutional Tribunal;[55] only the President, and not any of its members, can call COSENA into session;[56] and COSENA no longer has any role in the declaration of states of emergency or exception.[57] COSENA now acts in only an advisory capacity, when requested to do so by the President of the Republic.[58]
4. The set-aside of seats in the Senate for ex-Presidents was abolished, as was the appointment of former Commanders-in-Chief of the armed forces and a former Director General of the *Carabineros* to the Senate by COSENA.[59]
5. The Supreme Court was made responsible for the oversight of military courts, which were previously excluded from the Supreme Court's oversight.[60]

Consolidating civilian oversight: changes to the armed forces, 2010–15

It was not until Law No. 20,424 of 2010[61] brought about a totally new structural organization of the Ministry of Defence and the Ministry of the Interior that the security services in Chile could be said to be under effective civilian control.

The Minister of National Defence is at the apex of the Ministry, assisted by two new secretariats on one hand, and the newly created *Estado Mayor Conjunto* (Joint Chief of Staff) on the other. The Secretariat of Defence and the Secretariat of

53 Ibid., Art. 6.
54 Ibid., Art. 32(16) read with Arts 104 and 105.
55 Compare CP (1980), Art. 81 para. 1(c) with CP (as amended in 2005), Art. 92.
56 Compare CP (1980), Art. 95 para. 3 with CP (as amended in 2005), Art. 107 para. 1.
57 Compare CP (1980), Art. 40 with CP (as amended in 2005), Art. 40.
58 CP (as amended in 2005), Art. 106 para. 1.
59 Compare CP (1980), Art. 45 para. 3(a) and (d) with CP (as amended in 2005), Art. 49.
60 Compare CP (1980), Art. 79 with CP (as amended in 2005), Art. 82.
61 Law No. 20,424, 4 February 2010, DO (Chile).

the Armed Forces thus replaces the five secretariats in the Ministry before 2010. The Secretariat of Defence collaborates with the Minister on Defence policy matters,[62] and the Secretariat of the Armed Forces collaborates with the Minster on matters related to the bureaucratic and administrative functioning of the armed forces.[63] The staff of these secretariats is composed of both civilian officials and members of the armed forces.[64]

The Joint Chief is a permanent office mandated to provide ongoing advice to the Minister on matters relating to the readiness and deployment of the armed forces.[65] The President appoints the Joint Chief of Staff by decree, after informing both the Senate and the Chamber of Deputies. The Joint Chief must be a member of the military with the rank of at least general or vice admiral.[66] The Joint Chief of Staff is accountable directly and exclusively to the Minister of Defence. The Joint Chief of Staff exercises command of joint military operations of the branches of the armed forces both during times of war and during peace missions, for example those coordinated by the UN.[67] Defence policy is formulated by the Minister, with the country's strategic military needs and priorities defined by the Minister in light of this policy. The Joint Chief of Staff executes this policy.

The Commanders-in-Chief of the armed forces also play an advisory role to the Minister, through the *Junta de Comandantes en Jefe* (Board of Commanders-in-Chief).[68] The Minister must consult the Board on matters relating to subjects that affect the armed forces jointly or affect the distribution of resources and responsibilities among the branches of the armed forces.[69]

The chain of command under the 2010 arrangement is successive: each branch of the military is subordinate to its respective Commander-in-Chief, while the Commanders-in-Chief are accountable to the President of the Republic. The Joint Chief of Staff is accountable to the Minister of Defence, and the Minister of Defence, as with all Cabinet positions, serves with the confidence of the President of the Republic and can be replaced by the President alone at any time. The new structure is reflected in detail in Figure 2.3.

As an indication that SSR is ongoing in Chile, a constitutional amendment in 2011 provides that a law must transfer the responsibility for oversight over firearms and military arsenals to a civilian ministry or administrative agency, rather than leaving this in the hands of the armed forces.[70] This law was passed in 2015,[71]

62 Ibid., Art. 15.
63 Ibid., Art. 21.
64 Ibid., Art. 14.
65 Ibid., Art. 25.
66 Ibid., Art. 26.
67 Ibid., Arts 26 and 27.
68 Ibid., Arts 10–13.
69 Ibid., Art. 10 para. 2.
70 Law No. 20,503, 27 April 2011, DO (Chile).
71 Law No, 20,813, 21 January 2015, DO (Chile).

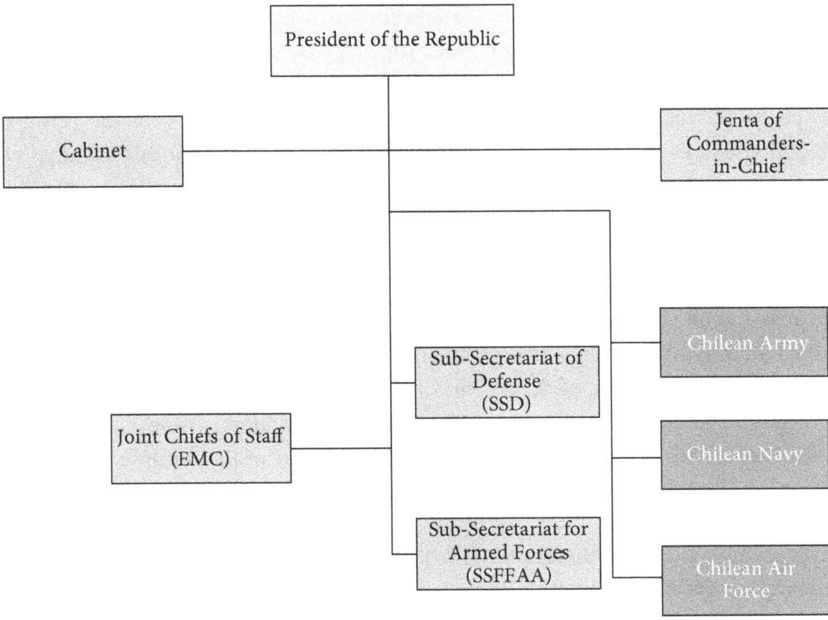

Figure 2.3: Defence structure and command in Chile: 2010–present.

and distributes responsibility for various functions in the oversight of arms and arsenals between the Ministry of Defence, the Ministry of the Interior and Public Security, and the *Ministerio Púbilco de Chile* or *Fiscalía de Chile* (Office of Public Prosecutions).

The military reacts: reasons for, and the value of, slow reform

The slow pace of constitutional reform, beginning in 1989 and continuing through to 2010, can be explained in part by the opposition mounted by Senators appointed by COSENA under the terms of the 1980 Constitution. It was only in 2005 that the composition of the Senate had changed sufficiently for constitutional amendments reducing the privileges of the security sector to pass into law.

A contributing factor to the slow pace of constitutional reform relates to the gradual loss of popular approval and support for the military. It is important to remember that the members of the Junta were not lustrated after 1989. On the contrary, many of them kept their jobs in the top rungs of the military hierarchy, and Pinochet remained Commander-in-Chief of the Army until 1998.[72] Many of

[72] Law No. 18,952, 27 February 1990, DO (Chile), transferred the personnel of the Junta government to the Ministry of Defence as part of the administrative management of the Ministry (Arts 8–10).

the revelations about the military's involvement in human rights violations and growing economic crisis were not made until 1983, and until then the military enjoyed some measure of popular and political support. The month of May 1983 was characterized by major protests around the country that were the result of the 'collapse of the financial system, the replacement of the economic administration team, a heavy foreign debt, and the generalized indebtedness of vast middle-class sectors'.[73] The vast social discontent brought together different organizations (from students to certain union groups) that promoted a collective expression known as '*Democracia Ahora*' ('Democracy Now').[74] In 1985, the Inter-American Commission on Human Rights published a report on the human rights situation in Chile, which denounced the detention and disappearances of more than 500 persons, unknown numbers of deaths, and thousands of people tortured.[75] Augusto Varas has also analysed polls from 1988 that demonstrated people associated the armed forces with 'the rich' and that 59.3 per cent of the polled sample maintained that more human rights violations had taken place during the dictatorship, and 73.1 per cent revealed some degree of distrust for the armed forces. Finally, Varas also highlights a Latin American poll from 1989 that revealed 76.9 per cent of the Chilean population considered the armed forces to have a poor ability to govern.[76] At the same time, the public's enthusiasm for military involvement in internal security issues began to wane, as changing strategic priorities refocused the military on regional cooperation and external security issues.

With former members of the Junta in leadership positions and the vestiges of military influence in the political processes, the military was able to preserve a measure of autonomy over certain of its internal affairs throughout the reforms of the 1990s. The military insisted on autonomy in career development, on training and education of military leadership, and the constitutional prohibition on creating military or police forces other than those expressly defined in the Constitution.

The military's resistance is reflected in the 1989 change to Article 94 of the 1980 Constitution, providing that the security services would be regulated by supreme decrees consistent with constitutional organic laws. The Government could not make changes to the personnel of the armed forces except in terms of enabling organic laws. Accordingly, after Patricio Aylwin was elected as President on 14 December 1989 but

[73] Manuel Antonio Garretón, *Incomplete Democracy: Political Democratization in Chile and Latin America*, trans. R. Kelly Washbourne with Gregory Horvath (University of North Carolina Press, 2003), 125; See also, Manuel Antonio Garretón, 'The Political Evolution of the Chilean Military Regime and Problems in the Transition to Democracy' in Guillermo O'Donnell, Philippe C. Schmitter, and Laurence Whitehead (eds), *Transitions From Authoritarian Rule: Latin America* (Johns Hopkins University Press, 1986), 95–122.

[74] Garretón, *Incomplete Democracy* (n. 73), 126.

[75] Informe de la Situación de Derechos Humanos en Chile, Inter-Am. Comm'n H.R., OEA/Ser.L/V/II.77, doc. 18 rev. 1 (1985).

[76] Augusto Varas, 'The Crisis of Legitimacy of Military Rule in the 1980s' in Paul W. Drake and Iván Jaksic (eds), *The Struggle for Democracy in Chile*, rev. edn (Rienner, 1995), 82–8.

before he took office on 11 March 1990, the Junta enacted the organic laws of the armed forces[77] and *Carabineros*[78] and promulgated forty-six other organic laws dealing with prerogatives of the armed forces and police. The Junta made sure to entrench these laws, as each law provided that it could be amended only with a 4/7 supermajority of Senators and Deputies—a supermajority that *Concertación* was unable to muster until the end of President Michelle Bachelet's term in 2010.

A number of features of the 1990 organic laws reflect the concerns of the military government as it faced the transition to democracy:

1. The law indexed the budget of the armed forces against an inflationary variable set out in the 1989 Budgets Law—the military regime's last budget. This eliminated deliberative debate in Congress about the military budget, guaranteeing a certain degree of financial autonomy to the military.
2. The law strengthened the social insurance system of the armed forces, providing an immediate severance package for each military officer leaving service. The severance benefit was increased to the equivalent of thirty months' salary—as opposed for the maximum of eleven months' salary allowed in the civilian labour system—while contribution amounts were reduced.
3. The law increased the guaranteed minimum appropriated to the military from funds generated from copper (Law on Funds Reserved from Copper).[79] Consequently, each branch of the military was allocated US$60 million annually for the acquisition of weapons systems and for the payment of debts to maintain old equipment.[80]

All of these new laws had one objective: to preserve as much autonomy from civilian control for the security sector. If the military's efforts to preserve its autonomy help to explain the slow pace of reform, the slow pace of reform may have had the effect of ensuring that the changes will be more robust in the longer term. As the military withdrew from political functions after 1989, they were expecting and began to prepare for retribution from the new civilian government. But the resistance the military was able to mount to the more immediate changes proposed by *Concertación* in 1989, for example, meant that changes to the structure of the military had to happen over two decades. The idea of change was thus allowed to

[77] Law No. 18,948, 22 February 1990, DO (Chile).

[78] Law No. 18,961, 27 February 1990, DO (Chile).

[79] Law No. 18,948, 22 February 1990, DO (Chile), Arts 96(99) and 98(101).

[80] This amount was the result of a reform to Law 13,196 of 1958 on the 'Restricted Law on Copper' under the dictatorship in October 1985, which came into effect in 1987. Such reform established that 10% of the exports of CODELCO, a state-owned copper company, and the revenue of its sub-products would be destined for the budget of the armed forces, which resulted in a sum of US$180 million annually. The organic constitutional law of the armed forces in 1990 ordered that during the transition that sum must not be decreased. See Guillermo Patillo, Fernando Bustamante, and Miguel Navarro, *Cuál debe ser el gasto militar en el Chile de los 90* (Centro de Estudios del Desarrollo, 1991), 41.

permeate the public and military consciousness gradually, without immediate action, fostering a culture more receptive to institutional change in the long run. This point is essential: the military were expecting a flood of widespread reforms and retribution that never came, and were ultimately faced with incremental statutory changes that they were happy to accept. A by-product of a 'Maginot line' of institutional autonomy the armed forces drew was the limit it put on opportunities for political or partisan abuse of the security services once the democratic government had assumed office.

Changes to the structure of the police and intelligence agencies

A significant challenge to establishing civilian oversight of the security sector in Chile has been the blurred line between the functions of the *Carabineros* and the armed forces. As described throughout this chapter, separating the functions of the two security services has been a gradual process. While the 2005 constitutional amendments made a significant break with the past in establishing operational control over the police in a separate executive ministry, an organic law passed in 2011 details precisely how the Ministry of the Interior and Public Security will exercise administrative control over the *Carabineros* and *Policía de Investigaciones.*[81] The law establishes two secretariats within the Ministry: the Secretariat of the Interior is responsible for the *Carabineros*, and the Secretariat of Crime Prevention is responsible for the *Policía de Investigaciones.* Each police force is accountable to its secretariat, but the leadership of both forces enjoy operational autonomy to command and manage their forces.

In general, the *Carabineros* did not make the same attempt to defend their autonomy as the military. The only example of the desire to resist civilian control was in 1994 when General Stange refused to resign despite President Frei's request. General Stange resigned two years later nevertheless, amid the *Carabineros*' decreasing influence on politics.

Reforming the internal security forces was not confined to the police, however. One of the early objectives of the democratic regime was dismantling Pinochet's secret internal intelligence machinery, *Direccion de Intelligencia Nacional* (DINA—National Intelligence Directorate), which, under the military regime, was supervised by the Army. Law No. 18,943 was an important compromise here: it dissolved the governmental intelligence agency (CNI) and transferred a part of its personnel to the private labour force contracted to the Army.[82] Law No. 18,889 facilitated the 'privatization' of security agents, allowing their

[81] Law No. 20,502, 21 February 2011, DO (Chile).
[82] Law No. 18,943, 13 February 1990, DO (Chile).

absorption into private security companies.[83] These private security companies had been established by the Junta in the first place many years earlier.[84] Apart from the few examples of political violence against members of the military in the early 1990s, the post-authoritarian period in Chile has experienced quite low levels of public violence. One explanation for this is in the existence of over 1,000 private security companies, employing about 125,000 persons as watchmen and guards, many of whom are former members of the Junta's disestablished intelligence agency.[85]

Providing viable and attractive alternative private-sector employment opportunities to members of disestablished intelligence agencies has proved to be valuable both in reducing the degree of opposition to the transition from these former security officers and, by moving these security officers into the private sector, reducing the incentives for them to remain involved in politics.

Conclusion: Timing Constitutional Change and Security Sector Reform

Chile's experience allows us to identify both the lessons learned and the mistakes made in the process of security sector transformation.

The slow change

A key element of Chile's success in transitioning from military oligarchy to democratic government and re-establishing effective civilian control over the security sector was the low degree to which the transition threatened the professional prospects of the high-ranking officers of the security services. This ensured that the cost of transition was low for the security sector, and that it had little to lose by accepting the transition. There were two factors that ensured this low degree of threat.

The first was that the members of the Junta, or at least their political representatives in the Renovación Nacional (RN), were active participants in the negotiations that led to the first post-Pinochet constitutional amendments in 1989. The compromise solution reached between RN and *Concertación* before Aylwin took office provided some assurance to the security sector that radical change to the structure and composition of the security services would not happen immediately. In this

[83] Law No. 18,889, 10 January 1990, DO (Chile).

[84] Decree-Law 194 of December 1973 reformulated by Decree-Law No. 3.607 of 1981.

[85] UNLIREC, *Control y regulación de las empresas de seguridad privada en América Latina y el Caribe: un análisis comparativo* (UNLIREC, 2011), 5.

light, the members of the Junta as well as the rank and file of the security services for the most part kept their jobs in the security sector. Those soldiers and spies whose agencies were disestablished were essentially compensated by opportunities in the private sector.

The second factor, related to the first, is that the changes that were made to the security sector after 1989 were incremental and moderately paced. During the 1990s and early 2000s, the Government made changes to the structures of administrative accountability of the security sector, such as redefining the chain of command, reshuffling Cabinet responsibility for the *Carabineros* from the Ministry of Defence to the Ministry of Public Security, and establishing legislative oversight committees and agencies. But no constitutional changes were made to the powers, functions, or institutional structure of the security sector until 2005, fifteen years after the end of the military regime. It is these changes that definitively reduced the political influence of the security sector and started to establish effective civilian control and oversight of the security sector. These changes were consolidated with further constitutional amendments and organic laws in 2010 and afterwards.

However, a consequence of the slow pace of reform and the Junta's influence in shaping the immediate post-Pinochet period was that very few members of the Junta or the Junta's machinery of government faced prosecution for the crimes they committed while in power. In 1978 the Junta passed a decree-law granting amnesty to the Junta for any crimes committed between 1973 and 1978.[86] The 1980 Constitution ensured the continuity of the amnesty law by affirming that Chile's legislative organs—the Junta at the time the amnesty law was decreed—could declare amnesty.[87] This law was not repealed by the post-1989 democratic governments, despite *Concertación*'s 1988 promise to do so if elected. One explanation for this is the strong influence the security sector retained in the Senate,[88] but even after the provision ensuring security sector representation in the Senate were removed in 2005, the law remains on the books as at the time of writing in 2016.[89] The democratic government's sensitivity to the strong position that the security sector maintained after 1990, and its desire to ensure that the transition was not threatening to the security sector, helps to explain the reluctance to bring criminal charges. This atmosphere of compromise is reflected in a Supreme Court judgment in 1990, holding that the amnesty law was neither unconstitutional nor in conflict with international law.[90] During Aylwin's Government, the only high-ranking member of Pinochet's security bureaucracy to face prosecution and conviction for

[86] Decree Law No. 2191, 18 April 1978, DO (Chile).

[87] CP, Art. 60(16).

[88] Louise Malinder, *Amnesty, Human Rights and Political Transitions: Bridging the Peace and Justice Divide* (Bloomsbury, 2008).

[89] CP, Art. 63(16).

[90] *Ivan Sergio Insunza Bascunan*, Supreme Court, Case No. 27, 640 (24 August 1990).

crimes committed while in office was General Juan Manual Contreras, former head of DINA. He was convicted of the murder of a Chilean diplomat in Washington DC in 1976.

As the 1990s wore on, however, this atmosphere of compromise and appeasement gradually changed, as the members of the Junta aged and retired, and their influence over politics faded. In 1998, the Supreme Court declared that the application of the Junta's amnesty law to human rights violations was unconstitutional,[91] allowing for prosecutions for the human rights violations of the Junta regime. In other cases, even without declaring the amnesty law invalid, the Supreme Court found ways to couch the crimes of which agents of the Junta regime were accused in order to circumvent its limitations.[92] Amid these decisions, over a thousand prosecutions have been launched against members of the Junta's security services for crimes relating to forced disappearances, torture, and killing, with final judgments against the accused in 279 cases and seventy-five persons serving prison sentences. After General Contreras served a seven-year sentence for the 1976 murder, he was tried and convicted in 2002 of human rights violations under Pinochet and sentenced to fifteen years in prison. Pinochet died in 2006, before a court was able to try him on allegations of human rights violations.

Separation of internal and external mission

An important part of the transition was the restriction of the role of the armed forces to matters of external security rather than internal security. During the dictatorship, it was almost inevitable that the armed forces would become embroiled in domestic or internal matters, in light of the fact that the Commanders-in-Chief of all three of the branches of the armed forces served on the governing Junta. It is an important step in reducing the political influence of the armed forces to refocus their mission on matters of external security, to ensure that there is neither incentive nor opportunity for them to involve themselves in matters of domestic or internal policy.

At the same time, the *Carabineros* and the armed forces under the Junta shared responsibility for ensuring the safety of the nation and eliminating threats to the bases of institutionality. There was thus no separation or distinction between the mission of the *Carabineros* and the armed forces. Combined with the expansive

[91] *Poblete Cordova*, Supreme Court, Case No. 469-98 (9 September 1998).

[92] See e.g. *Miguel Angel Sandoval*, Supreme Court, Case No. 517-04 (17 November 2004); *Diana Frida Aron Svigilsky*, Supreme Court, Case No. 3215-05 (30 May 2006); *Manuel Tomas Rojas Fuentes*, Case No. 3125-04 (13 March 2007). See generally Marny A. Requa, 'A Human Rights Triumph? Dictatorship-Era Crimes and the Chilean Supreme Court' (2012) 121 *Human Rights Law Review* 79.

definition of the 'bases of institutionality' in the 1980 Constitution, this gave the armed forces and the *Carabineros* a very broad mandate.

Establishing effective civilian control over the security sector involves a clear articulation of the mission and mandate of each branch of the security sector. Without such a clear statement of mission and mandate, or where as in Chile's case a broad mandate is shared between all the branches of the security sector, it will likely prove difficult for a civilian government to exercise effective control or oversight over the activities of the security sector. Ensuring effective oversight involves, for a start, a clear constitutional or statutory statement of the powers, functions, and mission of each of the security services, so that it is possible for civilian oversight bodies to determine if each service is doing its job.

Establishment of civilian bureaucracy

Finally, civilian oversight cannot be left to legislative committees or the executive government. It is important that civilian oversight of the functions of the security service be ongoing—and the best way to achieve this is through establishing a civilian command structure and bureaucracy for both the armed forces and the police.

Chile struggled in the post-Pinochet period with the fact that the Ministry of Defence was responsible for both the armed forces and the police. The separation of these two services, and the establishment of an effective civilian bureaucracy for the police took until several years after the fall of the Junta, but was an important step in defusing the concentration of power over the security services in a single Cabinet position and in reducing the influence of the former members of the Junta in the command of the security services.

The incremental changes to the chain of command and structure of both the armed forces and the police since 1990 have strengthened civilian control of the security sector by ensuring that officers in each force are accountable to civilian political office-holders, such as the relevant secretariat and ultimately the Minister of Defence or the Minister of Public Security. The Junta era had no civilian accountability to speak of, since the Commander-in-Chief of each of the security services was in government. There was thus no mechanism at all of government oversight of the security sector.

Even after 1990, the fact that the *Carabineros* were accountable only to the Minister of Defence was problematic. It is unsatisfactory that the Cabinet member responsible for matters of external security should be responsible also for matters of internal security, since these portfolios deal with very different subjects and issues and have different priorities. It was not until reforms in 2010 that lines of accountability within the security sector were structured in a way that maximizes civilian oversight and control of the security sector.

Overall, the present-day success of civilian oversight of the security sector in Chile has much to do with how long the process of reform took, and with the concessions made to the former military leadership throughout the transition. The price for this long, slow, and ultimately successful transition, however, is the lack of, or at least significant delay in securing, justice for the crimes committed by the Chile's former military rulers.

3

Argentina's Security Sector Reform

Democratization before Constitutional Transition

*Sandra Elena and Julia Pomares**

Introduction and Background

Argentina is one of only two countries in which a democratic transition was prompted by a defeat in war.[1] The surrender of the Argentine military to the British government on June 1982, ending the Malvinas War, had important consequences for the military regime: the military's image suffered in the collective estimation of the people, and the dominance of the Army within the security services was undermined, stoking growing tensions within the security sector. After the resignation of the commander-in-chief of the Army immediately after Argentina's defeat in the Malvinas, the new de facto government announced that general elections would be held by the end of 1983. The war played a crucial role in leading to the only transition in Latin America that was not a pacted transition.[2] The other country whose transition to democracy followed military defeat was Greece, whose attempt to foment a coup in Cyprus was thwarted by the Turkish invasion of Cyprus in July 1974.

After seven years of the cruellest military dictatorship, democracy in Argentina was restored in 1983. Raúl Alfonsín's victory in presidential elections in October marked the beginning of the now longest period of uninterrupted democratic governance since the creation of the Argentine state. The first administration of the transition faced a very difficult challenge; namely, the need to restore democratic institutions amidst a fragile social and economic situation. Against this background, the Alfonsín government set two key objectives: establishing strong civilian control over security and military forces, and prosecuting human rights

* We would like to thank Ana Ruival for her invaluable research assistance and Martín Böhmer, Ignacio Claut, Alberto Föhrig, and Marcelo Leiras for their comments. Finally, we are grateful to Horacio Jaunarena and Rosendo Fraga for their generosity in answering our questions (Mr Horacio Jaunarena, Former Secretary of Defence (1983–85), Minister of Defence, Secretary of the Office of the President and National Deputy, interviewed on 14 March 2014; Mr Rosendo Fraga, political analyst, interviewed on 7 March 2014).

[1] J.J. Linz and A.C. Stepan, *Problems of Democratic Transition and Consolidation: Southern Europe, South America, and Post-Communist Europe* (Johns Hopkins University Press, 1996).

[2] Ibid.

violations committed during a half-century of military interventions in civilian governments.[3] The two objectives were related. As part of the effort to establish civilian control of the armed forces, a new civilian Minister of Defence was appointed. At the same time, the democratic government tabled a bill in Congress repealing the Law of Self-Amnesty passed by the military government a couple of weeks before the presidential election. As its name suggests, the Law of Self-Amnesty was intended to ensure that leaders of Argentina's military regime would avoid criminal liability for their activities and conduct between 1973 and 1982. Repealing the law and paving the way for prosecutions was one way to ensure that members of the military regime would not remain in positions of power. The fate of the Law of Self-Amnesty had been a key issue of the presidential campaign.[4]

A few days after taking office, President Alfonsín signed three decrees that laid the foundations of the human rights policy of the first transitional government. Decrees 157 and 158 ordered prosecutions of leaders of both the military government (*Juntas Militares*) and former leaders of insurgent groups.[5] Decree 187 set up the *Comisión Nacional sobre la Desaparición de Personas* (CONADEP—National Commission on the Disappearance of Persons).[6] Its research, headed by Ernesto Sábato, was documented in the *Nunca Más* (Never Again) report, and delivered to Alfonsín in September 1984.[7] Furthermore, this research played a key role in raising public awareness of the atrocities committed by the de facto government and helped open the doors to the trial of the military juntas of the dictatorship which took place in 1985.

After 1985, enthusiasm for prosecutions seemed to wane. Several measures, such as the Full Stop Law in 1986 and the Law on Due Obedience in 1987,[8] limited prosecutions against the military. During Carlos Menem's first term as President, ten '*indulto*' decrees were approved, granting pardon to high commanders of the dictatorship and insurgent leaders. At this point, the emphasis appeared to shift towards internal control and oversight of the military, rather than judicial or criminal accountability. Menem's government continued the policy of reducing the budget allocated to defence affairs and appointed Martin Balza as the Army's General Chief of Staff. In 1995, Balza announced the military's first institutional

[3] R. Diamint, *La historia sin fin: el control civil de los Militares en Argentina* (Nueva Sociedad, 2008); Jaunarena, personal communication, 14 May 2014.

[4] For a detailed analysis of the consequences of the annulment of this law on the doctrine of the Supreme Court about the legality of laws enacted by the military government, see Martin Böhmer, 'La corte de los 80 y los 90. Un diálogo sobre el rule of law en Argentina' in R.J. Palermo (ed.), *SELA 2000: Estado de derecho y democracia. Un debate acerca del rule of law* (Editores del Puerto, 2001), 93–118.

[5] Decree 157, Presidential Order of Judging the Juntas Militares, 13 December 1983; Decree 158, Penal Prosecution of the Members of Insurgent Groups, 13 December 1983.

[6] Decree 187, Creation of the Comisión Nacional sobre la Desaparición de Personas, 15 December 1983.

[7] CONADEP, *Nunca más* (EUDEBA, 1984).

[8] Respectively, Law 23,492, 23 December 1986 and Law 23,521, 4 June 1987.

self-critique of its role during the dictatorship. Congress approved a law abolishing compulsory military duties in 1994.

Néstor Kirchner (2003–07) and his wife Cristina Fernandez (2007–15) set human rights policy as a cornerstone of their administrations. Kirchner overturned amnesties for military officers accused of human rights abuses and implemented several symbolic measures such as converting the Navy school into a memorial museum. Further, in 2007 the Supreme Court established that presidential pardons granted to former military officers were unconstitutional. At the time of writing, the involvement of the military in internal security affairs and a controversy about the Army's General Chief of Staff appointed by Cristina Kirchner (General Milani), accused of involvement in human rights violations, are on the media agenda. After more than three decades of democracy, a threat of a *coup d'état* is no longer an option. But civil–military relations are still the subject of public debate in Argentina.[9]

Timing and Sequencing

Although the military dictatorship was replaced by democracy in 1983, constitutional reform only took place in 1994. The legal reforms necessary to make changes to the structure and mandate of the security sector thus began with legislation enacted before the 1994 constitutional reform. Even though the armed forces did not retain any formal power after Argentina's democratic transition in 1983, Raul Alfonsín's and Carlos Menem's democratically elected governments faced four military rebellions and one attack by insurgent groups between 1987 and 1990. All failed to unseat the democratic government, but they highlighted the need to reduce the political influence of the security sector.

In this light, the leading political parties in Argentina in the 1980s—*Partido Justicialista* and *Unión Cívica Radical*—agreed on the need for a normative framework that set clear differences between the security and the defence sector. The latter would only take action in case of a foreign threat or cases of extreme national emergency. Civilian control through different bodies was also important for both parties although differences arose when defining whether legislative control was necessary or not. The main consensus that cut across party lines was the need to enact internal security and defence laws that would limit potential abuse while clarifying the functions of the different security services and establishing a civilian chain of command.

Security sector reform (SSR) was driven by four separate ordinary statutes: the National Defence law (1988)[10] and the Internal Security Law (1992)[11] passed

[9] This research covers the period between 1983 and April 2015.
[10] Law 23,554, 26 April 1988. This law replaced the Law on National Defence enacted in 1966.
[11] Law 24,059, 6 January 1992.

before the 1994 constitutional reforms, and the Law Restructuring the Armed Forces (1998)[12] and the Law Regulating Internal Intelligence (2001) passed after 1994. The consensus on the need for immediate legislative change—rather than waiting for constitutional reform—is indicated by the passage of the laws, in both houses of Congress, with the unanimous support of both Radicals and Peronists.

The first two statutes are the cornerstones of post-authoritarian security sector governance. The National Defence Law, enacted in 1988, was the first piece of legislation regulating the security sector since the return to democracy. Among other things, this law established clear differences between national defence and internal security issues and forbade the armed forces from taking action in matters of internal security. This clear-cut distinction between internal security and defence affairs was reiterated in the enactment of the Internal Security Law in 1992 (during Carlos Menem's first administration). The law placed Argentina among the few Latin American countries to exclude the military from taking part in internal security affairs.[13] Two other important laws of SSR—the restructuring of the armed forces and the regulation of intelligence affairs—would come several years later, by the end of the second term in office of Menem (1998) and during De La Rúa administration (2001) respectively. However, the regulations necessary for the implementation of these two laws were significantly delayed: regulations were promulgated only in 2006 in the case of the National Defence Law, while no regulations necessary for the implementation of the Law Restructuring the Armed Forces have been promulgated as of April 2015.

A consequence of the reform of the legal foundations of the security sector prior to the 1994 constitutional reform was that topics of SSR did not play any role in the constitutional debates, and have been left for resolution in the text of ordinary legislation.

The Institutional Structure of Security Services

During the years of the military dictatorship, the military did not differentiate between internal and external public order. Both matters were under the charge of the commanders-in-chief of the three armed forces (Army, Navy, and Air Force). All security matters, both internal and external, were within the mandate of the armed forces. This was part of an overall military strategy that was illuminated by the international context of the time. The junta took the position that by maintaining a strong military stance against guerrilla and communist opposition factions within the country, Argentina´s geopolitical position internationally, in the bipolar world of the Cold War era, would be enhanced. International

12 Law 24,948, 3 April 1998.
13 Diamint (note 3).

conflict with Chile (regarding possession of three islands in the Beagle Channel) and long-standing rivalry with Brazil over shared resources only served to justify the junta's claim that military control over both internal and external matters was necessary.

It was not until the National Defence Law was enacted in 1988 that the institutional separation of internal and external security forces was made a matter of law. Even before the enactment of the National Defence Law, several important policy changes were made to the organization of the security sector after the transition to democracy in 1983. The first of these key changes was to the chain of command. Restoring the democratically elected President to the position of commander-in-chief of the armed forces ensured that the ultimate head of the armed forces was now a civilian, rather than a member of the armed forces (Decrees 157 and 158, enacted in 1983). The President's role as commander-in-chief of the armed forces is now entrenched in the Constitution in Article 99.

Second, during the first months of the Alfonsín government, the Ministry of Defence was charged with the administrative control of the armed forces, marking a change from the military regime where the armed forces themselves administered their own affairs.[14] These changes also included the transfer of all the military industries (such as *Astilleros Militares* and *Fabricaciones Militares*) to the Ministry of Defence and the restoration of the *Secretaria de Inteligencia del Estado* (SIDE), the civilian unit for internal intelligence activities. All these bodies had been under the authority of the military before 1983.[15] These measures had a great impact on the organization of the security forces.[16]

A third aspect of the reorganization of the security sector had to do with restraining defence and security spending and ensuring that these budget items were subject to civilian political control and oversight. Military budget cuts became a crucial aspect of civil–military relations after 1983.[17]

The separation of the mission and mandate of the security services outlined in the 1988 National Defence Law, dealing with the armed forces, was reaffirmed in the 1992 Internal Security Law dealing with the internal security sector. While the main objective of the military is to safeguard the country from external threats, thereby limiting its function to external security, the mission of interior security

[14] With the enactment of the Law on Internal Security in 1992, these forces were then transferred from the Minister of Defence to the Minister of the Interior.

[15] Decree 32 of 1983. For a detailed historical analysis of the role of the military in internal intelligence activities, see M.F. Sain, *Condiciones institucionales del control parlamentario de las ctividades y organismos de inteligencia del estado* (CELS, 1997).

[16] As a consequence of the federal structure of the state enacted in the Constitution, each province has its own constitution and electoral rules for provincial authorities, independent judicial powers, and its own police force. That is why the federal police force (in charge of federal crimes and protection of boundaries) coexist with twenty-three police organizations. Unless stated so, when dealing with security sector institutions, this chapter focuses on federal forces.

[17] Jaunarena, personal communication, 14 May 2014.

forces is to secure the freedom, life, and assets of all the residents of the Argentine territory.

Defence and internal security forces

There are four federal interior security forces: the *Policia Federal Argentina* (Federal Police), who are responsible for federal crimes, as well as serving as the police of the City of Buenos Aires; *Gendarmeria Nacional* (National Gendarmerie), in charge of border patrolling; the Aeronautics Police; and the *Prefectura Naval* (in charge of ports). All these four forces have specific rules that guide the employment of their personnel and internal chains of command, among other factors. For example, Law 21,965 (1958) regulates all issues concerning the Federal Police members by setting out all the requirements, rights, and obligations of the members of the force. Resolution 1205 (2006) of the Ministry of Security sets the organization of the newly created Aeronautics Police (former Airport Police).

As in the case of the national defence system, the head of the interior security system is the President, who delegates the administration of the forces to the Ministry of Security. At the time of the transition in 1983, the Minister of Defence exercised the control of internal security forces, because the Under-Secretary of Internal Security reported to and was under the control of the Ministry of Defence. This was the position until the Interior Security Law of 1992 relocated the Under-Secretary of Security to the Ministry of Interior. In July 2002 the Under-Secretary was relocated again to the Ministry of Justice, Security and Human Rights (Decree 1, 210). Finally, a dedicated Security Ministry was created in 2010 (Decree 1,993).

The Minister of Security is counselled by the Internal Security Council composed of officials of the four internal security forces, the ministers of internal affairs and justice, and the chiefs of the different provincial police forces, among others. In line with other federal councils (e.g. the Federal Council on Education), this institutional mechanism seeks to coordinate national and provincial policies. The Council also has non-permanent members such as members of the legislature serving on congressional security committees.

Although Argentine legislation sets a clear legal distinction between national defence and internal security, the Interior Security Law establishes two situations in which military forces may take action in internal security operations. The law provides for the formation of ad hoc Crisis Committees composed of the Minister of Security, the governors of the provinces facing a crisis, and the heads of the four internal security forces. The Ministry of Defence, if required by the Crisis Committee, may authorize the deployment of military forces in order to cooperate with and provide assistance to internal security operations. This assistance could include transport, engineering, or communication tasks, among others. The law establishes that military forces' support may be required in situations of extreme danger in which internal security systems are considered insufficient by the President. In this case, after declaring the state of siege, the President can order the use of the military forces within Argentina.

During the first democratic government and until the passage of the Internal Security Law in 1992, the Minister of Defence exercised oversight and control of both the military and internal security forces. Although imperfectly aligned with the separation of internal and external functions, this structure did ensure that the security sector was under civilian, rather than military control. Civilian control of the military implies that civilians manage all relevant aspects of military and security policy. In the words of Ruth Diamint:

> civilian control implies the ability to really set the military policy, including the size, shape, structure, and quantity of arms of the military according to democratic values and the belief of the society. This control entails accepting the rules of democratic game. Democratic consolidation takes place when civilians effectively define security and defense policy and lead the armed forces.[18]

Under the current institutional structure, the Minister of Defence exercises administrative control over only the armed forces. National defence policy rests with the President, however, acting on the advice of the National Defence Council established in terms of the 1988 National Defence Law. The National Defence Council is an advisory body, assisting and counselling the President in the adoption of strategies, preparation of plans, and coordination of actions for the resolution of conflict or war. The National Defence Council comprises the President, the Vice-President, the Ministers of the National Cabinet, and the chief of the intelligence agency.

In addition to the National Defence Council, the President also relies for advice in the formulation of defence policy on the Ministry of Defence itself and the *Estado Mayor Conjunto* (Joint Chiefs of Staff). The Joint Chiefs of Staff is composed of officials from the three military forces and chaired by the Minister of Defence. Through this body, the military can contribute to defence policy, military planning, and lead military training and education. It is not mandatory that the opinion of the Joint Chiefs be followed on any issue.

There are restrictions on the President's power as commander-in-chief, however: for example, a declaration of war by the President must be approved by Congress, although the Constitution empowers Congress to authorize the President to declare war, make peace, allow the entry of foreign troops, deploy national military forces abroad, and declare a state of siege in case of necessity.

[18] Diamint (note 3).

Intelligence

The national intelligence system is organized into three different bodies. The main branch is the Secretariat of Intelligence. This body has the function of determining national intelligence policy based on guidelines given by the President, to whom the Secretariat is accountable. The National Intelligence Law[19] specifies that the National Directorate of Criminal Intelligence functions under the Secretary of Interior Security, while the National Directorate of Military Intelligence functions under the Defence Ministry. There are thus two distinct intelligence agencies for the police and military forces—a fact that has been criticized for generating a duplication of functions.[20]

The respective ministries and secretaries in charge of these three systems have the power to determine the internal organization of each of the intelligence agencies. As a result, there is a plethora of resolutions that define various aspects of each of the military, police, and national intelligence agencies.

Private security

It is important to mention that, in line with regional trends, the security sector also comprises a growing private security industry.[21] Except for a presidential decree in 1999,[22] there is no federal law regulating the private security industry. According to statistics from the Argentine Chamber of Private Security Enterprises, there were 1,200 registered private security enterprises in the country and 150,000 private security agents in 2012. This figure almost exceeds the personnel of the four federal security forces for the same year by 50 per cent (96,000).[23]

This growth in private security has gone hand in hand with increasing levels of public anxiety about predatory crimes. According to public opinion surveys, citizen security has been one of the top-ranking concerns since the late 1990s. Although the homicide rate in Argentina has not increased significantly over the last few years, the latest figures on robbery (as of 2011) place Argentina as the

[19] Law 25,520, 3 December 2001.

[20] M. Abregú, G. Palmieri, and S. Tiscornia, 'Informe sobre la Situación de los Mecanismos de Control de los Organismos de Seguridad Pública Interior en la República Argentina' in Hugo Frühling (ed.), *Control Democrático en el Mantenimiento de la Seguridad Interior* (Centro de Estudios del Desarrollo, 1998), 45–68.

[21] J.G. Paz, 'El Fenómeno actual de la Seguridad Privada en América Latina y su Impacto sobre la Seguridad Pública', Ponencia presentada en el V Congreso Internacional, 'Retos y Perspectivas de la Seguridad Pública', Guadalajara, Jalisco, Mexico, Universidad de Guadalajara, 28–30 November 2012.

[22] However, several provinces enacted laws regulating private sector security at the provincial level.

[23] Ministerio de Seguridad, *El Modelo Argentino de Seguridad Democrática* (Buenos Aires, 2012).

country with the highest rate in Latin America.[24] More than 40 per cent of robberies were violent and almost 80 per cent of the robberies were perpetrated with firearms.

Oversight

Legislative oversight

Legislative oversight of the security sector was a central issue in the debate of the Internal Security Law in 1992. Main political parties and civil society agreed that Congress should have a central role in the oversight and control of the armed and security forces. According to Miguel Angel Toma, President of the Defence Committee at Congress at that time: 'Parliamentary control is not against division of powers but within our legal framework; its goal is to exercise control over the enforcement of rights and freedoms.'[25] In spite of this initial consensus and political will, parliamentary control over national defence and security policies was very weak in Argentina during the transition and after.

The Internal Security Law of 1992 created the Bicameral Committee for Internal Security Forces Oversight, composed of eight national deputies and eight senators. The mission of this committee is to monitor security bodies so that they behave within the limits set by the legal framework. To fulfil this task, the law confers the following powers on the committee: to obtain information from any national, provincial, or municipal body or private body; to require the judicial branch to subpoena any person the committee considers relevant to its supervisory mandate; to require law enforcement to prevent persons being investigated by the committee from departing the country; and to propose to the executive branch measures to overcome deficiencies in the security sector.

The committee's powers appear very limited and it lacks the attributes that would allow it to exercise effective control of the internal structure, activities, and developments of the security and intelligence forces.[26] An important weakness is the fact that the committee does not have budgetary oversight over security bodies. It is worth mentioning that, since 2008, the Ministry of Justice has not published official crime statistics nor results of victimization surveys (in 2012 the System of National Crime Statistics was transferred to the Ministry of Security). Another weakness of legislative control is the lack of specialized knowledge of security,

[24] Programa de las Naciones Unidas para el Desarrollo, 'Informe Regional de Desarrollo Humano 2013–2014, Seguridad Ciudadana con rostro humano: diagnóstico y propuestas para América Latina' (New York, 2013).

[25] Ministerio de Seguridad, *Instituto Nacional Estrategicos de la Seguridad, Debate Parlamentario, Ley de Seguridad Interior, Ley 24.059* (Buenos Aires, 2012), 75.

[26] Sain (note 15).

defence, and intelligence issues on the part of political parties, congressmen, and public officials.[27]

Internal control

The principal ruling concerning the control of internal security forces acknowledges that it should be exercised by composite civilian bodies external to the organization of military and security forces. The military and internal security forces do, however, exercise internal disciplinary control and oversight over their members, in order to ensure that their conduct adheres to the laws and regulations in place.

In order to understand the organization of internal control in Argentine security forces fully, one should note that in general, the laws regulating these forces are actually quite old and were approved during dictatorial periods. Take, for example, the *Gendarmeria Nacional* (National Gendarmerie); the law ruling its organization, Law 19,349, is from 1971. Similarly, the Law of *Policia Federal Argentina* (Federal Police), Law 21,965, was enacted in 1979, and the *Prefectura Naval*, Law 18,398 was enacted in 1969. Law 26,102 of the Aeronautics Police is the most recent, having been enacted in 2006. These laws defined the institutional organization and structures of the security services, particularly in matters of hierarchy, training, and promotion systems.[28]

The political context in which these laws were enacted is visible in their substance. The statutes that pre-date the 1983 democratic transition, for example, do not impose clear guidelines for security sector discipline. Consider the Law of Federal Police: it fails to set out any procedures for the sanction of police misconduct (Article 600 of Decree 1886/83). With the exception of the provision allowing for the subpoena of police officers suspected of misconduct and formalities for the initiation of a case, there are no procedural formalities that need to be complied with.[29] More than this, the substantive definitions of misconduct contained in the law are so vague as to be largely inconsequential in practice: examples of such broad language include the requirement to 'adjust public and private conduct ethic norms according to the state of being a police officer'[30] and the imperative to 'not behave with moral weakness'.[31] There are also various subtle and opaque sanctions, such as transfers to distant locations

[27] Ibid.

[28] Centro de Estudios Legales y Sociales; Human Rights Watch, 1998, 33.

[29] Art. 601, Decree 1886/83. See also Centro de Estudios Legales y Sociales; Human Rights Watch, 1998, 33.

[30] Art. 8, sub-s. (a), Law 21.965.

[31] Art. 535, sub-ss. (a) and (u), Decree 1886/83. Centro de Estudios Legales y Sociales; Human Rights Watch, 1998, 29.

that are used as a form of punishment and allow for the manipulation of officers by authorities.[32]

Many authors consider that the discretion conferred by these rules allows security service members to sanction those subject to their command in an abusive and discriminatory way, thereby creating a so-called culture of administrative terrorism. This has led to the development of a corrupt system that suppresses any opposition to the hierarchal order of the security forces.

An important change regarding internal discipline occurred in 2008 when Congress repealed the Code of Military Justice (1951) and enacted a new statute. The 2008 law provides that members of the military must be prosecuted under ordinary criminal law in civilian courts for any civilian criminal offences. This is a significant advance for at least two reasons. First, it eliminates special military courts that have tended to shield members of the military from criminal accountability for human rights abuses and other criminal violations. Second, it effectively abolishes the death penalty in Argentina, as the 1951 Code was the only legal provision authorizing the imposition of a sentence of death.

Constitutional and Legal Issues

Argentina has a long tradition of democratic government interrupted by military *coups d'état*. During periods of military rule, the Constitution was set aside and replaced by an entirely different set of rules. For example, military governments shut down Congress, did not call elections, and did not respect rights recognized in the Constitution.

However, during democratic periods, the Constitution was restored and/or amended following legal procedures and, in general terms, respected. Since 1983, there has been consensus that government and all institutions of state should be bound by the Constitution, and political parties have declared their commitment to respecting the Constitution. Certainly, some may not agree with particular constitutional clauses, but rather than simply ignore those clauses, they propose amending the Constitution. This does not mean that constitutional violations do not occur; in fact, there are many examples of government decisions that have been challenged and overturned for infringing or failing to comply with the Constitution. For example, a recent attempt of the government to change the composition of the Judicial Council, as established by the Constitution, was overruled after the intervention of the Supreme Court of Justice.

It is important in this respect that the principle of constitutional supremacy is recognized. All judges in the country, therefore, have the power to determine

[32] Abregú, Palmieri, and Tiscornia (note 20), 20.

whether laws, decrees, administrative resolutions, and acts or omission of citizens or public officials are consistent with the principles, rights, and obligations established in the Constitution. Where a court concludes that any law or conduct or decision of the public administration is inconsistent with the Constitution, the law, conduct, or decision will be invalid and will have no legal force or effect. Although there are some exceptions, judicial decisions, including declarations of constitutional invalidity, have been respected in Argentina during democratic times.

The procedure for amending the Constitution is rigid. According to Article 30 of the Constitution, it can be reformed as a whole or partially. In order to start the amendment process, two-thirds of the members of each Chamber of the National Congress have to approve a law declaring the necessity of the reform. This law has to contain all the issues to be modified. The ensuing debate and final modification of the Constitution is completed by a special commission elected by the citizens.

The Argentine Constitution requires the enactment of laws for the regulation of the rights and principles established in it. The Constitution is divided into two sections: one refers to the rights of the people and the other to the rules governing public institutions. With regard to the rights of the people, the Constitution enumerates all rights including the right to work, to life, to exercise political rights, to enjoy a healthy environment, and many others. Although these rights are considered programmatic—that is to say, the state's obligation is to develop a legal framework setting out the specific conditions and mechanisms to achieve the rights over time—the rights are nevertheless justiciable. In the event of a violation of a constitutional right, it can be argued in court.

With regard to rules governing public institutions, there are several provisions relevant to the oversight of the security sector. On one hand, the Constitution regulates the high-level control of the military by the President, as commander-in-chief. As noted earlier, the President declares war with the approval of Congress, except where Congress authorizes the President to declare war or peace, to allow the entry of foreign troops into Argentina, to deploy troops abroad, and to declare a state of siege in case of necessity, in circumstances the Constitution itself sets out. The Constitution establishes limits on presidential prerogatives during these periods of siege or emergency. The Constitution prohibits the federal constituent units of the country (provinces) from establishing their own armed forces or declaring war on another province, and confers on the federal government alone the authority to set defence policy. In addition, although military conscription was ended in 1994, the Constitution imposes on every citizen the obligation to arm in defence of the country in the case of need.

On the other hand, because of the two-stage nature of Argentina's transition to democracy, constitutional rules regulating security services were not amended in the constitutional reform of 1994. Most crucial matters of national defence and internal security were dealt with in ordinary legislation enacted before the constitutional reform (the National Defence Law in 1988 and the Internal Security Law in 1992). By the time of the constitutional reforms in 1994, the security sector had largely been removed from civilian politics and neither exerted any influence over nor took part in the constitutional negotiations.

Some consultations with military leaders did take place leading up to the passage of the National Defence Law and the Internal Security Law. This practice continued after 1994 with the preparation of the Law Restructuring the Armed Forces in 1998 and the Law Regulating Internal Intelligence in 2001. With respect to all these laws, however, debates in Congress over the specific provisions of the law were limited to members of Congress, however, and the security forces had no influence over the text of the law after it had been submitted to the legislature for approval. In their analysis of the enactment of the National Defence Law, Barbuto and Sain state that:

> During the parliamentary debates, military leaders—particularly the leadership of the Army—expressed the need to retain some prerogatives in internal security affairs, especially with regard to internal intelligence. However, the failure of this position, which garnered very limited support among legislators, shows that the military did not have enough political power to impose conditions on civilian government.[33]

All four of the laws rely for the complete implementation on decrees and regulations issued by the executive power and relevant ministries and secretaries. These regulations organize the military, intelligence, and defence forces in such a way to allow the management and functioning of each of the security services in a manner consistent with the Constitution and to facilitate the fulfilment of defence and security objectives. An important consequence is that neither military nor security forces have the institutional capacity to self-regulate or self-define their institutional organization and structure. These decisions have to be made by a civilian authority in the respective ministry or secretariat or by the executive or legislative power. Although the laws were passed in 1988, 1992, 1998, and 2001, the Executive Decrees necessary for the implementation of certain parts of the National Defence Law were not promulgated until 2006. Regulations necessary for the implementation of the Law Restructuring the Armed Forces have not been promulgated, as of April 2015.

Perhaps because the security sector in Argentina was unable to exert any leverage or pressure to protect its interests during the process of legislative and constitutional reform, the military resorted to force. Uprisings took place during the last years of Alfonsín government (1987 and 1988) and during the first year of Menem (1990). Alfonsín's presidency also saw the attack by the insurgent

[33] M. Saín y V. Barbuto, *Las fuerzas armadas y su espacio en la vida democrática* (CELS, 2002), 3, own translation from Spanish.

group *Movimiento Todos por la Patria* (MTP) on military barracks of the *Tablada* Regiment in 1989. Some months later, Alfonsín resigned, stepping down from the presidency before the end of his mandate.

It is interesting to point out that in September 2014 heated public debate on these laws revived as military forces took part in operations against drug trafficking within Argentine borders. Various political leaders and security experts[34] have claimed that military involvement in internal affairs is a violation of the laws that regulate the military and posits a challenge to the separation of functions that has been settled for many years. However, the legislative committees overseeing security affairs have taken no action. Also, the controversy surrounding the accusations of human rights violations during the military dictatorship of the new head of the Army (General Cesar Milani) has revived the debate about the partisan role of the military. His support for Cristina Kirchner´s policies has been heavily criticized for giving the military a partisan cadence.

Amnesties

As with many of the issues regarding the security and military sector, the debate about amnesties for human right violations occurred prior to the constitutional debate. The prosecution of military leaders responsible for mass atrocity crimes was a crucial policy position of the Alfonsín administration. The prosecutions that followed were a historic step towards the strengthening of constitutional institutions and one of the few cases in the world in which a new democratic regime prosecuted former dictators for human right violations.

The policy of prosecuting former members of the military regime was tempered to some extent by recognition that consolidating the new democratic system might be threatened by overzealous prosecutions. In this light, the Alfonsín administration sought to limit the responsibility of the military for its role in the dictatorship. Congress approved two laws: *Ley de obediencia debida* (Law on Due Obedience) and *Ley de punto final* (Full Stop Law).

The Law on Due Obedience was approved in June 1987. It provided that intermediate and inferior officers in the armed and security forces were not guilty of human rights violations because they acted under direct orders of higher officials. This greatly limited criminal liability among military officers. Further, President Menem's ten '*indulto*' decrees of 1989 and 1990 pardoned over 1,200 people convicted of crimes committed during the military regime. The beneficiaries of the

[34] For experts' views, see e.g. an interview with Ruth Diamint (<http://www.lanacion.com.ar/1656427-rut-diamint-contar-con-los-militares-como-apoyo-del-poder-politico-no-es-conduccion-democrat>) and 'Narcotráfico: los riesgos de la lucha militar', *Clarin*, 29 January 2014 (<http://www.clarin.com/opinion/Narcotrafico-riesgos-lucha-militar_0_1075092501.html>).

indultos included members of the Military Councils, members of the junta, and several civilians responsible for the military rebellions during Alfonsín's presidency.

The Full Stop Law set a deadline for the institution of criminal proceedings for crimes related to political objectives during the military regime. The law provided new criminal prosecutions could be instituted up to sixty days from the date of promulgation of the law. After this date, no new cases could be prosecuted. The law was promulgated on 24 December 1986. The deadline obliged judges to accelerate processes in order to avoid falling outside this period.

Human rights violations and judicial remedies for them are still discussed in Argentina and play an important role in shaping Argentine politics. Eighteen years after President Menem passed the *indulto* decrees, the Supreme Court of Justice declared *indultos* unconstitutional. In the *Riveros Case* of 13 July 2007, the Supreme Court opened the way to initiate legal cases against those responsible for human rights violations that had benefited from pardons. In recent years, a new debate has surfaced in relation to the fairness of human rights cases that followed the *Riveros* decision, and the independence of the judiciary. Many experts as well as party leaders and legislators have questioned the independence of judges when deciding cases on human rights violations.

Lessons Learned

The democratization process that began in 1983 and ended with the approval of the new Constitution in 1994 was very successful in terms of securing democracy and excluding the military from power. The evidence of this is that Argentina has lived in a democratic regime for the past thirty years, the longest democratic period in the history of the country.

One of the keys for success, in terms of making the security forces obey civilians, was the total consensus among the relevant political parties. Major political parties were convinced that the security forces had to comply with democratic rules. They considered that civilians should command the military and security forces, and these forces should not have any power. Civil society organizations, as well as most important economic and social actors also supported this vision. In summary, there was a large coalition in support of democracy and a corresponding consensus opposing the idea that security forces should hold any political power.

Political consensus regarding the need to ensure criminal accountability for those leaders of the military and security forces who had participated in violations of human rights was also a key factor for success. Argentina followed a systematic programme for the investigation, indictment, trial, and punishment of those who committed atrocity crimes during the dictatorship. The conviction of military and security officials guilty of these crimes was a concrete result that provided a platform for a government committed to human rights.

The strong leadership of President Alfonsín was also a key to success. Alfonsín, along with his political party (Radical Party), had fought against the violations of human rights during the dictatorship and, when he took power, he strongly promoted a strategy of demilitarizing government. President Alfonsín had the legitimacy, strong belief, and popular support to implement the programme of criminal prosecutions for crimes committed during the dictatorship, but at the same time Alfonsín balanced these prosecutions with clemency. This ensured that the rank and file of the military was not aggrieved by comprehensive prosecution that might have risked alienating the security services from the new democratic government. Although the possibility of prosecution for these crimes has now been reopened by the repeal of the Full Stop Law and the Law on Due Obedience, and by the declaration that the *indultos* were unconstitutional, the restriction of criminal prosecution of members of the security services in the immediate aftermath of the transition to democracy may have helped to consolidate democracy in the long term.

It is also important that the prosecution of members of the security services respected the due process of law. This lent legitimacy to the process, showing that the prosecutions were not motivated by revenge but were carried out as a matter of justice. In summary, the most important characteristics of this process were: (i) serious investigation about the fate of '*desaparecidos*' and other human rights violations by a special commission—CONADEP—composed of very prestigious social and political actors; (ii) respect for due process of law; and (iii) an independent judiciary that judged with integrity and fairness.

This process emphasized that the violation of human rights and the failure to respect democracy has a cost in Argentina. All actors, including the security forces, learnt that acting against the law carries serious negative consequences: from life sentences to loss of social legitimacy and support. The result was conclusive: although there were some attempted *coups d'état*, these were rapidly controlled by civilians and the military quickly realized that it no longer had the power or the popular support to challenge democracy.

Another key to success were the institutional arrangements established by the National Defence Law and Interior Security Law. These laws created a clear separation between internal security and defence, banning the military from participating in any internal security operation. At the same time, the internal security forces recovered a certain degree of autonomy, as they were ultimately accountable to and commanded by civilians rather than by the military leadership, and have become the only force responsible for internal security. The fact that these laws were passed several years before the 1994 constitutional amendments meant that the military and security forces did not have any relevant role in debating the new Constitution.

In summary, the success of the Argentine transition was due to strong presidential commitment, political consensus, civilian control over the military, punishment for violations of human rights, proper institutional arrangements, and separation from internal and exterior security.

Nevertheless, the process had several drawbacks. Limiting the strength of the military has produced a military establishment that may be inadequate to meet the country's security needs. The new democratic government of Argentina was so concerned with how to ensure that military officials did not hold political power that it effectively gutted the military establishment. The military lacks any minimum training, equipment, and personnel to defend the country in case of war, or other intervention, such as preventing foreign ships fishing in Argentine waters.

The internal security forces still lack legitimacy, even thirty years after the democratic transition. Although the separation of functions between the military and internal security forces is important, in Argentina the perverse result of this separation has been an increase in internal threats to people's physical safety, in the form of increasing rates of violent crime. The democratic government's concern to eradicate the use of violence by the state against its own people has, in the view of many, prevented the internal security forces from effectively controlling crime. Therefore, the rates of crime and tumult increased without effective governmental control. This led to a privatization of internal security; currently the number of private security personnel almost doubles that of the governmental security forces.

Another result is the lack of professionalism in the internal security forces. Police and other security officials do not know how to use public force in a legitimate way. When they act, they usually produce more violence, and sometimes this includes killing people. This is why the national government strategy over recent years has been oriented towards refraining from using the forces. After thirty years of uninterrupted democracy there is no doubt about the exclusion of the military from ruling internal affairs. However, the consolidation of democratic security governance is still a work in progress in Argentina.

4
Stage-managing Security Sector Reform in Indonesia

Agus Widjojo (with *Andrew Ellis*)*

Introduction

Military reform in Indonesia after its transition to democracy in 1999 was heavily influenced by the legacies of the military's origins as freedom fighters and guerrilla units, the military's long-standing open and active influence in politics under authoritarian rule, and the specific use by the military of the separatist threats of Aceh, East Timor, and Papua as justification for its combination of civilian and military functions.

At the end of the Second World War, Indonesia proclaimed independence from occupying forces of Japan on 17 August 1945 and formed a government under the leadership of President Sukarno. In the years following the war, however, the Netherlands sought to re-establish colonial rule in Indonesia. Prior to the Second World War, armed struggle had played a comparatively minor role in the Indonesian independence movement, which had focused more on self-reliance, education, and non-cooperation with the Dutch colonial authorities.[1] In the years after the war, with no effective public administration, the independence movement was able to resist the reassertion of Dutch authority by mobilizing the people as a nation-in-arms. Armed units were formed in 1945, and a military ethos of independence from the new Indonesian government subsequently emerged.[2] Guerrilla warfare continued until 1949 when the Netherlands finally recognized Indonesian independence.

During its first decade of independence, Indonesia functioned as a parliamentary democracy. In 1959, it descended into authoritarianism in the guise of Sukarno's 'Guided Democracy'.[3] During the Sukarno period, the military was increasingly preoccupied with the growing influence of the Communist Party

* The author would like to thank Andrew Ellis for editing and enriching this chapter with various references and footnotes, and making the chapter more appropriately academic.

1 Herbert Feith, *The Decline of Constitutional Democracy in Indonesia* (Cornell University Press, 1962), 4–6.

2 Robert Lowry, *The Armed Forces of Indonesia* (Allen and Unwin, 1996), 46–7.

3 Zoltan Barany, *The Soldier and the Changing State* (Princeton University Press, 2012), 182.

of Indonesia (PKI), towards which Sukarno was sympathetic. The military accordingly removed Sukarno in 1965, leading ultimately to Suharto becoming Indonesia's second President in March 1968. The military quickly destroyed the PKI and emerged as the most powerful institution in the country. With Suharto as President, it was now able to develop ideas which it had originated in the 1950s and formally implement the doctrine of *dwifungsi* (dual function), which mandated a direct role for the armed forces in political life and military affairs. At the same time—partly fuelled by separatist threats in Aceh, East Timor, and Papua—the military pushed its vision of close cooperation between military and the civilian population as part of a 'total people's defence' strategy, in which military personnel were deployed throughout the country, allowing for the deep penetration of the military into Indonesian society, particularly in rural areas.[4]

Suharto's 'New Order' regime survived for three decades. Following a prolonged economic crisis in the 1990s and resulting street protests, Suharto resigned in 1998, paving the way for elections and a gradual process of democratization. As described in this chapter, establishing civilian oversight over the military after the collapse of the 'New Order' proceeded in similar fashion to Indonesia's broader democratization: gradually and in fits and starts, with some stable and positive progress in a transition that is still incomplete.

The Adoption and Amendment of the Indonesian Constitution: A Brief History

The 1945 Constitution of Indonesia was adopted alongside the Proclamation of Indonesian Independence on 17 August 1945. The Constitution was by design a concise document, whose framers wrote it virtually overnight in order to fill the vacuum of power created by the Japanese capitulation to the Allied forces. It was an emergency constitution, meant to be improved upon when the situation in the new republic permitted.[5] While it was not explicitly authoritarian, in practical terms the Constitution provided little obstacle to authoritarian rule.[6]

Notwithstanding the brevity of the 1945 Constitution, and the tight time frame within which it was written, a heated debate had been taking place within the independence movement over the philosophical and constitutional foundation for the new republic.[7] One major issue was the question of whether the republic should be

[4] Ibid., 183.

[5] Adnan Buyung Nasution, *Aspirasi Pemerintahan Konstitusional di Indonesia: Studi Sosio-Legal atas Konstituante 1956–1959* (Grafiti, 2001), 12–27.

[6] Harold Crouch, *Political Reform in Indonesia after Soeharto* (ISEAS, 2010), 44; Simon Butt and Tim Lindsey, *The Constitution of Indonesia: A Textual Analysis* (Hart Publishing, 2012), 4–6.

[7] Douglas E. Ramage, *Politics in Indonesia* (Routledge, 1995), 11–14.

Islamic or secular in nature. A second was the basic philosophy of the state:[8] some sought to base the state on the rights of the individual, while others advocated a form of nationalism known as integralism, which views the state and society as an organic unity in which social obligations rather than individual rights are paramount.[9] There was, however, a specific statement in the elucidation section of the 1945 Constitution[10] that Indonesia was a *Rechtsstaat*—a state based on law.[11]

As part of these debates, Sukarno, as leader of the independence movement, sought to embrace and provide a synthesis of the different currents of Indonesian nationalism through the enunciation of *Pancasila*, the five fundamental principles for the future Indonesian state: nationalism, internationalism/humanitarianism, democracy through consultation and consensus, social prosperity, and belief in God.[12] *Pancasila* formed the basis for the Preamble to the 1945 Constitution.[13]

Because the 1945 Constitution was short, its content relating to the relationship between the state and the military was limited. Article 10 stated that the President is the Supreme Commander of the Army, Navy, and Air Force, and Article 11 provided that the President declares war, makes peace, and concludes treaties with other states. In the appended elucidation section, these presidential powers were stated to be consequent on the President's position as Head of State. Article 30 on national defence provided that every citizen has the right and duty to participate in the defence of the country, and that further provisions governing defence will be regulated by law.

The 1945 Constitution was replaced in 1949 with a new constitution, alongside the agreement which ended the attempt by the Netherlands to regain colonial control over Indonesia. The 1949 Constitution was federal and parliamentary in nature, and was a much longer and more detailed document.[14] The chapter which covered national defence and public security contained seven articles.[15] A new federal law would regulate the right and duty of every citizen capable to assist in defending the independence of the United Republic of Indonesia. The military would have the duty to protect the interests of the United Republic of Indonesia. The government

[8] Nasution (note 5), 88–101; Mohammed Yamin, *Naskah Persiapan Undang-undang Dasar 1945* (Yayasan Prapanca, 1959), Vol. I.

[9] Butt and Lindsey (note 6), 7–11.

[10] Elucidation sections (*Penjelasan*) are often appended within Indonesian legal instruments. While these do not have the legal standing attached to the substantial texts, they do have significant influence in the interpretation of those texts.

[11] Constitution of the Republic of Indonesia, 1945, Section 6, Art. I. See also Butt and Lindsey (note 6), 11.

[12] John D. Legge, *Sukarno: A Political Biography*, 3rd edn (Allen Lane, 2003), 209; Mohammed Hatta, *Memoirs* (Gunung Agung, 1981), 221–2; Ramage (note 7), 11–14.

[13] The Preamble accordingly provides that Indonesia will be based on 'Belief in the One, Supreme God, just and civilized Humanity, the unity of Indonesia, and democracy which is guided by the inner wisdom in the unanimity arising out of deliberation among representatives, meanwhile creating a condition of social justice for the whole of the people of Indonesia.'

[14] Butt and Lindsey (note 6), 4.

[15] 1949 Constitution of the United Republic of Indonesia, Arts. 179–85.

would be responsible for defence, with a new federal law required to regulate the structures, duties, and powers given for management of defence policy and for organization of military duties. The President would be the Commander-in-Chief; the government could include a Minister of Defence, appointed and dismissed by the President in accordance with a federal law. The President could only declare war with the prior approval of both chambers of the legislature sitting in joint session. Under the provisions of a new federal law, the government could declare a state of war or a state of emergency in specified regions; moreover, regions could not establish their own armed forces, but could ask for federal assistance in maintaining security and public order.

The 1949 Federal Constitution, however, was short-lived. A product of an agreement between the Dutch and Sukarno governments, it sought to establish a federal republic composed of a number of states. The Dutch had intended this as a mechanism to weaken Sukarno's control and retain their influence in Indonesia, but popular opinion favoured a return to a unitary state and the 1949 Federal Constitution was replaced in short order in 1950 by the Provisional Constitution of the Republic of Indonesia (the '1950 Constitution'), re-establishing a unitary and parliamentary system.[16] The level of detail in the chapter on national defence and public security remained much the same,[17] but a number of changes were made over and above those necessitated by the return to a unitary state structure. The right and duty of every citizen to defend the independence of the Republic of Indonesia remained, as did the duty of the military to protect the interests of Indonesia. While government responsibility for defence remained, the new regulating law was now limited to the basis of the structures and duties of the bodies given the responsibility of managing defence. There was no specific reference to a Minister of Defence. The President would have the supreme power over the armed forces; in time of war, the government would place the armed forces under the leadership of a commander-in-chief. The President could only declare war with the consent of the legislature. The President could declare a state of emergency in specified regions. To maintain order and public security, a police force would be established, regulated by law.

Under the 1950 Constitution, an interim parliament was established,[18] and a series of governments were formed, all of them short-lived.[19] During the years which followed, attempts by government and top military commanders to institutionalize the military and subordinate it to civilian power met with resistance from regional commanders with whom President Sukarno's sympathies predominantly lay.[20] This conflict reflected the divergence between the desire to establish

[16] Feith (note 1), 99. This history is a major contributing factor to the continuing toxicity of the concept of federalism that remains embedded in Indonesian constitutional discussion to this day.
[17] 1950 Temporary Constitution of Indonesia, Arts 124–30.
[18] Feith (note 1), 93–5.
[19] The history and politics of this period are chronicled in detail ibid.
[20] Lowry (note 2), 47.

a professional military under civilian control, and the legacy and memory of the popular struggle for independence against centralized colonial rule. These competing visions were at the heart of the regional rebellions which broke out in the late 1950s, in what has been described as a conflict between 'administrators' and 'solidarity-makers'.[21]

Elections took place in 1955 both to parliament and to a specialist Constituent Assembly (*Konstituante*) which was intended to write a permanent document,[22] but this process did not fare well. From about 1956 onwards, Sukarno and his supporters voiced the view that it was the abandonment of the 1945 Constitution and the introduction of the parliamentary system which lay at the root of Indonesia's ills.[23] By 1959, the Constituent Assembly had not managed to reach an agreement on a new constitutional text. In the face of this impasse, President Sukarno moved to reintroduce the 1945 Constitution by decree, announcing the establishment of 'Guided Democracy'[24]—an executive-led autocracy in which the legislature played a limited and diminishing role[25]—and building *Pancasila* into the role of an all-encompassing national ideology.[26]

During the Guided Democracy period, there were three major political players: President Sukarno, the Indonesian Army (the TNI), and the PKI. Sukarno and the PKI grew steadily closer.[27] On 30 September 1965, a group of army officers, often suggested to have been inspired by PKI, attempted to kidnap seven senior officers and killed six of them, which triggered violence and turmoil culminating in the destruction of the PKI and the re-establishment of government authority by the military.[28]

In 1966, President Sukarno was succeeded by Suharto, a senior army officer who became the second President of the Republic of Indonesia. The transfer of power took place gradually: the military were keen to ensure that it was seen as a constitutional change of government.[29] The Suharto-era regime—known as the New

21 Feith (note 1), 113.

22 Nasution (note 5), contains a full study of the issues, conduct, and ultimate failure of the Constituent Assembly.

23 Andrew Ellis, 'The Indonesian Constitutional Transition: Conservatism or Fundamental Change?' (2002) 6(1) *Singapore Journal of International and Comparative Law* 123.

24 Legge (note 12), 346.

25 Etsi Yudhini, 'Indonesia's Presidentialism' in Andrew Ellis, Jésus Orozco, and Daniel Zovatto (eds), *Making Presidentialism Work* (National Autonomous University of Mexico and IDEA, 2009).

26 Ramage (note 7), 18.

27 Marcus Mietzner, *Military Politics, Islam, and the State in Indonesia* (ISEAS, 2009), 50–1.

28 R.E. Elson, *Soeharto: A Political Biography* (Cambridge University Press, 2001), 126, as quoted in the daily newspaper, *Kompas*, 1 November 1965. See also Salim Said, *Gestapu 65: PKI, Aidit, Soekarno dan Soeharto* (Mizan Publishing, 2015); John Roosa, *Pretext for Mass Murder: The September 30th & Soeharto's Coup D'État in Indonesia* (University of Wisconsin Press, 2006), 67; and State Secretariat of the Republic of Indonesia, *Gerakan 30 September Pemberontakan Partai Komunis Indonesia: Latar Belakang, Aksi, dan Penumpasannya* (State Secretariat of the Republic of Indonesia, 1994), 68–103.

29 Soedjati Djiwandono, 'Civil–Military Relations in Indonesia: The Case of ABRI's Dual Function', in D. R. Mares (ed.), *Civil-Military Relations: Building Democracy and Regional Security in Latin America, Southern Asia and Central Europe* (Westview Press, 1998), 52–3.

Order—operated under the 1945 Constitution, guided by the *Pancasila* ideology.[30] Suharto exercised control by ensuring that he was in charge of who served in Indonesia's legislature, the *Majelis Permusyawaratan Rakyat* (MPR), formalizing the rule that 20 per cent of the membership of the national legislature and provincial and local legislatures would be members of the military. President Suharto retained his own position as an Army general until 1976.

President Suharto's regime retained power until the Asian financial crisis hit Indonesia in 1998, which saw the collapse of the rupiah and massive inflation. The financial crisis evolved into a political crisis when mass demonstrations filled the streets of Jakarta. The growing demonstrations and the resignation of ministers from Suharto's Cabinet led to the resignation of President Suharto himself, in May 1998. He was succeeded as President by his Vice President B.J. Habibie, who responded to the crisis of politics, economics, and legitimacy by initiating a process of democratic reform, including preparing for early elections, lifting restrictions on the media and controls on mass organizations, and releasing political prisoners. In addition, President Habibie addressed the issue of East Timor, a former Portuguese colony which had been occupied by Indonesia in 1975, an action which had little and diminishing international acceptance, and where an active independence movement existed.[31] Habibie announced the holding of a consultative referendum on the future in East Timor in August 1999, in which the East Timorese rejected the government proposal for special autonomy within Indonesia in favour of independence.[32]

The depth of the economic crisis, the speed and scope of political change, and the uncertainty as to how much political change would be accepted by conservative elements (including the TNI), meant that there was little public discussion of constitutional change in the run-up to the elections, which took place in June 1999. These elections were generally judged as free and fair both within and outside Indonesia.[33] Only after these elections, in the three months before the MPR convened, did the Constitution become a central element of political debate. While the idea of a new Constitution briefly appeared on the agenda, the path that was chosen was instead to amend the 1945 Constitution, because a broad national consensus opposed changes to the national philosophy of *Pancasila* and the 1945 Constitution's Preamble. Although the 1945 Constitution was written as a temporary text, it gained enduring emotional significance for most Indonesians as a symbol of the struggle for independence, and as a founding pillar of the unitary

[30] Ramage (note 7), 18.

[31] One account in detail of the East Timor issue from 1975 onwards can be found in Don Greenlees and Robert Garran, *Deliverance: The Inside Story of East Timor's Fight for Freedom* (Allen and Unwin, 2002).

[32] Crouch (note 6), 21–8.

[33] Ibid., 6; Kevin Evans, *The History of Political Parties and General Elections in Indonesia* (Arise Consultancies, 2003), 125; National Democratic Institute, 'Election Statements 1999', <http://www.ndi.org/node/22214>.

state.[34] In a diverse and pluralistic nation like Indonesia, it was feared that a new constitution could pose a risk to the unity of the state, because it would practically mean creating a new Republic.

The process of amending the 1945 Constitution was conducted between 1999 and 2002 by the MPR, through two ad hoc MPR committees, Ad Hoc Committee I, which dealt with 'Amendments of the Constitution', and Ad Hoc Committee II, which dealt with 'Review of MPR Decrees and Other Non-Amendment' issues. These two committees were composed of representatives of all political groups within the MPR: elected legislators from political parties, but also military and police legislators, regional representatives, and functional group representatives. The three years taken to produce the amendments reflected the process of deliberation and consensus for MPR decision-making, as well as the depth and complexity of the issues being discussed.

A series of four constitutional amendments were passed in the annual plenary sessions of the MPR between 1999 and 2002,[35] with accompanying necessary MPR Decrees.[36] Together, the four constitutional amendments altered over three-quarters of the articles of the 1945 Constitution; in addition, they removed the elucidation section of the original document. The changes they introduced were ultimately significant and played an important role in establishing civilian control of the security sector and reducing opportunities for security sector interference in civilian government. However, each of the changes was incremental, and their careful timing and sequencing made it more likely that the goal of a depoliticized security sector and civilian oversight could be achieved. It is an open question whether this goal could have been achieved if the changes had been introduced in one amendment package, or in a different political situation, or conducted by different actors.

The first constitutional amendment, passed in 1999, introduced presidential term limits, and started to define the legislative process. In 2000, the second constitutional amendment laid down the framework for regional autonomy and completed consideration of the role of the legislature. It also addressed citizenship and human rights (including practically all the provisions of the Universal Declaration of Human Rights[37]), and updated Article 30 on state defence and security. The

[34] Andrew Ellis, 'Indonesia's Constitutional Change Reviewed' in Ross H. McLeod and Andrew Macintyre (eds), *Indonesia: Democracy and the Promise of Good Governance* (ISEAS, 2007), 22.

[35] Andrew Ellis, 'Constitutional Reform and the 2004 Election' in Thang D. Nguyen and Frank-Jürgen Richter (eds), *Indonesia Matters: Diversity, Unity, and Stability in Fragile Times* (Times Media, 2003), 53–70.

[36] The sources of law and the status of Indonesian legal instruments are currently laid out in MPR Decree 3/2000. Sources of law can be written or unwritten: *Pancasila* and the body text of the constitution are declared to be national sources of law. The decree lays down the hierarchy of laws: the constitution, MPR decrees, laws, government regulations in lieu of laws, ordinary government regulations, presidential decrees, and regional regulations.

[37] The important exception being that no right exists not to have a religion, which would be contrary to the inclusion within *Pancasila* of belief in God. Also, the inclusion of the right not to be

third constitutional amendment, passed in 2001 after the removal from office of President Abdurrahman Wahid and his replacement by his Vice President Megawati Soekarnoputri, made fundamental changes to the structure of the state. It shifted ultimate sovereignty from the MPR to the people; declared Indonesia to be a state based on law; created direct, single-round presidential elections; defined the presidential impeachment procedure; established a second regional chamber of the legislature; and addressed the conduct of elections, the management of state finances, and the judiciary.

The constitutional reform process was completed in 2002 with the fourth constitutional amendment, which introduced a run-off for presidential elections if no candidate achieved an absolute majority and sufficient support in enough regions in the first round, reconstituted the MPR with much more limited functions, addressed education and social welfare issues, and laid out a revised mechanism for constitutional amendments. The fourth amendment specified the existence of a Minister of Defence, but only in the context of being a member of a triumvirate responsible for assuming presidential powers in the event that both the presidency and the vice presidency became simultaneously vacant. The new provisions for constitutional amendments require that proposed amendments should be submitted in writing by at least one-third of the members of the MPR, be debated in a plenary attended by at least two-thirds of the members, and secure the agreement of 50 per cent plus one of the members of the MPR (replacing the previous requirement for the support of two-thirds of the members in attendance). Finally, the fourth amendment made the unitary form of the state in Indonesia unamendable.[38]

Overall, while the constitutional amendment process was not rooted in a grand design for the new state, it fundamentally changed the nature of the state, decisively departing from the integralist model that had been developed over the preceding forty years.[39] The amended Constitution contains a clear separation of powers, with a head of state and government elected for a fixed term and not subject to the confidence of the legislature, and an independent constitutional court. It is a system in which legislation requires both legislative and executive consent, and thus has inbuilt incentives for collaboration. It is easily categorized as a standard presidential system.[40]

tried under retrospective legislation proved controversial, rather to the surprise of MPR members: several civil society groups argued against it as enshrining impunity for New Order-era human rights abuses.

---

38 1945 Constitution of Indonesia as amended following the Fourth Amendment of 2002, Art. 37.

39 Butt and Lindsey (note 6), 19–20.

40 Ellis (note 35), 55.

Establishment and Role of the Indonesian Military up to 1999

The first Indonesian government was cautious in setting about building a credible defence force in 1945 because of the political context of transition from Japanese imperial power to the Allied power in 1945.[41] On the one hand, the Allied powers might have viewed the creation of an Indonesian defence force as Japanese-driven; on the other, the Japanese occupation army, which was still officially in charge of maintaining public security, might have rejected the defence force. The government started building a defence force by establishing the *Badan Keamanan Rakyat* (BKR—People's Security Agency). Although the first Cabinet after the Proclamation of Independence included a defence portfolio, Sukarno initially made no appointment to the position, mindful of possible rejection by the Japanese occupation army. The military viewed this decision as reflecting Sukarno's reluctance to build a defence establishment, including a credible defence force. In response, the informal military leadership and various armed elements deliberated and set in motion an effort to build a national army and its leadership, electing their first Commander-in-Chief from among their ranks. The fact that the organization and subsequent reorganization of the defence establishment were not based on government decree or policy left a marked imprint, creating a tendency for the military establishment to maintain independence from political authorities.[42] The doctrine of the Indonesian military contended that unlike other countries where the military was established by the political authorities, in Indonesia, the military had given birth to the Indonesian Republic.[43] The struggle for independence led the military to root its relationship with civilian authorities in the spirit of comrade-in-arms as opposed to the modern theory of civil–military relations, thereby justifying it taking a different position from the policy of the President as necessary.[44]

BKR evolved gradually into *Tentara Rakyat Indonesia* (TRI—the Indonesian People's Military), and then *Tentara Nasional Indonesia* (TNI— the Indonesian National Military). This marks the origin of the name given to the current Indonesian Joint Defence Force, the TNI. It was initially a single service, a Land Force. Subsequently the Navy and Air Force were established. The police, however, were initially created out of the civil service bureaucracy.

In the emergency circumstances in which the TNI overcame the rebellion of the PKI in East Java in 1948, the TNI was required to fill the vacuum left by civil servants who were either killed in the rebellion or were involved in it. The adoption

[41] Lowry (note 2), 193.
[42] Ibid., 47.
[43] Mietzner (note 27), 38–40.
[44] Nugroho Notosusanto, *The National Struggle and the Armed Forces in Indonesia* (Centre for Armed Forces History Department of Defence and Security, 1980).

of a guerrilla strategy in anticipation of a Dutch counter-attack also put TNI members in government positions when it was necessary to form an emergency guerrilla government at the end of 1948.[45] The non-military role of the TNI expanded beyond politics to include economics and national development.

The TNI drew strategic lessons from the experiences of the Second World War and the independence struggle. The defence of Indonesia could not depend on conventional warfare, and Indonesia's non-aligned approach in foreign affairs ruled out reliance on external alliances. Guerrilla warfare remained a prime component of defence strategy, building on the experiences of the independence struggle, necessitating deep military links in communities, and demanding close cooperation between the military, all levels of government, and the citizens.[46] Specifically, guerrilla warfare involved decentralization in the conduct of war and the need for the military to be integrated with the people as a source of information and logistics. In addition, key to the strategy was the continual creation and strengthening of commitment to the integrity of the nation as a whole: the concept of 'national resilience'.[47]

The declaration of a state of war and siege in 1957, as part of the response to regional rebellions,[48] saw the involvement of the military in domestic politics given institutional expression, with the first serving military officer to serve in Cabinet appointed in 1958.[49] When, under the return to the 1945 Constitution, the temporary MPR was established in 1960, it included functional group representation, including members from all three forces within the TNI (initially fifteen representatives from the Army and seven from each of the Navy and Air Force); the MPR also included five police members.[50] These representatives were appointed by the President on the recommendation of the Commander-in-Chief of the TNI.[51]

During the Sukarno era, the TNI thus saw itself increasingly not only as a defence and security force but also as a sociopolitical force.[52] There was continuing tension between the desire of government and top-level military officers to demobilize and professionalize the armed forces according to the modern concept of civilian supremacy, and the adherence of many regional commanders to the military traditions and models that had served well during the struggle for independence.[53] By the mid-1950s, however, these differences in opinion in the military had begun to fade. Army officers perceived declining public confidence in the competence

[45] Legge (note 12), 262.
[46] Lowry (note 2), 26–7.
[47] Ibid., 7–9.
[48] Feith (note 1), 547.
[49] Lowry (note 2), 183–4.
[50] Legge (note 12), 355.
[51] Lowry (note 2), 182.
[52] Ulf Sundhaussen, *The Road to Power: Indonesian Military Politics 1945–1967* (Oxford University Press, 1967), covers this period.
[53] Feith (note 1), 248–55.

of civilian governments, including the inability of politicians to reach agreement on a state structure for the longer term.[54] The military was united in the view that defence and security budgets were seriously underresourced.[55] At the National Military Academy in 1958, General Nasution, the Army Chief of Staff, introduced the concept of 'the middle way', which he distinguished from both military dictatorship and military non-participation in civilian politics.[56] As part of this middle way the Territorial Command system first set up in Java in 1948 was expanded and consolidated, establishing a military presence in communities at the local level throughout Indonesia.[57]

After Suharto replaced Sukarno in 1966, he introduced a policy to end the politicization and break-up of the various branches of the security services. The 'middle way' approach evolved into the *dwifungsi* (dual function) doctrine, which stated that the TNI existed not only as a defence and security force, but also as a sociopolitical force.[58] In 1969, Suharto reorganized all the armed services and the police force into the structure of an integrated defence force,[59] renaming it the *Angkatan Bersenjata Republik Indonesia* (ABRI—Armed Forces of the Republic of Indonesia). The integration of the police was in practice the most significant change because it ensured that there was no distinction between external defence and internal security.

Under the 1969 reorganization (which was achieved within the framework of the Defence Act enacted under the parliamentary regime in 1954), the Minister of Defence and Security held the position of Armed Forces Commander and had direct command over the Chief of National Police, which further eliminated any division of function among the security sector institutions. Criminal activities or violations of the law were viewed in the context of security and public order. An institution responsible for security and public order at the national level, *Komando Operasi Pemulihan Keamanan dan Ketertiban Masyarakat* (*Kopkamtib*—the Public Security and Order Restoration Operations Command), had been formed in 1965 with Suharto at its head, and fell under the armed forces.[60] The implication was that there was no boundary that distinguished between (operational) law enforcement and internal security and defence.

There was very limited space for the function of 'pure' law enforcement by the police when responding to riots and social unrest, especially in remote regions. In practice, social unrest during the New Order period was refracted through the

54 Mietzner (note 27), 43.
55 Feith (note 1), 403–7.
56 Mietzner (note 27), 46–9.
57 Ibid., 48.
58 See Nugroho Notosusanto (ed.), *Pejuang dan Prajurit, Konsepsi dan Implementasi Dwifungsi ABRI* (Penerbit Sinar Harapan, 1984); Bilveer Singh, *Dwifungsi ABRI, the Dual Function of the Indonesian Armed Forces* (Singapore Institute of International Affairs, 1995).
59 Lowry (note 2), 53.
60 Ibid., 55.

lens of internal security, viewed as lying on a slippery slope towards rebellion and threats to sovereignty, and thus to be dealt with by the military. Since the scope of the intelligence function tracked the scope of the function of the military as its parent organization, with the military role covering almost all the functions of government, military intelligence was in practical terms a national intelligence institution, and no division existed between internal and external intelligence.

Suharto again changed important elements of the institutional framework for defence and security through the passage of the Defence Act, enacted in 1982.[61] The positions of Minister of Defence and Commander-in-Chief were separated, with the latter as an *ex officio* Cabinet member reporting directly to the President.[62] This law also stated that ABRI played a formal sociopolitical role, in addition to a defence and security role.[63] ABRI was mandated not only to protect independence but also to promote socio-economic development and prosperity in line with the commitments of *Pancasila* contained in the Preamble to the 1945 Constitution. This sociopolitical role was given to ABRI as a whole with no formal distinction among its different branches, including the police. The reality, however, was that the Army carried out a majority of the political roles because from the beginning, it had always been the Army which lay in close proximity to political power (or its absence).

During the New Order period, not only were the armed forces often involved in internal security operations but internal security became their primary mission. The President exercised subjective civilian control over the military, and *esprit de corps* between the President and the military was very strong.[64] The legislature existed not to control the executive but to enforce and secure its policies; the relationship between the military and police leadership, on the one hand, and the legislature, on the other, was very good. The leadership of the security services and the general staff of the military were structured in the way that would be expected in a professional military. The military was ultimately seen as the central source of power of the New Order government and was perceived by the public as part of the 'benevolent authoritarian' state and as the guarantor of security and stability.

In stark contrast to earlier years, there were no long-standing or ongoing external security threats to Indonesia from roughly the beginning of the New Order period onwards. The creation of the Association of Southeast Asian Nations (ASEAN) in 1967 added to the process of trust-building with neighbouring countries. Relations with Malaysia, Singapore, the Philippines, Papua New Guinea, Australia, and other

[61] Law 20/1982 on Basic Provisions for the Defence and Security of the State of the Republic of Indonesia.

[62] Lowry (note 2), 55.

[63] Law 20/1982, Arts 26 and 28

[64] Samuel P. Huntington, *The Soldier and the State* (Harvard University Press, 1985 [1957]), 80–9. Huntington divided civilian control of the military into subjective civilian control, as maximizing civilian power over the military, and objective civilian control, as maximizing military professionalism.

neighbours have on occasions since been sour, but have never developed into a security threat. Indonesia has experienced a sustained period of external peace.

The model implemented by President Suharto was thus an example of what Samuel Huntington termed as subjective civilian control,[65] under which the civilian authorities put the military in the role of regime maintenance. ABRI formed the backbone of President Suharto's political power, and extensive military concern for, and study of, politics became the norm.[66] In the executive branch, the military was allowed to control the political situation, while in the legislative branch, together with the government party, the military was part of the single majority power which was able to secure the President's initiatives.

Aspirations to enhance professionalism within ABRI had existed since the 1980s, originating the spirit and context which later developed into proposals for internal reform. The difference with the actual TNI internal reform which took place after the resignation of President Suharto was that during the New Order period no ideas on dismantling the dual function doctrine were mentioned. The idea of dismantling the dual function only come to the surface after his resignation.[67]

The Approach of the Military to the Democratic Transition

Signs of public dissatisfaction with the Suharto regime began to emerge in the mid-1990s. The perception that declining approval for the government could tarnish the reputation of ABRI sparked active discussion within military circles from 1995 onwards, much of which focused on the level of support that the military should give to the governing party during the 1997 elections.[68] The most radical strand of thinking put forward at this time proposed a 'New Paradigm' for the role of the military, under which the military would recognize it would not always be at the forefront of political developments, would no longer seek to occupy positions in the government but only influence government decisions, would exercise influence indirectly and not directly, and would be ready to share responsibilities with civilian authorities.[69] However, this approach did not gain traction within ABRI at this time. Although in the lead-up to 1999 the armed forces undertook a policy 'to put the Police in front' in responding to domestic unrest and other riot control missions, in reality, the military continued to play the decisive role. This New Paradigm was later known in the internal TNI reform as New Paradigm I. It was the initial phase of the TNI gradually withdrawing

65 Ibid.
66 Leonard C. Sebastian, *Realpolitik Ideology: Indonesia's Use of Military Force* (ISEAS, 2006), 320–72.
67 Agus Widjojo, *Transformasi TNI* (Kata Hasta Pustaka, 2015), 7.
68 Mietzner (note 27), 101–5.
69 Ibid., 106–7.

from its sociopolitical role, but still under the dual function doctrine. Eventually this was followed by New Paradigm II when TNI was under the command of Admiral Widodo Adi Sucipto (1999–2002). The New Paradigm II was the actual document which prescribed that the TNI terminated the practice of the dual function doctrine by stating that:

1. Mission of TNI will always be mission of the state where in time of transition is directed to empower functional institutions,
2. Role of TNI is decided by the will of the people,
3. Together with other national components,
4. As part of the national system,
5. Through constitutional arrangements.

The elements of the New Paradigm II reflect the termination of the dual function doctrine, transforming the TNI into a professional military in a democratic political system and moving away from its past.[70]

After the fall of Suharto in 1998, the position of his successor, President Habibie, was weak. His nomination as Vice President had not been universally welcomed at the beginning, he had inherited the presidency rather than being elected to it, and as a civilian he did not have the presumptive support of the military. He thus found it politically desirable—even imperative—to leave the specifics of military reform to ABRI itself, which had major consequences for process and substance.[71] A document laying out the 'New Paradigm' for the military was published by Commander-in-Chief Wiranto, drawing very heavily on the ideas first put forward in internal discussions two years earlier.[72] This had a number of operational implications, including the separation of the police from the military, and the consequent reversion on 1 April 1999 of TNI as the name of the military.[73] In addition, the social-political branch of ABRI was dissolved in late 1998.[74] It also meant that as the laws for the 1999 elections were negotiated and drafted, it was agreed that ABRI representation in the 500-seat legislature would be reduced from 75 seats to 38 seats;[75] down from 100 prior to the 1997 elections. By the time the new legislature convened later in 1999, the group of legislators consisted of representatives of

[70] Widjojo (note 67), 399–406. See also *ABRI Abad XXI: Redefinisi, Reposisi, dan Reaktualisasi Peran ABRI Dalam Kehidupan Bangsa* (ABRI Headquarters, 1998) for New Paradigm I; see *TNI Abad XXI: Langkah-langkah Reformasi Internal Lanjutan TNI (Tahap II)* (TNI Headquarters, 2001), for New Paradigm II.

[71] Mietzner (note 27), 199–204.

[72] Crouch (note 6), 132–3.

[73] Rizal Sukma, 'Military and Politics in Post-Soeharto Indonesia', in Thang D. Nguyen and Frank-Jürgen Richter (eds), *Indonesia Matters: Diversity, Unity, and Stability in Fragile Times* (Times Media, 2003), 46.

[74] Crouch (note 6), 133.

[75] Law 4/1999 on the Structure and Composition of the MPR, the National Legislature, and Regional Legislatures, Art. 11.

the military and of the police, although it functioned as a single faction within the legislature.

The revision of the constitutional provision on national defence, Article 30, took place in 2000. By this time, it had been established as common ground between all of the factions within the MPR that *Pancasila*, the unitary state, and the presidential system were sacrosanct.[76] The discussion within Ad Hoc Committee I—in which the military and police representatives played an active role—addressed the need to clearly separate the military responsibility for defence from the police responsibility for law and order, the need for the two to be coordinated when appropriate, and the continuing relevance of the citizen defence concept as a support to the professional forces. The Committee considered the idea of creating three separate constitutional articles, on national defence, the TNI, and the police. However, in the draft that was finally reached, provisions relating to all three appeared as separate subclauses within a single Article 30 (which appeared to be more the result of a drafting technicality than the resolution of substantive disagreement).[77] The amended Article 30 provides that the 'defence and security of the State shall be conducted through the total people's defence and security system', with the TNI and the police as the main force, and the people as the supporting force, which appeared to give less emphasis than previously to the role of the citizen in defence and security.[78] It then clearly divides the functions of defence, protection, and maintenance of the integrity and sovereignty of the state—as duties to be undertaken by the TNI—from the functions of maintaining security and public order; protecting, guarding, and serving the people; and upholding the law—as duties to be undertaken by the police.

While there were many areas of the constitution where major disagreements among political factions still existed at this stage of the reform process, the amended Article 30 attracted little comment in the MPR plenary and was enacted as part of the second constitutional amendment. However, the title of the article, 'Defence' in the original 1945 Constitution, was changed to 'State Defence and Security' by the amendment. Although this had not been an issue that attracted much attention within the MPR, some people regarded this change as a set-back and contrary to the reality of the institutional change from 'the Department of Defence and Security' to 'the Department of Defence', which followed from the separation of the military and police.

At the same time, the restructuring of the TNI was achieved through two decrees enacted by the MPR in 2000, one covering the separation of the police from the Army, Navy, and Air Force,[79] and another laying out the respective roles of the

[76] Ellis (note 23), 127.

[77] Contemporary notes of sessions of MPR Ad-Hoc Committee 1 and MPR commissions and plenary sessions.

[78] Ellis (note 23), 133.

[79] MPR Decree VI/2000.

armed forces and the police.[80] With the passage of these MPR decrees, the TNI remained directly under the President, with the Commander-in-Chief appointed and dismissed by the President with the approval of the legislature.[81] Although the aim was to position the police under a ministry, it was not yet clear how this would be done. The police were thus also placed directly under, and responsible to, the President.[82] In the second of these decrees, the MPR also agreed that military representation in the legislature would cease in 2009.[83] In the final stage of the constitutional negotiations in 2002, the TNI and the police took the initiative to move this date forward to 2004. The idea of liquidating the military and police representation was initiated from within the TNI as part of the process of establishing itself as a professional, purely military, body. The TNI had realized both that its representation in the legislature served as a focus for public disapproval, and that in adopting this professional military approach its presence in the legislature created a conflict of interest between the role of its legislators and the relationship between civilian authorities and military commanders.[84]

The Military and Police Structure after the Constitutional Amendments

The legislative implementation of the new constitutional arrangements surrounding the military and policy was ambiguous in practice. The external political environment in which the implementing legislation was drawn up had been changed since 2000 by the impeachment of President Abdurrahman Wahid in 2001. Wahid had been replaced by his Vice President, Megawati Sukarnoputri, who had good links to senior TNI figures and, as Sukarno's daughter, a strong commitment to his legacy; in particular to the validity of the reintroduction of the 1945 Constitution in 1959. The Law on the State Police of the Republic of Indonesia[85] was agreed to soon after the end of the constitutional amendment process in 2002, as was a Law on National Defence.[86] It took two further years and a great deal of discussion, however, for agreement on the Law on the TNI to emerge.[87] That Law states clearly that the TNI carries out its duties based on the policies and political decisions of the civilian government[88] but retains elements of a role reaching

[80] MPR Decree VII/2000.
[81] Ibid., Art. 3.
[82] Ibid., Art. 7.
[83] Ibid., Art. 5.
[84] Agus Widjojo, 'Dari Dwifungsi Menuju Reformasi' in *Transformasi TNI* (Kata Hasta Pustaka, 2005).
[85] Law 2/2002 on the State Police of the Republic of Indonesia.
[86] Law 3/2002 on National Defence.
[87] Law 34/2004 on the TNI. TNI internal thinking at this time on its role may be found in TNI Headquarters (note 70). See also Crouch (note 6), 144–9.
[88] Law 34/2004 on TNI, Art. 5.

beyond national defence including, for example, assisting regional governments and police in the context of security and public order and assisting in search and rescue operations.[89] Many outside government and some elements within the TNI demanded the reform of the Territorial Command,[90] through which the military had exerted influence in regional and local political matters, but the government instead left it largely intact and practically still with its dual-function role.[91] Its retention implies that the government continues to see a role for the military in internal stability and security through its continued presence at village level.[92] Some therefore see the outcome of the constitutional reform process as a reflection of ambiguity, and of a reluctance to free the TNI from the responsibility of internal security.

The President, in the exercise of authority as Head of State and Head of Government, is assisted by the Minister of Defence in drawing up public policy for the defence of the state.[93] Under the amended Constitution, the Minister of Defence is specified as one of three ministers responsible if the presidency and vice presidency are simultaneously vacant;[94] this constitutional reference to the Minister of Defence makes it difficult to see how a future President could abolish the position. The first civilian Minister of Defence since the 1950s was appointed in 1999; the position has remained in civilian hands since, although two incumbents have been retired military officers.

The President is also *ex officio* the Supreme Commander of the TNI, a provision left unchanged by the constitutional amendment process.[95] Command structure responsibility is divided.[96] Defence policy and strategy and administrative support are under the coordination of the Ministry of Defence. The commander of the TNI is appointed by the President with the approval of the legislature.[97] The relationship between the Minister of Defence and the commander of the TNI is somewhat ambiguous, with the commander required to give considerations and opinions to the Minister on a range of policy and strategic planning issues.[98] The mobilization of military power is the responsibility of the President, subject to the approval of the legislature;[99] its use is the responsibility of the commander, under the authority of the President.[100]

89 Law 34/2004 on the TNI, Art. 7(2).

90 Crouch (note 6), 156–7 provides a description of the structuring of the Territorial Command.

91 Muhammad Asfar, *Wacana Penghapusan Koter: Pengembalian Fungsi Teritorial dari TNI ke Pemerintah Daerah* (Pusat Studi Demokrasi dan HAM (PusDeHAM), 2003); Sukma (note 73), 51; Crouch (note 6), 160–1.

92 Mietzner (note 27), 314–16.

93 Law 3/2002 on National Defence, Art. 16.

94 1945 Constitution of Indonesia as amended by the Fourth Amendment of 2002, Art. 8.

95 1945 Constitution of Indonesia, Art. 10.

96 Law 34/2004 on the TNI, Art. 3.

97 Ibid., Art. 13.

98 Ibid., Art. 15.

99 Ibid., Art. 17.

100 Ibid., Art. 19.

The Law on the Police placed the entire police function directly under the President, with the Chief of Police appointed by the President with the approval of the legislature.[101] When the police were first separated from the military, it was the clear intention within the legislature that they would eventually be placed under a ministry, and the initial provision placing them under the President was seen as only temporary, pending agreement on which ministry would be most appropriate. However, the Law on the Police institutionalized this temporary arrangement. This has suited the police as it enables them to write their own policies and budget and implement their own policies and strategies without day-to-day external supervision. With the TNI subject to the control of the Ministry of Defence, the police enjoy relatively less civilian oversight and control.[102] In parallel fashion, the police at regional level are reluctant to be accountable to regional governments. It has been suggested that in many respects the police are a kind of 'military-lite',[103] and have not yet developed a full professional civilian ethos.[104]

The National Resilience Council, *Dewan Ketahanan Nasional* (*Wantannas*),[105] is chaired by the President, with the Vice President, senior ministers, the Commander-in-Chief of TNI and the head of the national intelligence coordinating body as members. It has the duty of advising the President on the development of national defence policy and strategy, including the mobilization of resources and the assessment of risk. On a day-to-day basis, the Coordinating Minister for Politics and Security, a senior Cabinet appointment, has the function of coordinating all ministries related to politics and security, including home affairs, foreign affairs, defence, communications, and the law and justice functions, and also the TNI, the police, and the intelligence services. As a result, the *Dewan Ketahanan Nasional* has at present an almost redundant role, although historically it was formed with the intention of assuming a similar role to that of the US National Security Council. It is evident from the organizational structure where it consists of permanent members of institutions related to security functions, and non-permanent members comprising institutions relating to human security functions.[106] Hence it is more appropriately termed the *Dewan Keamanan Nasional* (National Security Council). Also worthy of note is the National Resilience Institute, *Lembaga Ketahanan Nasional* (*Lemhannas*), which was intended at the time of its inception by President

[101] Law 2/2002 on the State Police of the Republic of Indonesia, Arts. 8 and 11.

[102] Jacqui Baker, 'Professionalism without Reform: The Security Sector under Yudhoyono' in Edward Aspinall, Marcus Mietzner, and Dirk Tomsa (eds), *The Yudhoyono Presidency* (ISEAS, 2015), 127–8.

[103] Ibid., 117.

[104] Donald Horowitz, *Constitutional Change and Democracy in Indonesia* (Cambridge University Press, 2013), 233.

[105] Established by President Habibie through Presidential Decree 101/1999 under powers contained in Law 20/1982 on Defence, Art. 35, which updated previous powers which originated in 1946.

[106] Presidential Decree 101/1999 on National Resilience Council.

Soekarno on 20 May 1965 to function as a higher professional education institute to prepare senior government officials to sit in higher defence positions. This institute was originally called the National Defence Institute (*Lembaga Pertahanan Nasional*); in 1994, due to the change in orientation in foreign policy, the term 'defence' was changed to 'resilience'.[107] In 2001, it was restructured as a non-departmental government institute with a role in high-level leadership training and conceptual and strategic thinking in relation to national, regional, and international issues, with civilian leadership at ministerial level reporting directly to the President, through the Coordinating Minister for Politics, Law, and Security.[108]

Security sector personnel are prohibited from holding public office, elected or unelected, and from engaging in other political activities such as joining political parties or engaging in political associations.[109] One further change that is still missing from the reform agenda is the granting the individual rights of soldiers and police members to cast their votes in general elections. This right has been withheld, on the belief that soldiers' and police officers' direct participation in elections could damage the solidarity of soldiers and police personnel and undermine their non-partisan loyalty to the state, both legacies of the trauma of the past. As a matter of principle, active duty personnel cannot serve in other ministries or fill a civilian job position in the bureaucracy.[110] There are exceptions for positions in some specified ministries that require specialized expertise found only among security sector personnel.[111]

Finally, it was not until 2011 that new legislation on intelligence was enacted. The statute defines and increases the powers of the State Intelligence Agency, which reports directly to the President and is subject to external oversight by a special commission of the legislature.[112] However, commentators have suggested that the military and the Ministry of Defence were opposed to increases in civilian oversight of intelligence-gathering activities, and moved to replace the head of the State Intelligence Agency who had negotiated these changes with the legislature.[113] The process of reforming intelligence functions has not been as intensive as the reform of the military.[114]

107 National Resilience Institute of the Republic of Indonesia official website, <http://www.lemhannas.go.id>.

108 Presidential Decree 98/2016 on National Resilience Institute.

109 Law 2/2002 on the State Police of the Republic of Indonesia, Art. 28; Law 34/2004 on the TNI, Art. 39.

110 Law 34/2004 on the TNI, Art. 47(1).

111 Law 34/2004 on TNI, Art. 47(2).

112 Law 17/2001 on State Intelligence, Arts 42 and 43.

113 Stephen Sherlock, 'The Parliament in Indonesia's Decade of Democracy' in Edward Aspinall and Marcus Mietzner (eds), *Problems of Democratisation in Indonesia* (ISEAS, 2010), 107.

114 Fabio Scarpello, 'Indonesia's Flawed Intelligence Reform Process', *World Politics Review*, 7 June 2011.

Legislative Oversight of the Military and Police

With the change of role in the legislature—from being a rubber stamp that secured and enforced the policies of the executive during the authoritarian New Order regime to serving the democratic role of providing checks and balances and control over the executive power within a presidential system—there has been keen interest in legislative oversight of the security sector institutions, especially in the issues of deployment of military forces and of budgeting. The legislature undertakes oversight through its commission system.[115] Commission 1 handles the functions of defence, foreign policy, and intelligence, while Commission 3, responsible for law and human rights, covers police issues. Rules governing these commissions are part of the general rules that govern the legislative oversight of the executive, and include special investigative powers.[116] Under Standing Orders, legislative commissions are composed of representatives of all political parties who have seats in the parliament, proportional to party strength.[117] This mechanism for civilian oversight by the legislature places barriers in the way of the kind of partisan abuse of the security sector that took place under the authoritarian regime, especially the politicization of security sector institutions in general elections to influence the results in favour of the governing party.

However, the checks and balances that now exist have brought with them their own dangers.[118] Most members of the legislature have demonstrated a lack of familiarity with military matters.[119] Legislative oversight has also created opportunities for the practice of transactional politics between the members of the legislature and security sector actors who have access to financial resources, with the possibility of an accompanying politicization of security sector institutions. This in turn may influence the quality of the documents coming out of the legislative process, which may not serve the cause of security reform.

Military and Police Accountability and Amnesty

The 1945 Constitution gave to the President the general power of granting amnesty.[120] This power was altered by the first constitutional amendment, which requires the President to have regard to the opinion of the legislature in the granting of amnesty.[121]

[115] Sherlock (note 113), 166–7. In Indonesia, the eleven standing committees of parliament are referred to as Commissions (*Komisi*).
[116] 1945 Constitution of Indonesia as amended following the Fourth Amendment of 2002, Art. 20A
[117] Standing Orders of the Legislature, Regulation 1/2014.
[118] Sukma (note 73), 52.
[119] Mietzner (note 27), 318.
[120] 1945 Constitution of Indonesia, Art. 14.
[121] 1945 Constitution of Indonesia as amended following the Fourth Amendment of 2002, Art. 14.

Human rights abuses and violations were never admitted by the security sector prior to the transition to constitutional democracy. This led to impunity: no courts held trials of those accused of human rights abuses. After the fall of Suharto, some trials were held in military courts for alleged human rights violations during the transition period, but the few convictions that resulted were mainly of lower-level military personnel, and many of those were overturned on appeal.[122] Indonesia did see trials for human rights abuses in the form of an ad hoc court set up to hear cases for gross violations of human rights relating to the popular consultation in East Timor in 1999. The ad hoc court convicted six defendants; on appeal, all the TNI officers were acquitted and only two convictions stood: those of civilians, namely Abilio Soares (the Governor of East Timor) and Eurico Guterres (a pro-Indonesia militia leader).[123] Overall, transitional justice for abuses under the New Order and during the transition never got off the ground in Indonesia, despite persistent and widespread calls for it to do so. Interestingly, military accountability took place during the New Order period under President Suharto when a special military tribunal dismissed two general officers and several other officers when they were found to be responsible for the mishandling of a situation in Dili, East Timor, which resulted in fatalities. Another case was another special officers' tribunal which led to the honourable discharge of Lieutenant General Prabowo Subianto in relation to student kidnappings.[124]

To address transitional justice issues, the governments of Indonesia and the Democratic Republic of Timor Leste jointly decided in 2005 to establish a Commission of Truth and Friendship. The Commission was tasked with investigating (i) any violations of human rights surrounding the peoples' consultation in East Timor in 1999; (ii) institutions which were responsible for those human rights violations; and (iii) the forms of reparation to the victims of violence. The Commission was also mandated to recommend steps to establish peace and friendship between the peoples of Indonesia and Timor Leste. In 2008, the Commission concluded that organized violence had taken place against supporters of independence, and that violations had also been committed by the pro-independence side.[125] Although the Commission was given the authority to grant amnesty and rehabilitation in individual cases, it never actually did so. In essence, the Commission was political, with the mission to seek institutional responsibility and what went wrong, eventually submitting recommendations to both governments to heal the past and build friendship between the two peoples.[126]

[122] Crouch (note 6), 169–74.

[123] Mietzner (note 27), 321; Crouch (note 6), 172–3.

[124] Agus Widjojo, 'Contextual Analysis of Accountability for Core International Crimes' in Morten Bergsmo and Song Tian Ying (eds), *Military Self Interest in Accountability for Core International Crimes* (Torkel Opsahl Academic EPublisher, 2015), 107.a.

[125] Commission of Truth and Friendship (CTF), *Indonesia–Timor Leste, Per Memoriam ad Spem, Final Report of the CTF Indonesia–Timor Leste* (CTF, 2008); Crouch (note 6), 41.

[126] CTF (note 125), 310.

Internal Oversight of the Military and Police

Weak public and external oversight of the armed forces during the period of authoritarian government was matched by weak internal oversight. Although the issue of military justice has been a matter of public concern since the transition, few changes have occurred in the military justice system, under which the military has its own military courts and justice system. One initial change in the early days of transition was the holding of military trials in combat areas during the military stability operations in Aceh in 2000. Building on an MPR decree passed in 2000,[127] a provision was inserted in the Law on the TNI to shift the trials of soldiers committing public crimes to the civilian criminal justice system.[128] However, when the legislature sought to enact legislation containing the detailed arrangements that would make this work in practice, it met resistance both from within the TNI and from the government.[129] Despite a commitment by President Yudhoyono in 2006 to support such legislation, no agreement was reached during the legislative term ending in 2009, and at the end of the following legislative term in 2014, the issue was resolved by amendments to the Law on Military Discipline[130] which reframed alleged criminal offences by military personnel as in-house military disciplinary issues subject to the separate military justice system.[131] The attempt to change the system as a whole ultimately failed. Debate still exists between those who believe that military personnel charged with alleged criminal offences should be tried in the general court system, and those who consider that military justice system is already an integrated part of the Supreme Court.[132]

The separation of the police from the TNI required the establishment of a police complaints mechanism. The Law on the Police established *Komisi Kepolisian Nasional* (*Kompolnas*), the National Police Commission, the duties of which include advice on police reform and the receipt of public recommendations and complaints about police performance (although without investigatory or prosecution powers).[133] However, it took five years even to establish this body, and it has been considered as having had limited effect.[134] In contrast to countries such as Japan, where the Police Commission is a civilian political authority which oversees the police, in Indonesia the National Police Commission is placed within the police and has very limited authority.

[127] MPR Decree 7/2000, Art. 3(4)(a).
[128] Law 34/2004 on TNI, Art. 65(2).
[129] Mietzner (note 27), 309–11.
[130] Law 25/2014 amending Law 26/1997 on Military Discipline.
[131] Baker (note 102), 125–7.
[132] Widjojo (note 67), 545.
[133] Law 2/2002 on the State Police of the Republic of Indonesia, Art. 38(2)(c).
[134] Baker (note 102), 128–9.

External Perceptions of Security Sector Issues

In the early stages of the transition, there was a democratic euphoria in which it was held that the past practices of the New Order government were models of the wrong practice, and that all the opposites of the practice of the New Order government were best practices of democracy. The positions and policy frameworks of the leading political parties were generally pro-reform, with variations only on details. There was common ground to get the military out of politics, to end military-owned business as a massive source of out-of-budget funding, and to place the military under democratic control of the civilian authorities. To be sure, some parties still also voiced the role of the military as a stabilizing factor politically, including in the domain of internal security. Few of the civilian politicians had expertise and experience in security issues, and there was a lack of knowledge of building a professional military force in the context of a democratic system.

In its early stages, supporters of the transition process recognized the possibility that if badly handled, law enforcement or even security issues could develop. As lawyer and reformer Adnan Buyung Nasution wrote in 2004: 'The challenge for Indonesia is how to create an open, modern and democratic society in the midst of all the changes and rolled-over symptoms from the past regime in a way that is not perceived as a threat for the Indonesian nation.'[135] At the same time, old habits die hard: under the New Order regime, internal security, by the integration of the police into the structure of the armed forces, included the suppression of political opposition and gave the impression to the public that public safety, order, and security was well-managed because of the dearth of riots or demonstrations. However, in the new democratic setting where freedom of expression was protected, political protest became the order of the day. Those who still drew comfort from the memory of the stability of the past saw the TNI in its past role as a bulwark against internal disorder. The provision of the Law on the TNI that 'all of the mission of TNI will always be conducted by the decision of the political authorities',[136] was not accepted, not known, or forgotten in such circles.

The reputation of the military varied substantially, moving up and down during the reform period. The most important change in public perception was a consequence of the unwillingness of the Army, which still has felt itself independent from the Joint Defence Force Headquarters, to support the attempts by President Wahid during 2001 to prevent his removal from office by 'freezing' the legislature

[135] Adnan Buyung Nasution, 'National Unity: Respect for and Protection of Human Rights' in Thang D. Nguyen (ed.), *The Indonesian Dream* (Marshall Cavendish, 2004), 154.

[136] Law 34/2004 on the TNI, Art. 5.

and declaring a state of emergency. As a result, the favourable rating of the TNI in opinion polls rose from 28 per cent to 58 per cent in a little over a year.[137] By being perceived by the public as a non-partisan state institution that had just left the role of 'the benevolent authoritarian' and had implemented changes on its own initiative, the TNI had, at some key points, considerable political leverage to protect its interests. Although this change in public perception reflected the confusing situation, the case was that if the Army was unwilling to support President Wahid, it actually was still playing a political role. This was different from the stance of the Defence Force Commander who stated that the TNI perceived that the issue was a political issue. The TNI would not involve itself in the issue and wanted to see it solved politically by political elites.

However, the public's interest in security sector reform (SSR) issues appears to have declined over time. Even though a 2013 public opinion survey showed 32 per cent supported the proposition that 'democracies aren't any good at maintaining law and order',[138] a post-election survey in 2014 found that 'law and order' did not feature in the top five issues of public concern, which now focused on prices, corruption, and jobs.[139] There is also little evidence that the military or police had been politicized since 2004:[140] after the 2014 elections, a public opinion survey showed 77 per cent believed that the Army were able to respond neutrally and without political influence on election related issues, and 75 per cent believed that the police were able to do so.[141]

After the police were decoupled from the structure of the armed forces, it became evident that police training, experience, and professional standards often lagged behind those of the armed services.[142] While the police are still in the process of building capacity, they equally still face a challenge in gaining public trust: in 2006, 48.5 per cent of respondents to the World Values Survey had little or no trust in the police. In contrast, the figure for those with little or no trust in the TNI was 25.0 per cent. By 2013, asked to rate institutions favourably or unfavourably, the perception of the police appeared to have improved somewhat, with 36 per cent unfavourable and 58 per cent favourable; however, public support for the policy still lagged well behind that of the TNI, which scored 10 per cent unfavourable to 82 per cent favourable.[143]

137 Mietzner (note 27), 221.

138 Lembaga Survei Indonesia and International Republican Institute, *Survey of Indonesia Public Opinion* (LSI/IRI, 2013).

139 Lembaga Survei Indonesia, *Post Presidential Election Public Opinion Survey* (LSI, 2014).

140 Baker (note 102), 127.

141 Lembaga Survei Indonesia (note 139).

142 Theodore Friend, *Indonesian Destinies* (Belknap Press of Harvard University, 2003), 475.

143 Lembaga Survei Indonesia (note 138).

Conclusions and Lessons Learned

For the democratic transition to succeed, it was essential to gain the acceptance and acquiescence of the security sector for the wider process of change. In the Indonesian case, civilian politicians during the transition allowed the TNI itself to shape changes in its role through its own initiatives from 1998 onwards. In addition, in the final years of the old regime, it was the TNI that began the discussion which ultimately led to its decision to withdraw from politics and to refocus on national defence, while civilian politicians were busy trying to decide on a political system to replace the authoritarian system and were not focusing on military issues. The combination of the military's internal acceptance of the need for change of the military paradigm, which had broadly taken root before the constitutional reform process considered the issue, and the willingness of politicians to allow the military to shape that process, made the SSR aspects of constitutional reform far easier. Absent these conditions, SSR would have been much more difficult, both because of the MPR decision-making process of deliberation and consensus, and the participation of the military in that process.

The TNI was thus able to lead the first stages of internal reform while essentially enjoying the luxury of not being disturbed by politics. When the civilian political authorities established authority in 2004 as a result of the election, the TNI internal reform practically came to a stop: there was insufficient political will by the executive to push change, and the push and pull of multi-party politics militated against the legislature taking an effective role. The implication appears to be that if the TNI had waited for the political circumstances to evolve and for decisions by the new civilian authorities that ultimately emerged, very little SSR might have actually happened.

Additionally, the piecemeal approach to reform generally favoured gradualism in reform on oversight and mandate of the security sector. The importance of the 1945 Constitution as a symbol made it essential for the legitimacy of the process that it took the form of constitutional amendments rather than developing a brand new framework for the democratic era. However, the absence of a general reform blueprint meant that discussions of overall principles and frameworks for the security sector did not take place, which in turn prevented an integrated and comprehensive approach to SSR across all services. This meant incremental, but incomplete, progress; for example, the head of the TNI still reports directly to the President on issues relating to the mobilization and use of military force, and the TNI retains significant influence in the economy.[144]

Relatedly, timing and sequencing are critical, and key factors do not always align simultaneously to provide a fully open window of opportunity. The outcome of

[144] Barany (note 3), 205.

the reform process, the 1945 Constitution after the four amendments, took shape through the process of deliberation and consensus: it went well beyond what was envisaged in 1999 by many who subsequently accepted it, and it is highly unlikely that it would have gained support if it had been tabled as a proposal in 1999. Equally, momentum for reform existed in 2000 when the new Article 30 was agreed, but the pendulum had swung back with the passage of time and the impact of events (in particular, but not only, those surrounding the removal from office of President Wahid) by the time that the implementing legislation was debated and put in place.

Finally, there are two additional aspects of the Indonesian transition which are worth highlighting, although whether one can draw firm lessons from these features would require more research and investigation. The first is the calling of early elections in 1999 by Habibie, which gave momentum and support to the overall democratization project. For Indonesians, taking part in the first openly contested general elections since 1955, this event brought hope and support for the new political order.[145] Second, the 'thin' nature of the 1945 Constitution meant that many of the reforms could take place through ordinary laws and did not require constitutional amendment. Thus, issues such as the civilian accountability and command structure for both police and armed forces were dealt with through legislation, and avoided the often more polarizing stakes of constitutional reform. Where the follow-up to the legislation was speedy, the possibility of a lapse in the SSR process was reduced.

[145] E.C. Thompson, 'Indonesia in Transition: The 1999 Presidential Elections', Policy Report, No. 9. National Bureau of Asian Research (December, 1999).

PART II
POLICE STATES

Somewhat different from the military dictatorships discussed in Part I, Kenya, Ghana, and South Africa are more accurately described before their democratic transitions as 'police states'. In South Africa and Kenya, although the executive and other high-ranking government officials in each country were civilians (i.e. they were not active-duty security officers), the police and intelligence services were deeply committed to the ideology of the governing elite or otherwise invested in maintaining its power. In Ghana, a mixed or 'hybrid' form of military/civilian dictatorship exhibited clear personal and institutional connections to the security sector. In each case, the government was able to rely on the security services to root out and harass the opposition and ensure the continued electoral success of the ruling elite. Institutional structures in each country were ineffective in shielding security officials from manipulation by the civilian government, and formal government structures provided few opportunities to interrogate the connections between the government and the security services. The transition to democracy would thus have to focus, in each country, on reducing the structural and institutional pathways for the civilian government to abuse the security forces for domestic political gain. Alongside this prophylactic objective, new democratic systems would have to allow for effective oversight of the government's relationship with the security forces, both to bring to light and to correct any improper partisan abuse of the security forces. The three countries discussed in Part II have adopted various measures to achieve this objective, with variable success in each case.

5

Police Impunity in Kenya

*Richard Stacey**

Introduction

Josephat Mwenda was a Kenyan taxi driver who was shot in the arm by police during a traffic stop in 2015. Willie Kimani was the lawyer representing Mwenda in his claim against the police. In June 2016, Mwenda, Kimani, and their driver, Joseph Muiruri, disappeared after leaving court in Nairobi. They were found dead a week later. Four police officers have been charged with their murder.This is but one of a string of heinous abuses committed by the Kenyan police in recent years. Amnesty International reported that over 100 people were killed by police in 2002 in what could be described as extrajudicial executions.[1] In 2009, the UN Special Rapporteur on extrajudicial, summary, or arbitrary executions found that Kenya suffered from alarmingly high levels of extrajudicial killings and summary executions by members of the Kenyan police force,[2] and the Kenya Human Rights Commission, a non-governmental organization (NGO), documented around 500 people killed or disappeared by police in just a five-month period in 2009.[3] The Independent Medico-Legal Unit (IMLU), an NGO dedicated to seeking legal redress for victims of torture, found that 27 people were summarily executed by police in 2014 and 2015.[4]

The UN Special Rapporteur highlighted one of the reasons for the high level of police violence: 'internal and external police accountability mechanisms are virtually non-existent; there is little check on, and virtually no independent investigations of, alleged police abuses'.[5] The lack of police accountability and ineffective civilian control of police officers present significant challenges to the safety and

* The author would like to thank Lawrence Gitongo whose contribution during the authors' workshop was most helpful in formulating ideas for this chapter.

1 Amnesty International, 'Amnesty International Report 2003—Kenya', 28 May 2003, <http://www.refworld.org/docid/3edb47d92.html>.

2 Report of the Special Rapporteur on extrajudicial, summary or arbitrary executions, Philip Alston, Addendum, Mission to Kenya, UN Doc. A/HRC/11/2/Add.6, 26 May 2009.

3 Kenyan Human Rights Commission, 'The Cry of Blood: Report on Extra-Judicial Killings and Disappearances', September 2008.

4 Independent Medico-Legal Unit, 'Death on the Bullet: More People Dying from Police Bullets in Kenya', 5 October 2015, <http://www.imlu.org/index.php/shortcode/reports/typgraphy/send/3-reports/68-2017-extrajudicial-execution-report-full>.

5 Report of the Special Rapporteur (note 2), 7.

security of Kenyans. It is of some concern that the problem has persisted even after Kenya adopted a new Constitution in 2010.

Kenya's struggle to contain abuse by the police force is set against the background of high crime rates[6] and security threats from terrorist networks active in East Africa. The imperative to maintain an effective and capable police service, defence force, and intelligence service, sometimes at the expense of transparency, accountability, and legality, is strong. Indeed, the police have become involved in the war on terror: in 2014 the police detained nearly 4,000 people in counterterrorism operations, after a prominent Muslim cleric was killed in Mombasa allegedly at the hands of the police. However, the Kenya Defence Force (KDF) and the National Intelligence Service (NIS) have not been accused of anything like the level of abuse that the police have. This chapter provides a brief background to Kenya's recent political and constitutional changes. It then describes police misconduct in Kenya and seeks to explain why security sector reform (SSR) during the 2010 constitutional transition and in institutional changes since have been ineffective in moving beyond the long-standing problem of police abuse in Kenya. The chapter then goes on to describe reform and institutional structures in Kenya's military, suggesting how differences in the two security services may account for the lack of abuse and misconduct in the military.

Background

Kenya is in the midst of a slow process of transition, from authoritarian rule between 1963 and 1991, via a period of one-party dominance in a democratic system after 1992, to multi-party constitutional democracy after 2010. On gaining independence from the British in 1963, Jomo Kenyatta became Prime Minister. Almost immediately, Kenyatta began to centralize power. The 1963 independence Constitution was amended in December 1964, declaring Kenya a republic and replacing the Queen as head of state with an executive president, a role Kenyatta assumed.[7] In 1968, the Constitution was again amended to allow for direct election of the President, rather than indirect election by parliament.[8] Changes during the Kenyatta era also reduced the role and scope for opposition political parties; for example by prohibiting floor-crossing in parliament[9] and eliminating the upper chamber of parliament.[10] Kenyatta also established the

[6] A. Stavrou, 'Crime in Nairobi: Results of a Citywide Victim Survey', UN Habitat, Safer Cities Programme, Series No. 4 (Nairobi, 2002); R.W. Ngugi et al., 'Security Risk and Private Sector Growth in Kenya', Kenya Institute for Public Policy Research and Analysis Special Report No. 6 (Nairobi, 2004).

[7] Constitution of Kenya (Amendment) Act, 28 of 1964.

[8] Constitution of Kenya (Amendment) (No. 2) Act, 45 of 1968.

[9] Constitution of Kenya (Amendment) Act, 17 of 1966.

[10] Constitution of Kenya (Amendment) (No. 4) Act, 40 of 1966.

long-standing practice in Kenya of using his political position to benefit himself and his cronies. Most official jobs, including in the security sector, were given to people close to the President, from his Kikuyu tribe, or from his home region of Kiambu in central Kenya.[11]

Danial Arap Moi, Vice President under Kenyatta, ascended to the presidency in 1979 in a transition full of intrigue, tribal tension, and back-room dealings. Moi was able to sideline his opponents and overcome the Kenyatta clique's opposition to a member of the Kalenjin tribe taking power by playing powerful Kikuyu interests off against one another and ingratiating himself with opponents of the Kikuyu political elite.[12] To cement his position once in power, Moi amended the Constitution as Kenyatta did. In 1982 section 2A of the 1963 Constitution banned all political opposition and made Kenya a de jure one-party state.[13]

Amid this centralization of power, low-ranking soldiers from the Kenya Air Force staged an attempted coup in August 1982. Although the coup planners managed to capture some key installations including the state broadcaster, the coup was crushed within a day. Moi used the attempted coup as an excuse to purge the civil service. There were constitutional implications also: constitutional amendments abolished security of tenure for judges and the attorney general,[14] and extended the period of detention without trial from twenty-four hours to fourteen days.[15] Accusations of state-sanctioned political assassinations during this period were rampant.[16]

All of these measures were intended to personalize and centralize power in the office of the President.[17] Despite a formal liberalization of the political arena in the early 1990s, with the repeal of section 2A and the reintroduction of multiparty politics, power remained overwhelmingly in the office of the President. It was not until the late 1990s, when Moi bowed to international and donor pressure for fundamental constitutional reform,[18] that the locus of power began to shift and the transition to constitutional democracy could be said to have begun. The Constitution of Kenya Review Commission (CKRC) was established by statute under the chairmanship of constitutional lawyer Yash Ghai.[19] The CKRC began work after the 2002 elections in which Mwai Kibaki was elected President, and

[11] Charles Hornsby, *Kenya: A History since Independence* (Taurus, 2012), 230.

[12] Makau Mutua, *Kenya's Quest for Democracy* (Lynne Rienner, 2008), 66.

[13] Constitution of Kenya (Amendment) Act, 7 of 1982.

[14] Constitution of Kenya (Amendment) Act, 4 of 1988; Constitution of Kenya (Amendment) Act, 14 of 1986.

[15] Constitution of Kenya (Amendment) Act, 4 of 1988.

[16] Makau Mutua, 'Justice Under Siege: The Rule of Law and Judicial Subservience in Kenya' (2001) 23 *Human Rights Quarterly* 96, 102; Frank Matanga, 'Kenya: A Chequered Path to Democracy' (2003) 1 *East African Journal on Human Rights and Democracy* 31, 34.

[17] Richard Stacey, 'Constituent Power and Carl Schmitt's Theory of Constitution in Kenya's Constitution-Making Process' (2011) 9(3) *International Journal of Constitutional Law* 587, 592.

[18] Joel D. Barkan, 'Kenya after Moi' (2004) 83(1) *Foreign Affairs* 87, 89.

[19] Constitution of Kenya Review Act, 13 of 1997.

produced a draft Constitution in 2004. The draft was defeated in a popular referendum in November 2005.

Pressure for constitutional reform mounted again after the violence and bloodshed of the disputed 2007 elections. A new Committee of Experts on Constitutional Review was appointed in terms of the Constitution of Kenya Review Act, No. 9 of 2008, to draft a new Constitution. After the Waki Commission of Inquiry into Post-Election Violence found that the police played a major role in contributing to violence and allowing violence to occur,[20] it was clear that the constitutional transition would include police reforms.

The new Constitution was put to referendum in May 2010, approved by 67 per cent of voters, and entered into force on 27 August 2010. Before the 2010 Constitution, constitutional, legal, and institutional arrangements put the police force at the disposal of the political class in general, and the ruling party in particular, allowing them to maintain a grip on power despite political liberalization elsewhere in the system. This chapter takes the 2010 Constitution as the point of transition between the authoritarian police state and constitutional democracy, comparing and contrasting constitutional and institutional arrangements before and after the 2010 Constitution in analysing the successes and failures of SSR during Kenya's constitutional transition.

Policing in Kenya

Regime policing: 1963–2007

A distinction can be drawn between 'democratic policing' and 'regime policing'.[21] Key characteristics of democratic policing are the police's adherence to the law in the performance of their duties; police accountability for their actions, both to superiors and civilian government; and transparency that allows regular scrutiny and observation of police activities by civilian government, independent institutions, and civil society. More than these characteristics, however, democratic policing is distinguishable from regime policing by the fact that a democratic police service gives operational priority to the needs of citizens and society rather than to the needs of the state or political office-holders.[22] The Kenya Police Force (KPF) is more accurately described as a regime police force for most of its existence, as it

[20] Commission of Inquiry into Post-Election Violence (the Waki Commission), 15 October 2008, Part IV; Kempe Ronald Hope, 'In Pursuit of Democratic Policing: An Analytical Review and Assessment of Police Reforms in Kenya' (2015) 17(2) *International Journal of Police Science and Management* 91.

[21] David H. Bayley, *Patterns of Policing: A Comparative International Analysis* (Rutgers University Press, 1985).

[22] David H. Bayley, *Democratizing the Police Abroad: What to Do and How to Do It* (US Dept. of Justice, 2001), <https://www.ncjrs.gov/pdffiles1/nij/188742.pdf>.

was dedicated primarily to serving the interests of the ruling party and protecting its own vested interest rather than serving the public interest.[23]

Examples of police misconduct after 1963 are too many to mention, but, for the purposes of this chapter, the kinds of police misconduct can be divided into two broad species. The first is the deployment of the police for political reasons, such as the suppression or harassment of opposition parties or influencing the course of elections. This has long been a primary function of the police, in part a legacy of the colonial era, during which the primary police function of the King's African Rifles—a military force—was the pacification of dissidents and the suppression of recalcitrant indigenous communities.[24]

Regime policing continued after independence, with both Kenyatta and Moi using the police force as a tool to 'bludgeon critics into submission'.[25] The Akiwumi Commission of Inquiry into Tribal Clashes, investigating violence during the 1992 and 1997 presidential elections, found that the KPF, and in particular the 'Special Branch', had acted to 'sustain the continued ascendancy of the political party in power' by, for example, refusing to investigate allegations of misconduct by government officials, arresting supporters of opposition parties on 'trumped up charges', suppressing or refusing to act on information or reports of supporters of the government attacking or harassing opposition supporters (a 'conspiracy of silence'), and taking action 'deliberately calculated to assist' violence perpetrated against opposition political groups.[26] The pattern continued into the new Millennium, with political rallies planned by the opposition parties prior to the 2002 elections blocked by police anti-riot squads,[27] and journalists critical of the government routinely arrested and charged with criminal libel.[28] Investigations into the bloody aftermath of Kenya's disputed 2007 elections found that the police had been complicit in the violence, used excessive force, and committed criminal acts during the unrest.[29]

The second species of misconduct is police abuse of suspects, informants, or ordinary citizens. Such abuses usually go unreported and unpunished and have contributed to the culture of impunity that continues to shroud the police in Kenya and foster the perception that the police force is not primarily committed to serving the

[23] Joshua N. Auerbach, 'Police Accountability in Kenya' (2003) 3 *African Human Rights Journal* 275, 277; J. M. Migai Akech, 'Public Law Values and the Politics of Criminal (In)Justice: A Democratic Framework for Policing in Kenya' (2005) 5 *Oxford University Commonwealth Law Journal* 225, 235–6.

[24] J. Oloka-Onyango, 'Police Powers, Human Rights and the State in Kenya and Uganda: A Comparative Analysis' (1990) *Third World Legal Studies* 1, 3.

[25] Mutuma Ruteere and Marie-Emmanuelle Pommerolle, 'Democratizing Security of Decentralizing Repression? The Ambiguities of Community Policing in Kenya' (2003) 102 *African Affairs* 587, 592.

[26] Report of the Judicial Commission of Inquiry into Tribal Clashes in Kenya, 19 August 1999, paras 36–62.

[27] 'Police Block NARC Rally at Uhuru Park', *Daily Nation*, 19 December 2002.

[28] Akech (note 23), 240–1.

[29] Waki Commission (note 20), Part IV; Human Rights Watch, *Turning Pebbles: Evading Accountability for Post-Election Violence in Kenya* (HRW, 2011), <https://www.hrw.org/sites/default/files/reports/kenya1211webwcover_0.pdf>, 4.

public interest. Numerous reports of extrajudicial killings by the police confirm the alarmingly high incidence of this kind of abuse.[30] Just as worrying is that political officials indicated their support for the use of extreme force by the police. When eight alleged gangsters were gunned down by police in 2000, Kenya's Minister for Internal Security applauded the fact that these men had 'been sent out of the streets for life' and encouraged law enforcement officers to 'continue doing the same in a bid to reduce crime'.[31]

Alongside police abuse in Kenya is the police's general failure to fulfil its primary functions of investigating crime and maintaining public safety. Kenya's experience in this regard reflects a common dilemma of regime policing: while the ruling party relied on the police to remain in power, it could not allow the police to become too independent or too effective since it would not serve the interests of the ruling party if the police began to investigate government officials for crimes or misconduct. For this reason, the government tried hard to ensure that the police force remained under-resourced and unsupported, with police officers dependent on retaining the favour of the regime for their own welfare.[32]

In analysing the reforms made to policing in Kenya during the constitutional transition in 2010, it is important to set out the institutional, constitutional, and statutory circumstances that facilitated political dominance of the police and which gave rise to widespread occurrence of these two species of police misconduct before 2010.

The executive-dependent KPF: internal structure and presidential influence

Between 1961 and 2011, the KPF was constituted and regulated by the Police Act[33] and the 1963 Constitution of Kenya. Section 14(1) of the Police Act set out the mandate of the KPF as:

> the maintenance of law and order, the preservation of peace, the protection of life and property, the prevention and detection of crime, the apprehension of offenders, and the enforcement of all laws and regulations with which it is charged.

Beyond this broad statement, the statutory and constitutional scheme for the control, management, and institutional structure of the KPF of the police was thin on

[30] See e.g. reports by Amnesty International (note 1), the UN Special Rapporteur on extrajudicial, summary, or arbitrary executions (note 2), and the Kenya Human Rights Commission's Quarterly Human Rights Reports during the 2000s.

[31] Marsden Madoka, Minister for Internal Security, 3 April 2000, quoted in Kenya Human Rights Commission, (2000) 2(4) *Quarterly Human Rights Report*, 1.

[32] Alice Hills, *Policing Africa: Internal Security and the Limits of Liberalization* (Lynne Rienner, 2000), 41; Louise Skilling, 'Community Policing in Kenya: The Application of Democratic Policing Principles' (2016) 89 *Police Journal* 3, 6.

[33] Police Act 1961, Cap 84 (repealed 2011).

detail. Indeed, the vagueness of the language in these legal instruments provided the police with wide discretion in the performance of their duties.[34]

The pattern of wide discretion extended to institutional and organizational arrangements. The 1963 Constitution provided that the KPF would be headed by a national Commissioner, appointed by the President (section 108(1)). Section 5(1) of the Police Act provided that the Commissioner enjoyed wide powers to issue administrative 'Force standing orders . . . for the general control, direction and information of the Force'. While the Commissioner enjoyed this discretion to control and direct the KPF, the President had unfettered discretion to appoint and dismiss the Commissioner. Neither the Constitution nor the Police Act provided that the Commissioner served for a fixed term, and neither set out how the Commissioner could be removed from the position. Without any protections on the Commissioner's tenure—for example, a constitutional or statutory provision that the Commissioner could be removed only 'for cause' or through certain procedures—the Commissioner served entirely at the pleasure of the President.[35] The Commissioner was thus amenable to influence and manipulation by the executive for political reasons.

Arrangements for the appointment of lower-ranking police officers followed a similar pattern: section 108(2)(b) of the 1963 Constitution provided that officers could be appointed below the rank of Assistant Inspector by the Commissioner, and section 108(2)(a) provided that appointments above this rank would be made by the Public Service Commission. However, section 106(2) of the 1963 Constitution provided that all seventeen members of the Public Service Commission would be appointed by the President. The decision about who would fill every post in the police force, from top leadership to low-ranking officers, rested ultimately with the President.

Proliferating police units and overlapping mandates

The constitutional provision that the 'general control, direction and information of the Force' was to be determined by force standing orders issued by the Commissioner meant that the Commissioner (and ultimately the President) was largely able to determine the internal organization of the police force at will, without legislative control or scrutiny. The KPF was, and continues to be, divided into departments or specialized units established in force standing orders. The bulk of crime prevention and investigation functions were fulfilled by the Criminal Investigations Department (CID), but the KPF included a range of specialized units, including the paramilitary General Service Unit (GSU) dedicated

[34] Douglas Brown, *Criminal Procedure in Uganda and Kenya*, 2nd edn (Sweet and Maxwell, 1970), 28–9.

[35] Auerbach (note 23), 287–8.

to 'situations affecting internal security'[36] and, since 2003, the Anti-Terrorism Investigations Unit (sometimes referred to as the Anti-Terrorism Police Unit).

Section 5(2) of the Police Act allowed further that the force standing orders establishing these units did not need to be published; effectively allowing the KPF to cloak these institutional arrangements in secrecy. With no clear statement, in statute or otherwise, as to the role and mandate of each of the units, it was never particularly clear what each was supposed to do. From one perspective, this was not a major concern since all of these units were within the KPF and dedicated to the objectives set out in section 14 of the 1961 Police Act. However, from another perspective, the lack of clear and publicly available statements of the mission and mandate of each unit meant that the potential for mission creep was large. While the CID fulfilled the more customary police functions related to crime prevention and investigation under the 1963 Constitution, the GSU has developed into a militarized riot squad armed with 'light mortars'[37] and has been deployed by the government to buttress its political position in a number of ways. For example, the GSU aided in the colonial government's military response to the Mau Mau rebellion between 1952 and 1960,[38] suppressed the '*Saba Saba* riots' in Nairobi in July 1990 (protesting the government's refusal to allow opposition parties to hold public meetings),[39] posed as Maasai warriors and attacked Kikuyu people in Narok in 1993 in order to foment 'ethnic clashes,'[40] and physically dismantled schools serving Kikuyu communities in the Rift Valley in the early 1990s (the Kikuyu were seen as a political threat to Moi's Kalenjin presidency).[41] The GSU was even deployed overseas to quell civil unrest in Zanzibar in June 1961.[42] The GSU also played an important role as a 'counterweight' to the military: by having two heavily armed military forces in Kenya, the government was able to ensure that neither became powerful or independent enough to pose a challenge to the government's control of power. Indeed, the GSU was used to suppress a military junior officer's coup attempt in 1982.[43]

Alongside the GSU, the Special Branch was a second division within the KPF that fulfilled a specialized function. Established by the colonial administration as a

[36] Akech (note 23), 233, quoting the KPF Strategic Plan 2003–2007.

[37] Eruch Nowrojee, 'Kenya: Political Pluralism, Government Resistance and United States Response' (1992) 5 *Harvard Human Rights Journal* 149, 152; Irving Kaplan et al., *Area Handbook for Kenya*, 2nd edn (Government Printing Office, 1976), 380.

[38] David M. Anderson, 'The Battle of Dandora Swamp: Reconstructing the Mau Mau Land Freedom Army' in E.S. Atieno and J. Lonsdale (eds), *Mau Mau and Nationhood: Authority and Narration* (Ohio University Press, 2003), 155–75.

[39] Nowrojee (note 37).

[40] Kenya National Council of NGOs, 'Deception, Dispersal and Abandonment' (1995), 7.

[41] Jacqueline M. Klopp, '"Ethnic Clashes" and Winning Elections: The Case of Kenya's Electoral Despotism' (2001) 35 *Canadian Journal of African Studies* 473, 502.

[42] Statement to the House of Commons by Hugh Fraser, Under-Secretary of State for the Colonies, Hansard, HC Deb, 5 June 1961, vol. 641, § 648.

[43] Boubacar N'Diaye, *The Challenge of Institutionalizing Civilian Control: Botswana, Ivory Coast, and Kenya in Comparative Perspective* (Lanham, 2001), 128, 131.

branch of the CID, its function was to collect and process intelligence concerning resistance to the colonial government. After 1945, the Special Branch was scythed off from the CID and removed from the authority of the Commissioner of Police to the control of the Cabinet member responsible for law and order.[44] Without the Commissioner exercising operational command of the Special Branch, the government assumed direct operational control of it. The division became closely aligned to the political agenda of the government, standing alongside the GSU in quashing the Mau Mau rebellion, for example.[45] Moreover, the Special Branch became increasingly bold and brutal in its methods throughout the 1980s. An Amnesty International report in 1987 described widespread detentions and torture at the hands of the Special Branch,[46] leading commentators to conclude at the time that it operated above the law.[47] Moves to redefine its mandate more clearly as intelligence began in 1986, with the Special Branch officially renamed the Directorate of Security Intelligence. A decade later, the UN Special Rapporteur to the UN Commission on Human Rights concluded that the use of torture by the Special Branch to obtain confessions and to dissuade people from engaging in political activities was widespread.[48] In the fallout following the US Embassy bombings in Nairobi in 1998, the Special Branch was disbanded and replaced by the National Security Intelligence Service (NSIS), an intelligence agency entirely independent from the KPF.[49]

As the global threat of terrorism grew in East Africa after 1998, Kenya responded—with US and UK training and financial support—by establishing a third specialized branch within the KPF in 2003, the Anti-Terrorism Police Unit (ATPU).[50] Like the other divisions of the KPF, it was established at the Commissioner's discretion through the mechanism of force standing orders. The consolidated version of these standing orders, published in 2014, provides that the unit—now officially called the Anti-Terrorism Investigations Unit (ATIU)—is a unit within the CID. Its' mandate includes preventing, detecting, disrupting, and interdicting terrorist activities within the country and exhaustively investigating all terrorism-related cases.[51] However, the standing orders do not define the terms 'terrorist activities' and terrorism-related', or explain what is included in the ATIU's

[44] Oloka-Onyango (note 24), 11–12.

[45] Louis Leakey, *Defeating Mau Mau* (Methuen, 954), 112–13.

[46] Amnesty International, *Torture, Political Detention and Unfair Trials* (Amnesty International Publications, 1987).

[47] Oloka-Onyango (note 24), 26.

[48] UN Commission on Human Rights, 'Report of the Special Rapporteur, Mr Nigel S. Rodley, Submitted Pursuant to Commission on Human Rights Resolution 1995/37B', E/CN.41997/7, 10 January 1997, paras 128–138.

[49] National Intelligence Security Service Act, 11 of 1998.

[50] Beth Elise Whittaker, 'Reluctant Partners: Fighting Terrorism and Promoting Democracy in Kenya' (2008) 9 *International Studies Perspectives* 254, 257.

[51] Office of the Inspector General of the Police Service, *Service Standing Orders*, 12 February 2014, Part III (a).

mandate to 'disrupt' and 'interdict' these activities. As a result, the ATIU operates under a broad and vague mandate in terms of standing orders that can be changed at the discretion of a single official.[52] The Kenya National Commission on Human Rights (KNCHR) described the ATIU as 'an amorphous institution, filled with secrecy and corruption'.[53] Perhaps unsurprisingly, the ATIU has been widely accused of abuse, torture, and the use of excessive force.[54]

The overlapping and vague mandates of the divisions that constitute the KPF, alongside the influence the executive held over police leadership or the police itself, facilitated the abuse of the police force for political purposes. The confusion that stems from a multiplicity of units within the KPF is exacerbated by the existence of the Administration Police Force (APF), an institution entirely separate from the KPF. The APF was established by the Administration Police Act (Cap 85) in 1958. The Act set out the two broad functions of the APF: the ordinary police obligation to 'preserve the public peace, prevent the commission of offences and apprehend all persons in respect of whom he holds a valid warrant of arrest' (section 8(c)), and 'when called upon by any chief or sub-chief [to] assist him in the exercise of his lawful duties' (section 8(a)). The link between the APF and the force it replaced, the colonial government's 'Tribal Police', is clear here. The Tribal Police was left to police the native reserves, while the KPF operated in the urban areas. As a result, the Tribal Police was under the effective control of the chiefs rather than the central colonial government.[55]

The command structure of the APF reflects the institutional separation from the KPF. The 1958 Act provided that a Cabinet minister would act as the 'Commandant' of the force (section 5(2)), while the commissioners of the local districts would administer the APF in their districts (section 6). These commissioners, however, were appointed and dismissed directly by the President and were ultimately answerable to the President, as was the Police Commissioner of the KPF.[56] The executive thus had two distinct police forces to deploy as needed, with historically distinct areas of influence in the urban and rural areas respectively. The APF, however, was not confined to the rural areas even if it had expertise and influence there. On the contrary, its operations frequently overlapped with those of the KPF.[57] As an essentially duplicative police force, the APF 'served no identifiable purpose other than

[52] Although the Prevention of Terrorism Act, 30 of 2012 defines 'terrorist act', 'terrorist group', and 'terrorist property', these definitions are themselves quite broad and the Act does not mention the Anti-Terrorism investigations Unit at all.

[53] Interview with the Kenya National Commission on Human Rights, Nairobi, 21 November 2007, quoted in Jan Bachman and Jana Hönke, '"Peace and Security" s as Counterterrorism: The Political Effects of Liberal Interventions in Kenya' (2010) 109 *African Affairs* 97, 108.

[54] Amnesty International, *Kenya: The Impact of 'Anti-Terrorism' Operations* (Amnesty International Publications, 2005).

[55] Mathieu Deflem, 'Law Enforcement in British Colonial Africa: A Comparative Analysis of policing in Nyasaland, The Gold Coast and Kenya' (1994) 17 *Police Studies* 45, 54.

[56] Auerbach (note 23), 291.

[57] Akech (note 23), 237.

to bolster the coercive strength of the political executive'.[58] In this regard, the APF has intervened in the operations of the KPF to ensure that that political objectives of the executive are fully protected.[59]

The push for reform: 2007 elections and the National Task Force on Police Reforms

The violence that followed the national elections in 2007 renewed the commitment to constitutional reform in Kenya. After it emerged from the Waki Commission's report that the KPF and APF had been complicit in and guilty of post-electoral violence in 2007 and 2008, the government responded by appointing a National Task Force on Police Reform in 2009. Police reform in Kenya was thus very much rolled into the broader project of constitutional reform.

The broad mandate of the Task Force was to 'initiate urgent and comprehensive reform' including but not limited to the establishment of an independent police service commission and an independent police oversight commission.[60] Key findings in the Task Force's report (the 'Ransley Report') were that reforms must ensure police accountability and civilian oversight of the activities of the police.[61] The report made over 200 specific recommendations but highlighted a handful of these in the executive summary. These priority recommendations included:[62]

- the establishment in the Constitution of an independent police oversight institution, composed of civilians, with a clear legislative mandate and powers;
- decentralizing the command structure of the police, by making the process of appointing police officers competitive and transparent;
- reducing executive influence in the police by increasing operational autonomy.

While the Ransley Report did note that the overlapping functions, competition, and growing rivalry between the KPF and the APF was of some concern, it recommended closer coordination of the two forces. The Waki Commission, on the other hand, recommended that the APF and the KPF be integrated into a single police service operating under one command structure and administrative bureaucracy.[63]

58 Auerbach (note 23), 291.

59 S. Muiruri, 'Police Row as Graft Suspect Is Released from Cells', *Daily Nation*, 4 February 2003, describing how the APF secured the release of a suspect connected politically to the ruling party, despite being held for questioning by the CID.

60 Report of the National Task Force on Police Reforms (The Ransley Report) (Republic of Kenya, 2009), <https://www.scribd.com/doc/245815329/Ransley-Report>, 2–3.

61 Skilling (note 32); Hope (note 20).

62 Ransley Report (note 60), xxvi–xxviii.

63 Waki Commission (note 20), 434–5.

The 2010 Constitution and subsequent legislation have sought to reform the police service in Kenya against the background of two broad recommendations: greater institutional accountability and more effective civilian oversight.

The 2010 Constitution

Chapter 14 of the 2010 Constitution is dedicated to 'National Security'. Section 239 provides that Kenya's 'national security organs' are the KDF, the National Intelligence Service, and the National Police Service (NPS). The provisions in the rest of the chapter go on to describe the institutional structure, chain of command, mandate, and powers of each security organ. The 1963 Constitution had no corresponding provisions: the entrenchment of the security sector's fundamental organizational and institutional principles in the Constitution reflects an important commitment to a more democratic security sector than Kenya has had in the past.

Section 239(3) affirms this commitment by prohibiting partisanship or politically motivated action on the part of the national security organs:

> In performing their functions and exercising their powers, the national security organs and every member of the national security organs shall not—
> a) act in a partisan manner;
> b) further any interest of a political party or cause; or
> c) prejudice a political interest or political cause that is legitimate under this Constitution.

Section 239(5) provides further that the national security organs will be subject to civilian authority. The biggest challenge in Kenya, however, is not to establish civilian control over the police but to eliminate partisan political influence in the police and ensure accountability for police conduct.

In this light, the 2010 Constitution defines new institutional arrangements for the NPS and puts in place the basic architecture of a new command structure for the NPS (sections 243–247). The NPS is constituted by the Kenya Police Service (KPS) and the Administration Police Service (APS). The NPS is headed by the Inspector General of the NPS, appointed by the President with the approval of parliament. The Constitution ensures the Inspector General enjoys greater security of tenure than previously: the appointment is for a single, non-renewable four-year term, and the Inspector General can be removed only for reasons set out in section 245(6)–(7)).

The KPS and the APS are each headed by a Deputy Inspector General, appointed by the President on the recommendation of the National Police Service Commission. The NPS Commission is a new body established by section 246 of the 2010 Constitution. It plays an important role in the recruitment, appointment, and promotion of police officers and in maintaining discipline within the police service and ensuring that due process is followed by the police (section 246(3)). The Constitution provides that the Commission consists of a person qualified to be a high court judge, two retired senior police officers, three 'persons of integrity who have served the public with distinction', and the incumbent Inspector General and Deputy Inspectors General. The National Police Service Commission Act, 30 of 2011 (Cap 185C) provides for the appointment of the NPS Commissioners by an ad hoc selection committee, subject to presidential and parliamentary approval (section 6).

Post-2010 legislation

The 2010 Constitution enjoins parliament to enact national legislation to 'give full effect to' the constitutional provisions establishing the NPS and creating the office of the Inspector General. The National Police Service Act 2011 (Cap 85) is this legislation.

Two points are worth making about this statutory scheme. First, there remains considerable overlap between the functions of the KPS and the APS. The mandate of both services includes providing assistance to the public when in need, maintaining law and order, preserving peace, and protecting life and property (sections 24 and 27). The additional functions the KPS bears are largely devoted to the prevention, detection, and investigation of crime and the gathering of criminal intelligence. However, the Directorate of Criminal Investigations (DCI) is established separately from the KPS and the APS, and is under the 'direction, command and control' of the Inspector General (section 28) rather than either of the Deputy Inspectors-General or a third Deputy Inspector General. The role of the Director of Criminal Investigations, then, is confined to administrative and bureaucratic matters (section 34). The functions of the Directorate include collecting criminal intelligence, investigating crimes, detecting and preventing crimes, and maintaining law and order. It thus appears that there are three separate units within the NPS, responsible for many of the same functions, but under the control of three different individuals.

In the same vein, neither the 2010 Constitution nor the NPS Act say anything about the establishment of specialized or distinct units within the NPS. Nevertheless, this still happens in terms of the service standing orders which the Act provides the Inspector General may issue for the 'general control, administration, good order, direction and information of the Service' (section 10(1)(r) and (2)(b)). The service standing orders published in 2014 accordingly describe eleven distinct units within the KPS, including the General Service Unit. The standing orders provide that each of these units is 'established to support the . . . functions of the Kenya Police Service in accordance with Section 24 of the National Police

Service Act, 2011' (Chapter 6, Part I). One of the functions of the GSU is 'countering terrorism activities and insurgencies' (Chapter 6, Part I(h)(vii)).

The standing orders also describe the specialized units within the APS and the DCI. The Rapid Deployment Unit (RDU), for example, is the branch of the APS established in accordance with section 27 of the NPS Act to conduct counter-terrorism and counter-insurgency operations, among other things (Chapter 6, Part II(d)(v)). Finally, the DCI's Anti-Terrorism Investigation Unit is mandated to fulfil a range of functions related to preventing, detecting, disrupting, and investigating terrorist activities; collecting intelligence; and surveilling suspected terrorists (Chapter 6, Part III(a)).

These arrangements do little to assuage the concerns identified in both the Waki Commission and the Ransley Commission that the proliferation of distinct police forces and the duplication of functions has facilitated abuse, undermined accountability, and reduced the efficacy of oversight.

A second concern goes to security of tenure: while the Constitution provides that the Inspector General may be removed only for cause, the NPS Act provides that the President may remove either of the Deputy Inspectors General or the Director of Criminal Investigations at any time (sections 17 and 31).

Oversight

The Ransley Commission recommended that an independent, civilian oversight institution be established to scrutinize the actions of the police. The Independent Police Oversight Authority (IPOA) was in turn established by the Independent Policing Oversight Authority Act 2011 (Cap 88). Section 5 of the IPOA Act provides that its objectives are to:

a) hold the Police accountable to the public in the performance of their functions;
b) give effect to the provision of Article 244 of the Constitution that the Police shall strive for professionalism and discipline and shall promote and practice transparency and accountability; and
c) ensure independent oversight of the handling of complaints by the Service.

In pursuing these objectives, the IPOA is mandated to investigate any complaints against the conduct of the police made by members of the public or members of the NPS itself, to monitor the conduct of the police and investigate misconduct on its own motion, inspect police premises, and review the efficacy of internal disciplinary processes (section 6). In fulfilling its mandate, the IPOA has broad powers of investigation including subpoena, deposition under oath, and entry, search, and seizure (section 7).

The IPOA is to be governed by a Board. The Act sets out in some detail the qualifications the members of the Board must have, thus seeking to ensure that there is sufficient expertise on the IPOA to exercise effective oversight over police functions. The Chairperson of the Board, for example, must meet the requirements to be appointed a judge of the High Court of Kenya, while the other seven Board members must hold a university degree and have at least ten years' experience in the fields of criminology, psychology, law, human rights and gender, medicine, alternative dispute resolution, security matters, or community policing (sections 9(1) and 10(1)(a)).

The procedure for appointing the Board members aims at independence by limiting executive involvement. Accordingly, the President is required whenever there is vacancy on the Board to appoint a selection committee to appoint the Board (sections 11–12). Once established, this selection committee invites and considers applications to the IPOA Board and provides a shortlist of three names for Chairperson and eight names for appointment to the Board. The President makes the final appointment from this shortlist. The inaugural Board took office in June 2012.

The IPOA is not the only new oversight institution. Section 87 of the NPS Act provides for the establishment of an Internal Affairs Unit (IAU) to investigate complaints against the police received from members of the public or members of the police service, at the direction of Inspector General, at the request of the IPOA, or on its own initiative. The Director of the IAU is an officer with the rank of Assistant Inspector General or higher, although the Act does not explain how this Director is appointed. The Director, in turn, appoints a senior investigating officer in each county to be responsible for internal affairs in that county. Each county IAU officer reports to the Director, who reports directly to the Inspector General of the NPS. The IAU is housed in offices separate from the other institutions of the NPS, and the Act affirms that the IAU 'shall not be subject to the control, direction or command of the Kenya Police, Administration Police or the Directorate [of Criminal Investigations]'. Although the IAU is thus an internal rather than an independent oversight body, the Act attempts to ensure that its efficacy is not compromised by interference from the police force itself (section 87(11)). Indeed, the Act requires further that there be an 'effective relationship and regular reporting' between the IAU and the IPOA (section 87(10)). The NPS Commission also has a role to play here in ensuring that discipline within the police is maintained and to ensure that appointments and promotions are made on the proper grounds rather than on political or otherwise improper grounds.

The KNCHR, established first by legislation in 2002 and now entrenched by section 59 of the 2010 Constitution, fulfils a more general role as an ombudsman in Kenya. It is specifically mandated 'to monitor, investigate and report on the observance of human rights in all spheres of life in the Republic, including observance by the national security organs'. While the IPOA and IAU exist to ensure that the police continue to act according to the rules and principles set out in the constitutional and statutory provisions that govern them, the KNCHR focuses on the broader question of whether any conduct, including that of the police, undermines human rights in Kenya.

Finally, the 2010 Constitution provides for the establishment of a National Security Council (NSC) (section 240). The NSC is constituted by the President and Deputy President; the members of Cabinet responsible for defence, foreign affairs, and internal security; the Attorney General; the Chief of the Defence Force; the Director-General of the NIS; and the Inspector General of the NPS. The NSC plays an important oversight and coordinating role over all of the branches of the security sector.

The impact of the 2010 Constitution: unfulfilled potential

While these changes represent a marked improvement in the constitutional and statutory bases for the functioning, command, and oversight of the police, Kenya continues to be plagued by allegations of police misconduct. The silver lining to this dark cloud is that many of the examples of misconduct after 2010 do not appear to be consistent with 'regime policing'. That is, although police corruption, the use of excessive force, detention, and torture remain widespread, the underlying motivation of this misconduct is not primarily the maintenance of the ruling party and the suppression of political opposition.

The Anti-Terrorism Investigation Unit (ATIU or ATPU) and the General Service Unit (GSU) have been accused of using excessive force and torture in counterterrorism operations against Al-Shabaab inside Kenya, both before and after the 2010 reforms. A 2013 report by the Open Society Foundations and Muslims for Human Rights (MuHuRi) documented abuses by the ATPU in Mombasa in 2012 and 2013, including extrajudicial executions, detentions, and disappearances.[64] In 2014, Human Rights Watch released a report documenting ten cases of extrajudicial killing, ten cases of disappearances, and eleven cases of mistreatment, detention, or torture at the hands of the ATPU and GSU in the eight months between November 2013 and June 2014.[65] A report released by the KNCHR in September 2015 found evidence of twenty-five extrajudicial killings and eighty-one enforced disappearances as part of a pattern of human rights violations perpetrated by the ATPU, GSU, and the APS's Rapid Deployment Unit, that are 'widespread, systematic and well-coordinated and include but are not limited to arbitrary arrests, extortion, illegal detention, torture, killings and disappearances'.[66] The attitude within the security establishment echoes the Minister

[64] Open Society Justice Initiative and Muslims for Human Rights, *'We're Tired of Taking You to the Court': Human Rights Abuses by Kenya's Anti-Terrorism Police Unit* (Open Society Foundation, 2013).

[65] Human Rights Watch, 'Kenya: Killings, Disappearances by Anti-Terror Police', 18 August 2014, <https://www.hrw.org/news/2014/08/18/kenya-killings-disappearances-anti-terror-police>.

[66] Kenya National Commission on Human Rights, 'The Error of Fighting Terror with Terror: Preliminary Report of KNCHR Investigations on Human Rights Abuses in the Ongoing Crackdown against Terrorism', September 2015, 6, <http://www.knchr.org/Portals/0/CivilAndPoliticalReports/Final%20Disappearances%20report%20pdf.pdf>,.

for Internal Security's endorsement of police assassination of criminals over a decade earlier, with a Kenyan intelligence official arguing that extra-legal measures are justified and necessary because in combatting terrorism 'you can't go by the book'.[67]

The story with which this chapter begins makes it clear that it is not only antiterrorism police units that are guilty of extrajudicial killing. A 2014 report by the IMLU found that between 2009 and 2014, the police were responsible for 1,254 out of 1,868 gun deaths (67 per cent).[68] A follow-up report in October 2015 found that in 2014, 181 people were summarily executed by the police. At the time of the report's release in October 2015, this number was eighty-five.

Reasons for ongoing abuse

Perhaps it is naïve to have hoped that constitutional and statutory policing reforms would have eliminated police impunity and restored political accountability for police behaviour in just a few years. It may be that more time is required for the institutional changes made by the 2010 Constitution and subsequent legislation to bring meaningful changes to the performance of the police. However, more time will produce no more results unless existing obstacles to effective police oversight and accountability are eliminated. There are at least four problems that have arisen in this regard.

The first problem is the proliferation of police services and specialist units mandated to fulfil an overlapping set of functions. In investigating complaints related to police antiterror operations in the Nairobi suburb of Eastleigh, the IPOA noted:

> The monitoring exercise also established that there was no proper liaison or coordination between the various units of the NPS. For instance, as noted in the observations, in the process of searching residential areas, a building would be searched several times by different groups of Police Officers, whether by the Administration Police Service (APS), the General Service Unit (GSU) or the Kenya Police Service (KPS), during the day or night. This certainly inconvenienced members of the public who were forced to wake up several times to open their doors and/or premises for inspection.[69]

67 Open Society Justice Initiative and MuHuRi (note 64), 19.

68 IMLU, 'Guns: Our Security, Our Dilemma', 26 June 2014, <http://www.imlu.org/index.php/short-code/reports/typgraphy/send/3-reports/23-guns-our-security-our-dilemma-2014>.

69 IPOA, Monitoring Report on 'Operation Sanitization Eastleigh', publicly known as 'Usalama Watch', 14 July 2014, <http://www.ipoa.go.ke/images/press/MONITORING%20REPORT%20ON%20OPERATION%20(USALAMA%20WATCH)%2017%207%202014.pdf>.

In commenting on the police response to terrorist attacks in Mpeketoni in June 2014, the IPOA was even more strident in its condemnation of this functional duplication:

> The Authority's enquiries indicate that this discord between the units' command centers permeates even regular day-to-day operations of the police where there is widespread mistrust and rivalry. To some it seems the KPS and APS are in competition to outdo and sometimes undermine each other. This practice affects effective policing.[70]

The fact that multiple police agencies attempt to perform similar functions with similar objectives but without coordination has two effects. First, as the IPOA points out, the growing rivalry between the police units undermines the effectiveness of policing. Second, the constant intervention by numerous police units in the lives of the public has fostered public mistrust and antipathy towards the police. Despite the name change, the police continue to operate as a force rather than as a service, performing policing functions on the community rather than with it. The effectiveness of policing is reduced when the public do not see the police as legitimate, are exhausted by being policed, and are consequently unwilling to cooperate with the police.[71]

A second consequence of the duplication of functions is that the complexity of the IPOA's work has increased. It is more difficult for the IPOA to exercise effective oversight of the police where several police units are involved in police actions, and where there are no overarching or coordinating orders or centres of accountability. In order to oversee and monitor the work of these separate police units, the IPOA—as well as the IAU, NPS Commission, or KNCHR—must decode the administrative and operational arrangements and investigate the conduct of several organizations. This is not only time-consuming but also extremely complicated in circumstances where these organizations are working against one another in the same spheres of operation.

The second obstacle to the IPOA's work in particular is that police officers used to acting with impunity have not taken well to the increased oversight of their conduct. On 4 August 2016, the KNCHR issued a press statement describing how IPOA officers were threatened at gunpoint by a senior officer being summoned by IPOA for questioning in regard to allegations of misconduct. An IPOA officer was then detained in police cells for several hours. The KNCHR statement goes on: 'Refusal to cooperate with IPOA and intimidation of its officers by the police negates the spirit of the ongoing police reforms and in fact only serves to perpetuate the culture of impunity within the police service.'[72]

70 IPOA, Report Following the Mpeketoni Attacks (15 and 16 June 2014): Redacted version, 2014, <http://www.ipoa.go.ke/images/press/Mpeketoni-Report2.pdf>.

71 Skilling (note 32), 4–5.

72 Kenya National Commission on Human Rights, Press Statement: 'Harassment and Arrest of Officers of the Independent Policing Oversight Authority', 4 August 2016, <http://www.knchr.org/Newsroom/PressStatements.aspx>.

Relatedly, a third obstacle is the fact that the 'vetting' of police officers by the National Police Service Commission required by section 7(2) of the 2011 NPS Act has not progressed very far. Although scheduled to completed vetting in eighteen months, after about two years of work in October 2015 the Commission had vetted 1,364 out of roughly 35,000 police officers.[73] Institutionalized corruption continues to characterize the police in Kenya, with police routinely accepting bribes from criminals to disrupt prosecutions or to evade arrest.[74] Until the Commission has been able to complete the vetting process and at least make some moves towards rooting out corruption, or at least corrupt police officers, the culture of impunity will likely continue to impede the work of institutions like the IPOA and IAU.

Finally, and most significantly, in recent years the government has walked back some of the post-2010 institutional reforms. The Security Laws (Amendment) Act, No. 19 of 2014 (SLAA), amends the procedures for the appointment of the Inspector General of the NPA. Section 12 of the NPS Act, as it was initially passed in 2011, required that upon a vacancy in the office of the Inspector General the President would appoint an ad hoc selection committee constituted by one person each from the office of the President, the Public Service Commission, the NPS Commission, the IPOA, the KNCHR, the National Gender Commission, and the Law Society of Kenya. This committee would invite and consider applications for the position of Inspector General and prepare a shortlist of three people to be forwarded to the President. The person nominated by the President would assume the office of Inspector General upon confirmation by parliament.

Section 12(1) of the NPS Act as amended in 2014, however, now provides that the President will appoint the Inspector General directly, with the approval of parliament. The detailed provisions requiring the appointment of a selection committee and setting out its procedures for competitively selecting an Inspector General have been deleted. The High Court of Kenya upheld the constitutionality of the amended section 12, even as it admitted that the deleted provisions of the original section were better aligned with the spirit of police reform:

> While the competitive process and public participation that the previous provisions of section 12 engendered were more in keeping with the spirit of openness that Kenyans desired under the Constitution, it was expected that the provision for Parliamentary approval would provide an opportunity for public participation in the appointment, not only through the elected representatives, but also through the opportunities for such participation that Parliament

[73] Fred Mukinda, '63 Senior Officers Sacked Over Graft', *Daily Nation*, 15 October 2015.

[74] Skilling (note 32), 6. See also Transparency International, 'Global Corruption Barometer, 2013', <http://www.transparency.org/gcb2013/country/?country.kenya>.

was constitutionally required by article 118 of the Constitution to accord the public.[75]

More concerning, section 15 of the NPS Act originally provided an elaborate procedure to be followed for the dismissal of the Inspector General. Any person desiring the removal of the Inspector General could submit a petition to the NPS Commission, which could recommend the Inspector General's removal with a two-thirds majority of its members. Parliament would then consider the Commission's recommendation, and upon agreeing with it forward the recommendation to the President, who would appoint a five-member tribunal to make a final and binding recommendation as to the Inspector General's removal. Section 87 of the deleted all of these provisions, replacing them with a single provision providing that the Inspector General may be removed 'for the grounds specified under Article 245(7) of the Constitution'. This allows the President to unilaterally remove the Inspector General for cause, but without any provisions for interrogating the President's determination that the Inspector General has provided cause for his or her removal. The Inspector General's security of tenure is significantly compromised.

The amendments also sought to weaken the powers of the National Police Service Commission. First, section 95 of the SLAA sought to amend the NPS Act and establish a new National Police Service Disciplinary Board, with powers to investigate 'matters related to discipline' and take disciplinary action against police officers. This Board was to be staffed fully by members of the NPS itself, from the KPS, APS, and DCI. These provisions were struck down as unconstitutional by the High Court, however, holding that since section 246(3) of the Constitution provides that the NPS Commission is responsible for the recruitment, appointment, and discipline within the NPS, creating a parallel disciplinary procedure within the NPS would 'whittle down the powers and mandate of the Commission and create conflict and confusion'.[76]

While the establishment of an internal police disciplinary board was blocked by the court, other changes to the powers of the NPS Commission had already begun to chip away at its power. Amendments to the NPS Commission Act in 2014 deleted key oversight powers of the NPS Commission, including the authority to 'monitor and evaluate the performance of the Service' and 'ensure that the Service is efficient and effective'. These changes have not been challenged in court.

These changes have undermined the independence of the police and the effectiveness of oversight over the police. It is worrying that, despite a strong legislative commitment to police independence and oversight immediately after the enactment of the 2010 Constitution, the government has reversed course and attempted

[75] *Coalition for Reform and Democracy and Others v Republic of Kenya and Others*, High Court at Nairobi, Petition 628, 630 of 2014 and 12 of 2015, 23 February 2015, para. 83.

[76] Ibid., para. 86.

to recreate the conditions that facilitated executive dominance of the police and fostered a lack of police accountability prior to 2007. The fact that government is actively seeking these changes does not suggest that the political will to proceed with police reform exists.

The Kenya Defence Forces

Aside from the attempted coup in 1982, the military has remained largely uninterested in involving itself in politics. The KDF was, however, subject to manipulation for political purposes under the presidencies of Kenyatta and Moi. At the same time, there have been at least two instances of documented human rights abuses at the hands of the armed forces, in Wagalla in 1984[77] and the Mt Elgon region in 2006,[78] but the examples of military misconduct remain isolated and they pale in comparison to the widespread, persistent, and systematic abuses at the hands of the police. Moreover, during the 1990s the KDF leadership took a conscious decision to remain apolitical and to reduce political influence and abuse, and initiated internal reforms itself. By 2010, the new Constitution needed to do little more than confirm the institutional structures and rules the military had already committed to. Post-2010 legislation has given further effect to these constitutional achievements, but the government's attempts to amend this legislation threaten the military's independence and professionalism.

The KDF's internal reforms

As with many branches of the public service under Kenyatta and Moi, the leadership positions of the armed forces were filled by people loyal to the President and in many cases drawn from the same regions and tribes of Kenya as he was. The government ensured effective control of the military through this ethnic manipulation, promoting only officers of the government's preferred tribal identity. The government supplemented the military's ethnic loyalty to the government with a system of patronage, through which loyalty in military office was rewarded with land or high position in government or parastatal corporations on retirement. Any threat the military posed to the government was reduced through the 'counterbalancing' effect of the GSU as a rival military force.[79] Since the KDF was not the only armed military force in Kenya, the government did not have to rely exclusively on

[77] David M. Anderson, 'Remembering Wagalla: State Violence in Northern Kenya 1962–1991' (2014) 8 *Journal of Eastern African Studies* 658.

[78] Human Rights Watch, *'All the Men Have Gone': War Crimes in Kenya's Mt Elgon Conflict* (HRW, 2008), <http://pantheon.hrw.org/reports/2008/kenya0708/kenya0708webwcover.pdf>.

[79] Hornsby (note 11), 410–11.

the KDF for military support. As with the police, the challenge with the Kenyan military has never been establishing effective civilian control but eliminating political influence.

The first moves towards institutional autonomy came in 1996, when General Daudi Tonje was appointed as the Defence Forces Chief of the General Staff. Under Tonje, the KDF adopted a number of rules and principles, knows as the Tonje Rules, which limited the scope for political interference in the armed forces. The rules tied promotion to certain ranks to educational qualifications, such as a four-year university degree for senior ranks, and fixed the term of office for senior officers.

These changes limited the extent to which the government could co-opt the military by appointing senior officers on the basis of nepotism or cronyism, and ensuring a degree of independence and professionalism in the military. With changes meant to cement the independence and professionalism already in place, the military reforms sought in 2010 did not need to be as extensive as the changes to the police recommended by the Ransley Report or the Waki Commission. Rather, the arrangements set out in the 2010 Constitution and the Kenya Defence Forces Act, 25 of 2012 (Cap 199) confirm institutional rules already accepted and implemented by the military.

Constitutional and statutory provisions

The constitutional and statutory position after 2010

The 2010 Constitution provides that along with the NPS and the NIS, the KDF must not act in a partisan manner, further the interests of any political party, or prejudice a political interest or cause (s. 239(3)). Beyond this, section 241(2) confirms the division of the KDF into the Army, Air Force, and Navy; describes its chain of command of the KDF; and sets out its mission and mandate.

With regard to command, the Constitution provides that the President remains the Commander-in-Chief of the KDF (section 131(1)(c)), and that a Defence Council composed of the member of Cabinet responsible for defence, the Chief of the KDF, the commanders of the three branches of the KDF, and the Secretary of the Ministry of Defence shall be established (section 241(5)–(6)). There is some overlap in the composition of the Defence Council and the National Security Council established by section 240: the Chief of the KDF and the Cabinet member responsible for defence sit on both councils. While the two bodies exercise similar functions, the NSC plays more of a supervisory and coordinating role over all three of the security services. The NSC, for example, must 'exercise supervisory control' over the KDF, NPS, and NIS (section 240(3)), and must 'integrate domestic, foreign and military policies' in a way that enables effective cooperation between the branches (section 240(6)(a)). The Defence Council's role is confined to the overall policy, control, and supervision of the KDF (section 241(7)(a)) and to any other functions prescribed by national legislation.

The KDF Act 2012 recognizes the possibility of competition or duplication of functions between the NSC and the Defence Council. Section 18 of the Act sets out the functions of the NSC 'in relation to' the KDF, while section 20 sets out in more detail the functions of the Defence Council. These provisions emphasize that while the Defence Council is responsible for formulating the overall policy of the KDF, the NSC is responsible for integrating defence policy with foreign and military policy to ensure cooperation and effectiveness. The line between these functions is somewhat blurry, however. The ambiguity continues into the Act's provisions concerning the deployment of the KDF abroad. Section 240(8)(a) of the Constitution and section 18(c) of the Act provide that the NSC may deploy the KDF abroad, with parliament's approval, while section 20(1)(c) of the Act provides that the Defence Council may 'order any member [of the KDF] to proceed to any place outside Kenya' in accordance with the requirements of section 240(8) of the Constitution.

The Act provides further that the Chief of the Defence Force is 'responsible for implementing the deployment' of the KDF abroad, 'in accordance with an authorization by the National Security Council and Defence Council' (section 12(i)). This provision suggests that both the Defence Council and the NSC must authorize the deployment of the KDF abroad, but that once this has happened the Chief of the KDF retains operational control. While it remains to be seen whether these arrangements will lead to a struggle for control over the KDF, the overlapping membership of the NSC and the Defence Council will be likely to foster a high degree of coordination between the two bodies.

With regard to the mission and mandate of the KDF, section 241(3)(a) and (b) provide that the KDF is responsible for 'the defence and protection of the sovereignty and the territorial integrity' of Kenya, and must 'assist and cooperate with other authorities in situations of emergency or disaster'. Section 241(3)(c) provides that the KDF 'may be deployed to restore peace in any part of Kenya affected by unrest or instability only with the approval of the National Assembly'. The KDF is thus primarily oriented towards the defence of the nation from external threats. The deployment of the KDF in Somalia to neutralize Al-Shabaab fits with this orientation.

The KDF Act and amendments

One distinction between the KDF and the NPS is that the KDF Act provides clearly that the KDF consists of only the regular force, the reserve force, and the cadet forces. The functions of national defence rest primarily with one institution—the regular force—with the reserves and the cadets filling support and training roles respectively. The problems that flow from the overlapping and vague mandates of the numerous institutions that constitute the NPS do not arise in the context of the armed forces.

The KDF Act also sets out the chain of command for the military, distinguishing clearly between the functions of the Cabinet member responsible for the armed forces and the Chief of the Defence Forces. The Minister fulfils a largely administrative and oversight role in advising the president on matters of policy, monitoring the KDF's compliance with policies and directions issued to it, and reporting annually to the President and the legislature on the work, expenditure, and accomplishments of the KDF (section 10). The Chief of the Defence Force on the other hand is charged with the operational control of the KDF: for example, acting as principal advisor to the President on military and operational matters; formulating military strategy; exercising the control, direction, and general superintendence of the KDF subject to the general direction of the Defence Council; and implementing the deployment of the KDF when authorized by the NSC and Defence Council (section 12).

The Act codifies the Tonje rules concerning appointments and terms of office. Section 23 provides that in appointing the Chief and Vice Chief of the KDF and the heads of its three branches, the President must take into account whether candidates have a university degree (section 23(c)). Section 24 provides that each of these senior officers shall serve a non-renewable term of four years. It is of some concern, however, that section 26 provides that the President may remove any of these officers at any time before the expiry of the term of office. While term limits help to reduce the political allegiance that patronage and ethnically motivated appointments bred under Kenyatta and Moi, the ease with which the President may dismiss these officers undermines these benefits.

More worrying is that the statutory rules setting out the mandate of the KDF have been changed in recent years, suggesting that the political branches are less committed to maintaining the apolitical and independent nature of the KDF. An act to amend the KDF Act was passed in December 2016.[80] The amendments include:

- expanding the president's control over the Defence Cabinet Secretary by requiring the president and parliament acting together, rather than parliament alone, to delegate the performance of functions to the Cabinet Secretary (section 4(a))
- reducing parliamentary and executive oversight of the KDF by reducing the Cabinet Secretary's obligation to report on the operations of the Chief of the KDF and the work of the ministry (section 4(b) and (c))

[80] Kenya Defence Forces (Amendment) Act, 44 of 2016.

- adding a proviso to section 24 allowing the President to extend the term of office of the Chief of the Defence Force despite the provision in section 24 for a single four-year term (section 11)
- changing the conditions under which the KDF is deployed within Kenya in support of the NPS in cases of natural disaster or emergency, such that the Inspector General of the Police no longer exercises 'administration' nor 'command' over the KDF, but rather 'control and overall superintendance' (section 15)
- empowering the president, in addition to the NSC, to specify where the KDF may be deployed in support of the NPS within Kenya or to discontinue an internal deployment if it considers it expedient and necessary (section 16)
- extending the period that the president may call out reservists to assist the NPS during 'emergency, disaster, insurrection, hostilities, unrest or instability' from twenty-eight days to sixty days (section 34)
- restricting proceedings for any criminal offences alleged against members of the KDF to courts martial (sections 18–22, 30(b)).

Civil society reaction to the amendment was swift, loudly condemning what is seen as a threat to the institutional independence of the armed forces and opening the KDF to the same abuse that the proliferation of units with the NPS has bred.[81] As it stands, however, the KDF is far more effective and efficient than the police, and is dogged by fewer accusations of abuse and corruption. This is not to say that the KDF has maintained a spotless record after 2010: there have been complaints about abuses committed at the hands of KDF officers.[82]

However, these complaints number far fewer than those directed against the police, and do not reveal systematic and widespread abuse at the same level as the police. While this chapter does not make the claim that the clearer description of the mandate of the KDF, limiting the KDF to one primary force, and establishing a clear chain of command and oversight structures, have caused the KDF's better performance, there is certainly a correlation in Kenya between these institutional arrangements in the KDF and their lack in the NPS, and the difference in independence and oversight in the two security services.

Conclusion

The biggest challenge to attempts to establish effective civilian oversight over the police in Kenya continues to be the existence of multiple police services and police units. The KPS, APS, DCI, GSU, RDU, and ATIU share many of the same functions

[81] Kenya National Commission on Human Rights (note 66).

[82] Ibid.

and powers, and maintaining oversight over numerous organizations all involved in the same general activity through a convoluted and complex web of statute, standing orders, and institutional arrangements is difficult. Just the acronyms are confusing.

At the same time, the continued existence of these many organizations with overlapping mandates has bred an unproductive competition between them. Even without open rivalry, the intervention of so many police units to do the same job has worsened the already frayed relationship between the police and the public, leading to greater mistrust of the police and a greater unwillingness to cooperate with the police. Working against one another and a distrusting public has undermined the capacity of any of these police units to provide effective policing.

A second challenge has been the waning of political commitment to the project of police reform, demonstrated most clearly by the barrage of amendments to police legislation in 2014. While the apparent objective of Security Laws (Amendment) Act was to enhance the capacity of the police to meet growing threat of terrorism in East Africa, the effect of some of these changes has been to weaken the independence of the Inspector General, rendering the office beholden to the President and open to political influence, and to compromise the oversight powers of the National Police Service Commission.

With respect to oversight in particular, the job of the Independent Police Oversight Authority has been made difficult by the police's resistance to oversight and the culture of impunity that continues to pervade the police. To some extent this is a result of the fact that the mechanism Kenya chose to weed out corruption in the police—vetting by the NPS Commission—has been extremely slow. Indeed, the vetting process itself has been accused of corruption. The failure to deal effectively with corrupt police officers has meant not only that policing continues to be undermined by corruption but also that police officers accustomed to a lack of accountability and minimal civilian oversight remain in the Service and continue to violently reject the authority of institutions like the IPOA to scrutinize their conduct.

Kenya's transition to constitutional democracy has not followed through into comprehensive and lasting reform of the police service. While constitutional, statutory, and institutional changes have been made, these changes have failed to address core reasons for police impunity in Kenya. Worse, some of those changes have been reversed since their introduction. In these circumstances, the likelihood that police violence, detentions, and extrajudicial killings will continue is high.

6

Constitutional Reform and Security Sector Reform in Ghana

Ernest Lartey and Kwesi Aning

Introduction

The reform of the security system in Ghana has a peculiar characteristic. It is neither a post-conflict phenomenon (as in the case of Liberia[1] and Sierra Leone[2]) nor a post-apartheid experience (as in South Africa).[3] In fact, its underpinning peculiarity largely relates to elite political and economic consensus shared by both civilian and military elites through opportunism and manipulation. Further, as a product of post-colonial rule, the antecedence of the anti-colonial struggles and the immediate post-independence political imperative for multi-party democracy have also combined to shape the structural characteristics of Ghana's security sector, and the reforms that were carried thereof; namely, that the consensus around the 'reform' and 'constitutional' agendas goes a long way to keeping intact an elite bargaining process that provides a veneer of reform, constitutionality, and stability.[4]

It must be pointed out that there are some significant trajectories along which constitutional reform and security sector reform (SSR) was approached in Ghana.[5] The ongoing constitutional review and implementation process presents the

[1] For a detailed analysis on the Liberian security sector reform (SSR) process, see Thomas Jaye, 'Liberia: Parliamentary Oversight and Lessons Learned from Internationalized Security Sector Reform' (2010), <https://issat.dcaf.ch/download/10645/106742/Liberia_SSR.pdf>. Also see Thomas Jaye and Adedeji Ebo, 'Liberia' in Adedeji Ebo and Boubacar N'Diaye (eds), *Parliamentary Oversight of the Security Sector in West Africa: Opportunities and Challenges* (DCAF, 2008), 139–58.

[2] See a detailed discussion on the SSR process in Osman Gbla, 'Sierra Leone' in Adedeji Ebo and Boubacar N'Diaye (eds), *Parliamentary Oversight of the Security Sector in West Africa: Opportunities and Challenges* (DCAF, 2008), 223–42.

[3] More detailed analysis has been provided in Janine Rauch, 'Transforming Police-Community Relations in South Africa' in Chris Ferguson and Jeffrey O. Isima (eds), *Providing Security for People: Enhancing Security through Police, Justice, and Intelligence Reform in Africa* (GFN-SSR, 2004), 53–7.

[4] Robin Luckham and Eboe Hutchful, 'Democratic and War-to-Peace Transitions and Security Sector Transformation in Africa' in Alan Bryden and 'Funmi Olonisakin (eds), *Security Sector Transformation in Africa* (DCAF, 2010), 27–54.

[5] This is not to say that the SSR process in Ghana has finally reached its completion stage. With deepening democracy, public demand for more accountability and transparency in the security sector will continue to grow. The Freedom of Information Bill, when passed by parliament, will constitute another avenue for further accountability and transparency in the security sector.

opportunity to critically look into the security sector provisions and propose areas needing further reforms. However, most of the provisions on the security sector form part of the entrenched clauses and would require elaborate procedures, including a referendum, to amend. Currently, the crucial issue that seems to agitate the minds of most Ghanaians is the proposed removal of the indemnity clauses in the Constitution. The report of the Constitutional Review Commission (CRC) and the subsequent release of the government's White Paper have still maintained the indemnity clauses still within the entrenched provisions in the 1992 Constitution.[6]

Even though existing literature on the SSR experience in Ghana is growing, there is still more to be uncovered, especially in the areas of understanding the nexus between the military, police, and intelligence sectors, and their relationships to institutional modes of accountability and governance. Therefore, this chapter attempts to offer further insights into how the Ghanaian SSR experience has evolved within these three critical security sector domains. Before exploring further details about constitutional reform and SSR in Ghana, it is important to situate the governance and rule of law perspectives within their proper contexts. This will allow for a better understanding of the governance deficits, which then provided the rational for constitutional transition and SSR in Ghana. This concerns the period of military rule and the transition to multi-party democracy.

Effect of Military Rule on the Security Sector

Since the overthrow of Kwame Nkrumah in 1966 by the combined efforts of agents of the military, police, and intelligence, including the support of the Central Intelligence Agency (CIA) of the United States, Ghana experienced a cyclical process of democratic reversals through military *coups d'état*. This created 'a deepening crisis in critical sectors of national life . . . and neither civilian nor military regimes seemed able to protect themselves against their sudden removal [from office]'.[7] Between 1969 and 1992, when the country returned to constitutional rule, Ghana experienced four successive military *coups d'état*, all truncating the modest attempts at restoring democracy in the country. More importantly, it appears the military incursions did not only retard progress towards democracy but they also weakened the internal dynamics of the security institutions since almost all the coups involved a minimum number of troops, mainly of junior ranks, and faced little or no resistance from the military. In many cases 'no sooner has a coup

[6] See a remark made by Professor Albert K. Fiadjoe, Chairman of the Constitutional Review at two-day Media Engagement on the Report of the CRC and the Government White Paper on the report organized by the CRC in collaboration with the Ministry of Information (2012), <http://vibeghana.com/2012/08/15/removal-of-indemnity-clause-is-a-call-for-anarchy-crc/>.

[7] Eboe Hutchful, 'Military Policy and Reform in Ghana' (1997) 35(2) *Journal of Modern African Studies* 251–78.

commenced than commanders disappear, troops lay down their arms, and the military establishment capitulates'.[8]

Similarly, the military turned against their own, demonstrating a breakdown of command and discipline within the ranks and officer corps. It has been argued that:

> repeated interventions into politics since February 1966, involving at the beginning a number of senior and middle-level commanders but gravitating later to the junior ranks, had encouraged a cycle of political instability and policy uncertainty [in the country] . . . Coups that commenced with soldiers pointing their guns at political leaders had ended with the Armed Forces turning their weapons on themselves.[9]

This was precisely the case in the 1978 and 1979 *coups d'état* where the military countervailed their own forces after capturing political power from elected civilian authority. These trends produced excessive militarization of the other security agencies, such as the police and the intelligence services. For example, the military regime that succeeded the Nkrumah administration added a Military Intelligence Unit (MIU) to the range of intelligence organizations, ostensibly to provide regime protection.

Meanwhile, the efforts at restoring civilian democratic rule, especially in 1969 and 1979 respectively were both short-lived and deprived the country of the opportunity, first, to entrench democracy, the rule of law, and human rights and, second, to embark on genuine SSRs earlier than the 1990s, when they were finally introduced. As a result of these developments, political party activities were curtailed but remained in the politicization of the military and the security agencies. This development ensured that the country experienced prolonged governance deficits in its security system. A major set-back with all these military incursions into mainstream politics was the neglect of parliamentary practice which has contributed to the present curtailment of full parliamentary oversight of the security sector.

Institutional Structures and Separation of Powers

Ghana is presently governed under the Fourth Republican Constitution, which was adopted in 1992. This means that since the exit of the British colonial powers in 1957, the country has been evolving its republican status with varying degree of success. It should be recalled that a major set-back to its republican stability and

[8] Johnny Kwadjo, 'Changing the Intelligence Dynamics in Africa: The Ghana Experience' in Sandy Africa and Johnny Kwadjo (eds), *Changing Intelligence in Africa* (GFN-SSR and ASSN, 2009) 95–124.

[9] Ibid., 252.

electoral practice was the cycle of military *coups d'état* which reversed the original intentions of following a democratic path. Earlier attempts at constitutional transitions, especially in 1969 and 1979, had the military actors stepping aside in the elections and handing over power to the incoming civilian government. This was, however, not the case during the transition process supervised by the Provisional National Defence Council (PNDC) in 1992. The PNDC was a hybrid body which combined both military and civilian elites to govern the country for a little over a decade (i.e. between 1981 and 1992). It was transformed into a political party (the NDC) in 1992 and has since contested all general elections in Ghana. Therefore, together with the NPP, these two political parties remain the dominant force in Ghanaian politics today.

During the transition process in 1992, the PNDC regime committed itself to both military and civilian reforms. It has to be said that while internal reforms of the military and the security sector remained the preoccupation of the regime, military reform became a priority only after several external and internal pressures had pushed the regime to adopt democracy. These reforms embodied four major components embracing defence (military), intelligence, police, and civil affairs. Thus, the reforms involved a number of factors:

1. There was democratization of the internal structures of the military, in which the Armed Forces Defence Committees (AFDCs) were formed to perform the task of reshaping the relations of power between the senior officers and junior ranks. In spite of the fact that this effort yielded some positive results, such as making positions in the command hierarchy more elective and participatory, it equally undermined the rules and regulations of the armed forces and the declared intentions of the regime to restore political stability in the country. This meant that the influence of the AFDCs had to be curtailed in order to avoid fragmentations within the military command.[10] Subsequently, the AFDCs had to be replaced with key governance structures such as the Armed Forces Council (AFC), the Defence Administrative Committee (DAC), and the Defence Staff Committee (DSC).[11]
2. The National Intelligence Apparatus was restructured. The Military Intelligence was dissolved and the Special Branch was replaced by the new Bureau of National Investigations (BNI), which remained technically attached to the police but supervised under the presidency by the Chief of National Security. Coordination of national security was assigned to the National Security Council (NSC). Much as these reforms brought some level of coordination in the security and intelligence sector, the personalized

[10] Hutchful (note 7).

[11] Kwesi Aning, 'Security Sector Reform in Ghana' (2005), <http://www.bicc.de/ssr_gtz/pdf/ghana.pdf>.

controls of the process by the incumbent military President made it virtually impossible to allow for public oversight.[12]

3. While these processes were ongoing to restructure the security sector, considerations were being given to design appropriate ways of incorporating the security agencies, especially the military, into the new constitutional framework. Public opinion was divided on whether the military—apart from their traditional role of defence—could engage in political, legislative, and economic roles. While the proposed legislative role did not receive endorsement, the economic role was limited to the construction of public infrastructure such as roads and bridges. Participation in peacekeeping operations abroad were endorsed and a political role, even though not granted in its original form, received prominent attention in the reconstituted National Security Council (NSC). That said, apart from the armed forces being seen as a special security organ of the PNDC, there were also uncertainties—shared by at least the opposition parties—regarding how the military and the security agencies were going to be deployed, especially for the scheduled elections in 1992.[13] As a result, serving military and security officers and personnel were not permitted to hold elective positions or contest national elections. Again, to maintain the political neutrality and professionalism of the military and security establishments, partisan politics were not allowed within any security installations. However, the security personnel reserved the right to vote for any political party or candidate of their choice during general elections. In this regard, it is instructive to note that since 1992 the security personnel have been granted 'special voting' privilege by the Electoral Commission, allowing them to take part in voting prior to the voting dates of every general election in Ghana.
4. There was gradual political liberalization, allowing for civil society mobilization,[14] and political opposition in the affairs of the country had signalled the hope that a new constitutional order was in sight. This was confirmed in January 1991 when the PNDC regime announced modalities for the return to democracy. This diffused earlier suspicion by pro-democracy, human rights, and opposition groups that the regime was trying to legitimize its rule by deepening its hybrid nature through reforms in the security sector.[15]

[12] Hutchful (note 7), 259.

[13] Ibid., 263.

[14] Among the civil society groups that first emerged on the political scene were the Trades Union Congress, the Bar Associations, church groups, labour and student unions, as well as the Movement for Freedom and Justice (MFJ) which was created in 1990 as a forum to coordinate criticisms and protests by civil society groups.

[15] Hutchful (note 7), 262.

These four structural reforms would later separate the branches of the security sector into distinct military, police, and intelligence functions, and further reduce the militarization of civil affairs. However, the transformation into the separate branches did not immediately manifest at the turn of the 1992 Constitution. A few of the issues that militated against the attainment of this expected transformation in the security sector thus deserve closer examination.

Since independence, and throughout the military rule in Ghana, peacekeeping has been a prominent feature of the Ghana Armed Forces (GAF). In many respects, and as far as the 1992 transition regime was concerned, participation in peacekeeping by the military served two key purposes. The first was to use peacekeeping as a diplomatic tool to enhance the political image of the transitional regime abroad. This was evident, especially in the early 1990s when, at a period of dwindling defence budget, the GAF participated in the ECOWAS Military Observer Group (ECOMOG) missions in Liberia and Sierra Leone. The outcome of this course of action was the relative peace and stability still being enjoyed in the West African region. Second, the transitional regime saw peacekeeping engagements as an avenue to divert attention of the military away from the internal political economy. Thus, peacekeeping engagements became 'an important source of official patronage', allowing troops to supplement their meagre wages and upgrade their living standards.[16] This way, the military was able to offset some of their budgetary deficits for both capital and recurrent expenditures without depending much on the national budget. Thus, pressure on the national budget for military acquisitions was minimized in order to accommodate more 'development-based' projects for the country.

However, in spite of the extensive peacekeeping role which gave the military some degree of outward orientation, it did not take away the political affinity of the regime to retain the inward character of the armed force as its 'protective guard'. Thus, by virtue of operating under military rule, the military lost its distinct qualities of professionalism and overstepped its bounds of operating under the rule of law. Of significant note is the regime preservation orientation that allowed segments of the armed forces to be excessively preoccupied with internal security functions. For example, the 64th Infantry Regiment, which was a commando rapid-deployment force, was created—almost exclusively—to serve as the 'Praetorian guard' of the PNDC regime. Apart from its intimidating posturing, the excessive involvement of this commando rapid-deployment force in internal security created a downside of dragging the military and the presidency into many human rights abuses.[17]

[16] Eboe Hutchful, 'Ghana' in Omitoogun Wuyi and Eboe Hutchful (eds), *Budgeting for the Military Sector in Africa: The Processes and Mechanisms of Control* (Oxford University Press and SIPRI, 2006)72–99.

[17] Ibid., 74.

Similarly, the regime had militia groups that operated outside the mainstream military structure. For instance, the creation of the Committee for the Defence of the Revolution (CDR) and the Force Reserve Battalion[18] introduced divisions in the armed forces and entrenched militarization of civil affairs. This was evident as some CDR members worked closely with the National Commission for Democracy (NCD) on activities such as voter registration and local government elections.[19] It is important to note that a good number of the 'commandos' and the military were deployed by the PNDC regime to provide security, especially in areas where violence and rigging were anticipated during the 1992 elections. However, their heavy security presence and deployment during the elections, much as it helped to reduce the incidence of violence, was largely perceived as a means to intimidate voters and the general populace, especially in opposition strongholds.[20]

As already highlighted elsewhere in this chapter, all this process was supervised by the PNDC regime and, at some point, the regime did not even allow dialogue with the opposition groups regarding the future direction of the new Constitution. In the end, the opposition boycotted participation in the Consultative Assembly (CA) and subsequently did not take part in the 1992 parliament after it had thought that the elections were rigged in favour of the incumbent regime. The opposition believed that the perceived executive manipulation of the Interim National Electoral Commission (INEC) and political controls over the CA had undermined the attainment of credible elections.[21] The frustrations of the main opposition party (NPP) in the entire transition period, especially in the electoral process, were later published in a book its members authored, entitled *The Stolen Verdict*.

As indicated in the foregoing section, public opinion did not favour a direct political role for the military and security agencies in the new dispensation. This position was adopted in the 1992 Constitution.[22] Hence the military exponents in the PNDC regime who were still interested in contesting elections and taking up political appointments in the incoming dispensation had to officially renounce their military/security career. More importantly, the Constitution also set the agenda for separating military regime, military command, and political authority.

[18] The CDR was a special unit created by the PNDC regime to counterbalance the regular armed forces.

[19] International Foundation for Electoral System, *Ghana: A Pre-Election Assessment Report* (IFES, 1992).

[20] Kwesi Aning and Ernest Lartey, 'The Role of the Security Sector in Ghana's Democracy: A Case Study of the December 2012 Elections', *Kugenga Imani* (2013). <http://forums.ssrc.org/kujenga-amani/2013/07/11/the-role-of-the-security-sector-in-ghanas-democracy-a-case-study-of-the-december-2012-elections/#.U6FG18vW_IU>.

[21] Emmanuel Gyimah-Boadi, *Modelling Success: Governance and Institution-Building in Africa: The Case of Ghana's Electoral Commission* (The Consortium for Development Partners, n.d.).

[22] However, the political role of the military and the other security services was not completely abandoned. The creation of the service councils such as the armed forces, police, and national security councils in the Constitution seem to have compensated for this political role, even though not in elective capacities.

For instance, in previous practice whereby some regimes combined the roles of the Head of State, Minister of Defence, and Chief of Defence Staff all in a single person and this was effectively abolished. These roles have subsequently been separated into distinct offices to deepen professionalization of the military and the security agencies and enhance civilian oversight. As a result, the 1992 Constitution placed the raising of armed forces in the hands of parliament while political command of the armed forces rests with the President. The economic role of the security agencies, especially the military, was less prominent and not made explicit in the Constitution. For instance, the Constitution only states that 'the Armed Forces shall be equipped and maintained to perform their role of defence of Ghana as well as such other functions for the development of Ghana as the President may determine'.[23] Thus, even though the Constitution envisages a possible developmental role, it does not provide a direct economic role for the military. This position still remains unchanged even with the ongoing constitutional review and implementation process.

Further, the President is vested with the authority to appoint ministers who have direct jurisdiction over security matters such as Defence, the Interior, and National Security. These appointments must receive parliamentary approval. The President also appoints the Chief of Defence Staff and Chiefs of Army, Navy, and Air Force. Similarly, the President appoints the Inspector General of Police (IGP) and the National Security Coordinator. This is done through the advice of the respective service councils (in the case of the military and the police) and in consultation with the Council of State. The Armed Forces and the Police Councils give policy and strategy direction to the service chiefs who take charge of the administrative and operational responsibilities of the services.[24]

Ostensibly, it can be said that these reforms were conducted not because the regime wanted to release power to a new civilian administration but rather to reinforce the survivability of the regime and its long-term ambitions to become a major political player in the country. However, as argued by some analysts, the 'reforms contributed to suppressing praetorian tendencies within the armed forces, and produced one of the better-run armed forces and security sector in sub-Sahara Africa'.[25]

Chain of Command and Political Authority

As already indicated, the Police Council is the governing authority that sets policy directives for the administration and operations of the Police Service. The Vice

[23] See Art. 210(3) of the 1992 Constitution of Ghana.

[24] See Chapters 8, 15, and 17 of the 1992 Constitution of Ghana.

[25] Kwesi (note 11).

President chairs sittings of the council which comprises the Minister for Internal Affairs; the IGP; Attorney General or his representative; a member of the Ghana Bar Association; a representative of the Retired Senior Police Officers Association; two members of the Police Service appointed by the President acting in consultation with the Council of State, one of whom should be of junior rank; and two other members appointed by the President.

Table 6.1 shows the composition of the police, armed forces and the National Security Councils.

Clearly, by the nature of the composition, the President appointees far outnumber the other members not appointed by the President on the council. This,

Table 6.1: Composition of the armed forces, police, and the National Security Councils

Police Council[i]	Armed Forces Council[ii]
The Vice President Chairman	
(a) Attorney General, Ministers of the Interior and Foreign Affairs (b) Inspector General of Police (c) Representative of the Ghana Bar Association (d) Representative of the Retired Senior Police Officers Association (e) Two President appointees of the Police Service (f) Two other members appointed by the President	(a) Ministers of Defence, Foreign Affairs, and the Interior (b) Chief of Defence Staff, Service Chiefs, and a senior warrant officer (c) Two other President appointees
National Security Council[iii]	
President Chairman	
(a) Vice President (b) Ministers of Foreign Affairs, Defence, the Interior, Finance, and others (c) Chief of Defence Staff and two other members of armed forces (d) Inspector General of Police and two other members of the Police Service including Commissioner of Criminal Investigations	(a) Director General of Prisons Service (b) Director of External Intelligence (c) Director of Internal Intelligence (d) Director of Military Intelligence (e) Commissioner of Customs, Excise, and Preventive Service (f) Three President appointees

[i] See Art. 201 of the 1992 Constitution of Ghana which sets up the Police Council and defines its composition.

[ii] See Art. 210 of the 1992 Constitution of Ghana which defines the composition of the Ghana Armed Forces.

[iii] Art. 83(1) of the 1992 Constitution which sets up the National Security Council and defines its composition.

however, allows the President to have full handle of matters relating to internal security, police administration, budgeting and finance, and promotions of officers above the rank of Assistant Commissioner of Police. Thus, even though the President has no direct oversight role in this arrangement, the President takes ultimate responsibility—at least in theory—of issues pertaining to internal security. Prior to the 1992 Constitution, the position of Vice President did not exist and such governance structures were diffused and dictated to by the military regime, which ruled without a constitution.

Similar to the governing structure of the Police Service, the Armed Forces Council (AFC) also has the Vice President as the chairman, presiding over the Ministers for Defence, Foreign Affairs, and Internal Affairs. The other members include the Chief of Defence Staff, the Service Chiefs (Army, Navy, and Air Force) and a senior warrant officer, and two other persons appointed by the President acting in consultation with the Council of State. The AFC advises the President on matters of policy relating to defence and strategy including the role of the Armed Forces, military budgeting and finance, administration, and the promotion of officers above the rank of lieutenant colonel or its equivalent.

Again, the composition of the AFC indicates that political oversight of the military is firmly placed in the hands of the President. This is because, with the exception of the senior warrant officer, all the members including the Vice President are effectively appointees of the President. This political role of the President over the armed forces is further affirmed by the 1992 Constitution, which states:

> There shall be a President of the Republic of Ghana who shall be the Head of State and Head of Government and the Commander-in-Chief of the Armed Forces of Ghana.[26]

Significantly, while the Constitution places the exercising of political authority in the hands of the presidency and the executive, the authority to raise any armed forces in the country firmly resides with the legislature. Thus, the Constitution stipulates: 'No person shall raise an armed force except by or under the authority of an Act of Parliament.'[27] On the basis of this constitutional provision, the tendency of the President/the Head of State to create 'parallel' armed organizations outside the regular armed forces has been curtailed. It has also effectively abolished the existence of militias and many such groups from operating in the Ghanaian security system. Suffice to say that, unlike the military eras that preceded the 1992 transition in which the military operated over and above the law, the Ghanaian military now exhibits professional defence standards and capability, and has survived different democratic transitions since 1992.

[26] The 1992 Constitution of the Republic of Ghana, Art. 57(1).
[27] Ibid., Art. 57(2).

The National Security Council (NSC) is the apex body charged with the overall responsibility of overseeing and coordinating national security policy in the country. The NSC is composed of the President; the Vice President; Ministers for Foreign Affairs, Defence and the Interior; Chief of Defence Staff and two other members from the armed forces; IGP and two other members of the Police Service including the Commissioner of the Criminal Investigations Department; Director General of the Prisons Service; Directors of Intelligence Services; Commissioner of Customs, Excise and Preventive Services; and three persons appointed by the President. The President presides over meetings of the NSC, but in his absence the Vice President is mandated to play this role.[28]

The NSC is the nerve centre of Ghana's security system. It plays a pivotal role in the coordination of national security policy. It provides the forum for effective exercising of political control over the security establishments, and also serves as the interface for the strategic coordination between defence, internal security, and intelligence. By virtue of its composition, the NSC is constructed to reflect the totality of state security and the prominent players responsible for safeguarding the national security interest. The use of 'state secrecy' has made it unclear whether the NSC has been able to perform one of its distinct tasks of providing the much-expected national security policy framework for the guidance of the security sector. This concern has been shared by one security analyst, observing that:

> Despite the important role granted to the National Security Council, it has not been effective in terms of its mission in providing a security policy framework. Furthermore, it [National Security Council] is dominated by the security services that provide more than half of its members.[29]

Hence, the composition of the NSC is largely 'state-centric', making it assume the classical character of state security, which tends to lay more emphasis on regime and sovereignty survival. This presumption is further reinforced by the apparent lack of security policy framework that should guide the security sector in further areas of reforms, improved standards of performance, and accountability. In some respects, it is argued that rather than institutional and policy entrenchments, the transitional reforms were more driven by informal and personalized controls. Thus, even with the creation of formal structures including the NSC and the service councils (such as the Armed Forces and Police Councils), experts argue that such efforts did not replace personal and informal controls of the security agencies by the President.[30] This was evident when in 1996 the 1992 Constitution

[28] Ibid., Art. 83(2).

[29] Kwesi Aning, 'Security Sector Governance in Ghana' in Osita Eze and Jens-U. Hettmann (eds), *Security Sector Governance in West Africa* (Friedrich Ebert Stiftung, 2005), 7, 68–102.

[30] Ibid..

was amended to reduce the role of the Vice President on the Service Councils,[31] thus effectively making the President the Chairman of these councils.

An important feature of the intelligence reform process was the formation of the Joint Intelligence Committee (JIC) which is chaired by the National Security Coordinator. Other members of this committee include:

- Heads of the Intelligence Agencies
- the Commissioner of Police in charge of Operations and CID
- Senior Analysts from the NSC Secretariat
- Heads of Customs, Immigration and Prison Service.[32]

Unlike the service councils which have more political and strategic compositions, representation on the JIC is more limited to those involved in the technical functions of national intelligence, and focuses more on the operational aspects of intelligence coordination in the country. However, with this current structure, it is unclear what formal role the National Security Advisor plays in matters of national security and intelligence.

Previously, the intelligence agencies have existed as 'secret organizations'. They operated without clear legal backing and suffered from a legitimacy crisis as a result of excessive politicization by successive regimes. Being secretive also meant that abuses suffered at the hands of the intelligence institutions and personnel could not be remedied through formalized channels of the rule of law.[33] Even where the rule of law was seen to be followed, the outcome only reflected and reinforced the tendency of the regime to maintain personal control of the security agencies.[34]

Civil and Social Oversight

It is important to stress that opposition to military rule in Ghana did not only come from known political activists and entities, it was also instigated by several pro-democracy groups and civil society organizations. The most notable ones included the Trades Union Congress, the Ghana Bar Association, the National Union of Ghana Students, and the Movement for Freedom and Justice who

[31] By 1996 several provisions of the 1992 Constitution were amended to incorporate new reflections on the Constitution. One example of such amendment by parliament was a change in the position of the Vice President as the automatic chair of the Ghana Armed Forces, Police, and Prisons Councils. This specific amendment followed a personal confrontation that ensued between the President and the Vice President at a Cabinet meeting in 1995.

[32] The JIC is a technical body empanel by the National Security Coordinator, whose position is provided for by the Security and Intelligence Agencies Act 1996 (Act 526). See Kwadjo (note 8), 105.

[33] In many respects, this tendency had occasioned the many violent and illegal changes of government witnessed in the country after independence.

[34] As was the case with the 1996 episode where the Constitution was amended to reduce the role of the Vice President on the service councils.

methodically used the private newspapers and the private radio stations to mount campaigns and demonstrations to back their demands for constitutional rule and reforms in Ghana. Ghanaians advocated not only multi-party democracy but also institutional changes to forestall violent and illegal attempts to overthrow future constitutions by entrenching the rule of law, civil accountability, and human rights.[35]

These concerns propelled the framers of the new 1992 Constitution to incorporate measures such as political, legislative, judicial, and civil oversight of the security agencies. On one hand, there is a clear separation of powers between the executive and judiciary, and between the legislature and the judiciary. On the other hand, there is rather a hybrid separation between the executive and the legislature. This is because the President (once elected) is enjoined by the Constitution to appoint more than 50 per cent of ministers from parliament.[36] This constitutional structure and injunction has implications for both executive and parliamentary oversight of the security sector.

First, ministers of defence and the security agencies who are also members of parliament (MPs) can enrich both Cabinet discussions and parliamentary/committee debates based on their insights, especially through their participation in NSC and service councils' meetings. This is a significant advantage that is placed at the disposal of both organs of government by the Constitution. However, it appears that the executive has exploited this advantage more than the legislature. Part of the reason is that the legislature lost parts of its institutional memory and learning as a result of the many *coups d'état* in the country.

Second, this practice of legislative *hybridity* carries the potential to undermine effective parliamentary oversight of the security agencies due to the inherent conflict of interest in being a minister and an MP at the same time. Coupled with the catch phrase of 'secrecy and national security' and sometimes political party interest, this constitutional injunction has adversely impacted on the attitude of the legislature in performing its oversight functions of the security sector.

Notwithstanding these structural challenges as imposed by the Constitution, the parliament of Ghana has played a critical role in the reform of the security sector. Parliament was less robust in its oversight functions during the 1992 period, when the house was lopsided as a result of the boycott by the main opposition party (NPP). Significantly, the first parliament enacted the 1996 Security and Intelligence Agencies Act (Act 526), which has become the main reference legislation regulating security and intelligence coordination and oversight in the country. Parliament is recognized by the 1992 Constitution as the only organ responsible for authorizing the raising of armed forces and intelligence and police capabilities in Ghana.

35 Kwadjo (note 8), 105.
36 See the 1992 Constitution of Ghana, Art. 78(1).

However, effective oversight depends on committee work in parliament, and within the Ghanaian parliament, three bodies deserve some close examination as far as parliamentary oversight of the security sector is concerned:

1. *The Committee on Defence and the Interior* is concerned with the armed forces, police, immigration, and prison services and reviews the budgets of both the Ministry of Defence and the Interior. The Committee has two key powers, namely: (i) the conduct of investigations and (ii) inquiries into the activities and administration of ministries, departments, and agencies (MDAs) and public organizations and corporations as parliament may determine. Such investigations and inquiries may lead to proposals for further legislation. The Committee is also empowered to compel the attendance of witnesses to its sittings.[37]
2. *The Finance Committee* considers the budget of the Office of the President, including that of the National Security Council. It has the authority to advance contingence funds to support urgent and unforeseen expenditures.[38]
3. *The Public Accounts Committee* is mandated to oversee public accounts in general and also scrutinizes the Auditor General's report. Thus, the requirement to monitor military and security expenditures falls squarely under its ambit.[39]

It is noted that there is currently no specific parliamentary committee on intelligence. However, the responsibility of parliament exercising control over the budget and expenditure of the National Security Council and Intelligence agencies is performed by the Public Accounts Committee. Under the present constitutional dispensation, all ministerial appointments by the President, including the Ministers of Defence, the Interior, and National Security are vetted and approved by parliament. Presently, the position of Minister for National Security is vacant, and the role appears to have been assumed by the National Security Coordinator who is not of ministerial rank. This means that presently, parliament does not exercise direct oversight of that position and office.

With specific regard to defence and security budgets, the Defence and Interior Committee and parliament as whole have often shown support to the budgetary demands of the armed forces and the other security agencies, sometimes leading to sympathetic appreciation of the deteriorating conditions faced by the security institutions and the personnel. This has made parliament sometimes advocate for more budgetary support for the armed forces and the other security agencies.

[37] Kwesi Aning, 'Ghana' in Ebo Adedeji and Boubacar N'Diaye (eds). *Parliamentary Oversight of the Security Sector in West Africa: Opportunities and Challenges* (DCAF, 2008) 117–38.

[38] Ibid., 123.

[39] Ibid., 123.

However, it has turned out that the Committee and parliament have no real power to influence budgets of the armed forces and the security agencies.[40] Instead, it is the Ministry of Finance which can initiate such financial and budgetary adjustments for the defence and the security sector. Some experts have argued that such shortfalls in defence budgets are attributed to the manner in which national budgets are prepared, in which the process tends to be more inputs-driven rather than results-based, and often strictly controlled by the Ministry of Finance.[41]

Parliamentary work is severely affected by the regular turnover of MPs due to the competitive nature of the elections. The turnover makes it difficult to retain highly skilled and experienced MPs who can help entrench best practices of parliamentary oversight of the security sector in the prevailing democratic dispensation. The capacity of parliamentarians to be effective in their oversight functions is also hampered by lack of offices and research and resource support.[42] A few analysts have also argued that there is an unstated reticence on the part of some MPs, especially those in the government, to exercise oversight on matters relating to national security.[43]

The judiciary also assumes a critical role in the reform of the security sector. It plays a mediating role in the criminal justice system, by ensuring a balance between arrests, prosecution, and imprisonment. In Ghana, the Supreme Court interprets what constitutes legality and illegality as pertaining to the Constitution. Therefore, it acts as a check on the executive powers, especially in relation to issues bordering on fundamental human rights and freedoms.[44] With specific regard to intelligence reform, for instance, the intelligence and security agencies legislation[45] requires that persons dissatisfied with the action taken by the directors of the intelligence agencies reserve the right to submit a written complaint to the Chief Justice who shall refer the complaint to a tribunal of three persons to examine and make a determination on the issues raised in the complaint within sixty days.[46] Similarly, the directors of the intelligence agencies are required to apply to the courts for the issuance of warrants before they conduct certain surveillance operations.[47]

In recent times, the courts have made two critical rulings that have impacted on the operations of the security agencies:

1. The security agencies, especially the intelligence agencies, cannot impose restrictions on the free movement of people without recourse to the courts.

40 Ibid., 124.
41 Hutchful (note 16), 76.
42 Robert I. Rotberg and Jennifer Erin Salahub, 'African Legislative Effectiveness', The North-South Institute Research Report (2013).
43 Aning (note 37), 129.
44 See Chapter 11 of the of the 1992 Constitution of Ghana.
45 See Security and Intelligence Agencies Act 1996 (Act 526).
46 Ibid., ss. 21–27.
47 Kwadjo (note 8), 114.

2. Interrogation of persons within a security facility without the presence of a lawyer constitutes a violation of human rights and the Constitution.[48]

Significantly, these two rulings have sought to subject the security agencies to the dictates of the rule of law and respect for human rights, which hitherto were not properly followed. The Commission for Human Rights and Administrative Justice (CHRAJ) also performs a critical role in opening up the security sector for further scrutiny and transparency beyond the key organs of the state.[49]

In a similar vein, even though it is argued that there was little civil society presence[50] in security sector governance until the 1990s, a few of groups managed to direct sustained campaigns against military rule in Ghana (albeit amidst the prevailing culture of silence and fear and the 'precautionary measure of self-censorship').[51] Since the transition to democracy in 1992, most of these civil society groups have shifted their focus from the initial agitations against the military rule to a phase where they now concern themselves with deepening democracy and the respect for the rule of law and human rights. This includes efforts at building capacity, especially of parliamentarians and other civil groups, to improve their oversight functions in the security sector. Others have also focused on peace-building, human security, and community safety by providing advocacy, expertise, and training to support security agencies and other civil personnel and organizations in fighting crimes, addressing low-intensity conflicts, and peacekeeping engagements.[52]

Currently, civil society inputs remain integral in the ongoing constitutional review process, making it more inclusive and less politicized. Apart from their excessive reliance on donor support and limited capacity to engage, a major challenge with civil society participation and oversight is that many of them appear to lack the capacity and the sustained interest to engage in security issues.[53] There is also the risk of being 'labelled' or 'branded' a pro-government or anti-government

[48] See further details in Kwesi Aning, Emma Birikorang, and Ernest A. Lartey, 'The Processes and Mechanisms of Developing a Democratic Intelligence Culture in Ghana' in Philip H.J. Davis and Kristian C. Gustafson (eds), *Intelligence Elsewhere: Spies and Espionage Outside the Anglosphere* (Georgetown University Press, 2013), 212, 199–218.

[49] See Chapter 18 of the 1992 Constitution of Ghana.

[50] Dr Kwesi Aning who is a security expert in Ghana has identified a few civil society organizations who have remained constructive in security sector engagements in Ghana. They include the media, religious bodies, African Security Dialogue and Research (ASDR), the Foundation for Security and Development (FOSDA), the Ghana Centre for Democratic Development (CDD), and the Centre for Security Studies (CSS). Increasingly, however, institutions such as the Kofi Annan International Peacekeeping Training Centre (KAIPTC) and others have gained expertise in security sector engagements both within Ghana and abroad.

[51] Aning (note 37), 128.

[52] Kwesi Aning and Ernest Ansah Lartey, 'Parliamentary Oversight of the Security Sector in Ghana: Lessons from Ghana' (2008), <http://www.agora-parl.org/sites/default/files/lessons_from_ghana.pdf>, 14.

[53] Aning (note 11), 8.

advocate, depending on the perspective offered on security policy in the country. This has the potential to undermine objective contributions to security policy and reforms.[54] In spite of these notable challenges, civil society engagement in the security sector has helped to improve civil–military relations in Ghana.

Constitution-building and Legal Issues

Preceding Constitutions—especially those of 1960, 1969, and 1979—all had provisions on the security sector. However, their legal effects were rendered null and void as a result of the military coups that truncated their dispensation midstream. The Acts of parliament that set up the security agencies—such as the Armed Forces Act 1962 (Act 105),[55] the National Security Service Act 1963 (Act 202), and the Police Services Act 1970 (Act 350)—still remained in force after the introduction of the 1992 Constitution. Nevertheless, the Police Service legislation, for instance, has undergone several amendments, and different commissions of inquiry into the police administration[56] have made recommendations which have cumulatively influenced the orientation and organization of the Ghana Police Service.[57] The Police Service Act of 1970 (Act 350) is one of the important pieces of legislation regulating the conduct of the Ghana Police Service. This Act incorporated all previous Acts and Decrees relating to the Police Service. An important provision in this piece of legislation is that it provides a mechanism for the Ministry of the Interior to regulate the operations of the non-state security providers such as private security companies.[58] Notably, all these pieces of legislation preceded the adoption of the 1992 Constitution. This therefore means that while these statutes existed before the Constitution, the new Constitution provided for a more effective and democratic means for their implementation through the newly created councils and strengthened of parliamentary oversight.

[54] Aning (note 37), 128.

[55] Just recently, an Accra High Court presided over by His Lordship Utter P. Derry, ruled in March 2009 that the Armed Forces Act of 1962 (Act 105) is inconsistent with the provisions of the 1992 Constitution of the Republic of Ghana. According to the court, the aforementioned Act is outdated and probably needs to undergo some review process in order to align it with the current Constitution. See *Modern Ghana*, 27 March 2009, <http://www.modernghana.com/news/208521/1/court-throws-out-ghana-armed-forces-request-orders.html>.

[56] Kwesi Aning, 'An Overview of the Ghana Police Service' (2006) 2(2) *Journal of Security Sector Management*.

[57] Aning reviews (ibid.) the legislative and constitutional instruments regulating the Police Service and identifies the following instruments: Security Services Act 1963 (Act 202); 1969 Republican Constitution, Chapter 13; The Police Service, ss. 142–4; Police Service Act 1970 (Act 350); Police Force (Amendment) Decree 1974; 1979 Republican Constitution, Chapter 17, ss. 172–5; and 1992 Republican Constitution. The article also reviews all the various Committees of Inquiry within the Police Service. See ibid., 13.

[58] Aning (note 56), 7.

However, one of the significant developments in the SSR agenda in Ghana relates to the adoption of the Security and Intelligence Agencies Act, which for once gives a legislative basis for the operations of the national intelligence agencies in the country. The Security and Intelligence Agencies Act (Act 526) adopted in 1996 serves as the operative instrument for the effective and transparent implementation of national security as was envisaged in Articles 83–85 of the 1992 Constitution. The major reforms which were introduced by this legislation include:

1. subjecting the intelligence agencies to the authority of the National Security Council;
2. ensuring parliamentary and judicial oversight;
3. centralizing the three existing intelligence services (i.e. the Bureau of National Investigations, Research Department and Military Intelligence) under the control of one body (the NSC);
4. empowering the President to appoint a Minister for National Security;
5. authorizing the President to appoint a National Security Coordinator who will function as the professional head of the NSC.

In addition, the Act makes provision for the Minister to submit an annual report to parliament regarding the operations of the intelligence agencies. Similarly, the National Security Coordinator is required under section 33(1) of the Act to keep books of accounts which will be audited by the Auditor General on an annual basis. It is believed that reforms in the intelligence sector were a fundamental priority to address the perennial problem of military coups in the country.[59]

Contrasting the provisions in Article 83 of the 1992 Constitution and the Security and Intelligence Agencies Act 1996 (Act 526), one notices a conspicuous omission in the composition of the NSC regarding the positions of the Minister of National Security and the National Security Coordinator. Suffice to say that these two positions were a creation of the Act, which was adopted after the 1992 Constitution. Making an addition to the composition of the National Security Council to accommodate these two positions in the security and intelligence agencies Act would have meant amending Article 83 of the 1992 Constitution. While this exercise was possible, it could have only been done through a referendum since Article 83 is an entrenched provision in the Constitution. However, this anomaly is somewhat remedied with the allowance for more presidential appointees on the NSC.[60]

Between 1992, when the present Constitution came into effect, and 1996, when the security and intelligence agencies legislation was promulgated, the intelligence community had been streamlined and placed under the NSC Secretariat which was controlled by the Office of the President through the Office of the National

[59] Aninig (note 11).
[60] Aning and Lartey (note 52), 3.

Security Adviser. This process effectively separated intelligence activity from police investigative processes, making national intelligence a distinct operation independent of the police administration. As noted by Johnny Kwadjo, members of the intelligence services no longer used police ranks. Instead, those belonging to the internal service carried 'normal public service designations, while those of the external service carried normal Foreign Service designations. Members of the new Defence Intelligence, however, maintained their respective military ranks'.[61]

More importantly, by bringing the intelligence agencies under the purview of the Constitution and the legislative instrument, the intelligence agencies were stripped of their traditional anonymity and became subject to the law. Obviously, this process effectively terminates the existence of 'shadow intelligence' organizations not operating under the law or democratic oversight.[62]

Indemnity Provisions in the 1992 Constitution

The indemnity clauses in the 1992 Constitution remain one of the controversial issues in the country today. The controversy began with the formulation of the Constitution during the transitional phase in 1992 and has continued even at this stage of the review process. Even though the Constitution reflects liberal aspirations in the political governance of the country, it equally offers specific protection for actors and parties who truncated previous constitutions and spearheaded the transition process in 1992. The chapter on 'Transitional Provisions' is part of the entrenched provisions in the Constitution and has an elaborate provision on actors and actions covered under indemnity. The indemnity clause is an entrenched provision and covers all previous constitutional and human rights violations suffered as a result of military coups since February 1966. What this means is that with the coming into effect of the 1992 Constitution, it is unlawful for any individual or group of persons to take legal action against any member of the previous military administrations for constitutional and human rights violations. Similarly, it is also unlawful for any court in Ghana to entertain cases brought before it on issues touching constitutional and human rights violations during military rule. Of significant note about this indemnity clause is the imposition of an indefinite time limit within which the provision can be amended.[63]

In as much as the indemnity provisions may sound highly intimidating to individuals and even to the entire transitional justice system, it was seen as a compromise strategy to facilitate a peaceful transition from the revolutionary era to the democratic process. Possibly, if those guarantees were not enshrined in

[61] Kwadjo (note 8), 103.
[62] Ibid., 106.
[63] See Part 34 of the chapter on transitional provisions in the 1992 Constitution of Ghana.

the Constitution, the transition and the subsequent consolidation of the democratic process could have suffered another set-back as was previously experienced,[64] and the modest gains in SSR during the transition period could have been eroded.

Opinions were divided as to whether the indemnity clause should be expunged from the Constitution during the ongoing constitutional review process. In the view of the CRC, however, it was still unsafe to remove the indemnity clause in the Constitution. The Chairman of the CRC notes that 'the removal of the Indemnity Clause (IC) from the 1992 Constitution would lead to anarchy in the country'.[65] The CRC further notes that by removing the IC, all governments since 1966 would become illegal, and that immediate steps would have to be taken to hand over the reins of government to the Convention Peoples Party. This would lead to criminalizing all those who have participated in governments since the overthrow of the first republic and would also bring unnecessary interruptions in national affairs.[66]

Significantly, due to these indemnity clauses which were introduced as precondition of the political transitions, SSR in Ghana did not require a complete rebuilding of the security sector, thus the Constitution only adopted the status quo arrangements that had been set before the transition. All the members and the institutions of the armed forces, intelligence, and the police services that operated during the military eras were 'rolled over' into the new constitutional dispensation without any major restructuring and rebuilding. However, in 2000, the NPP administration, after winning the elections, initiated efforts to reintegrate the 'commando' unit into the mainstream armed force and instituted the National Reconciliation Commission (NRC). It is argued that:

> as a result of the amnesty [indemnity] that was constitutionally entrenched during the previous administration, victims had no recourse to the courts for their grievances and a truth commission was believed to be the only way to secure some measure of accountability and acknowledgement, as well as to reveal the full extent of past violations.[67]

[64] As noted by Professor Albert K. Fiadjoe, Chairman of the CRC, the principle underlying the IC in the 1992 Constitution is nothing unusual as the 1969 and 1979 Constitutions contained similar provisions. Section 3 of the First Schedule of the 1969 Constitution and ss. 15 and 16 of the First Schedule to the 1979 Constitution indemnified the persons responsible for bringing about the changes in government on 4 June 1979—Rawlings' first coup; 13 January 1972—the Acheampong coup; and on 24 February 1966—the Kotoka coup.

[65] Professor Albert K. Fiadjoe, made this remarks at the end of a two-day media engagement on the report of the CRC and the Government White Paper on the report organized by the CRC in collaboration with the Ministry of Information, <http://vibeghana.com/2012/08/15/removal-of-indemnity-clause-is-a-call-for-anarchy-crc/>.

[66] Professor Albert K. Fiadjoe, CRC Chairman, ibid.

[67] Nahla Valji, 'Ghana's National Reconciliation Commission: A Comparative Assessment', International Centre for Transitional Justice, Occasional Paper Series (2006).

However, as it turned out, this exercise was heavy politicized and was viewed by the sceptics as an attempt by the NPP government to discredit the PNDC, NDC, and former President Rawlings.[68]

Key Lessons

Ghana's constitutional reform and SSR processes present a unique opportunity to draw some key lessons that could help inform future reform processes in the security sector. In the first place, it was a reform process that was largely supervised by a military regime in which the initial motivation for the SSR was for the narrow interest of regime protection, but later expanded to embrace wider reforms leading to democratic constitutional rule and civil oversight. Thus, contrary to the general belief that reform in the security sector is usually imposed from outside, Ghana's experience shows a classic case of a process that was initiated primarily from within the security sector. In this regard, even though ownership was not properly implanted in the process, it offered a home-grown solution which was wholly peculiar to Ghana. Historically, this was partially made possible because the constitutional transition was anchored on existing state and security structures that had not completely collapsed.

Second, the SSR process was initially underpinned by the philosophy of regime preservation. Therefore, starting from the revolutionary era to the PNDC period, there was a conscious effort by the political regime to shift the process from a radical to a gradual tinkering of human rights and rule of law principles within both the civil and security sectors. This was done to curtail the coup legacy that had plagued the military and the country since independence.

The third lesson was that the aim of demilitarization meant that priority attention was given to military/defence reform. The assumption was that military reform—which also encompassed the main government machinery—would ultimately provide the enabling political environment necessary to conduct similar reforms in the other sectors such as the police and intelligence. This is not to say that military reform was done before the other reforms. In fact, in reality, the implementation of these reform processes followed concurrent and overlapping steps.

Finally, peacekeeping engagements remain instrumental in the reform process. Apart from the fact that it provides sound financial outlay for the maintenance and sustenance of the military and the security services,[69] it has provided the military

[68] Ibid., 2.

[69] The financial 'properties' of peacekeeping engagements have been the most reliable sources of deficit financing in terms of military equipment and defence acquisition in Ghana. However, there is lack of proper accountability regarding the use of the peacekeeping account. Even though parliament has jurisdiction to oversee disbursement of this account, it has not been able to do so until today (see Hutchful (note 16) and Aning (note 11)).

and the country an alternative avenue to exercise part of their defence capabilities abroad. This has been useful in rechannelling their energies and interests away from internal politics.

In spite of these positive lessons, the success of the Ghanaian SSR experience has been hampered by three key factors. First, the personalized controls which sometimes characterized the reform process by the supervising PNDC regime appeared to have created a 'psychological room' that allows the coup legacy to linger. Succeeding governments under the present constitutional dispensation sometimes appear jittery about the security infrastructure around them. This creates the tendency to fortify security arrangements around the presidency of succeeding governments, which tends to reinforce the tradition of regime security as opposed to human security.

Second, as a result of the protracted military rule, the initial SSR process did not involve any parliamentary oversight. In the process, the late start of the exercise of parliamentary oversight of the security sector has inhibited parliament's capacity to reduce the governance deficit in the security sector. Even though parliament has set up committees to deal with specific security issues, it still cannot influence budgetary allocations to the security sector. In addition, effective procedures do not exist for intelligence oversight in parliament.

Third, the SSR process was implemented in a 'depressed environment' which did not allow for effective and constructive participation of civil society. The imposition of the 'culture of silence' prior to the transition and even in the early stages of the constitutional dispensation did not facilitate open and transparent dialogue. Thus, even though the military actors took ownership of the SSR and constitutional process, the prevailing culture of silence did not permit the same level of ownership and participation to resonate with some of the key political actors and the civil population. In the end, the exercise was generally perceived as being promoted to entrench the political interest of the military regime.

Conclusion

Like many African countries, Ghana's political process has been punctuated by periods of instability, not least because of the exploitative colonial legacy but also the effect of self-induced autocratic tendencies that had overshadowed earlier attempts at democratic pursuit. Even though the military had been the main player in these democratic punctuations, it got involved in those situations partly because of the excessive politicization that undermined military discipline and command.

Even though democracy was reinstituted in Ghana in 1992, efforts to reform the security sector had begun earlier in the 1980s when SSR was piloted under the PNDC military regime. Under that regime, significant progress was made to instil military discipline in the barracks and maintain stability in the country, but that achievement was not accompanied by oversight on the part of the civilian public. Therefore, the legitimacy and genuineness of the SSRs was left in doubt, not least in the perspective of some segments of the military itself and also from the point of view of the political opposition parties and civil society groups.

Significantly, the accompanied restructuring of the intelligence sector seemed to have added some gains in military reform, leading to—not least—greater disposition towards the rule of law. In all this, parliamentary oversight of the security sector arrived late. It was not until 1992 that parliamentary processes began to impact on the security sector. Even then, much as authority for oversight was guaranteed by the Constitution and the Security and Intelligence Act 1996, it lacked the ability and the attitude to proceed with its oversight functions of the security sector. Its ability has been hampered by the turnover of MPs as a result of competitive elections, party influence, and limited research and office support.

7

Security Sector Reform and Democratic Transition in Parallel

The South African Case

Richard Stacey and Christina Murray

Introduction

In 1987, Nelson Mandela had been in jail in apartheid South Africa for twenty-four years. The African National Congress (ANC), the anti-apartheid organization to which Mandela belonged, was illegal. Many of its leaders were in exile abroad. The ANC's armed wing, uMkhonto we Sizwe (MK), was engaged in an armed struggle against the security machinery of the apartheid government. That year, however, members of the apartheid government's National Intelligence Service (NIS) began to meet with Mandela in prison, and ultimately decided to meet with members of the ANC in exile, to discuss ways to end the armed struggle.

On 12 September 1989, at the Palace Hotel in Lucerne, Switzerland, two operatives of the NIS met with two senior ANC members. One of these men was the chief of the ANC's Department of Intelligence and Security (DIS), Jacob Zuma. The other man was Thabo Mbeki. Both these men would go on to serve as President of a democratic South Africa. The meeting was authorized by the State Security Council (SSC), a Cabinet and security services committee of which the President was the chairperson.[1] It became clear to both sides during this meeting and those that followed that a negotiated end to apartheid was possible.

In February 1990, President F.W. de Klerk rescinded bans on the ANC, the Pan-Africanist Congress (PAC), and the Communist Party (SACP). The security apparatus that had policed South Africa's apartheid laws now no longer had an enemy. With the release of Mandela on 11 February 1990, the subject of discussions between the ANC and the apartheid intelligence services shifted rapidly to practical matters such as the repatriation of exiled ANC, PAC, and SACP members with special indemnities against prosecution for anti-apartheid activities, and the initiation of formal discussions at the political level.[2] Political negotiations proceeded in fits and starts,

[1] Allister Sparks, *Tomorrow Is Another Country* (University of Chicago Press, 1996), 111.

[2] The Indemnity Act 35 of 1990, for example, which empowered the State President to indemnify specific people against arrest and prosecution for crimes committed during the struggle against

but culminated in the adoption of South Africa's interim Constitution in 1993.[3] The security services—military, police, and intelligence services—did not play a direct role in these negotiations, although close links between political principals and the security services were maintained, notably with NIS chief Niel Barnard.

The substantive questions of reforming the apartheid security services were negotiated in separate, parallel discussions between the leadership of the various security services and liberation armies that existed in South Africa, and within the Transitional Executive Council (TEC), the multi-party authority established in October 1993 to oversee the period until President Mandela's inauguration on 10 May 1994.

This case study examines the reform of South Africa's security services through these 'security negotiations', within the broader context of South Africa's 'constitutional negotiations'. The bulk of these negotiations occurred before 27 April 1994, when South Africa's interim Constitution took effect. Three issues dominated the discussion:

1. *Integration and amnesty*: Several military and civil security forces existed in South Africa prior to the constitutional transition. The South African Defence Force (SADF) and the South African Police (SAP) stood alongside the 'homeland' police forces, established by statute in the nominally independent homelands or bantustans. In addition to these 'statutory' forces, MK and the PAC's armed wing, the Azanian People's Liberation Army (APLA), were active in and outside the country.[4] The question of amnesty for the actions of all of these organizations in the struggle against and in support of apartheid was high on the agenda.
2. *'Desecuritizing' government*: The apartheid government had maintained control over the country largely through a heavily securitized system consisting of a policy-making organ (the State Security Council) and comprehensive bureaucratic machinery (the National Security Management System). Members of the security services were centrally involved in both institutions.
3. *Transitional peacekeeping*: An effective and legitimate security force was needed to ensure stability in the run-up to the April 1994 elections. There was substantial political violence in the early 1990s, particularly in the

apartheid, was a product of NIS/ANC talks and allowed exiled opposition leaders to return to South Africa.

[3] Constitution of the Republic of South Africa Act 20 of 1993. See also Richard Spitz and Matthew Chaskalson, *The Politics of Transition: The Hidden History of South Africa's Negotiated Settlement* (Witwatersand University Press, 2000).

[4] It is interesting to note that the post-apartheid integration of MK and Defence Forces armies was the second time that South Africa has faced the problem. British and Afrikaner forces were integrated into the Union Defence Force after the second Anglo-Boer war ended and the Union of South Africa formed in 1910.

KwaZulu-Natal region. The security negotiations aimed to establish transitional security arrangements capable of providing effective police services.

The negotiated arrangements of the interim Constitution yielded to the 1996 Constitution, deliberated and approved by a Constitutional Assembly (CA) democratically elected under the interim Constitution. The security services played only a peripheral role in the CA and the post-1994 constitutional process. This case study therefore focuses on the period up to 1994, and the impact of this transitional period on security sector oversight since under the 1996 Constitution.

Institutional Structure of the Security Services

South Africa's Apartheid Security Services

South Africa's apartheid system was based on the central idea of racial segregation. Legislation set out the racial classification of South African society, and sought to separate white, black, coloured, and Indian people from one another in all aspects of life.[5] Political rights were differentially conferred based on colour: in 1951 the Separate Representation of Voters Act[6] created an entirely white electorate for the first time, by removing from parliament's lower house four seats set aside for election by the coloured voters in the Cape Province. The 1983 Constitution[7] established a tricameral legislature with separate chambers for white, coloured, and Indian South Africans, but not black South Africans.

The keystone of apartheid's political architecture was the Homelands policy. The Bantu Homelands Citizenship Act[8] declared that black South Africans were no longer citizens of the Republic of South Africa, but rather of one of several nominally independent 'Homelands' carved out of the South Africa. The Bantu Homelands Constitution Act[9] empowered the government to create and grant political independence to bantustans. The homeland states of Transkei,

[5] The core pieces of this statutory system were the Population Registration Act 30 of 1950, the various Group Areas Acts (41 of 1950, 77 of 1957, and 36 of 1966), the Natives (Abolition of Passes and Co-ordination of Documents) Act 67 of 1952, and the Native (Urban) Areas Act 21 of 1923. In terms of the Population Registration Act, the four racial classifications of apartheid were (i) African (or Black), (ii) Coloured, (iii), Indian/Asian, and (iv) White. See also the Mines and Works Act 12 of 1911, reserving skilled occupations for white and coloured people; the Industrial Conciliation Act 11 of 1924, prohibiting black trade unions and industrial action by black people; and the Immorality Act 5 of 1927, Prohibition of Mixed Marriages Act 55 of 1949, and Immorality Act 23 of 1957 (later the Sexual Offences Act), prohibiting interracial relationships.

[6] Separate Representation of Voters Act 46 of 1951, later re-promulgated as Act 50 of 1968.

[7] Republic of South Africa Constitution Act 110 of 1983.

[8] Bantu Homelands Citizenship Act 26 of 1970.

[9] Bantu Homelands Citizenship Act 21 of 1971.

Bophuthatswana, Venda, and Ciskei (TBVC states) were granted political independence from South Africa during the 1970s and 1980s[10] and established their own police forces and armies.

The apartheid security services were dedicated to enforcing these racist laws. Several pieces of 'security' legislation were passed to facilitate this and to aid state suppression of opposition.[11] Working through this legal framework, apartheid South Africa claimed throughout to respect the rule of law. The state made a deliberate effort to ensure that apartheid's machinery was erected by legislation. In addition, the white minority was fully enfranchised and the architect of apartheid, the National Party (NP) government, won regular legislative elections contested within the white minority electorate. Elections held in the TBVC states under the watch of the NP government and the South African security services lent formal legitimacy to the Homeland governments. This semblance of democracy and the formal adherence to principles of the rule of law does little to temper apartheid South Africa's classification as an authoritarian government heavily reliant on draconian legislation and an elaborate security apparatus.

After the NP government banned the ANC, PAC, and SACP in 1960,[12] the ANC established MK and began an armed struggle against the government.[13] By the late 1960s, the NP government was convinced that it faced a 'Total Onslaught' of anti-apartheid forces (or 'Revolutionary Onslaught' by the 1980s), to which it responded with a two-pronged 'Total Strategy':[14]

- The first prong was maintaining security itself, both inside the country and in the 'frontline' states to the north of South Africa.

[10] See, generally, Roger Southall, *South Africa's Transkei: The Political Economy of an 'Independent' Bantustan* (Monthly Review Press, 1983); Roger Southall and Geoffrey Wood, 'Control and Contestation: State Security in South Africa's Homelands: A Report to the Truth and Reconciliation Commission' (1997); W.M. Tsotsi, *Human Rights in the Homelands of South Africa* (Institute of Southern African Studies, 1992).

[11] See e.g. the General Laws Amendment Act 37 of 1963 which provided for detention without warrant or trial for up to ninety days; the Criminal Procedure Amendment Act 96 of 1965, which doubled the time of detention without trial to 180 days; the Suppression of Communism Act 44 of 1950, which empowered the State President to declare an organization unlawful if he was 'satisfied' that its activities were calculated to further the ends of communism; the Internal Security Act 74 of 1982 which, among other things, allowed magistrates to prohibit gatherings and empowered the Attorney General to order that an arrested person not be released on bail; and the Public Safety Act 3 of 1953, which empowered the President to declare a state of emergency if circumstances, in his opinion, threatened public safety or public order and ordinary law was inadequate to ensure public safety or maintain public order, and to make such regulations as appeared to the President to be necessary for providing for the public safety and maintaining public order.

[12] See the Unlawful Organisations Act 34 of 1960 and the Internal Security Act 74 of 1982.

[13] The ANC and SACP planned military strikes against the apartheid government through 'Operation Mayibuye', for which Nelson Mandela was eventually sentenced to life in prison (Report of the Commissioner of the South African Police for the Year Ended 30th June 1964 (1965), 8).

[14] Annette Seegers, *The Military in the Making of Modern South Africa* (Tauris, 1996), chapter 5; Noel Stott, 'From SADF to SANDF: Safeguarding South Africa for a Better Life for All?', Centre for the Study of Violence and Reconstruction, Violence and Transition Series Vol. 7 (2002), 6.

- The second prong of Total Strategy was the commitment to achieving effective bureaucratic management of the country and placating opposition by ensuring economic and social development. This would require close and vigorous management from a militaristic administration.

Violent resistance to the apartheid government increased significantly in the 1970s and 1980s, and the apartheid security forces were engaged both within and outside the country in efforts to undermine the armed struggle being waged by the ANC and other liberation groups. The apartheid government was committed to using security legislation, the police, and the court system as the primary mechanism for undermining opposition based inside the country,[15] with the SAP assuming responsibility for internal security.[16] The Police Act 7 of 1958 identified 'internal security' as the SAP's functional priority.

The SADF sought to define itself as a professional military, engaged in protecting the state from external threats. In 1977 the SADF insisted that the responsibility for combatting internal and urban unrest lay with the SAP,[17] but by the 1980s it had become clear that the SADF would have to participate in 'joint action' with the SAP to quell opposition and violence within South Africa, and that the two would have to cooperate as part of a coordinated security community. A joint declaration in the early 1980s by the SAP and SADF stated that the SAP was primarily responsible for riot control and counter-insurgency, while the SADF would play a supporting role until armed conflict emerged. At that point, the SADF would take over, with the SAP in a supporting role.[18] The NIS and the national Department of Foreign Affairs provided support and backup to both the SAP and the SADF.[19]

The security community, however, was by no means monolithic.[20] A number of different forces existed, and their mandates and scope of operations overlapped and blurred into one another. First, the Security Branch (SB) was established within the SAP in 1947, and quickly became the elite division within the SAP. Two former heads of the SB subsequently became Commissioner of Police.[21]

15 See the Report of the Commission of Inquiry into Security Legislation (the Rabie Report) (Government Printer, 1982): '[A]ctivities which theater the internal security of the Republic should, as far as circumstances permit, be combatted as crimes. Such a line of action is, so long as it can be maintained, is preferable to a situation where subversive activities are combatted by military measures.'

16 Stott (note 14), 6.

17 Gavin Cawthra, *Policing South Africa: The SAP and the Transition from Apartheid* (David Philip, 1993), 26; and *Brutal Force: The Apartheid War Machine* (International Defence Aid Fund, 1986), 223.

18 Major General A.J. Wandrag, 'Political Unrest: A Police View' (1985) 7 *Strategic Review for Southern Africa* 9.

19 Seegers (note 14), 163.

20 Annette Seegers, 'Current Trends in South Africa's Security Establishment' (1992) 18(2) *Armed Forces and Society* 159, 159.

21 Seegers (note 14), 125.

Second, while the SB was in the business of gathering intelligence on insurgent and anti-apartheid activities, so too was the Department of Military Intelligence (DMI), housed within the Department of Defence.[22]

Third, to end rivalries between agencies with an intelligence-gathering mandate, the NIS (originally the Bureau of State Security) was established in 1969, both to gather intelligence and to consolidate other security agencies' intelligence. Both the SB and DMI were obliged to share intelligence with the NIS, which had a direct line to Cabinet. The NIS consisted mostly of former members of the SB, but by the late 1980s had been transformed into an organization that valued professional and academic qualifications, and focused on long-term strategy rather than short-term security.[23]

Fourth, in 1967 the SAP began training specialized riot police, and by 1976 each SAP division had a riot squad. These riot squads were trained at a base used primarily for training the SAP in counter-insurgency (COIN) tactics. The COIN-trained policemen received basic infantry training from the SADF alongside training in specialized counter-insurgency policing. One such COIN unit was codenamed 'Koevoet' [crowbar]. Under the supervision of the SAP, it operated in northern Namibia to undermine the insurgent activities of the South West African Peoples' Organization (SWAPO).[24]

Fifth, once it became clear by the mid-1980s that the SAP was unable to contain urban unrest in the black townships of South Africa, and that the SADF was unable to help because 'township duty' was unacceptable to most SADF conscripts, the SAP recruited and hastily trained black men as 'municipal police' and 'special constables', to serve in the townships. These auxiliary police forces were initially under the control of local (black) town councils, and were deployed to guard town councillors and council property. The SAP took command of the auxiliary forces in 1989.[25]

Finally, the SADF made regular military incursions into the 'frontline' states between 1976 and 1989, largely under the auspices of the Directorate of Special Tasks (Spestake). These were intended to destabilize neighbouring governments supported by communist governments in the Soviet Union and Cuba (Angola and Mozambique), and to strike at ANC and MK members in exile (Botswana, Lesotho, Zimbabwe, and Swaziland).[26]

The mission of each of these security forces was to eliminate opposition to the apartheid state and suppress violence directed at the state. Less clear, however, was the division of labour and the scope of operations of each of the services. The SAP attacked insurgents through Koevoet in Namibia and fulfilled an

[22] Ibid., 131.
[23] Ibid., 131, 250.
[24] Ibid., 225–6.
[25] Cawthra, *Policing South Africa* (note 17), 62.
[26] Seegers (note 14), 210–16.

intelligence mandate through the SB. The Department of Defence housed its own intelligence unit also, but the NIS was established to consolidate intelligence activities and to run its own intelligence operations. The SADF operated beyond South Africa's borders, but frequently acted not against foreign military forces but against South African opposition groups with operations in foreign countries. The SADF was also deployed inside South Africa when necessary. There was no clear articulation of the mandate and scope of operations of each service, and no clear distinction between the internal or external orientation of the services.

Chain of Command: South Africa's 'Securocrats' and the Securitized Government Structure

During apartheid, the leadership of the security services became directly involved in determining the policies that would govern and direct their activities. At the same time, the civilian executive government circumvented the ordinary chain of command and communicated directly with security personnel, without a civilian ministry acting as an intermediary. Members of the government responsible for the security services were not required to be civilians, and several were active members of the security service they headed.

This close relationship between the apartheid government and the security forces was a result of the government's reliance on the security establishment, disjointed as it was, for advice on how to hold the apartheid ruling structure together. Total Strategy required the involvement of security sector leaders at a high-level of civilian politics. The SSC was the vehicle through which this occurred. The SSC emerged as a response to the infighting and rivalries between various security agencies that existed.[27] Its function was to advise the government, at the request of the President, on the formulation of national policy to ensure national security, on policies to combat particular threats, and on the manner of implementing policy. The SSC included the President as chairperson; the Ministers of Defence, Foreign Affairs, Law and Order, and Justice; as well as high-ranking members of the security forces.[28] The SSC was established by legislation,[29] which enhanced its status and position. Through a 'silent coup', the 'securocrats' became

[27] Report of the Commission of Inquiry into Matters Relating to the Security of the State (Abridged) (the Potgieter Commission). (Government Printer, 1971), 33–4; Security Intelligence and State Security Council Act 64 of 1972.

[28] Gavin Cawthra, *Reconceptualising Security for the Twenty-First Century: South Africa's Experience in Remaking Defence* (Universidad Torcuato di Tella, 2000), 4; Justin Sylvester, 'Parliamentary Oversight of Defence: South Africa in the Democratic Era', Pakistan Institute of Legislative Development and Transparency, August 2011.

[29] State Security Council Act 64 of 1972.

the de facto Cabinet.[30] The SSC was supported by a secretariat staffed mostly by NIS members.[31]

The National Security Management System (NSMS) emerged in 1979 as a highly centralized and militarized bureaucratic structure to execute the SSC's policies. The NSMS was a hierarchy of geographically based units and subunits, with twelve Joint Management Centres (JMCs) ultimately reporting directly to the SSC.[32] Following the two elements of Total Strategy—security and socio-economic development—each NSMS entity at each level in the hierarchy comprised a security committee and a committee of economic and social affairs.

Political Transition: Forging an Integrated National Defence Force

Timing, Sequencing, and Participation By the Security Sector in Political Negotiations

The pressure on the South African government from opposition groups and armed resistance mounted throughout the 1980s. ANC-led guerrilla and sabotage activity rose from 19 incidents in 1980 to 136 in 1985.[33] Many of these incidents involved the destruction of the state's administrative assets, such as official buildings.[34] The government relied on the SADF and the SAP to respond to this pressure, and imposed a state of emergency from July 1985 to March 1986, and again from June 1986 until the start of constitutional negotiations in 1991. Emergency regulations made no distinction between the SAP and SADF, endowing the 'security forces' with sweeping powers of arrest, detention, and interrogation, and indemnifying them from sanction for their actions during the emergency.[35] The effect of the state of emergency was drastic. In 1983, 453 people were detained under security legislation and emergency regulations. In 1985 this number was nearly 8,000 people, and in 1986 an astonishing 29,132.[36]

[30] Laurie Nathan, 'The 1996 Defence White Paper: An Agenda for State Demilitarisation?' in Jacklyn Cock and Pemy McKenzie (eds) *From Defence to Development: Redirecting Military Resources in South Africa* (David Philip, 1998) 39, 51; Stott (note 14), 7; Stephen Ellis, 'Review Essay: Truth and Reconciliation Commission of South Africa Report, Volumes 1–5' (1998) 42 *Transformation* 57, 62.

[31] Deon Geldenhuys and Hennie Kotze, 'Aspects of Political Decision-Making in South Africa' (1983) 10 *Politikon* 33; Seegers (note 14), 166.

[32] Cawthra, *Policing South Africa* (note 17), 31–2.

[33] Tom Lodge, 'State of Exile: The African National Congress of South Africa' in Philip Frankel, Noam Pines, and Mark Swilling (eds), *State, Resistance and Change in South Africa* (Southern, 1988), 230; available at <https://www.jstor.org/stable/3991845?seq=1#metadata_info_tab_contents>.

[34] Seegers (note 14), 247–8.

[35] Cawthra, *Policing South Africa* (note 17), 29.

[36] South African Institute of Race Relations, *Race Relations Survey 1986* (SAIRR, 1986), 517.

During this period, disagreements emerged within the security establishment and within the NP government about the way forward. The SADF, for its part, objected to being used as a police force, arguing that troops were trained for combat rather than for maintaining internal law and order.[37] The SAP favoured the use of force to maintain law and order, and prioritized strikes against political opposition (i.e. the first element of Total Strategy) rather than establishing effective government capable of delivering socio-economic development (i.e. the second element of Total Strategy). Armoured vehicles designed for use in war zones began to patrol townships, curfews were imposed, meetings were banned or broken up, and troop cordons sealed troublesome areas. The security forces killed over 700 people between 1984 and 1986.[38]

The costs of policing the townships during the emergency were high. While the SAP claimed in 1988 that the ANC had come to accept that it could not win an armed struggle,[39] members of the NP and security establishment had come to realize that neither could the state win an armed struggle. In 1987, the Department of Constitutional Development and Planning, which played a leading role in the economic and social affairs committees of the NSMS, produced a document entitled *Ons Skrik vir Niks* [We Fear Nothing]. The document criticized the detention of opposition leaders, arguing instead for the unbanning of political organizations and the repeal of apartheid legislation like the Group Areas Act, which had become unenforceable. The SAP itself admitted that it did not have enough uniformed police officers to maintain law and order.[40]

The NIS, too, began to follow a different approach, gradually withdrawing from participation in the entities of the NSMS and thinking about long-term, macro-level resolution of conflict in South Africa rather than the daily security objectives of the NSMS, SAP, and SADF. By the end of the 1980s, the dominance of the SSC and the securocrats who staffed it had eroded, and in 1989 the Cabinet overruled an SSC decision for the first time.[41] As the SSC and the NSMS lost influence, P.W. Botha suffered a stroke, resigned, and was replaced as State President by F.W. de Klerk in August 1989. De Klerk had no background in or links to the SAP or SADF. By early 1990 de Klerk began to shift the balance of political power away from the securocrats. New rules stipulated that the SSC, while left in place, had to be staffed by elected politicians, leaving no place for career soldiers. A Cabinet Committee for Security Affairs (CCSA) was established as the site of decision-making power on security issues. General Magnus Malan, a career solider, was replaced as Minister of Defence by Roelf Meyer, a civilian and later the NP's chief negotiator.

37 General Jannie Geldenhuys, cited in Christopher Coker, *South Africa's Security Dilemmas* (Center for Strategic and International Studies, 1987). 14.

38 Cawthra, *Policing South Africa* (note 17), 33.

39 Annual Report of the Commissioner of the SAP (1988), quoted ibid., 35.

40 General P. J. Coetzee, speaking for the SAP in October 1986, quoted in Seegers (note 14), 249.

41 Cawthra, *Policing South Africa* (note 17), 36.

The portfolio was later held by Kobie Coetsee, the Minister of Justice from 1980 until 1993 who had met secretly with Mandela in hospital in 1985. The NSMS was also dismantled and replaced with a National Coordinating Mechanism focused on socio-economic development rather than security.[42]

The apartheid state's security forces thus played a central role both in the decision to enter into negotiations to end apartheid, by making it clear that continued suppression of armed opposition was unsustainable, and in the initiation of political talks between the government and the ANC. The first meeting official meeting between the ANC and the NP government took place in Cape Town from 2 to 4 May 1990, producing a roadmap for negotiations known as the Groote Schuur Minute. It set out plans for the release of political prisoners, the return of exiles under indemnity, and the repeal or amendment of security legislation. Relevant to the issues facing the security sector, the Minute recognized that MK was not a private army but was, rather, a politically directed military force under the formal command of the ANC leadership. The SADF took part in the Groote Schuur meetings, but was not included directly in any political negotiations for the next three years.[43]

After the framework for negotiations had been erected at Groote Schuur, the negotiations about constitutional transformation and security sector reform (SSR) largely diverged into two parallel streams. The SADF and MK began to meet bilaterally to discuss technical military issues arising from the Minute, mostly concerning the integration of the opposing armed forces.[44] The leadership of both armed forces had sought to split the negotiations into these separate streams because, although SADF and MK negotiators were in constant contact with their political principals, they were not confident that civilian political negotiators (Roelf Meyer for the NP and Cyril Ramaphosa for the ANC) had sufficient understanding of military matters to successfully protect their interests during negotiations.[45] For its part, the SADF stressed that it was a professional force, by definition disinterested in political affairs. Partisan politics within the SADF were forbidden by the statutes that established the SADF: as a result, the SADF could have no interest in participating as a party in political negotiations between the ANC and NP.[46]

While the constitutional negotiations focused on the broader issues of establishing a framework for transferring power and redefining the South African constitutional and political system, they did touch on the disestablishment of the SADF and the creation of a transitional peacekeeping force in the run-up to the April 1994 elections. Discussion of this issue during the constitutional negotiations

[42] Seegers (note 14), 267, quoting A.P. Stemmet, administrative head of the NSMS on 5 March 1990.
[43] Seegers (note 14), 272.
[44] Philip Frankel, *Soldiers in a Storm: The Armed Forces in South Africa's Democratic Transition* (Westview Press, 2000), 2.
[45] Ibid., 3.
[46] Seegers (note 14), 271–2.

necessarily involved members of the respective armed forces, especially as civilian leaders seemed increasingly incapable of managing violence outside the negotiating chamber.[47]

It must be emphasized too that there were several distinct armed forces in existence in South Africa in the early 1990s: MK and APLA were liberation armies engaged in an armed struggle against the state and its security forces, while the various 'homeland' police forces and armies operated in support of the homeland governments established and propped up by the South African government. Each of the armed forces had a different agenda, and it would be simplistic to ascribe a single set of coherent goals to 'the security sector'. Nevertheless, the security negotiations were dominated by two entities: the SADF and MK. Tensions and differences of opinions had existed between the SAP and the SADF since the mid-1980s, and in the early 1990s the SAP showed itself reluctant (or institutionally incapable) to participate in plans to secure the transition to democracy.[48]

The SADF and MK, moreover, agreed early on that the homeland police forces, as well as the other non-statutory forces like APLA would be largely excluded from the security bilaterals.[49] The TBVC military and police forces, and the other non-statutory forces such as APLA, did not make a distinct contribution to the process. Although the Transkei's leader (and leader of the Transkei Defence Force), General Bantu Holomisa, attempted to build support within the ANC, PAC, and SADF simultaneously, he eventually allied the Transkei Defence Force with MK. The other homeland security forces did the same.

The Armed Forces' Political Leverage

The conventional view within the SADF in 1989 was that the military was 'holding the umbrella' over the changes in the country, and that without the military watching from the wings, negotiations could not proceed.[50] Once negotiations began, however, neither the SADF nor MK suspended military operations. The threat of military options allowed both the NP and the ANC to strengthen their bargaining positions. The ANC, for example, formulated a military contingency plan known as 'Operation Vula' to be launched if negotiations failed. The guerrilla forces would remain in place until it was clear that the dismantling of the apartheid state was irreversible.[51] Similarly, de Klerk

[47] Ibid.

[48] Mark Shaw, 'Point of Order' in Steven Friedman and Doreen Atkinson (eds), *The Small Miracle* (Raven Press, 1994), 209–11; Frankel (note 44), 4.

[49] Frankel (note 44), 2.

[50] Deputy Minister of Law and Order (i.e. the civilian head of the police), 18 May 1989, quoted by Seegers (note 14), 251.

[51] Sparks (note 1), 122–3.

viewed the SADF as an insurance policy against an unfavourable negotiated outcome.[52]

In August 1990, Nelson Mandela announced the suspension of the armed struggle. By the early 1990s, as a result of both the government's reliance on the SADF and the suspension of the armed struggle, the SADF had significant autonomy. Its professed commitment to professionalism and non-partisanship, however, dictated that it would not participate directly in the constitutional negotiations, but it was able to insist that it negotiate directly with MK about the structure of the new, post-election defence force.

Amnesty

Amnesty was a critical issue in the constitutional process. Indeed, there was no way the constitutional negotiations would have gone ahead without an agreement on amnesty for the members of the security forces of the apartheid state and the armed forces of the ANC and other liberation organizations. On the issue of amnesty, more than any other in the transition, the demands of the armed forces on both sides influenced the actions and discussion of the political principals. The principle of a general amnesty was agreed at an early stage between MK and the SADF during the security negotiations, but the details were left to subsequent articulation.

Once the general principle was accepted that some form of amnesty would preclude Nuremburg-style trials in post-election South Africa, the security negotiations were able to proceed to discuss the technical details of integration, peacekeeping, and reorganization.[53] The security negotiators essentially left the details of amnesty to be worked out by the political actors at the constitutional negotiations. The ANC in particular, however, was not prepared to tie itself to a specific amnesty deal, insisting instead that these details should be worked out by a democratically elected legislature. Nonetheless, the broad outlines of this amnesty were included in what has come to be known as the 'post-amble' to the interim Constitution, in a section headed 'National Unity and Reconciliation':

> In order to advance such reconciliation and reconstruction, amnesty shall be granted in respect of acts, omissions and offences associated with political objectives and committed in the course of the conflicts of the past. To this end, Parliament under this Constitution shall adopt a law determining a firm cut-off date, which shall be a date after 8 October 1990 and before 6 December 1993,

[52] Sylvester (note 28), 13; Peter Batchelor and Susan Willett, *Disarmament and Defence: Industrial Adjustment in South Africa* (Oxford University Press, 1998), 56.

[53] Batchelor and Willett (note 52), 25.

and providing for the mechanisms, criteria and procedures, including tribunals, if any, through which such amnesty shall be dealt with at any time after the law has been passed.

The Promotion of National Unity and Reconciliation Act 34 of 1995 established South Africa's Truth and Reconciliation Commission (TRC). It provided that amnesty would be granted by the Amnesty Committee of the TRC on an individual basis, provided that the act for which amnesty was sought was politically motivated and that the applicant made a full disclosure of all the relevant facts.[54] The TRC was an important compromise between prosecution and blanket amnesty, necessary to convince security forces on both sides to go along with political transition but still allow for the prosecution of members of the security forces who did not meet the requirements for amnesty. The TRC was intended neither as a mechanism of prosecutorial fact-finding nor as an exercise in providing oversight over members of the security forces during the transition. Rather, the TRC process aimed to provide an accounting of the atrocities of the apartheid era, as part of the process of national reconciliation and rebuilding.

Design and Choice of Laws

During the negotiations, the NP and the ANC were for the most part in agreement that the post-election security sector should not have the influence that it had held in policy-making through the SSC, and in administration through the NSMS. The ANC set out its position in a 1992 policy document entitled *Ready to Govern*. This document committed the ANC to a handful of core principles for the security sector, including:[55]

- National security and personal security shall be sought primarily through efforts to meet the social, political, economic, and cultural needs of the people.

[54] Promotion of National Unity and Reconciliation Act 34 of 1995. Not all parties were happy with the Act, and the Truth and Reconciliation Commission it established: the Azanian People's Organization (AZAPO) challenged the constitutionality of the Act on the grounds that the grant of amnesty for crimes committed infringed the right of the victims of those crimes to have justiciable dispute settled by a court of law (s. 22 of the interim Constitution). The Constitutional Court agreed that the grant of amnesty may infringe this right, but that such infringement was justifiable in terms of the general limitations clause of the interim Constitution (s. 33) in order to promote national unity and reconciliation (*AZAOPO and Others v President of the Republic of South Africa* 1996 (8) BCLR 1015 (CC); 1996 (4) SA 672 (CC)).

[55] *Ready to Govern: ANC Policy Guidelines for a Democratic South Africa* (1992), section Q (copy on file).

- The security forces should be 'bound by the principles of civil supremacy and subject to public scrutiny and open debate' and should be 'accountable and answerable to the public though a democratically elected parliament'.
- Security institutions should 'respect human rights, non-racialism and democracy'.
- The security forces should be politically non-partisan and 'reflect the national and gender composition of South African society'.
- The Defence Force 'shall be defensive in its character, orientation and strategy, and its force levels will be adjusted accordingly'.
- The Defence Force 'shall not be engaged in any internal policing role except in extreme circumstances and where so authorised specifically by parliament', and 'the primary function of policing will be the prevention of crime and to guarantee the personal security of citizens'.
- The police force 'shall be structured as a non-militarised service function'.

The ANC's principles of SSR were based on an understanding of 'security' that encompassed developmental security as well as security against aggression. Underdevelopment, poverty, lack of democratic participation, and the violation of human rights were all recognized as threats to security.[56] There is a superficial similarity in this approach to the second element of the apartheid government's Total Strategy approach—although while the NP government had sought to militarize all aspects of the state, the ANCs approach was to demilitarize and broaden the concept of security. Perhaps because of this superficial similarity, but also because the NP's security strategists had developed expertise in protecting a minority government rather than in macro-level policy development, planning, and evaluation,[57] the NP did little to develop a competing or alternative policy vision for the post-apartheid security sector.

Indeed, de Klerk's actions in 'desecuritizing' the state tend to suggest that the NP government was similarly committed to at least the first of the ANC's *Ready to Govern* principles, and wanted to ensure that the security forces did not have significant influence over policy-making or bureaucratic administration. Together with sidelining the SSC and dismantling the NSMS, de Klerk took steps to end conscription, reduced military spending by 16 per cent in both the 1990–91 and 1991–92 budgets, and shifted the NIS from the portfolio of the Minister of Justice to the President's office.[58] The parties negotiating the transition to a new national defence force had to decide on the legal mechanism to effect these changes from the apartheid legal system to the new, integrated, national defence force.

[56] Annette Seegers, 'The New Security in Democratic South Africa: A Cautionary Tale' (2010) 10 *Conflict, Security and Development* 263, 270.
[57] Ibid., 273.
[58] Seegers (note 14), 267.

Security Sector Legal Framework Prior to the Transition

Although the security sector in apartheid South Africa held considerable influence in policy-making through the SSC, and in the bureaucracy through the NSMS, this influence was never cemented in the Constitution. Rather, the logic of Total Strategy ensured that the civilian NP government relied heavily on the security forces for support, and ultimately for policy guidance. There was never a serious concern that the military or police forces would remove the civilian authorities. On the contrary, the SADF made claims to being a professional and apolitical military uninterested in political intervention which, even if it had held such ambitions, was a force of citizen-soldiers that did not have the manpower to pursue independent political objectives.[59]

Nonetheless, the SADF's influence in policy was facilitated by the absence of constitutional rules governing its operations or structures for effective civilian oversight. The Defence Act 44 of 1957 was enacted to regulate the defence force, but South Africa's 1961 Republican Constitution said nothing about the military. Further, a 1966 commission of inquiry recommended that the chief of the SADF replace the civilian Secretary of Defence as the head and chief accounting officer of the Department of Defence. At the same time, the Minister of Defence was removed from the chain of command and made responsible only for matters concerning defence policy.[60] The result was that operational command of the SADF was in the hands of the chief of the SADF, who reported directly to Cabinet. The 1961 Constitution, moreover, established no formal mechanisms through which parliament could exercise oversight of the executive, much less the SADF itself. In any case, the National Party's dominance of parliament meant that it rarely challenged the government.

Moreover, this left the apartheid government free to amend the Defence Act as needed to achieve its security objectives. In 1974, an amendment criminalized anti-conscription activities,[61] and another in 1976 retroactively authorized the deployment of conscripted servicemen abroad without Cabinet approval.[62] The 1976 amendments put the determination of whether threats to the country justified the deployment of the armed forces in the 'opinion of the State President'.[63]

One of de Klerk's first acts as State President in 1989 was to overhaul the existing Cabinet and executive structure to remove the channels of influence that the security sector had held. De Klerk has been criticized, however, for not taking these reforms far enough: elements of the NSMS were left in place up until 1994,

59 Ibid., 271–2.
60 Sylvester (note 28), 11–12.
61 Defence Act 44 of 1957, s. 121.
62 Ibid., s. 95. See also Seegers (note 14), 212.
63 Defence Act 44 of 1957, s. 1(1).

ensuing that at least some of the autonomy and influence of the SADF and SAP was protected.[64]

With respect to the SAP during apartheid, its powers and functions were set out, as with the SADF, in an ordinary piece of legislation, the Police Act 7 of 1958. This statute, and numerous amendments made to it over the years by parliament, conferred on the SAP the broad powers that the NP government considered necessary for the SAP to assist in the suppression of opposition to the government.

The apartheid intelligence service, the NIS, succeeded the Bureau of State Security established by the Security Intelligence and State Security Council Act 64 of 1972. As with the SADF and the SAP, the intelligence service was subject only to the provisions of ordinary legislation, which in the context of a system of parliamentary supremacy, allowed the government to adapt the powers, scope, and mission of the security services as necessary.

Restructuring of the Security Services During the Transition

Defence force

In March and April 1993, members of the SADF, South African Air Force, and MK met openly to discuss the future of the armed forces. Representing the apartheid security sector were the chiefs of the SADF, Army, Air Force, DMI, and NIS. Representing MK were the commander and chief of staff of MK, the chief and adjutant chief of DIS, the head of the ANC's legal team, and Nicholas Haysom, a noted constitutional lawyer and activist.[65]

At this first meeting, the government security forces adopted the position that MK personnel returning to South Africa should place themselves under the control of the existing military command structures. MK rejected this, accepting that while its forces and armaments would have to be subjected to oversight and control by external structures, this should be the multi-party TEC that that political negotiators had proposed, rather than the SADF. Further, MK adopted the position that the SADF should itself submit to the direction and control of the TEC. This evolved into an agreement between the sides that a subcouncil of defence would be formed within the TEC to exercise control over the security force, even as the SADF and MK remained distinct entities.

From 26 May to 10 June 1993, a second round of talks between security leadership of the two sides took place. Regarding command and control of the distinct, pre-integration forces, agreement was reached on the establishment of a Joint Military Coordinating Council (JMCC), under the authority of the TEC's

[64] Seegers (note 14), 267.
[65] Frankel (note 44), 7.

subcouncil on defence (SCD). While the security leadership concluded the agreement, frequent consultations with political principals in both the NP and ANC took place.[66] However, since the TEC was slated to come online only in October 1993, and the JMCC would emerge only in January 1994, there was little time for coherent command structures to develop.

The SADF's primary objectives in designing a post-apartheid defence force were (i) political stabilization leading up to elections; (ii) a non-political and professional post-election defence force protected against a return to the Total Strategy and securitized structure of the apartheid years; (iii) adherence to international standards; (iv) a two-tier structure distinguishing between full-time and part-time forces; and (v) amnesty. MK was committed to (i) an integrated defence force, to the command positions of which MK would have access according to the general principles of power-sharing being articulated in the constitutional negotiations; (ii) career mobility for MK troops in the lower ranks; (iii) the institutionalization of values of democracy and non-racialism in the new defence force; and (iv) amnesty for members of MK.[67] In this regard, at least, the sides reached agreement that the new national defence force would be founded on values of civilian supremacy over the military and civilian oversight, constitutional accountability to elected officials, adherence to the principle of representation, and having a non-political nature, and respect for human rights.[68]

These agreements were subsequently reflected in the Transitional Executive Council Act 151 of 1993. The SCD was mandated to 'oversee any planning, preparation and training for a future South African defence force' (section 16(2)(g)), and was to be kept informed on a continuous basis of all activities of each armed force in the country (section 16(2)(a) and (b)). All armed forces in the country—statutory and non-statutory—were compelled to recognize the authority of the SCD if they wished to be represented on it and participate in its operation (section 16(1)(ii), read with section 4(1)(b)). Importantly, the command structures of the armed forces were to remain independent on routine matters of internal administration and day-to-day management, but subject to the monitoring and oversight of the SCD (section 16(5), read with section 13(2)(b)). Importantly, the deployment of troops by the SADF was not a 'routine' matter, and was thus not a decision the SADF leadership could take without TEC approval. This ensured mutual monitoring of opposing armed forces through the mechanism of the SCD.[69]

The TEC Act further authorized the establishment of the JMCC, which became operational in January 1994. It was headed by the chief of the SADF and MK chief of staff. The SADF welcomed the JMCC as a tool for shaping the post-election

66 Ibid., 11.

67 Ibid., 20–3.

68 Report of the Transitional Executive Council Sub-Council on Defence, Working Group 2 (2 June 1993), cited in Frankel (note 44), 22.

69 Frankel (note 44), 32–3.

defence force to its advantage as far as possible before elections, while MK preferred to delay taking binding decisions on matters of defence until after the elections, when it anticipated it would have greater leeway as an electoral winner. As it turned out, most decisions on details were delayed until after the elections, in order to reach quick decisions on the more pressing matter of securing peaceful elections.[70]

The South African National Defence Force (SANDF) officially replaced the SADF at midnight on the evening of 26 April 1994. When all South Africans went to the polls for the first time on 27 April 1994, it was under the watch of the brand new SANDF.

Police

Since the ANC did not have a police force, the question of integration into the SAP did not arise. Reorganization of the SAP had already begun in the late 1980s, after a commission of inquiry: the SB was disbanded and its officers moved into the Criminal Investigation Branch, the riot squads were scythed off from the Uniform Branch and reformed as the Internal Stability Division, a community policing branch was constituted, and a Police Board was appointed, including civilians and other non-SAP experts, to investigate police misconduct.[71]

The biggest police-related issue that affected negotiations was the status of the KwaZulu Police force (KZP). KwaZulu was a semi-autonomous Bantustan headed by Chief Mangosuthu Buthelezi of the Inkatha movement (later the Inkatha Freedom Party or IFP). Buthelezi was also the KwaZulu Minister of Police. The KZP was in essence little more than a branch of the SAP, and was commanded by officers seconded from the SAP. By the early 1990s, it had a force of around 4,000. The KwaZulu and Natal region saw significant political violence in the early 1990s, which the KZP was nominally mandated to address. However, a commission of inquiry headed by Judge Richard Goldstone, who would later sit on South Africa's Constitutional Court, found that the SAP and KZP had been complicit in the violence, often participating directly in the use of force against opponents of Inkatha (including the ANC and MK) and refusing to arrest or charge members of Inkatha for their role in violence. Evidence emerged that the SB had trained members of KZP at bases outside South Africa and supplied arms to KZP.[72]

The IFP refused to surrender control of the KZP in the run-up to elections, on the argument that it could not prepare for an election while engaged in a war against political violence. This demand was effectively met in the 2 June 1993

[70] Ibid., 35–7.

[71] Seegers (note 14), 275.

[72] Second Interim Report of the Commission of Inquiry Regarding the Prevention of Violence and Intimidation (Goldstone Commission), quoted by Cawthra, *Policing South Africa* (note 17), 174; ibid., 66.

agreement of a TEC working group that existing KZP security forces would remain in place until after the election. This was sufficient to placate Buthelezi, who withdrew the IFP from political negotiations but accepted that elections would go ahead in April 1994.

Intelligence

Neither the NIS nor the ANC's DIS was concerned about issues stemming from integration: these two organizations had been in contact since the mid-1980s, and were agreed on integration after the elections.[73] The primary concern of both organizations was to overcome a common enemy: the Army's Department of Military Intelligence (DMI). The coalescence of NIS and DIS interests enabled the two to dominate discussions about the future intelligence services. The NIS and the DIS strongly supported the merger of the two services into an integrated service, with separate divisions focusing on external and domestic intelligence.

The Position Under the 1996 Constitution

Unlike the apartheid constitutions, the 1996 Constitution is supreme, and all law and conduct inconsistent with it is unconstitutional and invalid (section 2). The 1996 Constitution also sets out principles that broadly govern the organization and mandate of the security services. Section 199(1) provides that the security services consist of a single defence force, single police service, and intelligence services established in terms of the Constitution. While section 199(4) does provide that the security services must be structured in terms of national legislation, leaving it somewhat to the national legislature to determine the details of the various security services' structures, sections 200–04, 205–08, and 209–10 set out specific rules for the mandate, command structure, political responsibility, and civilian oversight of the defence force, police service, and intelligence services, respectively. A member of Cabinet is responsible for the direction of each of the services (sections 201(1), 206(1), and 209(2)).

Unlike under the apartheid constitutions, the national legislature no longer has the freedom to alter the mandate, structure, or rules governing the security services by ordinary legislation. It is worth setting out briefly how each of the security services transitioned out of the apartheid security state into the democratic era, and noting the legislation that structures and controls each service as envisaged by the 1996 Constitution.

[73] Seegers (note 14), 280–1.

With respect to the SANDF, the 1957 Defence Act was repealed and replaced by the Defence Act 42 of 2002, which is the legislation that now regulates and governs the SANDF. Among other things, the Act sets out the command structure of the SANDF, establishes the Department of Defence, regulates the use of the SANDF outside and within the borders of the Republic, and sets out the powers and functions of the SANDF and its various officers. It does so within and subject to the provisions of the 1996 Constitution.

With respect to the police, the South African Police Service Act 68 of 1995 'provides for the establishment, regulation and control of the South African Police Service' (SAPS). The Act continues the trends begun towards the end of the apartheid era, establishing a civilian secretariat of police to monitor and evaluate the performance of the SAPS and report back to the member of Cabinet responsible for the police.

Finally, with respect to the intelligence services, the disparate pre-transition services have been absorbed into a single State Security Agency (SSA) established by the Intelligence Services Act 65 of 2002. This consolidation of the NIS and DIS, along with PAC's Pan African Security Service and the intelligence services of Venda, Transkei, and Bophuthatswana, was effected by the Intelligence Services Act 38 of 1994, the National Strategic Intelligence Act 39 of 1994, and the Committee of Members of Parliament on and Inspectors-General of Intelligence Act 40 of 1994 (now the Intelligence Services Oversight Act). The division of labour between the two was defined by the National Strategic Intelligence Act. The South African Secret Service and the National Intelligence Agency have since been absorbed into a single entity, the SSA, established by the Intelligence Services Act 65 of 2002. The Act also establishes the South African National Academy of Intelligence in order to provide training and qualification for the intelligence agencies or department.

Civilian and Social Oversight

Unlike the apartheid era, the interim and 1996 Constitutions provide a set of rules and principles that govern the operation, status, and structure of the security services. Two principles run through the constitutional framework: (i) respect for human rights and the rule of law, and (ii) civilian control and oversight of the security services and accountability to elected officials. With respect to civilian oversight itself, the 1996 Constitution contains more specific protections. Section 199 provides:

> (7) Neither the security services, nor any of their members, may, in the performance of their functions—
> (a) prejudice a political party interest that is legitimate in terms of the Constitution; or
> (b) further, in a partisan manner, any interest of a political party.

(8) To give effect to the principles of transparency and accountability, multi-party parliamentary committees must have oversight of all security services in a manner determined by national legislation or the rules and orders of Parliament.

The sections relevant to each security force provide that a member of Cabinet will be responsible for the direction of each service, and that parliament must have oversight of their activities through multi-party parliamentary committees.[74] Under this broad constitutional framework, statutory frameworks have been established for the control and oversight of each of the security forces.

Defence

Section 202(1) of the 1996 Constitution provides that the President, 'as head of the national executive', is Commander-in-Chief of the SANDF. This suggests that executive decisions about the command of the SANDF are taken in Cabinet, and are in theory full Cabinet decisions. In this light, the command of the SANDF must be exercised in accordance with the directions of the member of Cabinet responsible for defence, under the authority of the President (section 202(2)). A civilian secretariat for defence must be established by legislation, and function under the direction of the member of Cabinet responsible for defence (section 204). The Constitution requires in addition that the President report promptly and in appropriate detail to parliament when the defence force is employed (section 201(3)).

A 1995 amendment to the Defence Act of 1957 established the Defence Secretariat for the first time.[75] The 2002 Defence Act states that civilians are responsible for determining defence policy, which the SANDF executes faithfully and without prejudice or partisanship, and that the Secretariat ensures democratic and civilian management of, and enhances parliamentary and ministerial control over, the SANDF. Section 2 of the Act provides that the SANDF will operate on the principles of non-partisanship, civilian control and direction, and a commitment to fundamental rights.

The Secretary of Defence, appointed by the Minister of Defence, may not be a member of the SANDF (section 7(3)). The civilian Secretary is the Head of the Department of Defence, its chief accounting office, and the principal advisor to the Minister on policy matters. The Secretary must monitor compliance with policies and orders issued by the Minister, and reports to the Minister' (section 8(f)).

[74] Constitution of the Republic of South Africa, 1996, ss. 199(8), 201(1), 206(1), and 209(2). The committees must be joint committees of Senate and the National Assembly.

[75] Defence Act (1957), as amended by the Defence Amendment Act 72 of 1995.

The parliamentary Joint Standing Committee on Defence (JSCD) was established by section 228 of the interim Constitution.[76] Although the JSCD still exists, the 1996 Constitution makes no mention of it, and its continued existence rests in the discretion of parliament. Indeed, since the JSCD was largely a transitional body, it has been far less active in recent years.[77] This is explained also by the fact that the Portfolio Committee on Defence, a separate committee of the National Assembly, has assumed much of parliament's oversight functions of defence. The portfolio committees deal with a range of issues within a single portfolio of government affairs. The Defence Portfolio Committee scrutinizes legislation dealing with defence; maintains oversight of the Cabinet's actions, including the implementation of legislation; and inquires into matters of defence policy.[78]

A third parliamentary committee in this family is the Standing Committee on Public Accounts (SCOPA). Established by Part 10 of the National Assembly Rules, SCOPA is mandated to oversee the financial affairs of all executive organs of state, and not only those related to defence. SCOPA was originally praised for its independence and assiduousness in the fulfilment of its mandate.[79] After it investigated possible irregularities in the South African government's Strategic Defence Package ('the Arms Deal'), however, it was publicly chastised by members of government and the Portfolio Committee on Defence, and its composition was altered to reflect the ANC's preferences.[80]

Police

The ANC's commitment during negotiations to a clear institutional and functional distinction between the police and defence forces was carried through without controversy to the interim and 1996 Constitutions.[81] The disestablishment of the various special police forces (including homeland and municipal police forces), begun during the negotiation process, was institutionalized in the 1996 Constitution's provision that there be a single police service.

The 1996 Constitution provides also that the police service (SAPS) must be structured to function at national, provincial, and, where appropriate, the local level. A member of Cabinet must be responsible for policing and determine policing policy after consulting provincial governments and taking into account policing priorities as determined by provincial governments. The provinces, in turn, exercise some decentralized control over police functions (section 206). The

76 Cawthra (note 28), 8.
77 Ibid.
78 National Assembly Rules, rule 201(1).
79 Paul Holden, *The Arms Deal in Your Pocket* (Jonathan Ball, 2008), 43.
80 Ibid., 57.
81 Gavin Cawthra, *Securing South Africa's Democracy* (Palgrave Macmillan, 1997), 86.

delegation of power to provinces was most likely to have been an attempt to satisfy the binding principle set out in the interim Constitution that the provinces have no fewer powers for providing provincial services than under the interim Constitution.[82]

Control is exercised by a National Commissioner, appointed by the President. Neither the Constitution nor legislation specify that the Commissioner must or must not be a member of the SAPS (section 207).

Section 208 provides that a civilian secretariat of police services must be established by national legislation to function under the Cabinet member responsible for policing. Section 3 of the South African Police Services Act 68 of 1995 provides that the Secretariat is responsible for functions necessary or expedient to ensure civilian oversight of the SAPS and monitoring and reporting to the Minister on the implementation of police policy. These functions were greatly expanded in 2011 by the Civilian Secretariat for Police Service Act 2 of 2011 (section 6(1)). The Secretary for the Police Service, appointed by the Minister to head the civilian Secretariat, must not be a member or a former member of police service.

Intelligence

Section 209(1) of the 1996 Constitution provides only that the President may establish intelligence services in terms of legislation. The SSA was established by the Intelligence Services Act 65 of 2002 to encompass the existing intelligence agencies.

Section 210(b) of the 1996 Constitution provides that national legislation must provide for the civilian monitoring of intelligence services by an inspector appointed by the President and confirmed by a vote supported by two-thirds of the National Assembly. The Office of the Inspector General for Intelligence (OIGI) is established by the Intelligence Services Oversight Act 40 of 1994. Further, this Act establishes the parliamentary Joint Standing Committee on Intelligence (JSCI), consisting of fifteen members appointed on the basis of party representation in parliament. The statutory establishment of the JSCI purports to offer it some protection against the kind of political manipulation that befell SCOPA; however, the Act allows on the other hand that the JSCI may conduct its business in secret.

The role of the OIGI is to monitor the activities of the intelligence agencies and intelligence divisions of the SAPS and SANDF, and to submit reports to the JSCI as well as to Cabinet. Although section 210(b) of the Constitution provides that legislation must provide for the 'civilian monitoring' of intelligence activities, the

[82] Constitutional Principle XXI(6), Sched. 4 to the interim Constitution.

Intelligence Services Oversight Act does not stipulate that the Inspector General must not be a member of the intelligence services.

The National Intelligence Agency, however, has 'established for itself a record of misbehaviour in domestic affairs', including:

> interference with the work of the Justice Ministry; interfering with the work of the Safety and Security Ministry; spying on government officials and private individuals; interfering in the so-called succession battle over the presidential office.[83]

As a result, a Ministerial Review Commission on Intelligence was established to strengthen oversight and controls, among other things.[84] The Commission points out that the secrecy that surrounds the work of the JSCI, the secrecy of ministerial regulations that govern the intelligence services, and secret budgets and secret Auditor General's reports, are inconsistent with the principles of transparency and accountability outlined in the Constitution.[85]

Conclusion

In the twenty years since the end of apartheid in South Africa, while there have been significant isolated cases of abuses committed by the security services, there has been no ongoing pattern of abuse. Moreover, in the few cases that have occurred there has usually been an accounting of the incident to the civilian authorities. This concluding section draws important lessons and warnings from these cases of abuse, as well as from the largely successful experience of civilian control and oversight of the security services in South Africa since 1994.

First, the SANDF has not involved itself in politics or pursued its own political agenda. The attempt to desecuritize the structures of government in South Africa, and remove the soldiers from politics to the barracks, was successful. This outcome is surprising to the extent that one might have expected a military so closely involved in the formulation of policy, and central to the initiation of political negotiations, to have sought to retain a hand in post-transition politics. However, the SADF during apartheid was opposed to its deployment as a force for domestic stability, and preferred to define its mission as the defence of the country's national borders. This external orientation is consistent with the SADF's leadership's insistence that it was a force of professional soldiers, unconcerned with matters of politics or policy. The SADF had been brought into the policy arena through

[83] Seegers (note 56), 274.
[84] Ministerial Review Commission on Intelligence, Intelligence in a Constitutional Democracy: Final Report to the Minister for Intelligence Services (10 September 2008).
[85] Ibid., 57–8.

the establishment of the SSC, only because its input was crucial to continued suppression of apartheid's opponents. Once it was no longer needed for this purpose, the SADF was quite prepared to exit the halls of policy. The professionalism of the SADF before the transition, and the SADF's own sense of mission and mandate—even if that mission and mandate was altered by a government that was forced to rely on the army to prop up its failing policies—are an important factor in why the SADF was effectively removed from politics, and why the SANDF has remained distant from politics ever since.

It is also relevant that the SADF and MK had sufficient autonomy during the transitional period to hold their own negotiations. The fact that the security negotiations and the political negotiations took place in parallel helped to shield the military from the influence of their political counterparts and ensure that the close link that had grown up during the operation of the SSC between the military and the government was broken.

The experience of the police and the intelligence services has been less than exemplary. A number of 'spy scandals' have emerged in recent years, highlighting the abuse of the intelligence services for political motivations. The intelligence services have been deployed by members of the respective forces without the knowledge of their superiors or of the civilian leadership of each institution, to spy on political opponents and orchestrate political outcomes favourable to them or to their political superiors. In the wake of these scandals, a Ministerial Review Commission on Intelligence was established to strengthen oversight and controls, among other things.[86] The SAPS attracted the national and international spotlight in August 2012 for the shooting of thirty-four mineworkers at Marikana. The massacre forms part of a trend of increasing police brutality over the last ten years.[87] While both the Marikana incident and the spy scandals have come to light and are or have been the subject of civilian commissions of inquiry, the concern is that these abuses occurred because of a lack of civilian oversight in the first place.

The failures of civilian oversight of the intelligence community and the SAPS can be traced to two primary factors. The first is that the system of parliamentary oversight may fail to be effective in the context of a legislature dominated by a single party, and where rules requiring multi-party oversight committees are open to manipulation by the dominant party. SCOPA's failure highlights these dangers.

Second, the procedures by which the heads and senior leadership of the security services are appointed are important. Where a dominant political party has a largely unfettered discretion to appoint these senior office-bearers, there is

[86] Ministerial Review Commission on Intelligence (note 84).

[87] David Smith, 'South Africa Reports of Police Brutality More than Tripled in the Last Decade', *The Guardian*, 22 August 2013.

a greater likelihood that members of parliament belonging to or sympathetic to the dominant party will be reluctant to hold the party's deployees to account for their actions as leaders of the security services. However, even in the context of a dominant-party democracy, if the leaders of the security services are not seen as a political appointee of a single party, there may be greater propensity to hold them to account to parliament more willingly.

South Africa's successes in breaking the link between the security services and the government rests largely on a robust set of constitutional rules, reflected in statutory provisions and regulations that must adhere to the principles of the Constitution. The fact that the military removed itself from the discussions leading to the composition of these rules is significant. The failures of oversight can largely be attributed to the ease with which systems of oversight have been manipulated to suit the ruling party, and the unconstrained propensity of politicians to appoint security officials over whom politicians are themselves reluctant to exercise oversight. In theory, it would not be difficult to entrench the rules for appointment or the parliamentary committee system in legislation to guard against these breakdowns in oversight. However, the making of these changes now depends on political will that may be lacking.

PART III
POST-AUTHORITARIAN REFORM
Ruptures, Conflict, and Managed Transitions

Part III presents a snapshot of five countries in the Arab region, in different stages of transition at the time of writing following the Arab Spring in 2010–11. Egypt and Tunisia both adopted new constitutions in 2014, following widespread popular uprisings against long-standing authoritarian regimes. In both cases, a secret police and intelligence establishment previously committed to the prior regime eventually turned on it and forced out the authoritarian ruler. While Tunisia stands as a model of success in the region, Egypt has arguably experienced a slide backwards into authoritarianism. There are key lessons to be learned from comparing these two cases. In Yemen and Libya, civil insurrection rages on with no clear path to constitutional democracy. In Iraq, the collapse of military forces in the face of ISIS indicates that dismantling the military machinery that supported an oppressive regime, as happened at the hands of the United States, must be managed carefully lest the efficacy of the security services is undermined. Each of these case studies offers lessons for security sector reform following a sudden or violent rupture with the previous regime.

8

Constitutional Reform Processes and Security Sector Reform

Principles for Practice: Iraq Case Study

Zaid al-Ali

Following a troubled history through much of the twentieth century, Iraq's security forces quickly and easily accepted the principle of civilian oversight following the 2003 war. That principle was codified in a number of legal documents, most importantly in the 2005 Constitution. However, despite that important advance, Iraq today suffers from a number of important difficulties, many of which are perhaps as challenging as any of those from which it has suffered during its past.

Iraq's political system is now under the control of a constellation of political parties and operates on the basis of consensus. The 2005 Constitution establishes a parliamentary system that leaves no-one in overall charge, and that provides little guidance on how the security services should be administered. Meanwhile, the legislative process has essentially broken down, leaving security forces without much of the legislation that they need to govern their mandates and duties. In addition, a plethora of security institutions and bodies have been created since 2003, each of which is under the control of specific political parties, most of which are deeply suspicious of their rivals from other parties. This is compounded by the fact that most of these parties—many motivated by greed and corruption—lack a unified vision and a sense of duty to improve governance in their country.[1] The result is a deeply dysfunctional security framework that lacks a governing philosophy and in which individual institutions generally do not cooperate with each other or share information.

Hence, although Iraq's security institutions all function under civilian control and oversight, the civilians in question are not representative and are not transparent in their activities. The Army, the police, and intelligence services are all extremely vulnerable to being used for partisan purposes, something which has itself damaged the state and the security sector's legitimacy in the eyes of ordinary people.

[1] See Zaid al-Ali, 'Iraq's Rot Starts at the Top', *The New York Times*, 10 August 2014; Zaid al-Ali, 'The Only Way to Solve Iraq's Political Crisis', *The New York Times*, 5 May 2016; and Martin Chulov, 'Post-War Iraq: "Everybody Is Corrupt, from Top to Bottom. Including Me"', *The Guardian*, 19 February 2016.

Background

From the Ottoman period to the monarchy

The territory that eventually became Iraq had been part of the Ottoman Empire for several centuries. In 1912, there were 1,200 officers of Iraqi origin in the Ottoman Empire.[2] These individuals were educated in the Empire's military academies, which had been modernized by German officers, some of whom also lectured at the academies. The curriculum reflected the ideologies that grew from Kaiser Wilhelm II's expansionist and militaristic ambitions. Many of these Iraqi officers were heavily influenced by the debates and developments that they witnessed in Istanbul before the start of the war. The Young Turk movement advocated in favour of more ethnocentric politics which would place their own ethnic group at the centre of all policy-making within the Ottoman state.[3]

After the Ottoman Empire's defeat and subsequent collapse at the end of the First World War, many of its officers who were of Iraqi origin returned home and were joined by some officers from other Arab countries. Iraq was then under British occupation, and the new authorities had decided to install a monarchy in Baghdad and to crown their wartime ally Faisal Bin Hussein as King. As the newly established Iraqi officers were set up in their positions, they set out to influence the state's policy in important ways.[4] In that sense, Iraq is perhaps unique in that the seeds of its militaristic tendencies were planted even before the modern Iraqi state was created.

The young Arab (and Iraqi) officers carried many of the discussions that they had been party to in Istanbul back to Baghdad after the war, eventually adapting them to advocate in favour of a pan-Arab ideology. A national educational curriculum was established to imbue Iraq's youth with a sense of belonging to a much larger nation, and with significant hostility towards France and, especially, the United Kingdom as colonial powers that conspired to prevent Arab unity. Eventually, notions such as sacrifice, militarism, and violence were deliberately incorporated in

[2] See Ahmed Hashim, 'Saddam Husayin and Civil–Military Relations in Iraq: The Question for Legitimacy and Power' (2003) 57(1) *Middle East Journal* 13.

[3] For a discussion on the evolution that took place within the Ottoman Empire during this period, see Andrew Mango, *Ataturk: The Biography of the Founder of Modern Turkey* (Overlook Press, 2002).

[4] Perhaps the most prominent individual from within that category, Sati' al-Husri, an Ottoman officer whose family originated from Aleppo, Syria, arrived in 1920. He was appointed Director General of the Ministry of Education and was instrumental in establishing Iraq's modern educational system. Al-Husri was eventually sidelined and other officials pushed the educational system in favour of a more overt form of militantism. William L. Cleveland, *The Making of an Arab Nationalist: Ottomanism and Arabism in the Life and Thought of Sati' al-Husri* (Princeton University Press, 1971).

the national curriculum's narrative.[5] These developments imbued the population with a deep sense of chauvinism and pro-military tendencies that would eventually have a deep impact on Iraqi society.

Throughout the 1920s and the 1930s, senior government circles debated the role that the new Iraqi Army should play. There was agreement that the Army should be used to inculcate a sense of national identity among the country's various and disparate groups, but there was also significant realism about the challenges that had to be faced to satisfy that objective. Amongst other things, many of the country's large tribal confederations rejected any form of national conscription as an affront against their own authority.[6] In addition, the tribes were sufficiently well armed to defend themselves against any attempt to impose the state's writ by force.[7] Finally, in the 1920s and 1930s, as a result of its close association to the United Kingdom and its interests, the new Iraqi state's security forces did not enjoy the type of popular legitimacy that would have allowed it to influence the popular discourse on issues relating to identity.

Following its repression of the Assyrian revolts in 1933,[8] the Army began asserting its role as the guardian of national unity. For the first time, Iraqis from various parts of the country volunteered to join its ranks. Imbued with greater self-confidence in its own role, the Army forced seven changes in government between 1936 and 1941, culminating in the Rashid Ali coup in 1941, which had as part of its objective the deposing of the Iraqi monarchy and bringing an end to British influence.[9] The United Kingdom invaded in April 1941, defeated the putschists, reinstated the monarchy, and reoccupied the country militarily until 1947. During the following period, British officials paid closer attention to the workings of Iraqi institutions. They dismissed a significant part of the military's officer class and exiled some of the individuals who were responsible for establishing the national

[5] Sami Shawkat, who also served as the Ministry of Education's Director General in the 1930s, regularly praised the virtues of the Army and of military life. See Reeva Spector Simon, *Iraq between the Two Wars: The Militarist Origins of Tyranny* (Columbia University Press, 2004).

[6] See Hanna Batatu, *The Old Social Classes and the Revolutionary Movements of Iraq: A Study of Iraq's Old Landed and Commercial Classes and of its Communists, Ba'thists and Free Officers* (Princeton University Press, 1983).

[7] Iraq's tribes led a revolution against the UK occupation in 1920, which, although unsuccessful, caused significant financial and human losses on the British side. See Abbas Kadhim, *Reclaiming Iraq: The 1920 Revolution and the Founding of the Modern State* (University of Texas Press, 2012).

[8] The United Kingdom had raised armed divisions that were composed of Assyrian Christians from northern Iraq. They were better armed and remunerated than the remainder of Iraq's security services, and were also used to put down rebellions on other parts of the country, stoking significant sectarian tensions in the process. In June to August 1933, following a demand by the Assyrian's spiritual leader for autonomy within Iraq, the Iraqi military was involved in a number of armed confrontations, culminating in a massacre of between 600 and 3,000 Assyrians. See Sargon George Donabed, *Reforging a Forgotten History: Iraq and the Assyrians in the Twentieth Century* (Edinburgh University Press, 2015).

[9] The coup was led by a number of pro-German officers. Salah al-Din al-Sabbagh, one of the coup leaders, was educated at the Ottoman Military College in Istanbul. See Peter Wien, *Iraqi Arab Nationalism: Authoritarian, Totalitarian and Pro-Fascist Inclinations, 1932–1941* (Routledge, 2008).

curriculum. The British also sought to amend the curriculum itself but found that the relevant Iraqi officials were deeply uncooperative.[10]

The republican period

Irrespective of the United Kingdom's efforts, the wheels of insurrection were already in motion. Encouraged by their Egyptian counterparts' successes in 1952, and motivated by the catastrophic socio-economic conditions that were prevalent in Iraq of the time,[11] a group of Iraqi officers seized power in July 1958, established a republic, and executed members of the former ruling elites including the Royal Family. The country was directly ruled by a military officer (General Abdel Karim Kassem) for the first time. For the following ten years, a number of radical trends struggled against each other, often violently, to take control over the country. The Baath Party gained power for a few months in 1963, and then seized it again in a July 1968 coup that brought this period of volatility to an end.

The Baath Party's main objective was to consolidate its hold on power. In order to achieve that aim, it sought to expand the armed forces' capabilities (which it could then use to protect its own power) while at the same time moving to consolidate its own political control over the military itself. Both these objectives were prioritized after Saddam Hussein (who had never served in the military and greatly distrusted the professional officer class) gained full control over Iraq's security portfolio and even more so after he seized the presidency in a 1979 palace coup. From that point, the party's leadership targeted potential threats within the military through rotations, retirement, purges, and executions. It also established a number of mechanisms to prevent sedition within the military, including oversight of military units by internal intelligence services, through the establishment of parallel military structures, and through ideological indoctrination and military academies.[12]

The Baath Party was ruthless with respect to its political opponents, including the Iraqi Communist Party, Islamist groups, the Kurdish parties, as well as imaginary enemies within the Baath Party itself. The level of repression was so severe that virtually everyone who was politically active and who had not been captured by the regime was driven into exile, where they lived in terror of the possibility of assassination by Iraq's intelligence services. The resulting distrust and paranoia

[10] See Simon (note 5) chapter 7.

[11] World Bank, *The Economic Development of Iraq: Report of a Mission Organized by the International Bank for Reconstruction* and *Development at the Request of the Government of Iraq* (Johns Hopkins Press, 1952), 1.

[12] 'Previously, our political discussions would revolve around socialism, Arabism and the struggle against western imperialism. After Saddam Hussein acquired full control over the state, all those discussions ended and we were given classes on Saddam's character and on his bravery.' Interview with former military officers, Baghdad, June 2004.

that this treatment imbued in the exile community was to have an incalculable impact on the country, and on the role of the security sector, after 2003.

The military was also occupied with a number of conflicts that were forced upon it by the Baath Party leadership and by Saddam Hussein in particular. In 1980, Iraq's ground forces invaded Iran, resulting in an eight-year conflict, hundreds of thousands of dead, many through the use of chemical weapons. Despite a massive military build-up, the conflict ended in 1988 with a stalemate and a peace agreement that left Iraq with nothing to show for its efforts and its sacrifices.[13] In August 1990, Saddam Hussein ordered his Army, which by that time was the fourth largest in the world, to invade Kuwait, which the Iraqi state then purported to annex. The United Nations Security Council immediately imposed the most comprehensive sanctions regime ever devised to compel Iraq to withdraw from Kuwait. An international military coalition led by the United States eventually declared war and forced Iraq to withdraw from Kuwait, destroying much of its military capacity as well as the state's civilian capacity in the process. In addition, the international sanctions remained in place reportedly to compel Iraq to destroy whatever might remain of its weapons of mass destruction, causing economic collapse and bringing hardship to the entire population, including the military's officer class. The Iraqi Army was reduced to a shadow of its former self, its capabilities greatly reduced, and its morale brought to the lowest point possible. Some special forces were still relatively well equipped but were in no position to resist a serious security threat by a well-organized military force.

The 2003 invasion and what followed

Following the March 2003 invasion and subsequent occupation of Iraq by the United States and the United Kingdom, there was no question of the Iraqi military ever playing a significant political role. The military's direct involvement in politics in 1958, which led to the Baath Party's and Saddam Hussein's dictatorship, and subsequent submission to the Baath Party, caused the military to lose all political credibility among the general population. In that context, the US and UK occupation, and their Iraqi allies on the ground, were determined to establish a constitutional system that would place the military and remaining security services firmly under civilian control.

In May 2003, the United States and the United Kingdom established the Coalition Provisional Authority (CPA) to administer the country during the period of formal occupation. There was some debate as to what should be done with what remained of Iraq's security forces. Senior US officials in Washington

[13] Joost Hiltermann, *A Poisonous Affair: America, Iraq and the Gassing of Halabja* (Cambridge University Press, 2007).

intended to use the regular armed forces to police the country, and over 30,000 soldiers from the regular Army had been placed on notice that they would be called upon for this purpose. However, the CPA had in fact decided to establish an entirely new state, with a new system of government, new institutions, and almost entirely new political leaders. The CPA disbanded the armed forces with a view to establishing entirely new police, intelligence, and military services. Regrettably however, most of the CPA's decisions were made on the basis of a narrow understanding of Iraq's situation, and also without considering possible the consequences of its actions.

Amongst other things, the United States and the United Kingdom installed in power a constellation of political parties, most of which had previously been based in exile and had a very poor political culture. In addition, the CPA established Iraq's first post-2003 government on an ethno-sectarian basis. What this meant was that all major policy decisions had to be made on a consensus basis (which was extremely difficult, if not impossible, in most circumstances given the number of parties that had to sign off on each individual initiative). The result was near-total paralysis, lasting for more than a decade now. Second, individual positions in government and in state institutions were allocated to political parties based on a broad understanding of the size of their respective constituencies. Thus, different security portfolios were under the control of different political parties and groups, which did not trust each other, which in turn meant that there was precious little cooperation between institutions on security matters.

Iraq's weak rule of law made matters significantly worse. The security sector's legal framework that governs its functioning is lacking in detail and is often contradictory, leaving enormous ambiguities in how specific institutions should function. In addition, the courts play almost no role in overseeing the security sector. Claims are never brought before the courts to challenge the constitutionality or legality of specific actions, or in order to clarify mandates. Courts also almost never hold officials to account for abuse of authority, incompetence, or corruption. Finally, Iraqi state officials almost never question instructions that they receive from superior officers. Regardless of whether instructions are legal, or in conformity with the Constitution, officers apply them unquestioningly. The result is that Iraq's governing elite has been able to manipulate the security sector for its own political and financial gain. Indeed, although former prime minister Nouri al-Maliki (who governed Iraq from 2006 to 2014) formally advocated in favour of a state of law and eschewed sectarianism, he deliberately set out to capture security institutions to intimidate his opponents.[14] The security sector was also a major source of revenue for political parties, given how much of the state budget was allocated to each

[14] Michael Knights, 'Yes, Iraq is Unraveling, and It's About to Become Obama's Problem All Over Again', 15 May 2013, *Foreign Policy*, <http://www.foreignpolicy.com/articles/2013/05/15/yes_iraq_is_unraveling> (once in power, the new Prime Minister set out to capture the state and divide and conquer opponents. To quote Knights, the government set about 'alienating the Sunnis and occupying their

institution.[15] The practice of buying command positions in the military was rife and has resulted in corrupt officers ascending to the leadership of divisions, brigades, and battalions. These officers then engage in theft, fraud, and extortion.[16]

Constitutional and Legal Issues: Constitution Building and Process

The 2004 Interim Constitution

Following the 2003 war, the 1970 interim Constitution was set aside, without ever actually being formally repealed. In 2004, an interim Constitution, entitled the Law for Administration for the State of Iraq for the Transitional Period (the 'Transitional Administrative Law' or the 'TAL') was adopted to govern the interim period and until a permanent constitution entered into force.[17] The TAL incorporated a number of key principles from some of the orders that the CPA had been issuing since April 2003 (see section, 'Institutional Structure of Security Services, and Separation of Powers and Functions'), and was also deliberately designed in reaction against the system of government that existed prior to 2003. It provided that the 'Iraqi Armed Forces shall be subject to the civilian control of the Iraqi Transitional Government' (Article 5), that Army personnel 'may not stand for election to political office' (Article 27(c)), and that an Army officer must have left his or her post at least eighteen months earlier to occupy political office (Article 28(b)).

One pre- 2003 institution that the TAL did not eschew was the tradition of maintaining a 'commander in chief of the armed forces'. Under Iraq's 1970 interim Constitution, in keeping with the state's heavily presidential system of government, the President was the Commander-in-Chief (القائد العام للقوات المسلحة). The TAL, however, established Iraq as a parliamentary democracy, in which the presidency was left with very few powers. In that sense a decision had to be made as to which office should hold that function. Article 39(b) of the final version provided as follows:

> The Presidency Council shall carry out the function of commander-in-chief of the Iraqi Armed Forces only for ceremonial and protocol purposes. It shall have no

communities with a heavy-handed, military-led approach that [did not] differentiate between diehard militants and the mass of peaceable civilians').

[15] For more on Iraq's anti-corruption framework, see 'Failing Oversight: Iraq's Unchecked Government', International Crisis Group, Middle East Report No. 113 (26 September 2011).

[16] Michael Knights, 'The Iraqi Security Forces: Local Context and US Assistance' (2011) 4 *Washington Institute for Near East Policy* 1, 4.

[17] For an account of how the TAL was drafted, see Larry Diamond, *Squandered Victory: The American Occupation and the Bungled Effort to Bring Democracy to Iraq* (Times Books, 2007); and Feisal Amin al-Istrabadi, 'Reviving Constitutionalism in Iraq: Key Provisions of the Transitional Administrative Law' (2005–6) 50 *New York Law School Law Review*.

> command authority. It shall have the right to be briefed, to inquire, and to advise. Operationally, national command authority on military matters shall flow from the Prime Minister to the Minister of Defense to the military chain of command of the Iraqi Armed Forces.

The drafters clearly understood the need to diffuse power over the armed forces and as such distributed authority over three different offices, namely the President, the Prime Minister, and the Minister of Defence. Importantly as well, Article 39(b) makes clear that while the Prime Minister has ultimate authority over the armed forces, he or she cannot issue instructions directly and must do so through the Minister of Defence, who himself must also respect the military chain of command. While this provision appears to have been well conceived, the TAL was only in application for two years and had limited impact on this area.

The 2005 Constitution

The Iraqi Constitution was negotiated and drafted during 2005, and, in so far as security sector reform (SSR) is concerned, it represents more of a punctuation mark than a turning point. In January 2005, a parliamentary assembly was elected for the purpose of organizing the drafting of Iraq's permanent Constitution. That assembly appointed a fifty-five-member constitutional drafting committee (which was later expanded to seventy members), which commenced work in May 2005. The committee worked until an agreed deadline in August 2005, at which point the committee had the option of extending the drafting process by another six months or submitting the draft for public debate. The committee had made significant progress in relation to some issues (namely, human rights) but had not reached agreement in relation to others (namely, the federal system of government). Instead of extending the deadline, the process was literally hijacked by the US Embassy in Baghdad and two to three political parties (who together represented no more than 20 per cent of the population) who favoured finalizing the draft as quickly as possible and shifting from a federal system, in which the central government played an important role in governance, to one in which the central government played almost no role.[18] Thus, the negotiations continued with only some of the parties present, with some of the sessions actually taking place at the US Embassy. The parliament which was elected for the purpose of organizing the drafting process was not allowed to discuss what was taking place, to debate the draft, or even to vote on it. Although a referendum took place on 15 October 2005, this essentially informal

[18] See Zaid al-Ali, 'Constitutional Legitimacy in Iraq: What Role Local Context?' in Rainer Grote and Tilmann Röder (eds), *Constitutionalism in Islamic Countries: Between Upheaval and Continuity* (Oxford University Press, 2011).

and illegal redrafting of the text continued until 13 October 2005. The result was that the people were voting on a text that they had never seen. Nevertheless, the final text was eventually approved by around 80 per cent of the population.[19]

Despite the historical context, most of the attention during the entire drafting process was dedicated to designing the federal system of government, and scant attention was given to security sector issues. The constitutional drafting committee did not include any officials from the security sector. It is unclear whether any such officials advised during the constitutional drafting process at any point, but whatever advice may have been given was hardly determinant given how the drafting process was taken over by a small number of parties in August 2005.

The final version of the Constitution established a federal system of government that was parliamentary at the central level. Many of the Constitution's essential features are incomplete. The most obvious example is the upper chamber of parliament, which is intended to represent the country's federal regions and provinces. The Constitution says nothing about how the body is to be composed or elected, leaving the issue for the lower chamber of parliament to decide (Article 65).[20] Some analysts have argued that Iraq's constitutional negotiators were deliberately ambiguous on these issues and that that approach should be viewed as a positive development, mainly on the basis that it allowed for a final agreement to be reached within the necessary time frame.[21] There is no question that ambiguity can be useful to paper over disagreements on matters of general principle, including issues relating to identity and religion.[22] However, while ambiguity can be useful in relation to some issues, it can be deadly in relation to many others, including how security sector institutions should be governed.[23]

As soon as a constitution enters into force, its most important institutions will have to work under the framework that it imposes. On these issues, constitutional negotiators can adopt a number of approaches, including (i) establishing clear constitutional rules that must be followed by future parliaments and

[19] An unofficial translation of the Iraqi Constitution, and of all previous Iraqi constitutions, is available at <http://zaidalali.com/resources/constitution-of-iraq/>.

[20] At the time of writing, which is to say more than ten years after the Constitution entered into force, the lower chamber has not passed the necessary legislation and the upper chamber has therefore not yet been composed.

[21] See Haider Hamoudi, *Negotiating in Civil Conflict: Constitutional Construction and Imperfect Bargaining in Iraq* (University of Chicago Press, 2013).

[22] The negotiators successfully adopted that approach in relation to the status of Islam, which was granted the same status as the 'principles of democracy' (see Article 2 of Iraq's final Constitution). While that specific construction is yet to be understood, it allowed for what could potentially have become a major point of contention to be deferred until a later date. For more on how constitutional ambiguity can allow for deeply divided societies to successfully negotiate fundamental texts, see Hanna Lerner, *Making Constitutions in Deeply Divided Societies* (Cambridge University Press, 2011).

[23] The Iraqi Constitution has been heavily criticized for its lack of detail and clarity in relation to a number of issues. See e.g. Zaid al-Ali, *The Struggle for Iraq's Future: How Corruption, Incompetence and Sectarianism Have Undermined Democracy* (Yale University Press, 2014); and Yash Ghai and Jill Cottrell, 'A Review of the Draft Constitution of Iraq' (3 October 2005), <https://media.law.wisc.edu/s/c_8/ftfkf/arotcoi.pdf>.

government;[24] (ii) establishing broad principles that will have to be fleshed out in subsequent legislation in the immediate future; and (iii) remaining silent on the issue, therefore leaving the issue to be determined as soon as possible after the Constitution is completed. For the second and third of these approaches to be successful in a given country, one would have to be reasonably confident of the state's capacity to produce the relevant legislation and regulations within a short period of time. Iraq nominally followed the second of these approaches, without anticipating the fact that the parliament would be incapable of passing the necessary legislation to govern the security sector (or any other major area of contention for that matter). The result is that, aside from a small number of exceptions, the only legal texts that govern the security sector are found in the Constitution or in legislation that pre-dates it.

Thus, the 2005 Constitution only includes three provisions that are specifically dedicated to the security sector, none of which is particularly detailed or well-conceived. The military's mandate is defined solely as being to 'defend Iraq', without specifically defining what 'Iraq' consists of in this context (Article 9(1)(a)). In the chapter on the state's federal system of government, Article 110 sets out the exclusive powers of the federal government, which includes to 'establish and manage armed forces to secure the protection and guarantee the security of Iraq's borders and to defend Iraq' (Article 110(2)). While that wording provides some clarity as to what the armed forces' mandate consists of, it does not exclude the possibility that they could be used for other purposes as well. The intelligence sector is provided with a far more detailed mandate. The Constitution provides for the existence of a National Intelligence Service (NIS) (see section, 'Institutional Structure of Security Services, and Separation of Powers and Functions'), which is responsible for 'collecting information, assessing threats to national security, and advising the Iraqi government' (Article 9(1)(d). That wording suggests (without specifically saying so) that the Service does not have any authority to take direct action on its own, and that it will have to work in cooperation with law enforcement agencies (namely the police) to make arrests or prevent criminal activity including threats to national security. Meanwhile, the police or internal security forces are simply never mentioned in the Constitution.

The Constitution also confirms the principle of civilian control. It provides that the armed forces are 'subject to the control of civilian authority . . . shall not be used as an instrument to oppress the Iraqi people, shall not interfere in political affairs, and shall have no role in the transfer of power' (Article 9(1)(a)). The NIS is also 'subject to legislative oversight, and shall operate in accordance with the law and pursuant to the recognized principles of human rights' (Article 9(1)(d)). The principle of civilian control is repeated in the Constitution's section relating to the Council

[24] The German Basic Law is a good example of this type approach. See the Basic Law's Chapter 10 on financial issues. A translation of the Basic Law is available at <http://www.constituteproject.org>.

of Ministers, which states that the state's 'security institutions' (left undefined) and the NIS are 'subject to oversight by the Council of Representatives', and that the NIS is 'attached' to the Council of Ministers (Article 84). Although the concept of civilian control appears fairly well supported by these provisions, the fact that the Constitution never defines what the consequences of being subject to 'oversight' or being 'attached' are has created significant uncertainty, which has contributed to the security services' general lack of capacity (see section, 'Institutional Structure of Security Services, and Separation of Powers and Functions').

Perhaps most importantly, the 2005 Constitution maintains the position of a 'Commander-in-Chief of the Armed Forces' from the pre-2003 presidential system. Under the 1970 interim Constitution, the President of the Republic was *ad officio* the Commander-in-Chief of the Armed Forces (Article 56).[25] As explained below (see section, 'Institutional Structure of Security Services, and Separation of Powers and Functions'), while some of the relevant legislation from that period indicated that that position was not purely ceremonial, the Minister of Defence was ultimately responsible for administering the Ministry and the armed forces (the President exercised ultimate control through his appointment powers which he used to ensure that whoever occupied the position was personally loyal to him; often the Minister was directly related to the President through familial ties). The 2005 Constitution maintains the position of Commander-in-Chief, the difference being that the position is now granted to the Prime Minister (Article 78). The relevant provision does not provide any detail as to whether that position was ceremonial or whether it entitles the Prime Minister to exercise real functions, and it also does not mention the Minister of Defence or the chain of command. Given that much of the pre-2003 legislation which defined how that position was designed to operate in practice was either repealed or ignored, this created an opportunity for the incumbent Prime Minister to abuse his authority over the armed forces to further his own political ambitions.

Al-Maliki exploited that ambiguity to establish and staff an Office of the Commander-in-Chief, which he used to circumvent the formal chain of command and direct military and security operations himself. Under his command, counterterrorism units were used to silence the political opposition and to intimidate segments of the general population. Al-Maliki's divisive rule and mismanagement of the security sector explains in large part why the Iraqi government lost control over large parts of Iraqi territory to the self-proclaimed Islamic State in June 2014. Iraq's security sector was in such a state of disarray that the Islamic State was able to invade and occupy Tikrit, a city of 200,000 people, with an initial force of only thirty.[26] It was also there that more than 1,000 Army cadets were left defenceless

[25] An unofficial translation of the 1970 interim Constitution is available at <http://www.zaidalali.com>.

[26] See Zaid al-Ali, 'Tikrit: Iraq's Abandoned City', *The New York Review of Books*, 4 May 2015.

and without arms by the military's command, leaving them to be massacred by a small number of Islamic State fighters. Al-Maliki was eventually forced from office in August 2014 by a parliamentary majority that granted confidence to Haider al-Abadi (a cadre from al-Maliki's own party). In August 2015, a parliamentary fact-finding committee found that a number of senior political and military officials were responsible for the fall of Mosul and recommended that they be tried in court. The officials in question included former Prime Minister al-Maliki, and former Army chief Babakir Zebari.[27]

Amnesties

On the issue of amnesties, all the ruling authorities that have been in power since 2003 have adopted an unrelenting and vindictive approach to the former Baath Party. In its Order No. 1, which was issued on 16 May 2003 (which is to say merely two months after Iraq was fully occupied), the CPA banned individuals who belonged to the Baath Party's four most senior ranks from ever holding future employment in the public sector again (section 1(2)), regardless of whether these individuals were guilty or even suspected of criminal activity in the past. In addition, Order No. 1 provided that:

> [i]ndividuals holding positions in the top three layers of management in every national government ministry, affiliated corporations and other government institutions (e.g. universities and hospitals) shall be interviewed for possible affiliation with the Baath Party . . . Any such persons detained to be full members of the Baath Party shall be removed from employment.

This applied regardless of what type of rank they held in the party and, once again, irrespective of whether there was any suggestion of criminal activity on their part (section 1(3)). The Iraqi Governing Council, an Iraqi executive authority that was established by the CPA and existed alongside it until the CPA itself was dissolved, established a Debaathification Commission by virtue of Decision 21 (18 July 2003), without saying anything about how the Commission would carry out its work. In a subsequent decision, the Governing Council ordered that committees should be established in all ministries to identify Baathists and remove them from their positions.[28] The TAL later confirmed the Commission's existence by mentioning it by name (Article 49(a)).

The 2005 Constitution followed suit, first by banning the Baath Party as a political entity (Article 7(1)), and second by providing that the Debaathification

[27] Ahmed Rasheed and Stephen Kalin, 'Iraqi Panel Finds Maliki, Others Responsible for Fall of Mosul', Reuters, 16 August 2015.

[28] Decision 58 (30 September 2003).

Commission 'shall continue its functions' (Article 135(1)) and that the parliament should dissolve the Commission 'by an absolute majority after the completion of its function' (Article 135(2)). In 2008, the parliament passed the Accountability and Justice Law, which renamed the Debaathification Commission as the High National Council of Accountability and Justice (Article 28), and redefined its mission as being to 'cleanse the public and mixed sectors, civil society organizations and Iraqi society from the Baath Party system' (Article 3(2)).[29] The new law allowed for the reinstatement of some former Baathists, while at the same time leading to the dismissal of others from the security services. Altogether, the combined effect of the CPA-era legislation and the 2008 law was that tens of thousands of government officials were dismissed at a time when increased government efficiency should have been a priority. These policies also had the effect of worsening community relations, and possibly also contributing to the security crisis in the country.[30]

Institutional Structure of Security Services, and Separation of Powers and Functions

The Iraqi Army

Much of the legislation that existed prior to the 2003 war relating to the Army was either explicitly abrogated or was simply no longer applied by virtue of the fact that the institutions that they purported to govern were no longer in existence. Indeed, shortly after the invasion and subsequent military occupation of the country was complete in April 2003, the US-led CPA,[31] which at the time was recognized as the highest civilian authority in the country, issued its Order No. 2 in May 2003, which dissolved a huge number of bodies including the Ministry of Defence, the Ministry of Information, the Ministry of State for Military Affairs, the Iraqi Intelligence Service, the National Security Bureau, the Army, the Air Force, the Navy, the Air Defence Force, etc.[32] Iraq's police force operates under the Ministry of the Interior, which was not formally dissolved following the 2003 war (see section, 'The police').

Prior to 2003, by virtue of Bylaw 23 (3 December 1979), the Ministry of Defence was formally under full control of the military. The Army's Chief of Staff, military intelligence, the Department of Military Public Accounts, the Department

[29] Law 10 (14 February 2008).

[30] See the report by Miranda Sissons and Abdulrazzaq al-Saiedi, 'A Bitter Legacy: Lessons of De-Baathification in Iraq', International Center for Transitional Justice (March 2013), <https://www.ictj.org/sites/default/files/ICTJ-Report-Iraq-De-Baathification-2013-ENG.pdf>.

[31] The CPA's official website is still available for historical purposes. See <https://govinfo.library.unt.edu/cpa-iraq/index.htm>.

[32] All of the CPA's Orders are available in English at <https://govinfo library.unt.edu/cpa-iraq/regulations/>. They were all translated into Arabic and published in Iraq's Official Gazette, which is available at <http://www.iraqld.iq>.

of Officer Administration, and the military court of appeals were all established within the Ministry (Article 4). The Bylaw confirmed that the President of the Republic was the Commander-in-Chief of the Armed Forces (Article 1), and insisted that this translated into 'real and effective leadership' (Article 2). It also confirmed that the Minister of Defence was the 'highest authority in the ministry and was responsible for its general policies and affairs', and that the Minister was responsible for 'developing the armed forces and its preparedness for conflict, training, administration and discipline to successfully meet its combat obligations' (Article 3(1)). The Minister was also obliged to present reports on the state of the armed forces and their combat capabilities to the Commander-in-Chief of the Armed Forces (i.e. the President of the Republic) (Article 3(4)). The Office of the Chief of Staff was also established as the body that 'controls the armed forces through which the commander in chief of the armed forces and the Minister of Defense can exercise control' (Article 8). The Bylaw also establishes a number of councils, committees, and departments that are responsible for various issues relating to the ministry's work, including the armed forces council (Articles 5 and 6), the administrative department (Article 11), the inspections department (Article 13), etc. Finally, the Bylaw provides the Minister with the authority to issue the 'necessary regulations to achieve this Bylaw's objectives' (Article 28), without having to refer to the Commander-in-Chief.

The 1979 Bylaw remained in force until 2003 when the country was invaded by the United States and the United Kingdom. Although Order No. 2 dissolved the armed forces, it did not explicitly repeal the 1979 Bylaw, which created a significant amount of uncertainty as to its formal status. That uncertainty did not dissipate when the CPA issued Order No. 22, for the purpose of establishing a new Iraqi Army. Section 3(2) of Order No. 22 defines the military's role is 'the military defense of the nation, including defense of the national territory and the military protection of the security of critical installations, facilities, infrastructure, lines of the communication and supply, and population'. It also clearly establishes that the Army shall not engage in 'domestic law enforcement functions, nor intervene in the domestic political affairs of the nation'. Order No. 22 also includes sections governing the conduct of military personnel, disciplinary measures,[33] terms and conditions of service and enlistment, rank structure, pay and allowances, leave, termination of service, and the prohibition against political activities. All this was followed by Order No. 23 (7 August 2003) which established a code of military discipline for the new Iraqi Army.

More importantly, on 21 March 2004, the CPA issued Order No. 67, which established a new Ministry of Defence. Order No. 67 did not specifically mention the 1979 Bylaw, but included a general provision indicating that '[a]ny laws or

[33] Section 5 of Order No. 22 provides that for non-military crimes (e.g. offences committed under the Penal Code No. 111 of 1969), Army personnel are subject to the jurisdiction of ordinary civilian courts, as provided pursuant to the Code of Criminal Procedure No. 23 of 1977.

regulations inconsistent with the provisions of this Order are hereby suspended to the extent that they are inconsistent with the provisions of this Order' (section 3). Order No. 67 transferred control of the new Iraqi Army to the Ministry of Defence (section 2) and provided that the Minister of Defence's mission is the 'management and employment of the [armed forces] . . . [and to] exercise direction and control (including commissioning and appointments) over the [armed forces]' (section 4). In conformity with Iraq's status as an occupied nation, Order No. 67 provided that the armed forces should be 'under the operational control of the Commander of Coalition Forces' (section 4(2)). In comparison with the 1979 Bylaw, Order No. 67 was far less detailed. It did not provide for the establishment of specific councils or committees, but merely provided that the Minister of Defence should staff the Ministry 'as needed' (section 4(6)(d)) without providing any indication as to how necessity was to be defined in that context. Finally, and also in contrast to the 1979 Bylaw, Order No. 67 specifically provided that members of the armed forces 'may not hold or stand for election to political office or complain for candidates' (section 9(2)), and that former Army officers who wish to hold political office will have needed to have resigned at least eighteen months prior (section 9(3)).

Over the following ten years, the military evolved into an extremely problematic institution. In response to a challenging security environment, including persistent terrorist threats, the Army deployed across the country, setting up checkpoints to control the flow of people, and carrying out military operations in various districts. Although that task should have belonged to the country's police force, the military was reluctant to cede any significant authority to the Ministry of the Interior, ostensibly because of the police's lack of capacity, but in reality mainly because of a lack of trust between the two institutions. At the same time, the military's budget grew significantly during this period, increasing opportunities for corruption. Anti-corruption efforts generally failed, and the Ministry of Defence and the armed forces were regularly cited as being amongst the most incompetent and corrupt institutions in the country.[34] However, because of the country's political paralysis (described earlier in this chapter), no subsequent legislation relating to the military was enacted from 2004 until 2015.

Instead, the Army was heavily politicized by Nouri al-Maliki, who was Prime Minister from 2006 to 2014. Through his Office of the Commander-in-Chief, al-Maliki issued direct orders to military commanders (often via cellphone), established military units that were personally answerable to him, and appointed and dismissed officers at will. Former members of the Baath Party were dismissed from their positions unless they were considered to be personally loyal to al-Maliki, in which case they were allowed to stay on.[35] He also refused to nominate a

[34] See al-Ali (note 23); Ali A. Allawi, *The Occupation of Iraq: Winning the War, Losing the Peace* (Yale University Press, 2008).

[35] See Sissons and al-Saiedi (note 30).

Minister of Defence during his second term in office (2010–14), preferring to exercise those powers either directly himself or through an acting minister, who was never confirmed by parliament. Finally, al-Maliki made sure to shield loyalists from accountability, leading to a desperate lack of capacity and increased levels of corruption.[36]

After the self-declared Islamic State invaded and occupied a number of Iraqi cities (including Mosul, Iraq's second largest city, and Tikrit, which is a two-hour drive from Baghdad) in June 2014, the 2015 Ministry of Defence Law was adopted. That disaster illustrated how desperate Iraq's security situation under the post-2003 arrangement had become and created a sufficient impetus for the parliament finally to adopt some new legislation to improve the security services' performance. Unfortunately however, the 2015 Law presents few improvements in comparison to the previous legal framework. Although it reaffirms the principle of civilian control over the Army, it centralizes control in the Prime Minister's hands even more firmly than in the past, in a way that could easily either slow down reforms or cause any individual reform initiatives to break down in the event of a disagreement between the Prime Minister and the Minister of Defence.

The 2015 Law establishes that the Ministry's mission is to provide the Army with modern weapons; establish advanced research and technical centres to provide information and studies to the Commander-in-Chief of the Armed Forces, the Minister of Defence and the Chief of Staff; and provide the Army with technical staff to develop military and scientific institutions (Article 3). The Law, for the first time in the post-2003 era, defines the role of the Commander-in-Chief. It states that the Commander leads and supervises the Army, guarantees the protection of Iraq's sovereignty, determines national objectives relating to national defence, unifies national efforts to achieve national defence, and finally ensures that the state, including its armed forces, is capable of defending the nation (Article 4). The Minister of Defence, defined as the highest official in the ministry, is responsible for administering its affairs, for ensuring that all civilian and military staff in the Ministry carry out their functions properly, and issues regulations, internal instructions, decisions, and orders relating to the Ministry's objectives (Article 5). Importantly however, in a departure from previous legal frameworks, the Prime Minister must ratify all of the Minister's regulations and international instructions (Article 13(2)). Article 6 lists all the Minister's other authorities and

[36] See e.g. D.J. Elliott, 'The Missing Links: A Realistic Appraisal of the Iraqi Military', *Defense Industry Daily Staff*, 12 July 2011; Michael Knights, *The Future of Iraq's Armed Forces* (al-Bayan Center Publications Series, 2016), 15–20 ('By the time Daesh began to grow stronger in 2012 the ISF was increasingly a hollow and brittle force that could be badly damaged by one major blow. Morale was lowered by the low quality of leadership and the lack of training, by the negative effects of corruption on military price, and by the vulnerability of soldiers and policemen to assassination and intimidation.').

responsibilities, which include advising the Commander-in-Chief (including on appointments), overseeing the execution of contracts relating to the Army's offensive capabilities, and issuing directives to the Army's Chief of Staff (within the context of the National Security Strategy). The 2015 Law also provides for the existence of a Defence Council, which is entirely composed of military officers and ministry staff, and which is responsible for developing and determining military doctrine, and presenting studies to build and develop the armed forces to the Commander-in-Chief (Article 8).

The police

The Iraqi police have traditionally been under the control of the Ministry of the Interior. Following the 2003 war and occupation, the US-led CPA did not dissolve the Ministry nor did it abrogate the legislation in force relating to the Ministry or the police's operation. As a result, Law 183 (17 November 1980) is still in force, and has not been amended, despite the fact that it still requires for Baath Party members to play an official role in ministerial committees relating to the country's security.[37] Also, Law 183 was passed at the start of the war with Iran, and many of its provisions reflect a military mindset. The Law provides that the Ministry's general mission was to implement the state's general policy to 'maintain internal security' and to do so 'in light of the war and the revolution's aims' (Article 1). More particularly, the Ministry is responsible for (i) protecting life and public and private monies from danger; (ii) crime prevention; (iii) the implementation of laws and regulations that relate to the Ministry's work; and (iv) cooperating with ministries of the interior in Arab countries and in friendly nations and to cooperate with relevant international organizations (Article 2). Although the legal framework was left intact, in 2003 the Ministry was purged of much of its senior staff. In the years that followed, many of the most senior staff members were former exiles, and many were accused of both corruption and human rights abuses.[38] Perhaps most egregiously, the police are notorious for their use of bomb detectors, which have been proven to be fake.[39] Although the owner of the company that sold the devices to the Iraqi state was given the maximum penalty for fraud by a court in London in 2013, the devices were still in use throughout Baghdad in 2016.[40]

[37] See e.g. Article 7(1)(c) which requires for a Baath Party official to be a member of the Ministry's Internal Affairs Committee.

[38] See e.g. Jeffrey Fleishman and Asmaa Waguih, 'Detainees in Iraq Suffer Abuse, Says Government', *The Los Angeles Times*, 19 June 2005.

[39] See al-Ali (note 23).

[40] See 'Residents Hold Protest Blaming Leaders for Baghdad Carnage', AFP, 12 May 2016.

The intelligence sector

As already indicated, prior to 2003, Iraq ran a number of intelligence agencies, all of which ultimately reported to the President of the Republic. All these agencies were dissolved by virtue of Order No. 2, and in the years that followed, a new network of intelligence agencies were established. However, whereas the pre-2003 system was defined by the fact that it was entirely designed by the Baath Party and for the purpose of maintaining a single person in power for as long as possible, the post-2003 system lacked any type of coherence. The main defining feature of the post-2003 era is the fact that the intelligence sector does not appear to have been deliberately designed, that a plethora of different agencies appeared mainly without any legislation to regulate their activities, and that each appears to be under the control of specific political groupings. The end result is that these bodies' mandates overlap to a very significant extent, and that they do not appear to coordinate with each other.

The first intelligence agency to have been established was the Ministerial Committee for National Security (مستشارية الأمن الوطني العراقي), by virtue of Order No. 68.[41] Section 1 provides that the Committee's role is to 'facilitate and coordinate national security policy among the ministries and agencies of the Iraqi government tasked with national security issues. It is the primary forum for Ministerial-level decision making on these issues.' Section 3 also established the position of National Security Adviser (NSA), who is described as being the 'primary adviser . . . on national security matters' to the head of the government. Although Order No. 68 provides that the NSA's term should last five years (section 3(3)), it does not clearly establish whether there is a limit to the number of terms that a single individual can serve in that position. Neither the Ministerial Committee nor the NSA are mentioned in the 2005 Constitution, and no subsequent legislation was passed to further regulate its activities.

Over time the NSA established its own intelligence agency, namely the National Security Service (NSS) (جهاز الأمن الوطني). There does not appear to be a single legal text that provides for the NSS's formal establishment, but judging from the funds that have been allocated to its offices in the annual state budget, it appears to have over 10,000 staff members. According to the NSS's website, the service's mandate includes collecting information on terrorist organizations, maintaining a database of information, overseeing 'suspicious' activities by civil society organizations and foreign companies, and investigating financial and administrative corruption, as well as economic crimes, money laundering, and arms and drug trafficking. Little is known about the NSS's activities and what it actually does.

By virtue of Order No. 69, the CPA also provided for the existence of the NIS (جهاز المخابرات الوطني). The Order was formulated as a 'delegation of authority' in

[41] The Ministerial Committee's official website is available at <http://www.nsa.gov.iq/>.

favour of the Iraqi Governing Council.[42] The Order attaches a proposed Charter, which had been discussed between the Governing Council and the CPA, as Appendix A. The draft Charter does not appear ever to have been formally adopted; there is certainly no record in Iraq's Official Gazette of any legal document ever having been issued or adopted by the Governing Council that would have legally established the NIS. Nevertheless, the NIS was formally established in 2004 and was provided with a staff and began exercising its functions.

The body was granted constitutional status by the 2005 Constitution, which stated that its mandate was to 'collect information, assess threats to national security, and advise the Iraqi government. This Service shall be under civilian control, shall be subject to legislative oversight, and shall operate in accordance with the law and pursuant to the recognized principles of human rights' (Article 9(1)(d)). The Constitution also provides that the NIS should 'operate in accordance with the principles of human rights and shall be subject to the oversight of the Council of Representatives', although it should be 'attached' to the Council of Ministers (Article 84). A new draft law, which was never formally published, was prepared and approved by the Council of Ministers in 2006 and was referred to the Council of Representatives.[43] The draft was not prioritized by the Council of Representatives however, and does not appear ever to have been formally considered for a vote. In 2009, some representatives expressed concern at the NIS's size, particularly given that no legislation had been passed to organize its activities, and expressed scepticism that the draft would ever have been adopted.[44]

The NIS continued functioning throughout this period however, and appeared to be applying the principles established in the draft Charter. The Charter's Article 4 provides some information relating to the NIS' mandate:

> The Iraqi National Intelligence Service has the authority to collect intelligence and conduct related intelligence activities regarding:
>
> - Threats to the national security of Iraq.
> - Terrorism and insurgency.
> - Proliferation of weapons of mass destruction, narcotics production and trafficking, and serious organized crime.
> - Espionage and other acts threatening to Iraqi democracy.
>
> Intelligence collected under this article may be disseminated to appropriate government entities both within and outside of Iraq. Any other dissemination of

[42] See Raad al-Kadiri and Chris Toensing, 'The Iraqi Governing Council's Sectarian Hue', Middle East Research and Information Project (20 August 2003).

[43] See Council of Ministry Decision No. 11857 (21 November 2006).

[44] See 'Passage of NIS law unlikely' (نمألا نوؤشل ةلودلا ةرازو نوناق عورشم رارقإ مدع حيجرت ينطولا), Radio Sawa, 8 August 2009.

> intelligence will be strictly limited to what is essential to the national security of Iraq. All intelligence activities will be strictly required to further national security, and will be subject to the oversight provisions of this Charter.

The draft Charter also provides that the NIS should not take any actions that undermine political parties (Article 5), should not take actions based on most forms of discrimination (Article 6), should respect human rights (Article 7), should not have the power to arrest people (Article 12), and should cooperation with 'appropriately authorized government authorit[ies]'. The draft Charter also establishes the position of Director General of the NIS. Once again, the draft Charter provides that the Director General should serve for a five-year term, without clearly establishing term limits (Article 14). There is significant confusion, however, on how the Director General's mandate relates to the role of the NSA. As already mentioned, Order No. 68 provides that the NSA is the 'primary adviser . . . on national security matters', meanwhile the draft Charter provides that the Director General should be the 'principal adviser to the head of government . . . for intelligence matters related to the national security' (Article 15).

Both the NSS and the NIS have serious problems with their legal standing. The parliament has not passed any legislation to define their mandates or working methods, as a result of which both institutions have been regularly accused of operating illegally, and of serving as slush funds for particular political parties (as of September 2018).[45] Also, there is clearly significant overlap between the NSS and the NIS's mandates and it is very unclear how these two bodies cooperate, or even if they are even in communication with each other. The parliament's Security and Defence Committee has been studying draft legislation that could regularize both institutions' work for many years without making any significant progress.[46] After the Islamic State invaded and occupied much of Iraq in June 2014, former Prime Minister Nouri al-Maliki was forced from office, and discussion on SSR accelerated. Al-Maliki's replacement, Prime Minister Haider al-Abadi considered whether the NSS and the NIS should be merged, but this never appears to have taken place.[47] Also, as at the time of writing, no legislation has been passed relating to any of the country's intelligence agencies,[48] partly because of substantive

[45] See e.g. 'State of Law Coalition: The NSS's Work Is Legal but the NIS Is Operating Without a Legal Basis and Without the Government Being Aware of its Activities' (نائب عن الائتلاف: عمل وزارة الأمن الوطني قانوني وجهاز المخابرات يعمل بدون معرفة الحكومة), *al-Bayyna*, 10 September 2018.

[46] See e.g. Falah al-Shamari, 'Abbas al-Bayati: The Security and Defense Committee Will Present Laws to Govern the Ministry of the Interior, the NIS and the NSS for Discussion' (عباس البياتي: لجنة الامن والدفاع ستقدم قانون وزارة الداخلية وقانون جهاز المخابرات وقانون جهاز الامن الوطني للمناقشة), Iraqi Media News Agency, 18 March 2013.

[47] See 'The Government Considers Merging the NIS and the NSS' (الحكومة تدرس دمج جهاز المخابرات ومستشارية الامن الوطني), Mawazin News, 22 February 2015.

[48] See 'Next Saturday: Draft NIS Law Will Be Passed in the Parliament' (السبت المقبل: تمرير في البرلمان), Sumer News, 28 March 2016.

disagreements[49] but also because of Iraq's idiosyncratic political system, which requires a consensus to be reached between all the parties that are represented in parliament before any reforms can be passed.

In addition to these agencies, a number of other intelligence services exist within other ministerial bodies. For example, in 2006, the Ministry of the Interior established a Federal Information and Investigation Agency (وكالة الوزارة للاستخبارات والتحقيقات الاتحادية), which is also responsible for many of the same areas that the NSS and the NIS cover, including gathering information on and combatting terrorist organizations, gathering information on Arabs and foreigners living in Iraq and following their movements, gathering information on organized crime centred on Iraq's archaeological heritage, etc.[50] The Ministry of Defence also established a Directorate General for Intelligence and Security (المديرية العامة للاستخبارات والأمن), which collects intelligence both at home and abroad, where it is based in Iraqi diplomatic missions, and provides security for ministry facilities.[51] The Directorate's existence is provided for in ordinary legislation, including the 2015 Ministry of Defence Law (Article 9(1)(f)).

Militias

Prior to 2003, the Kurdistan region of Iraq had suffered from repression by Baghdad, and in response maintained irregular forces known as the Peshmerga (which translates as 'stare death in the face'). The Peshmerga (and other local forces) were involved in a large number of conflicts with the Iraqi military, and have been in full control of the region's security since 1991.[52] A number of other militias and armed groups were formed during the 1980s and 1990s and, although none of these were based in Iraq during that time, they all moved back to the country following the 2003 war. The most prominent of these groups is the Badr Brigades, previously associated with a political party known as the Islamic Supreme Council of Iraq (itself previously known as the Supreme Council for the

49 Osama Najah, 'Eavesdropping Provision Delays Approval of the Draft NIS Law' (بند "التنصت" يعوق إقرار قانون جهاز المخابرات العراقي), al-Sabah al-Jadeed, 14 December 2015.

50 The National Information and Investigation Agency's website is available at <http://moi.gov.iq/PageViewer.aspx?id=28>.

51 The Directorate General for Intelligence and Security does not maintain a website.

52 Importantly, the Peshmerga are not a united force, with each of the region's two main political parties (the Kurdistan Democratic Party and the Patriotic Union of Kurdistan) maintaining their own separate divisions. Efforts to merge the two separate forces into a single unit have by and large failed. See e.g. Mario Fumerton and Wladimir Van Wilgenburg, 'Kurdistan's Political Armies: The Challenge of Unifying the Peshmerga Forces', Carnegie Endowment for International Peace, 16 December 2015, <https://carnegieendowment.org/2015/12/16/kurdistan-s-political-armies-challenge-of-unifying-peshmerga-forces-pub-61917>.

Islamic Revolution in Iraq).[53] After the 2003 war, one of the issues that needed to be resolved was how these forces should be incorporated in a national security strategy. CPA Order No. 91, issued in June 2004, sought to integrate militias into the Iraqi security forces. Many individuals (so-called *dimaj* appointees) with connections to influential politicians, tribes, and militias were appointed to positions in the Iraqi Army, in some cases relatively senior ones, notwithstanding their lack of formal military education or training. In many cases, the *dimaj* appointees did not know how to wear their uniforms and were regarded by colleagues as incompetent.[54] Second, Article 9(1)(b) of the Constitution contemplates that a law would grant the Peshmerga some formal status, by indicating that the 'formation of military militia outside the framework of the armed forces is prohibited', but no such legislation was ever passed, leaving the Peshmerga's status ambiguous at best.[55]

This difficult situation was complicated further when in June 2014, in response to ISIS's invasion and the collapse of Iraq's regular security institutions, a number of additional irregular forces (popularly referred to as 'Popular Mobilization Forces' (الحشد الشعبي)) were formed to respond to the growing threat. Although exact details as to their formations and numbers are not always reliable, experts agree that the number of PMU forces currently stands at around 50,000. Although these fighters were regarded as being essential in the war to reclaim Iraq's territory from ISIS, there is significant concern in Iraq about these forces' legal status. This includes the fact that most of them operate without any sense of accountability for their actions, and second that they often do not operate in full cooperation with Iraq's regular armed forces.[56] An effort was made during 2015 to draft and pass a 'national guard law' (الحرس الوطني), which would incorporate these forces into a broader security framework. However, while a draft was prepared at the time, it has not been adopted as a result of Iraq's ineffectual political system.[57] In the meantime, the Council of Ministers issued a decision to establish a Popular Mobilization Commission (هيئة الحشد الشعبي), which is headed by the NSA.[58]

[53] The Badr Brigades were accused of committing atrocities in the post-2003 period, including running assassination squads. See e.g. Lionel Beehner, 'Iraq's Militia Groups', Council on Foreign Relations, 26 October 2006; and Susannah George, 'Breaking Badr', *Foreign Policy*, 6 November 2014.

[54] Michael Knights, Lachlyn Soper, Andrew Lembke, and Barak Salmoni, 'The Iraqi Security Forces: A Status Report', 13 June 2011, Washington Institute for Near East Policy, <http://www.washingtoninstitute.org/policy-analysis/view/the-iraqi-security-forces-a-status-report>.

[55] Saad N. Jawad, 'The Iraqi Constitution: Structural Flaws and Political Implications', LSE Middle East Centre Paper Series No. 1, November 2013, 16 ('in practice the Ministry of Defence has had no authority over the Kurdish armed force, the Peshmerga, which is officially regarded as part of the Iraqi military and is financed by the central government').

[56] Some of these fighters have been accused of committing atrocities. See e.g. 'Iraq: Possible War Crimes by Shia Militia', Human Rights Watch, 31 January 2016.

[57] The full draft of the draft national guard law is available at <http://bit.ly/1XphtAe>.

[58] Council of Ministers Decision 138, 2005. The Popular Mobilization Commission maintains a website, available at <http://al-hashed.net/>.

Civilian and Social Oversight

The issue in Iraq is not how to enforce civilian control over the security sector; security forces are completely under civilian control. Rather, the issue is how to prevent abuse by the political class, or a part of the political class, against the civilian population or against political rivals.

Article 61(5)(c) of the Iraqi Constitution confers on the Council of Representatives the power to 'approve' the appointment of 'the Iraqi Army Chief of Staff, his assistants, those of the rank of division commander and above, and the director of the intelligence service, based on a proposal from the Council of Ministers'. In addition, according to Article 80(5), the Council of Ministers 'recommend[s] to the Council of Representatives that it approve the appointment of . . . the Chief of Staff of the Armed Forces and his deputies, division commanders or higher, the Director of the National Intelligence Service, and heads of security institutions'.

With those responsibilities in mind, the Council of Representatives established a Security and Defence Committee, which is composed entirely by civilians. The Council's bylaws provide that the Committee's responsibilities include overseeing all of the security services' activities (including the intelligence sector) and to propose legislation relating to security issues (Article 89).[59] The Committee's website provides details of some of its activities, which includes regular hearings with senior security officials,[60] and discussions on security-related legislation, including the draft Ministry of the Interior law and the draft national intelligence law.[61] This type of activity has had very little impact on the performance of Iraq's security institutions. The pace of legislative reform is frighteningly slow, and there is no indication that evidence provided by security officials to the Council of Representatives has ever led to any reforms or improvements of any kind.

Constitutional and Legal Issues: Design and Choice of Law

Iraq's amendment procedure is relatively rigid as compared to most other countries. Article 126 of the Constitution provides that the President of the Republic and the Council of Ministers collectively, or one-fifth of the Council of Representatives members, may propose to amend the Constitution. There are also limits on the type of amendments that may be proposed. Amendments that take away from the

[59] An Arabic version of the Council of Representatives' bylaws is available at <http://ar.parliament.iq/LiveWebsites/Arabic/Council-Bylaws.aspx>.

[60] See e.g. 'Security and Defense Committee Meets with Head of Baghdad Operations', 17 February 2016, <http://ar.parliament.iq/LiveWebsites/Arabic/Container.aspx?ActivityID=59709>.

[61] See e.g. 'Security and Defense Committee Discusses Draft Ministry of the Interior Law', 21 February 2016, <http://ar.parliament.iq/LiveWebsites/Arabic/Container.aspx?ActivityID=59790>.

powers of the regions and that are not within the exclusive powers of the federal authorities are prohibited except by the approval of the legislative authority of the concerned region and the approval of the majority of its citizens in a general referendum. In addition, the amendment threshold is demanding: an amendment requires 'approval of two-thirds of the members of the Council of Representatives, the approval of the people in a general referendum, and the ratification by the President of the Republic within seven days'. Although some amendments were drawn up by a joint expert committee in 2009, they were never debated or formally presented. Since then, the issue of constitutional reform has essentially been forgotten.

9

The Arab Spring Region in a Constitutional Era

A Few Instances of Short-lived SSR

Philippe Droz-Vincent

Introduction

The Arab Spring, also dubbed by numerous local actors the Arab Revolutions (*thawrat*), was an era of upheavals against authoritarian rule undertaken by mobilized civil societies. Nine years after the beginning of the uprisings in Tunisia, it is clear that diversity in political trajectories paints a more accurate picture than generalizing images such as 'the Arab Spring', 'Winter', or other season. However, a common set of processes in relation to security sector reform (SSR) vindicate a common treatment and the use of the neologism 'the Arab Spring region' in relation to constitutional transitions. Common factors revolve around the crucial role of the security sector in the transitions, with its multifaceted components, from the armed forces to the Ministry of the Interior to the intelligence services and various paramilitary forces. Each case can be regarded as independent, yet common questions revolve around the reactions of the various components of the security sector and the crucial role of the armed forces in channelling changes in transitional settings.

The SSR agenda was opened up in new ways in 2011. Transitions in the Arab world began by the sudden surge of massive societal mobilizations against authoritarian rule, largely taking place in public spaces, that exerted a strong 'stress test' on security institutions, first of all on the Ministry of the Interior's forces that were at the forefront of regime maintenance. However, when regimes asked their militaries for 'upgraded' or 'enhanced' repression, the latter's reaction (to shoot or not to shoot at protesters) was an essential determinant of the trajectories of transition. Much more than in any previous experiments in transition in Latin America or Asia, the centrality of the military question exerted significant influence, either via its oppressive presence or, conversely, its complete absence in transitional processes, or at least in bargains to re-institutionalize the new polities.

This chapter explains that the complex questions of SSR and democratic control of the armed forces were, for the first time, seriously raised in the Arab world, at critical junctures for regimes and in the context of massive political shake-ups in 2011. It took these specific moments to initiate changes in the former authoritarian stasis, but at a heavy price of instability and with an assertive role for military institutions when existing regimes stayed afloat. Second, the dynamics of transition proved very complex, and included institutional disarray, even state decay, and divergent trajectories away from initial hopes. Third, with one exception, Tunisia, regime reformations then left these hopes of SSR and control incomplete, even extinguished, behind the resurgence of military regimes or 'law and order', counter-revolutionary, and anti-terrorist strategies.

The Moment of Transition and the New Prospects for SSR in 2011: Reopened Agency and Heavy Structural Constraints

The Arab Spring upheavals represented a big shake-up that allowed new questions about SSR to be raised, either formally (with open demands for SSR and efforts to integrate reform into constitutional debates) or informally (as a subtext in numerous difficult steps in the transitional processes).

Two structural factors combined to foster change and put SSR on the agenda. First, there was a new societal awareness and an explosion of public discourse and debate, at least from 2011 to 2013. This was a novel phenomenon in polities where public discourse was severely constrained by so-called red lines (*al-khutut al-hamra*), namely, topics no-one could broach without encountering the risk of repression, such as the security apparatus, the Army, Presidents, and their dynastic practices. There was a new societal awareness and a will, among broad sectors of society, to take their fate into their own hands. For the first time after 2011, some people dared to talk about the role of the military, call for reforms of the Ministry of the Interior—a reviled sector in all countries for its repressive role—and, despite persistent constraints, talk about constitutional articles dealing with the military in Egypt. Demonstrations against militias and the general insecurity in Libya, open debates regarding the military in the so-called National Dialogue in Yemen, and fresh proposals for SSR in Tunisia continued unabated for some time. Even during the period of open military rule in Egypt between February 2011 and June 2012, the high command was hypersensitive to public criticism and bowed under pressure—or gave in amidst concessions, for instance when the former Minister of the Interior, Habib al-Adli, and some of his aides were jailed (February 2011) or when Mubarak and his sons were arrested (April 2011)—and Egyptian generals closely monitored media discussions and public opinion.[1] The deeper the military was involved in politics, the more it was subject to criticism.

[1] Interviews with Egyptian university teachers and journalists close to the military, Paris, June 2013.

Second, the Arab uprisings shook established institutional equilibria, especially in the security sector, as coercive forces were crucial to maintain authoritarian balances. The literature of the 2000s on the enduring stability of Arab authoritarianism conveyed the false impression of an institutional stability: in fact, the so-called stability (a better phrase would be 'enduring rule') was based on the management of contradictions as a way to survive, by limited political contestation, economic liberalization, and cautious societal opening while maintaining the central role of security institutions. In addition, authoritarian leaders often stemmed from a military background. The authoritarian regimes of the Middle East and North Africa were security (*mukhabarat*) or police states rather than military regimes. Authoritarian regimes were built upon strange equilibria with leaders often hailing from the military but having 'de-militarized' their respective political systems, with the military playing the role of regime pillar in times of crisis and isolated in a kind of political 'quietism' (against the background of huge privileges and as an untouchable sector) in 'normal' authoritarian times, along with the Ministry of the Interior which acted as the first line of defence and the day-to-day tool of repression.[2] The system/equilibrium was given some coherence by the dominating and hyper-centralized role of the executive at the top, whose power comprised networks linked to the executive (the President in our cases) and the over-extended role of intelligence services (*mukhabarat*). Such arrangements were put into disarray in 2011 by the Arab Spring, but that does not imply that democratization was *ipso facto* in motion.

As a consequence of these two factors, for the first time, in 2011 SSR in the Arab world became an endogenous debate driven by domestic actors. This was a fundamental reversal of a trend of the 1990s and 2000s, when SSR was an external discourse with little traction on internal, domestic processes. At that time, SSR was promoted by Western powers with very different agendas, from the United States to the European Union and individual Western states, in relation to democracy promotion. The emblematic case was the Palestinian Authority's security forces, along with some incipient programmes in Lebanon and Yemen. Yet, SSR did not gain much traction on the ground or affect military–civilian relations.[3] For instance, adhesion to increased modernization and professionalism of the armed forces collided with the fact that the security sector was the crucial pillar of authoritarian regimes.

The transition paths of countries in the Arab world displayed two very distinctive characteristics that weighed heavily on the prospects for SSR. On the one hand, the setting was much messier in the Arab world in the 2010s—with social

[2] For more details, see Philippe Droz-Vincent, 'From Political to Economic Actors: The Changing Role of Middle Eastern Armies' in O. Schlumberger (ed.), *Debating Arab Authoritarianism* (Stanford University Press, 2007).

[3] The best summary is the report by Y. Sayigh, 'Security Sector Reform in the Arab Region: Challenges to Developing an Indigenous Agenda', Arab Reform Initiative, Thematic Paper (December 2007).

mobilizations still in motion and, with Egypt after 2011 acting as a trendsetter with a very shaky and prolonged transitional process—than in the transitions of the 1980s and 1990. The latter were largely implemented from above with a negotiated pact between elites (for example, in Brazil, Chile, Ecuador, Paraguay, Peru, Hungary, and Poland), and with differences in the mode of transition ranging from extrication to transaction. The new societal awareness was exemplified by re-mobilizations on Tahrir Square in Egypt against the military in 2012 and against the Muslim Brotherhood rule in 2013. However, civilian mobilization lacked organization (activism was not synonymous with organization) and capabilities (such as agenda-setting). As a consequence, the bargaining talks between the actors involved took place in a context of uncertainty underplayed by those promoting change, even when they limited themselves cautiously to speak of 'transitions from authoritarian rule' rather than 'transitions to democracy'. 'Transitologists' do not consider uncertainty to be the central phenomenon of change, assuming that revolutionary situations will naturally end in a way described as a transition, an element that might have some validity in the 'third wave' of the 1990s, but that has much less validity for the Arab Spring region in the 2010s.[4] Conversely, in such a messy setting, the experience of having gone through the phase of popular and street politics in 2011–13 had a powerful uniting effect for the forces of the status quo or counter-revolution (the police, the judiciary, the media, the bureaucracy) around the military (and General al-Sissi) in Egypt in 2013–14.

On the other hand, the second characteristic, with respect to institutions, was the unique role of the military, as differentiated from the over-extended Ministry of the Interior and the intelligence services. The military faced different challenges from some earlier transition experiences. Arab militaries were not enfeebled by defeat (Greece in 1974, Argentina in 1982) or collapse (Portugal in 1974); indeed, in most of the Arab World in 2011, the military remained a powerful stakeholder. Arab armies were not trying to extricate themselves from politics and were not fighting a last-ditch battle after years in direct power, as were many armies in Latin America in the 1980s. Still, as Alfred Stepan recalled, no experts in Latin American studies thought that transitions were foreordained and that the military would retreat easily from politics.[5] In the Arab world, however, the military moved on to the changing stage in 2011 as a proactive actor, either triumphant (Tunisia, Egypt) when it maintained its existing role or at least powerful (Yemen). Further, Arab armies were not subordinated to a civilian authority (as in Spain) or to a single party (as in Eastern Europe or Russia), and their role in the polity was greater and much more encompassing than the corporate autonomy of a military corps, even one

[4] The influential textbook by J. Linz and A. Stepan, *Problems of Democratic Transition and Consolidation* (Johns Hopkins University Press, 1996), chapter 5, considers actors and contexts of transitions and then concludes with a typology of six different possible constitution-making environments.

[5] A. Stepan, *Arguing Comparative Politics* (Oxford University Press, 2001).

endowed with a vague yet encompassing concern for public order and national security (as in Argentina, Brazil, and Peru). The massive role played by the military in Egypt and Yemen (and, conversely, by the evaporation of the military corps and the ensuing lack of institutionalization of a security sector in Libya) clearly distinguished the Arab world from comparative cases where the officer corps could be interventionist but gradually became one stakeholder among others in the hard bargains of a transitional process.

Transitional Dynamics: The Military, Revolutionary Situations, and the Challenges of Reinstitutionalization

In the process of regime change in the Arab world, endogenous factors, such as the security sector and social mobilization, played a crucial role. Much depended on the reactions of the security sector—endowed with a primarily domestic role of regime maintenance and in direct line of command with the executive—and the ability of some parts of it, particularly the armed forces, to dissociate themselves from the fate of the regime under pressure. There were two types of case, depending on the role of the military corps—as distinguished from the Ministry of the Interior's forces, paramilitary forces, intelligence services, and the praetorian guards or special forces that might be part of the military in nominal terms only, but who were in fact directly dependent on the executive.

On the one hand, the first type of cases included those where the military maintained some coherence to act under the guidance of its senior officer corps (Egypt, Tunisia). What was striking with the 'stress test'[6] exerted by the 2011 uprisings was the security sector's resistance and the strong repression it carried out and the simultaneous fragility of the entire authoritarian equilibrium and how quickly, in some cases, it unravelled before determined protesters vying to control symbolic public spaces (Tahrir Square in Cairo, Taghayir Square in Sana'a, Benghazi centre, the Habib Bourghiba Avenue in Tunis, etc.). When the executive vacillated, there was a swift dissipation of power and its adornments—including the dominant party when there was one—as well as its coercive arm (the Ministry of the Interior's forces), leaving the armed forces, when they remained intact, acting in a vacuum.[7] The military, when it remained intact in transitional settings (the paradigmatic examples were Tunisia and Egypt), found itself in a political void after

[6] On the notion of 'stress test', see my chapter, Philippe Droz-Vincent, 'The Military Amidst Uprisings and Transitions in the Arab World' in F. Gerges (ed.), *The New Middle East* (Cambridge University Press, 2014); and 'A Return of Armies to the Forefront of Arab Politics', Istituto Affari Internazionali, IAI Working Papers (July 2011).

[7] Interviews with Tunisian military officers in charge of various military districts, Tunis, October 2011. The former Tunisian Chief of Staff, General Ammar, recalled in a TV interview that the military had power drop into its hands with the fall of the Ben Ali regime, due to the very void left.

social mobilizations succeeded in overthrowing incumbent autocrats. The officer corps was a specific body with the ability to respond as a coherent institutional actor and to endow its role with some narrative of the state (the military as the embodiment of the state, with a historical role in state- and nation-building). These features enabled the military to act as a whole and speak for the state when the regime collapsed. It was thus very different from the Ministry of the Interior, which was reviled for its taking part in repression.

The foremost change was the reordering of forces at play, with the disappearance of the encompassing authoritarian grip of the executive, the new presence of the military, and the looming presence of the Ministry of the Interior's weight (along with other institutional parts of the former regime, in Egypt called *al-fouloul*, the remnants, such as the bureaucracy, the judiciary, the media, some entrepreneurs, etc.). The ability of the military to stay cohesive as a corps and display a nationalist narrative of the state might be a blessing (Tunisia) but at the same time it had the potential to be a curse (Egypt).[8] In 2011, the huge Egyptian senior officer corps enjoyed secure employment, high salaries, sponsored housing, healthcare, education, and numerous other advantages, especially for retired officers, all benefiting from pervasive military patronage in the civilian sector, along with its own economic enterprises geared towards the civilian market. Just how well-off were the Egyptian armed forces was suggested by the Supreme Council of the Armed Forces lending, in December 2011, US$1 billion to the Egyptian state to help the government solve a budget crisis.[9] As a result, political change made the military corps feel nervous or unsettled. In 2011–13, Egyptian military officers tried to safeguard their interests, privileges, and autonomy by projecting an image of themselves as the guardians of political order. They jumped into a new emerging political scene populated with youth leaders, party blocs, intellectuals, Muslim Brothers, Salafists, occupying the driver's seat and playing king-maker. Size mattered: by comparison, the military in Tunisia was very small and endowed with an ultra-loyalist officer corps, although there was a sense of anxiety in 2011 among Tunisian officers faced with an uncertain future and the prospect of new relations with civilians.[10] In both cases, Egypt and Tunisia, the military was the guardian and the controller of the transition and the hand of restraint, but the prospects for SSR differed between Tunisia and

[8] We differentiate militaries according to their degree of coherence and their self-produced narrative; in their textbook on transitions informed by cases of the 1990s, Linz and Stepan make a distinction among variables that affect transitions between 'hierarchical militaries', where the officer corps as a whole sees itself as a permanent part of the state apparatus with enduring interests and permanent functions, and 'non-hierarchical militaries' where some parts (some colonels or majors) of the military are ruling (but the military-as-institution keeps aside and can play a role to extricate the military as a whole from government).

[9] Philippe Droz-Vincent, 'Le militaire et la politique en Egypte' (July–September 1999) 165 *Maghreb-Machrek* 16–65.

[10] Interviews with military officers during an informal dinner with the Minister of Defence, his staff, and former officers, Tunis, October 2011.

Egypt, dependant on the size of the corps and the degree of militarization/military penetration of the polity.

In the second type of case, the military disintegrated in the face of massive public demonstrations because it lacked coherence to begin with (Yemen) or because it was not an institutional actor at all (Libya). Although Gaddafi himself came to power from within the Army via a coup in 1969, he harboured a strong distrust towards the military (and numerous dangerous coups came from within the military) and he reshaped it after 1974 according to the nebulous concept of the 'People's Army' (*al-chaab al-musallaha*). Instead, he relied on his own tribe, with a large number of junior officers headed by a core of loyal colonels, in the military and security services (police and intelligence) and in numerous paramilitary forces ('the people's military', 'security battalions', 'revolutionary guards', 'people's guards', 'military committees', etc.). No coherent military institution existed and, in February 2011, the entire Libyan security edifice imploded: parts of the Libyan Army defected to the mobilized opposition. Helped by easy access to weapons, civilians formed their own militia: Gaddafi had transformed Libya into a veritable arsenal of arms of whatever calibre.[11] Conversely, the most loyal units were at the forefront in fighting the opposition and trying to retake lost towns. The end result was an eight-month-long civil war which lasted until NATO intervention tilted the balance.

Similarly, the Yemeni military gave the superficial impression of being more cohesive than its Libyan counterpart but was in fact more of a coalition of warlords than a real army, with one *primus inter pares*, Ali Abdallah Saleh. The purpose of the security apparatus was mostly internal regime maintenance and had little to do with foreign or even domestic threats (when they remained localized). Tellingly, and despite the military's extraordinary budget, the Yemeni Army was not able to put down the al-Houthi rebellion in the northern province of Sa'ada in 2004–10. There was no real coherence to the military apparatus or even a commonly accepted chain of command, except that of senior officers related personally to Saleh. Only the all-pervasive corruption gave the security sector some degree of unity. Military officers controlled webs of patronage, especially through the largely autonomous Military Economic Corporation that was formally placed under the supervision of the Ministry of Supply, was allotted part of the state apparatus's import quota, and was heavily involved in land deals.[12] The 'informalization' of the chains of command further worsened in the 2000s with the rise of Saleh's sons, nephews, and relatives who received posts in the

[11] Interviews with former members of the Libyan National Transitional Council, Brussels, March 2012.

[12] Glenn E. Robinson, Oliver Wilcox, Stephen Carpenter, and Abdul Ghani al-Iryani, *Yemen's Corruption Assessment*, USAID (ARD, 2006). And in the 2000s, the reinforced Republican Guard under the command of Ali Abdallah Saleh's eldest son got sporting clubs, housing, and preferential hospital treatment.

defence and security establishment. That sphere included numerous organizations, most importantly the Republican Guard, Special Forces, Central Security Forces (CSF) (theoretically related to the Ministry of the Interior but in fact independent), the Counterterrorism Unit within the CSF, Emergency Police, Presidential Guard, along with numerous intelligence services (with identical duplicated tasks). In early March 2011, after some loyalist military units violently stormed Sana'a's university campus and opened fire on demonstrators, the armed forces fractured into two halves. General Ali Mohsen al-Ahmar, the commander of the First Armoured Division and powerful head of the Yemeni Army in the north-west, and other northern commanders announced that they had joined the revolution. The result was a split after May 2011, especially in Sana'a and Taiz, between defectors' units and units loyal to President Saleh, signalling the loss of the Saleh regime's monopoly on the coercive apparatus and, consequently, the beginning of transition.[13]

In these cases, SSR was not just a process of reforms whose importance was derived from broader transitional processes. It was the very basis of all political reforms, a kind of infrastructural precondition for rebuilding the polity by displacing self-generated militias or military/security high commanders turned warlords.

Regime Reformation 'with' the Military: From the 'Exceptional' (Tunisia) to the 'Hard Core' of Military Politics (Egypt)

The crux of the problem in the Arab Spring region became the transition from street politics, military coups backing popular revolts, or army fragmentation and civil war, to political processes and some form of reinstitutionalization. The point of departure was the fall of the authoritarian regime, namely its symbolic figures at the top of the regime. What massive social mobilizations provoked, notwithstanding any prospect of transition to democracy, was a 'revolutionary situation'—to borrow from Charles Tilly, following Trotsky—whose defining feature is 'the presence of more than one bloc effectively exercising control over a significant part of the state'.[14] Revolutionary situations do not presuppose revolutionary outcomes, namely the displacement of one set of power-holders by others; a revolutionary situation can occur without a revolutionary outcome. In 2011, it was a situation where power was diffused among numerous power-holders, among them street

[13] President Saleh reluctantly signed the transition plan on 23 November 2011. And phase one ended with early presidential elections on 21 February 2012 in an election with only one candidate (the former Vice President, yet a figure without much power in the Saleh regime), Abded Rabbo Mansur Hadi.

[14] Charles Tilly, *From Mobilization to Revolution* (Addison-Wesley, 1978), 190.

politics, the armed forces, and what remained from the 'old regime', and no longer defined along prevailing institutional chains of decision-making.[15]

The big problem was then how to move from revolutionary settings toward the reinstitutionalization of political processes—an important part of which was the debating of prospective constitutions—and the rebuilding of political structures. The difficulties of this process were clearly highlighted, even in the thus far best-case scenario, Tunisia, by the innumerable intricacies of the three-and-a-half-year constitutional process which concluded, after numerous delays, in January 2014. Elsewhere things were considerably worse. In Libya, the election of a constitutional assembly in February 2014 did not prevent the collapse of political processes three months later. In Yemen, the National Dialogue ended in January 2014 and was to give way to a constitution drafting process, with the formation of a constitutional committee in March 2014. However, it was pre-empted by a coup by a peripheral actor, the Houthis (also known as Ansar Allah). Egypt's experience with building a constitution was instructive in showing how ephemeral gains might be. The formative moments were an amended Constitution (19 March 2011); a provisional constitutional declaration superseding the former (30 March 2011); a supplement to the constitutional declaration (June 2012), then reversed by presidential decrees (November 2012); a new Constitution (December 2012); and, finally (at least so far!), a revamped Constitution (January 2014).

We can illuminate the transitional settings by cross-tabulating the differences between military reaction to the 'stress test' of societal mobilizations in public spaces by the variation in the state of the polity: along the columns, the military reactions vary from a small loyalist military entering the fray, a big military filling the void with its institutional heft, an exploded military, a fractured military, and a fractured and recombined military; and organized by rows, we characterize the state of the polity with bureaucracy, political parties, civil society actors, and mobilizations (see Table 9.1). The presence and number of plus and minus signs indicates the degree to which a given characteristic was present or absent.

Civilian supremacy was unique to Tunisia among our case studies. The Tunisian military not only refrained from interfering but actually endorsed and supported the rebuilding of the Tunisian polity. In a rare public address on 24 January 2011, Chief of Staff, General Ammar—an unknown figure prior to the Arab Spring who emerged as the head of the most highly respected institution in Tunisia—promised both to uphold Tunisia's revolution and that the military would not play a political role beyond guaranteeing stability until elections were held in October 2011. The institutional statist tradition was hijacked but not destroyed by the Ben Ali

15 Of course, various power-holders do not have the same power and power should be understood as not confined only to hard coercive power. As stated by Tilly (ibid., 193), there are many reference points available, such as power over the means of production, power over symbols, and power over means of violence.

Table 9.1: The policy mix of Arab transitions

	Small military maintaining coherence: Tunisia	**Huge military maintaining coherence: Egypt**	**Exploded military: Libya**	**Fractured military: Yemen**
Mobilizations	+	+	+	+
Bureaucracy	++	+	--	-
Parties	+	-	--	+
Civil society	+++	=	=	++
State of the polity	Cohesive	Fragmented and polarized	Militia politics	Dangerous stalemate

regime: a sense of the state was preserved by numerous actors, mid-ranking bureaucrats, lawyers, university professors, jurists, trade unionists, civil society activists, human rights defenders, etc., along with military officers. These actors were able to revive the Tunisian statist tradition after the fall of the Ben Ali regime, through the '*Instance supérieure pour la réalisation des objectifs de la révolution, la réforme politique et la transition démocratique*' (the High Commission for the Realization of the Revolution's Objectives, Political Reforms and Democratic Transition). Furthermore, that reinstated political space was dominated by civilians. The main difficulties in Tunisia came not from a huge military lobbying for preserving some interests but from the institutional weight of parts of the former regime (the Ministry of the Interior and the justice apparatus).

In Egypt, the military remained in the driver's seat. The transition was led by the military, one that was not well-geared towards politics—given that the Army was not a *political* actor under Mubarak—and was clearly perplexed by the new Egyptian transitional setting. At the same time, the military was triumphant, in stark contrast to the Ministry of the Interior, reviled for participating in repression on behalf of the Mubarak regime. We will devote a detailed analysis to Egypt as it is the most interesting case in terms of what happened following the initial 'triumph' of the Arab uprisings.

The three-step protracted Egyptian transitional process

First, the Supreme Council of the Armed Forces (SCAF) in direct power followed the basic subtext laid out in the final hours of the Mubarak regime. Mubarak offered to amend several constitutional articles in a last-ditch attempt to save his regime. In February 2011, the SCAF dissolved Egypt's rubber-stamp parliament, suspended the 1971 Constitution (and thereby became the de facto ruler of Egypt), and set a schedule for new elections, beginning with parliamentary elections; in the initial timetable, these were due to take place in June followed by a presidential election in the summer of 2011. The SCAF tasked a committee, whose members it selected according to unknown criteria, with amending several articles of the Constitution to prepare for fair elections. In the end, the changes they introduced dealt essentially with state-of-emergency laws and the electoral system that had originally been designed to allow the Mubarak regime to select the winners; the SCAF did not allow the committee to initiate more extensive changes.[16] On 19 March 2011, three weeks after their public release, the resulting hurriedly written eight constitutional amendments were presented to Egyptian voters in a referendum. The turn-out was impressive by the Egyptian standards of the 1990s and 2000s and the proportion of the 'Yes' vote was overwhelming.

Then, on 30 March 2011, the SCAF announced on its Facebook page a 'provisional constitutional declaration' of sixty-three articles, mostly drawn from the 1971 Constitution superseding the amended Constitution and acting as the basic law prior to the drafting of a new Constitution. It incorporated the amended articles along with scores of others, and its Article 56 protected the SCAF as a legitimate and constitutional ruler through the parliamentary elections and until a new President was elected.[17] The SCAF acted with a mixture of proclaimed disinterest in the name of Egypt—the military leadership as a patriotic actor dedicated to Egypt and strongly frustrated when it did not receive the gratitude it thought it deserved[18]—and at the same time sought to manage the process, even by repeatedly changing the roadmap for transition. Despite strong criticism—beginning in April 2011 with a 'Friday of warning', huge gatherings dubbed the SCAF's head, Marshal Tantawi, a dictator and called for '*isqat al-muchir*' (the fall of the Marshal) and several anti-Tantawi Facebook pages appeared—the SCAF sought to shape an outcome that would protect military influence and privileges in the Egyptian polity. The SCAF inserted ideas into the public debates to gauge how people would react to them and then, adjusting and calibrating to that response, it sometimes returned with another idea. There was no formal political dialogue between military and interim civilian leadership, but rather an interplay and often a show of force with the SCAF confined to the Ministry of Defence in Cairo's Abbasiyya neighbourhood, issuing decrees sent over to the civilian interim Cabinet. While

[16] Interview with one member of the constitutional committee, Paris, April 2013.

[17] The SCAF consulted some Egyptian leaders on an ad hoc basis but ignored calls to bring together various political forces to oversee the process; he convened a national dialogue only after the constitutional declaration was issued; nobody knew who drafted the declaration.

[18] Interviews with three Egyptian scholars (of various political leanings) advising the SCAF, Paris, April 2013. The military strongly believes it is responsible for the fall of Mubarak (and denies the crucial role of social mobilizations without leaders) and in some sense harbours a feeling of knowing more than others what is best for Egypt. And, when the SCAF faces huge demonstrations, it answers that these phenomena are not representative of Egypt and that the so-called 'silent majority', a mythical term, in fact supports its stance.

some generals spoke to the media to justify their decisions, the SCAF remained opaque and failed to consult with others. All political forces were keenly interested in the electoral process with the Muslim Brotherhood having learned that elections worked to its advantage, and the still-weak liberal and leftist opposition complaining about, boycotting, or demonstrating against, important state institutions (justice institutions and the Ministry of the Interior). Between them, and playing on their contradictions and inabilities, was the military.

Beginning in June 2011, the political debate centred on the sequencing of political processes, either to proceed with elections in order to end military rule—favouring the Muslim Brotherhood who were eager to enter the corridors of power and were well aware of their own electoral potential—or to slow down the pace of electoral preparations and prioritize drafting and ratifying the Constitution, a more appealing alternative for liberals and the left wing who feared being wiped out by Islamists. At the same time, the convoluted electoral process fuelled suspicions about the SCAF's real intentions among both liberals and the Muslim Brothers. The transitional agenda became fluid, due to the SCAF's patchy attempts to drive it. There was careful and slow public disclosure regarding the process of the transition and a readjustment of military preferences according to public reaction. Leaks by some SCAF generals stressed that Egypt's new Constitution should grant the right to protect public interest and freedom from parliamentary oversight to the military in its budget (June 2011). Then posters went up (and rumours circulated) in Cairo and Alexandria touting Marshal Tantawi for President (September 2011). The SCAF denied involvement; thereafter, the El-Selmi document (of 'supra-constitutional principles', from the Deputy Prime Minister, November 2011) seeking to carve out an influential place for the armed forces was aired. Faced with large demonstrations, 'the million marches' (*al-milioniyyat*), the SCAF made a major concession by scheduling presidential elections by the end of June 2012 and not in 2013 as was previously announced.

The transition toward the parliamentary and presidential elections was prolonged. Exhaustion set in over delays, turning points, changes to the roadmap, and the military trying to tailor the process according to its interests. The SCAF could only reach tactical and very temporary agreements over serious negotiations with political groupings, as its aggressive approach turned the entire process into disarray. The military constantly changed tactics to drive its agenda on, between concessions (when the public outcry grew too great) and violent reactions (the Maspero massacre of Copts in 2011; the Mahmud Street clashes in November 2011, not to mention the trial of civilians, the military police maltreatment of protesters, the infamous 'virginity tests' for arrested women, etc.). For instance, the influential Muslim Brotherhood campaigned for the 'Yes' vote as a religious duty in March 2011 and accepted the 'provisional constitutional declaration' as it was enticed into the SCAF's plan to put parliamentary elections first. Conversely, the

SCAF was convinced of the supposed ability of the Muslim Brotherhood to control the streets, but the Muslim Brotherhood opposed the El-Selmi document in November 2011 and took part in huge demonstrations. Then, two weeks before parliamentary elections, the Brotherhood refused to support protests for fear of cancellation of the ballot by the SCAF. In January 2012 with the final results of parliamentary elections, relations (or what was called in Egypt at the time, the Muslim Brotherhood–SCAF 'power-sharing') went sour when the SCAF woke up to the fact that a parliament invested with a strong popular mandate could assert itself. The SCAF compelled the majority Freedom and Justice Party (FJP, an offshoot of the Muslim Brotherhood) to acknowledge that forming the next interim Cabinet was the SCAF's prerogative and that presidential powers (in the hands of the SCAF) included the right to appoint 90 members (out of 270) of the incoming High Chamber (*majlis al-shura*) with a role in selecting the members of the constitution drafting committee. In addition, the SCAF circulated the idea of a 'constitutional pact' granting the military autonomous jurisdiction over its internal affairs and budget, creating a National Security Council with representation of the military (hence giving the military a say in discussions pertaining to national security, foreign policy, etc.) and giving the military immunity from prosecution under civil law.[19]

Constitutional processes and presidential elections progressed. In March 2012, the FJP put forward a presidential candidate, reneging on a previous pledge, and called for demonstrations in Tahrir Square until the transfer of power from the SCAF to an elected President was completed. For the military, the presidency was also an essential position: the SCAF had resisted any diminution of Egypt's presidential system in the hope that an SCAF-friendly President would be elected, what it called 'a consensus candidate'. The election of such a President would also endow the SCAF with the ability to interfere indirectly in the constitutional process. In April 2012, the State Court judged that the constitutional committee was 'unrepresentative', suspended its activities, and thereby relegated the FJP to the tedium of hard parliamentary work without much clout in constitutional processes. In fact, the latter was taken outside parliament, as political parties negotiated possible criteria for a second constitutional assembly directly with the SCAF. Then on 7 June, the SCAF allowed the Islamist-dominated parliament to form a more representative constituent assembly. A week later, the Supreme Constitutional Court dissolved parliament owing to the now-unconstitutional electoral law. On 17 June 2012, on the second day of the two-day presidential election, the SCAF unilaterally issued a 'complementary constitutional declaration' granting itself legislative

[19] The Muslim Brotherhood were advocating that the newly elected parliament be granted absolute sovereignty to draft the Constitution; the liberals wanted a supra-constitutional declaration promising respect for religious minorities and the broader vision of a democratic state; and the military wanted to benefit from these diverging agendas to oversee the drafting and work out a deal in which it would continue to enjoy its prerogatives by playing on the other camps.

powers, a strong role in the constitution-making process, and a tutelary position to the elected President.

The result was a stalemate with the SCAF insisting it was unwilling to rule, but at the same time refusing to surrender decision-making powers to civilian politicians. The longer this situation endured, the less likely that some very necessary institutional decisions could be taken in a turbulent political scene whose main characteristic was extreme divisions. Moreover, it was becoming more difficult for the SCAF to see what kind of reassurances it could get and from whom, and thus the SCAF position turned into a classic prisoner's dilemma that partly explained the Army's remaining near the centre of political power.

Inaugurating a second step, on 12 August 2012, after a terrorist attack in the Sinai, newly elected President Morsi repealed the SCAF's supra-constitutional declaration, thereby arrogating the SCAF's legislative as well as executive powers to himself by decree until a new parliament was elected and a new constitution was ratified. He also removed the top leadership of the SCAF, most importantly Minister of Defence Marshal Tantawi and Chief of Staff General Anan.[20] The ease with which President Morsi managed to force the SCAF out of power confirmed the military's fatigue and the Army leadership's broad-mindedness—particularly among the younger generals around the top leaders of the SCAF,[21] for instance General al-Sissi—in entering into a tacit deal with the newly elected President Morsi in order to extricate themselves from power and let civilians govern Egypt. Conversely, President Morsi believed that these younger officers, some of whom were religious, posed less of a threat to him than the older generals who had served Mubarak.[22] The regime's drive towards allowing more civilians to occupy political posts, a new feature in Egypt since 1952 with a civilian elected President and Vice President, did not happen. The 2012 Constitution was rushed through at a time of legal cases pending against the Muslim Brotherhood-dominated constitutional assembly, and the prerogatives of the military were preserved (in Articles 195, 197, and 198). As an indication of the tacit agreement between the military and the Muslim Brotherhood, the articles in the 2012 Constitution dealing with the exemption of the military budget from civilian oversight and military tribunals were identical to Articles 9 and 10 of the El-Selmi document that the Muslim Brotherhood had previously condemned. The 2012 Constitution gave in to all the demands of the military, including an autonomous budget and complete autonomy for its own affairs,

[20] In Tantawi's place, Morsi promoted General Sissi, the SCAF's youngest member who ousted him on 3 July 2013. Powerful generals across the security sector who shared an anti-reform stance and a defiance of elected civilian rule were also removed.

[21] Others put the problem the other way: the military went to Morsi to offer such a deal. Interviews in Paris, January 2014.

[22] This was a kind of wishful thinking among inexperienced Muslim Brothers, as officers are first and foremost military officers endowed with a sense of corporatism. Interviews in Geneva with retired officers in contact with active officers, January 2014.

immunity from prosecution in civilian courts, and a veto in high politics by being required to approve crucial decisions.

The now 'satisfied' top brass kept a low profile. During the preceding SCAF rule, the military had managed to maintain coherence (despite some rumblings in the ranks)[23] but it had lost much credibility: the SCAF's rule had exacted a heavy price on the military. The essential task of General al-Sissi during Morsi's rule was to restore the military's credibility, and the stunning fact was how successful the military had been in restoring its popularity, in translating its own narrative into a kind of legitimacy to guarantee a role of guardian of the Egyptian polity, and in making Egyptians completely forget almost two years of calamitous misrule by the SCAF. However, the viability of the military acting as a silent partner was only possible if the Muslim Brotherhood ruled Egypt smoothly, with military direct intervention remaining an option in case of failure; military support was not a foregone conclusion, as alluded to by numerous officers in the Egyptian press during Morsi's rule.[24]

In a third step, at the end of 2012, Morsi's incompetence—his disastrous economic policies, though in some part engineered by state institutions he was unable to control; his inability to deal with the rise of militant Islamic groups in the Sinai, a highly strategic region for the military; his threat to use force against Ethiopia; his suggestion that Egyptians could join jihad against the Syrian regime; his stubbornness highlighted by his failed attempts to acquire super-constitutional powers; his authoritarian tone and lack of sensitivity, especially to issues of minority rights—was dividing the country and leading to polarization and chaos. After November 2012, Morsi's constitutional declaration and assertion of unchecked power split the country: the National Salvation Front versus the Muslim Brotherhood, the judges and the prosecutors against the presidency, etc. New challengers, especially the well-organized *Tamarrod* (rebellion) movement in May–June 2013, were moved by a deep sense of frustration against Morsi's government, which had come to treat people the same way the Mubarak regime did. The mobilizational momentum was also manipulated by the military intelligence close to the Minister of Defence and its former head, General al-Sissi. In January 2013, court decisions sentencing football supporters in Port Said to death sparked violence and mobilizations at the time of the anniversary of the 2011 uprising. In response, Morsi declared a state of emergency which the military refused to enforce.

The military elites gave the impression of allowing Morsi the opportunity to mend his ways; in December 2012, on Facebook, the SCAF invited the President for what it called a 'social dialogue' but then cancelled its invitation. The Army leadership issued declarations stating its neutral stance but at the same time suggesting that it would not let the country fall into the abyss. In the end, the generals decided to ride the wave of change rather than wait and let Egypt fall again into massive

[23] 'Egyptian Army Officer's Diary of Military Life in a Revolution', *The Guardian*, 28 December 2011.
[24] Interviews with active military officers, Paris, January 2014.

upheaval which potentially would have led the Muslim Brotherhood to call on the military to re-establish order. The Army overthrew Morsi on 3 July 2013 during a massive popular uprising that gave the military some legitimacy to jump in: it was a coup but with popular support and with lots of ambiguities, as many Egyptians who deeply resented Morsi still did not want him overthrown by the military. The Army could not have acted in the absence of such a specific setting.

Regime Decays under the Threatening Prospect of a Fractured Security Sector (Yemen) or 'Without' a Security Sector (Libya)

In Libya, as a consequence of the unravelling of the Gaddafi regime through civil war (and international intervention) and of the collapse of all institutions, the weak Libyan military first among them, new (civilian) actors came to the fore, most visibly organized in militias or 'brigades of revolutionaries' (*kata'ib al-thuwwar*), as they called themselves. It was a 'civilian' process taking place in a 'civil' society that organized itself into self-defence units and 'cannibalized' the official (state) security sector. The security sector evaporated or (alternatively speaking) was recreated from below by civilians-turned-militiamen with the help of former officers and retired officers. Its few remaining institutional elements came out of the civil war in a weak position with the rise of militias. The main driver of militia creation was not ideology but rather fragmentation and localism: local leaders, entrepreneurs, notables, religious leaders, former officers, etc., formed militias in cities besieged by Gaddafi's loyalists. Some of them, especially those with Islamist/Salafist leanings, were more ideological than others. Specifically, and as an exception, in the eastern part of Libya, some Army units (and the feeblest part of Gaddafi's regular Army) kept some cohesiveness and defected *en masse*. After March 2011, Benghazi was protected by NATO's no-fly zone, which provided rebels with a relatively secure area; a few former military commanders there set up a 'New (or Rebel) National Army' under the command of the defecting Minister of the Interior, General Abdul Fatah Younes, who was assassinated under mysterious circumstances, hence signalling strong internal oppositions in the rebels' camp. Yet, the New National Army had no control over, and was far weaker than, the autonomous militias/revolutionary brigades.

No real state-building process meant there was no reinstatement of a state monopoly on force. The National Transitional Council (NTC), until its replacement by the elected General National Congress (GNC) in August 2012, played a very successful role as an external arm—the political face of the revolution—for a Libyan revolution comprising a series of disconnected and uncoordinated local uprisings. The NTC could boast a number of tangible economic and democratic successes with the restoration of previous levels of oil production—which fell dramatically during the uprising—and the GNC elections in July 2012. However, it did not act as a government, in particular in preventing competition between militias, registering the huge number of weapons and ammunition circulating in the country, or reinstating the state monopoly on violence. In addition, the GNC did not even capitalize on the wave of popular rage against militias. For instance, among many instances of militias' misbehaviour, following days of violence in Tripoli and Benghazi in November 2013, clashes between Misrata militiamen and protesters resulted in at least 46 civilians dead and over 600 wounded, generating public uproar against militias.

In December 2011, the NTC set up the Warriors' Commission, an inter-ministerial body under the guidance of the Prime Minister, to register fighters and channel them into employment in the Ministries of the Interior and Defence or return them to civilian life. Perhaps no more than 20,000 revolutionaries fought, but 120,000 to 150,000 were registered by the Warriors' Commission (out of 215,000–250,000 requests). That process institutionalized the role of militias. Furthermore, the pressing security agenda in Libya led the NTC/GNC to rely on some brigades or local military councils to negotiate local rifts and impose local ceasefires. The government allowed coalitions of various militias with different ideological leanings and tribal compositions to be integrated into the security forces, such as the most powerful security forces in Libya, the Libya Shields Forces (*Quwwat Der'a Libya*), acting nominally under the authority of the Ministry of Defence or the Supreme Security Committees (SSC, ranging from 90,000 to 120,000 members) under the Ministry of the Interior. In reality, militias integrated within the Army or police were answering only to their commanders. The NTC even appointed some commanders of the most powerful militias to key government ministries, where they carved out their own fiefdoms.

The Libyan case represents a kind of 'perverse institutionalization'[25] pushed to the extreme, with the central government's acquiescence. Militias filled the institutional and political void left unoccupied by the NTC, then the GNC. Furthermore, there was no Ministry of Defence after the fall of Gaddafi, as the latter had coordinated his highly fragmented security forces through networks of personal acquaintances, not through institutions. In the post-Gaddafi Ministry of Defence, everything had to be done from scratch as new power-holders discovered, from laws on pensions and services, the disbursement of salaries, to establishing a pyramidal hierarchy, and all this under the heavy constraint of addressing the demands of the genuine or alleged 'revolutionaries' to vet security and military personnel who served under the former regime. There was a programme of capacity-building requested by the Justice, Security, and Defence Programme agreed in Paris in February 2012 between the NTC and its external backers, but the logic of militias

[25] S. Valenzuela, 'Democratic Consolidation in Post-Transitional Settings', Notre Dame, Kellogg Institute, Working Paper No. 150 (December 1990).

overwhelmed it and state institutions did not displace militias as the basic structure of politics.

The dynamics of the political system (before its implosion) were unable to sustain a programme of SSR and the short-cut answer of foreign backers and observers was that Libya was rebuilding 'hybrid forces'. In fact, the security sector was not really a hybrid as it was dominated by militias. Militias served as tools to extract concessions from the government: any relatively small group of armed men could extract whatever concession they desired from the state by storming an official building or even the General National Congress (GNC), or cutting an oil pipeline or a road to Tripoli, to ask for increased pensions for warriors, for fighters to be sent abroad for medical treatment, for more seats in parliament or the constituent assembly, or for whatever reason. In October 2013, the Prime Minister was abducted from his office for five hours for relatively trivial demands. Militias could get more important concessions at gunpoint, as in May 2013 when various militias forced the GNC to vote in a 'Political and Administrative Isolation Law', barring people who worked for the Gaddafi regime from public positions. Furthermore, militias directly controlled or extracted resources: Misratans controlled a Mediterranean port; Zentanis 'protected' oil infrastructures and smuggling in the Nafusa region across the Tunisian border; and numerous other armed groups in the south manned checkpoints on trading roads.

In the face of such challenges, the government was inclined to compromise and hesitated to take bold action for fear of being targeted by militias; and when one militia succeeded in getting a concession, even a minor one, it was immediately copied by numerous other groups across the country. Libyan society strongly resented militia violence and felt imprisoned by it. Yet, at the same time, Libyans had rational reasons to keep militias operating (to get jobs, funds, etc.). Militias took root in the Libyan local landscape. Civil war has a great transformative potential in social relations. It generates new groupings and new social hierarchies; SSR can be seriously impaired by such a social restructuring when militias become embedded in society. Local authority becomes militarized or influenced by militia, with new forms of governance that reflect the role of armed groups.

The Libyan central government remained very weak and timorous in a potentially wealthy country, unable to use its money to build its power, in contrast to the classic rentier economies such as the Gulf emirates. It has been a patronage machine but not a centralized one, co-opting clients by handing out money or favours, and much more so in the hands of clients who might be more appropriately considered 'stakeholders'. The government acted as a kind of technocratic body with no sense of the state (i.e. not struggling for its own differentiation amidst rival centres of power to build its own monopoly).[26] The militias, in turn, looked upon the

[26] See the process of European state-building as described by C. Tilly, 'War-Making and State-Making as Organized Crime' in Peter Evans, Dietrich Rueschemeyer, and Theda Skocpol (eds), *Bringing the State Back In* (Cambridge University Press, 1985).

government as a form of easy prey or a golden goose.[27] They played on the strong distrust in Libya of a strong centralized authority, the spectre of 'the evil centre' that might become a tyrannical power in the hands of a leader, and on the unease of the government to impose its will. Militias brandished their legitimacy as 'real fighters/revolutionaries (*thuwwar*): Zintanis recalled bitter fighting and their capture of Saif al Islam Qadhafi; Misratans claimed they sacrificed thousands in one of the deadliest battles of the eight-month civil war and captured Qadhafi; and eastern regionalists like Ibrahim Jadhran used a sort of regionalist populism, while in fact controlling oil facilities as part of the Petroleum Facilities Guard. All this is hardly conducive to SSR given that there is no political sphere functioning independently of militias. As a consequence, and although numerous societal protests resented these trends, the constitutional process suffered long-term delays in Libya.[28] Conversely, militia politics benefited from the absence of a rebuilt security sector to thrive and even to dominate (civilian) politics.

In Yemen, the degree of institutional disintegration in 2011 as a consequence of authoritarian path dependence and revolutionary state collapse was high, but not to the same degree as in Libya. Armed violence resulted from the fracturing between two warring camps drawn from the Saleh regime's former power-holders. Hence, there was not an implosion of the whole security sector giving way to multiple rag-tag militias as in Libya. After Saleh reluctantly signed the UN-sponsored Gulf Cooperation Council initiative for regime transition in Yemen, power was gradually transferred to Vice President Abed Rabbo Mansour Hadi, who was elected President in a single-candidate referendum in February 2012.

To implement the vague guidelines on SSR in the Gulf Cooperation Council transition agreement, a Committee on Military Affairs for Achieving Security and Stability was established with US and Jordanian help and chaired by newly elected President Hadi. Jordan had an enduring relationship with Yemeni armed forces. The Committee was created to alleviate tensions and risks of fighting between rival camps. It was assisted by two technical committees (Defence and the Interior), with help from technical advisors (from the United States, European Union, and United Kingdom) tasked with offering some concrete plans for SSR. SSR reform began with the replacement of the top brass of the military and security apparatus—it removed twenty senior military commanders, most of them Saleh's relatives—by presidential decrees in April and May. In September 2012 the CSF and intelligence apparatuses were reshuffled in order to remove the remainder of Saleh's relatives from them. President Hadi's moves were buttressed by a UN Security Council's

[27] Discussions with former members of the NTC, Brussels, March 2012.

[28] With the UN Support Mission in Libya (UNSMIL), the GNC resolved in February 2013 the long-standing dispute over the manner in which members of the sixty-member constitution-drafting assembly would be elected. In January 2014, the GNC took the decision, despite protests, to extend its legislative mandate to December 2014, beyond the original February 2014 deadline in the draft Constitution. See the various reports by the UNSMIL on its website, <http://unsmil.unmissions.org/>.

resolution (No. 2051, 12 June 2012) that threatened sanctions against those who opposed presidential decrees, after Saleh's loyalists balked at leaving their posts, complaining that this amounted to the exclusion of one side in favour of the other. President Hadi earned criticism from both sides (Saleh and Ali Mohsen) as he was accused of favouring his allies—the Minister of Defence was a trusted ally from his home province of Abyan. Furthermore, the Islamist-tribal group al-Islah was accused of pursuing a hidden agenda, given that the Minister of the Interior was drawn from it.

SSR entails not just important personnel questions, a side-product of personalized authoritarian regimes with dynastic trends (*tawrith al-sulta*). It also entails a thorough revamping of the command structure and defence laws, elements that did not exist in the Yemeni military under Saleh's reign. In December 2012, Presidential Decree No. 104 announced a major revamping of the armed forces' organizational structure, to be valid for a five-year transitional period, until a new comprehensive law could be enacted. In particular it disbanded both the Republican Guard and the First Division. Saleh's eldest son, Ahmed Ali Saleh, was the chief of the Republican Guard, the most powerful unit in Yemen's armed forces. The Republican Guard had been built to counterbalance the potential threat from the First Division, led by General Ali Mohsen. Mohsen was named an adviser to President Hadi while Ahmed Ali Saleh was sent to the United Arab Emirates (UAE) as Yemeni ambassador. These reforms were complemented, in February 2013, by a major overhaul of the Ministry of the Interior's internal structure. Finally, at the low and mid-levels, efforts were made to streamline recruits and introduce some degree of professionalism.

However, the main military stakeholders (who controlled units) refused to comply in most cases. Soldiers went on strike or stormed official buildings in protest. New commanders nominated by Hadi could not overcome the entrenched loyalty of units to their prior commanders. SSR on paper never led to changes in reality in Yemen and networks built by Saleh and Ali Mohsen (or other commanders) could not be erased simply by new organizational charts. The challenge was also the implementation of reforms that had to go further and deeper than President Hadi's decrees, which played a forerunner role in SSR restructuring. Former President Ali Abdallah Saleh had managed the security sector through a series of unconstitutional laws and decrees, granting him exclusive power and establishing a kind of virtual security sector above the law: parliamentary oversight and internal auditing oversight were neutralized by the links senior officers had with the presidency. Therefore, the whole apparatus of control had to be revamped which entailed the need for broad political consensus. Furthermore, in 2012–13, in a context of terrorist attacks and significant advances for al-Qaeda in the Arabian Peninsula (AQAP) in some southern provinces, SSR was caught between a rock (the political resistance of former senior figures of the Saleh regime, quite different from the Egyptian military's corporatism) and a hard place (the necessity of having an efficient military tool not overly weakened by reforms and reshuffles).

Beyond its technical aspect, SSR is always strongly related to the workings of the whole political system and the latter's ability to put SSR on the agenda in an (relatively) apolitical way. This was not the case in Yemen, despite a few initial bright spots, as the rebuilt political system went awry. A National Dialogue conference (*al-mu'tamar al-hiwar al-watani*) was initiated in March 2013, initially planned for six months and then extended for another four in the face of bitter disagreements over key issues, especially the southern question and the Houthi rebellion. It was tasked with dealing with all the problems of the country and agreeing on the content of a new constitution to be adopted by referendum in 2014. Its 565 participants were tilted heavily toward politicians but with some younger members, although certainly not in proportion to their importance, and with a solid representation of women, representing the north and the south. The National Dialogue committee had nine working groups, including one on the armed and security forces, engaged in wide consultations in the country and reported through a well-resourced website with the help of—and heavy pressure from—the UN Special Envoy, Jamal Benomar. In September 2013, the Military and Security Working Group approved its final report on time and offered a series of 'major questions relevant to the Constitution' concerning the Army and security organizations.[29] The main problem was that the National Dialogue gave the impression of aiming at the creation of a whole new Yemeni polity, whereas its focus lay in a very pressing, short-term context: the resolution of two conflicts, the southern question and the al-Houthi uprising. It could not give new momentum to state rebuilding in general in Yemen, and the ensuing Constitutional Draft Committee (March 2014–January 2015) delivered a draft Constitution that provided the trigger for the Houthi takeover (see later in this chapter).

State of Play: Meagre Outcomes, Some Remaining Hopes, and a Pressing Need for SSR

Heterogeneity is the basic outcome nine years after the beginning of the Arab Spring, arising from similar questions of control in the four cases examined here. Most dauntingly, with the exception of Tunisia, the context that allowed the topics of SSR to be raised has been lost in new types of revamped authoritarian regimes (Egypt) or in war settings (Libya, Yemen).

[29] In January 2014, in the closing ceremony of the National Dialogue, President Hadi pledged to form commissions to draft the new Constitution; a document of some 1,400 recommendations was agreed upon. Delegates agreed that President Hadi, who was sworn in for a two-year term according to the transitional plan in February 2012, should remain in office until a new Constitution had been approved and elections held.

The Tunisian process seems the most promising, notwithstanding an enormous shortcoming that impedes civilian 'advancement' in SSR. In Tunisia, the Ministry of Defence is an entirely civilian organization, acting with the advice of the Chief of Staff whose position has remained vacant since the resignation of General Ammar in 2013. Furthermore, the three Chiefs of Staff of the different services do not serve on a unified general staff that might concentrate power in military hands. Power has been channelled through the hierarchy of the Ministry of Defence. The new 2014 Constitution's Article 18 set up provisions to ensure civilian control. Just as important in parallel, a culture of oversight must also be institutionalized, with the defence budget opened for public scrutiny as well as parliamentary oversight of the military sector by dint of parliamentary committees. Most importantly, all of this is welcomed by a generation of officers in command for whom the language of democratic governance is not alien.[30]

The paradox is that the Tunisian problem is not, as in the other cases discussed, to curtail the role of the military but to reinforce it in terms of means in a context of acute security threats (in the northern part of the Algerian–Tunisian border and in Mount Chaambi) and terrorism. The military, since the revolution, has fulfilled a number of essential internal security tasks—securing borders, establishing camps for refugees from Libya, countering incursions from Libyan or Algerian armed groups, guarding public institutions—using 18,000 out of 43,000 forces personnel available to perform these tasks. Moreover, the military has taken over control of some internal security functions from the Ministry of the Interior, with military officers playing a role in security operations especially when things got out of hand.[31] This is not comparable to an invasion of security functions by military officers, however. As a corollary of the more open (democratic) political system, the military has been pulled into some political controversies, and retired officers have been more inclined to speak in public debates. Senior officers have striven to keep the Army out of politics and to remain within strict constitutional limits, yet public criticism of the military has remained a sensitive topic as highlighted by the increasing number of charges of 'army defamation', in particular against bloggers.

The main shortcoming of SSR in Tunisia was that the new Constitution said nothing about the Ministry of the Interior and the intelligence services. They were governed by more than 1,700 laws and amendments[32] and the organization of the Ministry of the Interior was byzantine, with fiefdoms that did not answer to civilian authorities but were autonomous and impervious to control. The 2011 White Paper on Police Reform focused on enhancing its capabilities, not on promoting its democratic governance. More generally, the 'organizational anarchy'

[30] Interviews, Tunis, August 2013.

[31] Interview with a retired military officer with very close connections to active officers, Paris, January 2014.

[32] For the maze of legislation related to the security sector, see Haykel Ben Mahfoudh, Jonas Loetscher, and Arnold Luethold, *La Législation du secteur de la sécurité en Tunisie* (DCAF, 2012).

that was cultivated by the Ben Ali regime—which ensured that decision-making was left exclusively to the executive—has remained in place and serves to perpetuate the institutional inertia of some parts of the state apparatus. Beyond the sacking of some high-level police officers by the initial al-Sebsi transitional government and then by the al-Nahda government,[33] there have been no far-reaching legal and institutional reforms of the police. The political police have been reintegrated into the regular police. Discussions were held about the handling of the archives of the political police, as highlighted by a 2012 conference convened by the non-governmental organization (NGO) 'le Labo' Démocratique' and the Swiss think-tank DCAF. After the fall of Ben Ali, police unions were formed advocating for reforms, a new feature in Tunisia. As a consequence of the new openness, they have aggressively lobbied and even pressured decision-makers and the judiciary (even storming a courthouse in February 2018) on the question of police abuses, blocking SSR reforms. The Ministry of the Interior has withdrawn from interfering in electoral processes and, in 2015, the creation of a Ministry of Local Affairs weakened its extensive grip. However, the police force remains the most reviled sector in Tunisia. It continues to be oblivious to the public interest and is accused of being involved in torture, although human rights provisions have been inscribed into its regulations. The police culture has not been reformed, and the Ministry of the Interior has concentrated on merely cosmetic changes: it created a Facebook page and introduced a new police uniform. The July 2015 Counterterrorism Law, hastily finished after two serious terrorist attacks (the Bardo Museum and Sousse), was considered too comprehensive and risked infringing civil liberties, although police unions lobbied for stricter provisions. In addition, the Ministry of the Interior has remained unreformed, with ministers more eager to appease the security sector with salary increases and looser legal control in a context of increased terrorist threats.

Parliament after 2014 has not produced legislation on the security sector beyond a single law in 2017 on custom procedures in a sector heavily affected by cross-border smuggling and protection rackets. Fundamentally, the reform of the Ministry of the Interior has been paralysed by the absence of consensual (and removed from party politics) political will. Furthermore, in a highly polarized Tunisian political landscape between al-Nahda and networks of so-called secularists and old (Ben Ali) regime elites in Nida' Tounes, the competitive yet cooperative consensus and 'pacted politics', limited to distributing posts, has slowed down reforms to a halt.

[33] Al-Nahda was very concerned, when appointing a Minister of the Interior during the coalition caretaker government, not to generate the impression of exerting revenge on a sector it considered part of the old regime. In 2012, the Nahdawi Minister of the Interior, Ali Laarayedh, who was tortured and imprisoned for fifteen years, faced difficulties in removing some senior officers, such as the head of the *Brigades d'intervention* (formerly *Brigades de l'Ordre Public*) involved in the killing of protesters in 2011. He was then accused of partisan control (Islamicizing) of the police and backtracked on many reforms.

There has been some weak political will to introduce forms of transitional justice: Decree Law 35 in 2011 by the High Independent Authority for Elections, prohibiting candidacies of individuals linked to the former Ben Ali regime; the establishment of the Ministry of Human Rights and Transitional Justice by the al-Nahda-led government at the end of 2011 yet weakened by mistrust between secularists and Islamists; then, after the ousting of the al-Nahda government, and in a deal between political forces to adopt the Constitution, the Organic Law on Establishing and Organizing Transitional Justice (December 2013) to investigate violations of human rights between July 1955 and December 2013. A significant step was the nomination of the members of the Truth and Dignity Commission in June 2014. Again, however, despite significant achievements (with the collection of 60,000 testimonies of abuse and galvanizing televised hearings), the working of the Commission lost its momentum in a highly politicized Tunisia and against fading public interest. In any event, the question remains highly sensitive and political, short of accomplishing any standard of transitional justice.

By comparison, Egypt left the path of reform to re-enter that of authoritarianism with an untouchable military at the top. In the aftermath of the 2013 coup, Egypt displayed the strong tutelary influence of the armed forces evident in the reopened constitutional process. After the removal of President Morsi, a fifty-member committee/Constituent Assembly was formed to reform the 2012 Constitution, following a constitutional declaration issued by the interim President. In fact, the constitutional declaration was handed over by the SCAF (and General al-Sissi) after limited consultations with what it called 'people of trust' (who remain unknown). The 2014 Constitution approved by referendum bore the weight of the military's reinforced influence, with additional gains for the military when compared with the 2012 Morsi Constitution. The military and the police were granted extensive autonomy and, in the Chapter 8 of the Constitution the military was a branch unto itself with provisions much more neatly defined than those of the police. The Minister of Defence would be a serving officer and approved by the SCAF for the next two presidential terms. A National Defence Council, with the military controlling a majority of the seats, would discuss the military budget to be included in the state budget under one line, as explicitly stated in Article 203. Military courts would have wide jurisdiction on civilians, as defined in broader language and enshrined in more specific and compelling terms than in 2012. A National Security Council would allow the military to have a say in crucial political decisions. In addition, as a corollary and directly related to the hegemony of the military through the SCAF, the much-needed reform of the Ministry of the Interior has been a second-order issue and talks of reforms have been buried. Finally, to square the circle, General (then Marshal) al-Sissi, was elected President in June 2014.

The al-Sissi regime has revealed itself as a regime dominated by the military and a 're-militarization' of power unknown previously in Egypt, at least since 1956. The military has remained a key (if not *the* key) component of the new Egyptian regime, and the one giving structure to the new political equilibrium. Talk of a 'deep state' (to borrow the Turkish model of the so-called *parallel devlet*) points to the reality of the alliance between of the Army, state institutions, and, in particular, the '*fouloul*', the remnants of the Mubarak regime within some state institutions. Some state institutions were very conservative indeed—none more so than the Ministry of the Interior—but they have not developed a coherent sense of purpose around a given project as the military have done. The al-Sissi regime expanded the role and influence of the security services. Systematic repression aimed at repressing political opponents (the Muslim Brotherhood, young revolutionaries) and, most importantly, ending the unprecedented wave of street mobilizations and local activism in Egypt (unorganized but with a sense of anger, betrayal, and dispossession that can at some turning points fuel huge protests, even uprisings). Over this period, by clamping down on activism of all kinds, the military-led regime has sought a general depoliticization of the Egyptian political space and the silencing of all dissident voices (intellectuals, bloggers, media anchors, universities, NGOs, mosques' preachers, soccer fans).

The military has preyed on the strong expectations among Egyptians of a better socio-economic situation (with its ability to get massive Saudi and Emirati economic aid) and of stability (*al-istiqrar*) in the context of unspecified external and internal threats against Egypt while equating the Muslim Brotherhood and various jihadists and all oppositional voices with 'terrorist organizations'. Many topics have been 'securitized' in the context of new repressive laws; the law on the right to public meetings, processions, and peaceful demonstrations; the university law; a decree bringing mosques and preachers under government control; the association law on NGOs; the penal code amendment; the anti-terrorism law; etc. The prevalent atmosphere of fear, chaos and insecurity in the region, seen nowhere in the world, with the rise of ISIS in Iraq and Syria (2014–17) and its enduring consequences in Libya, in the Sinai, or Egypt in general, and more generally four conflict-affected countries (Libya, Yemen, Syria, Iraq) in the area, have played into the hands of the al-Sissi regime's counter-revolutionary propaganda. Hence, all talk about SSR in Egypt, prudently aired in 2011, was sidelined and forgotten.

Here arises the question of whether or not it could have been possible to prevent the military from playing such a definitive role. The question is difficult to answer, given the mistakes made by civilian political actors, particularly the inexperienced Muslim Brotherhood. The crux of the problem in Egypt was not just that the military was a political actor in its own right, trying to extricate itself from power and at the same time wanting to preserve some prerogatives and immunize itself from prosecutions, as in Latin America in the 1980s. It remained the most powerful institutional actor and its very presence impaired the development of other civilian political forces and processes. This had to do with the preserved balancing role of the military in post-Mubarak Egypt. What was essential in Egypt from 1967 until 2011 was not the military's interventionist potential per se (*coup d'état*), but its capacity to act as a 'balance-holder'—to borrow from international relations—in an authoritarian equilibrium under the strict control of the executive. All polities consist of nested and changeable groups, but this notion is more important in authoritarian polities that are based on a systematic mechanism of political exclusion of some groups and conversely the co-option of clients/cronies and supposedly loyal groups. An authoritarian regime is also an equilibrium based on a winning coalition whose support is essential for the incumbents to remain in power. This, of course, was keenly felt by Mubarak himself when the military opted out and refused to repress the crowds on his behalf in 2011. This way of governing Egypt with an authoritarian equilibrium/coalition had a historical depth or 'path dependence'. Nasser and Sadat restructured the Egyptian polity by giving a key role to the executive and the state—key posts in the state were also given to ex-officers—in restructuring society and economy. Conversely, they excluded the military from direct politics by 'demilitarizing' the polity.[34] Nasser restructured the domestic political arena to prevent workers, peasants, and urban middle classes from independently mobilizing; and he subordinated private capital to state managers. Sadat opened up the Egyptian authoritarian system by promoting a private sector of entrepreneurs (*infitahiyyun*) with crony (*tufai'liyya*) ties to the regime. Mubarak fragmented the Egyptian political order to survive in power by playing divide-and-rule tactics among domestic opposition and interest groups. The opening of the system was gradually reversed by a de-liberalization in the 1990s. This was in parallel with a retreat of the state, which abandoned Egyptian society to itself and to its own survival strategies, governing it with increased brutality through the police apparatus. Equilibrium was maintained with the weight of the military as the pillar of the regime even if it appeared to be a silent political actor following the executive's will. Hence the military, though often invisible, was deeply embedded in the Egyptian polity. After 2011, the military has kept and even reinforced its role as the 'balance-holder' in Egypt's emerging political equation. Then, in 2013, under a legitimizing discourse of defending the Egyptian state under threat, the Army as a whole moved to occupy centre stage and act, prompted by some of its constituent parts, chief among them the military intelligence and the department of morale affairs (i.e. propaganda).

In polarized Libya, the dark side of 'perverse institutionalization'[35] of militias in the security sector was the risk of a return to civil war, with numerous and non-overlapping divisions: Islamist-leaning forces versus 'liberals' (at least for external observers), centralists versus federalists, urban versus rural, regions and cities between themselves, official army or former officers versus 'hybrid forces'/militias created by revolutionaries, etc. By mid-2014, political conflicts over legislative elections (the newly elected House of Representatives (HoR) due to succeed to the

[34] N. Cooper, *The Transformation of Egypt* (Croom Helm, 1982).
[35] Valenzuela (note 25).

GNC) and the resentment of eastern officers (those who defected *en masse* and kept some cohesiveness around Benghazi) coalesced into the relaunching of a full-scale civil war between two warring camps. The wave of assassinations of military and security cadres in 2012–14 in eastern Libya, especially in Benghazi, was never really investigated but seemed like a way to displace ancient and prospective elites; the former were very carefully targeted, in particular with sophisticated devices detonated beneath cars. From May to June 2014, a coalition of officers headed by retired General Khalifa Haftar launched a military campaign (Operation Dignity, '*Karama*') to cleanse some radical Islamists from Benghazi, prompting the majority of Islamist-leaning revolutionary brigades to align against it, and *Karama* was joined by the brigades from Zintan and supported, though acting independently, by the newly elected HoR. Then a coalition of Misrata brigades in Operation Dawn Libya ('*Fajr Libya*') launched an offensive against Zintani brigades in Tripoli with the support of former members of the GNC. Multiple factions coalesced into two rival yet disparate camps (Karama + the HoR versus Dignity + the GNC) assuming the characteristics of a civil war, furthermore with the support of regional actors (Egypt, Saudi Arabia, and the UAE versus Qatar, Turkey, and Sudan). Polarization receded to the point that a year later, both coalitions no longer existed, but the offensive of General Haftar and his self-proclaimed Libyan National Army (LNA) has continued, hence introducing a new context of war detrimental to constitutional talks and SSR reforms.

Some kind of political solution entailing the rebuilding of a Libyan state (whatever its specific form, perhaps far from the Weberian role model) is required to extricate Libya from the grip of militias and the recurring risks of civil war, and to relaunch SSR reforms. After numerous failures, the most promising attempt occurred in December 2015, when a UN Support Mission in Libya (UNSMIL)-brokered Libyan Political Agreement was reached: a Presidential Council (PC) was born out of it in March 2016, along with a government (Government of General Accord, GNA). The implementation of signed agreements has remained problematic but a new Prime Minister (Fa'iz al-Sarraj) has settled (in a naval base) in Tripoli, under the protection of four to five influential Tripoli-based militias. Yet the Libyan military has remained wholly fragmented at a level that even Gaddafi did not reach, between forces rallied to the GNA, those loyal to the HoR, those close to the GNC, those remaining autonomous, and Haftar's alliance. In 2018, the so-called and self-designated Libyan National Army under General (then named Marshal) Haftar was not loyal to the GNA, was only a national army in name, and was part of a coalition of militiamen. Haftar and some officers around him have been dreaming about rebuilding some central power in Libya based on the military (or more accurately the al-Sissi) model in neighbouring Egypt. The dangers for Libya lie in the fact that the threat of ISIS (flourishing in a context of state decay) and the absence of a central authority controlling frontiers (hence flows of refugees coming from Africa or even Syria to reach the shores of Italy) has bred desires for intervention among foreign powers desperately looking for a central government. This has led external powers to prioritize security gained through rapid reforms from above (state-building) over the long rebuilding of a Libyan security sector by taking into consideration the bottom-up processes signalled by the rise of militias in Libya. SSR reforms entail a twin-goal process of demobilizing militias while transforming (or even creating/reinstitutionalizing) the security sector from scratch. In parallel, some external actors (Italy, France) have also bet on the support of some militias/strongmen (Misratans) or the self-proclaimed Libyan National Army (General Haftar), with a dangerous tendency among foreign powers to disconnect counterterrorism and border control from other forms of engagement in order to support political dialogue and state reformation in Libya. In Libya, SSR risks remaining a talking shop only, played out by powerful militias in the absence of a political solution and some form of state rebuilding.

In Yemen, the transitional process was disrupted by a peripheral actor that overturned it. The Houthi rebellion had started as a Zaydi revivalist movement led by the al-Houthi family. It had originated in issues concerning regional identity, rather than being a solely religious and sectarian movement, and then morphed into a northern Zaydi rebel movement (or *Ansar Allah*) that had waged six wars against the Saleh regime (2004–10). The Houthis participated in the UN-backed National Dialogue (see earlier), but at the same time they retained their arms and completed their control over northern governorates. Benefiting from the general discredit of the Hadi government and the whole political process, the Houthis took power in September 2014 in Sana'a with the backing of military units and tribal forces loyal to former president Saleh. They pressured Hadi—who fled to Saudi Arabia—and then marched south. Yemen left the constitutional path examined in this chapter and entered civil war with a regional dimension after Saudi Arabia and the UAE intervened with a coalition in March 2015 to roll back the Houthis, reinstate the Hadi government in Aden, and retake the north. Then Yemen entered full-scale war, which is beyond the scope of this chapter.

Conclusion

The numerous tools and paths of SSR relating to other countries addressed elsewhere in this book are of interest and relevance for those concerned with Arab issues. Nonetheless, critical gaps remain between lessons learnt in the comparative cases addressed here and outcomes in the Arab region.

The crux of the problem lies in how the previous weight of the security sector (with its multiple components, with different relations to the polity and roles in the regimes) has translated itself into the transitional process in Arab cases, either with its full weight or, conversely, its total absence (and the subsequent rise of militias or commanders turned stakeholders or warlords). The problem was more complex and less clear-cut than in the comparative cases of Latin America and Spain, where the crux of the matter was the relations between the military as a corps and a civilian tradition reinvigorating itself. This was highlighted by the fact that in Latin America and to some extent in Spain (with the European example as a counter-model to the Franco dictatorship), a tradition of constitutionalism had persisted in a pattern of alternating civilian and military rule, with a memory of civilian politics in churches, labour unions, political parties, judiciary institutions, civil society, etc. The same holds true for the 'exceptional' case, Tunisia, with strong cultural (bilingualism), social (migrations), and economic ties with Europe, especially France, in a country endowed historically with a small and 'contained' (i.e. kept weak), hence legalist, military willing to go back to the barracks. Furthermore, military politics in Latin America was linked to the shift (albeit brutal) of the military towards full involvement in civilian politics, and was less related to the building of enduring authoritarian regimes. For instance, none of the military rulers in Latin America planned to hand over power to their sons in dynastic regimes (as in Egypt, Yemen, and Libya). In Latin America, military politics took the classic and simplistic form of seizure of power by *coups d'état* and corporate rule, not that of authoritarian leaders hailing from the military and 'civilianizing' complex authoritarian regimes. In the Arab world, there were no routinized cycles of alternation between civilian and military rule as in Nigeria, Thailand, or Turkey. The Army had to be 'disembedded' from its long-standing role in the state, in the political regime, and from its enduring encroachment in the economy and society (including national education and media). This embeddedness of the military in the polity was seen nowhere to the same degree in Latin America even during military rule.

That does not mean that the essential element of civilian politics and institutionalization could not be created in the Arab world. Such a possibility was highlighted by the South African constitutional negotiations: the quality of the leadership and adaptable institutions helped manage a profound organizational transformation and deny predictions of a Yugoslavia scenario unfolding there in the 1990s. Also relevant is Ghana, where the elite consensus towards creating economic growth has helped address the question of how to reform a system of power plagued by previous military interventionism, and hence to introduce SSR reforms. Civilian control or SSR constitutional reforms have to be built upon that sense of breach that occurred, albeit briefly, in the Arab world in 2011. There needs to be a strong, committed (civilian) leadership with a sense of strategy allowing adequate timing of events if the transition/changes—be they small and technical or more substantial constitutional steps—are to take root.

On the one hand, transitions and SSR take many years to reach a critical mass: they often require patience, and entail set-backs and renewed efforts. Latin America was the heartland of hard military politics with very different types of military regimes (personalized, less formalized, or in alliance with civilian elites), and yet the issue of democratic control of the armed forces was grappled with decisively, as exemplified by the range of topics addressed and bargained. Thus, Latin America nowadays offers a set of standards of civilian control of the military over questions of transitional justice, national security councils, ministries of defence, budgets, military service, etc. Setbacks might occur as in Brazil with President Bolsonaro in 2018, but they do not invalidate this general trend. Yet, compared to these cases, in the Arab world in 2019, the difficulty remains to find a 'before' and 'after', hence the sense of continuity or 'counter-revolutions' felt by some local actors (especially in Egypt). There is a sense that counter-revolution is occurring in Egypt, of intricate complexities and state decay continuing in Libya, and opportunities lost to war in Yemen (and never available in Syria). The Arab world is a long way from the stage reached by the other cases studied in this book. That may be related to the question of time, but also to deeper problems.

On the other hand, comparisons point to even deeper differences. Previous processes were transitions by imposition in Latin America where the military determined the transition or an agreed transition in Spain: the military came to think that it had to confront its institutional weight with that of the re-emerging democratic system even if some generals would have preferred a controlled/guided model of democracy. There came a point when the military in Latin America or Spain did not consider the regime but, instead, the strengths and weaknesses of a given administration, and no longer felt a responsibility for the polity. It adopted a hands-off attitude towards the transition and concerned itself only with its own interests, degree of autonomy, and privileges that it tried to win. As a corollary, in most cases, after some dangerous periods, the capacity to advance SSR in the military and the police was strongly affected by the existence of a functioning political system, endowed with high levels of public support and success in managing the economy, and especially by the full support of major civilian elites to civilian supremacy and democracy. Therefore, the military came to realize gradually that there were no alternatives to the advancement of its professional or institutional interests outside a democratic system and it was not able to find allies for a counter-project. In a sense, it *had* to put up with SSR and democratic reform of the armed forces. The perception of the absence of alternatives helped pave the way for SSR better than the advancement of technical reforms.

Quite differently, in the Arab world in 2011–18, the setting was much more fragmented, and the political systems were in limbo, with the notable exception of Tunisia and its tradition of constitutionalism, and notwithstanding the dangerous shortcomings of a negotiated transition (between al-Nahda and Nida' Tounes). In Egypt, the political system remained weak and heavily polarized and the military managed to hijack the transition by riding the demand for change, and positioned itself centre-stage, as exemplified by the rise of Marshal/President al-Sissi. In Libya, the political system was subdued by militias. In Yemen, the National Dialogue was a way to recreate politics, but it was strongly tilted towards the old elites, with the looming presence of high commanders turned warlords, and it was ultimately overwhelmed by a peripheral actor, the Houthis. The military, or parts of it, could then apply its institutional weight on the polity, with a military perspective focused on creating stability (*istiqrar*) and enforcing law and order strategies. In Tunisia, the difficulty of reinvigorating civilian politics with a broad democratic project is also compounded by the risks of heightened politicization and even polarization, risks curtailed by the relatively small size of its Army.

SSR is the action of civilians on the military corps and the security sector. SSR also entails restraining civilian politicians from being able to use the military to maintain power. This danger is highlighted (and raised to another level where a large army exists) and even pushed to the limit by Iraq after 2007–08, where a Prime Minister elected as a weak and compromise candidate (Nouri al-Maliki) could use the military and the security sector as a political asset, until his sacking in 2014 after ISIS managed to take control of the second city of the country (Mosul) and defeat the northern part of the new Iraqi Army. Conversely, Ghana shows that it is possible to pull back from the brink of conflict after the politicization and ethnicization of security organs. The problem is not just civilian control—the Franco regime tamed the military and was a civilianized regime—but open control. This is quite different from informal bargaining, taking place behind closed doors, between the military or parts of the security sector and the political elite in authoritarian settings; it means open control through open constitutional and parliamentary channels. Counter-examples of great interest are those where the military keeps a strong behind-the-scenes/subterranean influence, as in Pakistan and, to some extent, in Indonesia, and where it retains the means (the intelligence services in Pakistan) to return centre-stage regularly.

Conclusion

Security Sector Reform and Constitutional Transitions: Challenging the Consensus

Zoltan Barany, Sujit Choudhry, and Kent Roach

Introduction

Security sector reform (SSR) is central to the democratic transitions currently unfolding across the globe as a diverse range of countries grapple with how to transform militias, tribal forces, and dominant military, police, and intelligence agencies into democratically controlled and accountable security services. SSR is likely to be a key element in shifts from authoritarian to democratic rule for the foreseeable future, since abuse of the security sector in some form is a central technique of autocratic government.

Because SSR is an indispensable part of a larger process of democratization—which in turn entails the creation of a constitutional democracy—SSR in principle can also have an important constitutional dimension. Indeed, underlying and uniting the involvement of a broad variety of international and domestic actors is a consensus, among scholars and practitioners, about how SSR is related to the larger process of constitutional transitions towards democratic rule. This consensus concerns both *substance* and *process*.[1]

[1] An important statement of this consensus is in Samuel P. Huntington's classic work, *The Soldier and the State: The Theory and Politics of Civil-Military Relations* (Harvard University Press, 1957). Huntington's theory of 'objective civilian control' requires that the military and security sector must provide security to a democratic system without undermining the democratic system of government (83–4). Key to achieving this effective civilian control of the security sector, and strict professionalism on the part of the security establishment, 'Civilian control is undermined if [the armed forces] stray outside the military sphere or if the civilians make it impossible for them to discharge their professional responsibilities' (S.P. Huntington, 'Civilian Control and the Constitution' (1956) 50 *American Political Science Review* 676, 678). For our purposes, important elements of Huntington's criteria of objective civilian control are that the security sector is isolated from other institutions of the social and political structure, and that they remain indifferent to the political ideologies of society.

Challenges to Huntington's orthodoxy have emerged before now, however. Morris Janowitz's proposal for 'pragmatic civilian control' recognizes that while the security sector must remain professional and functionally capable of providing security, it also recognizes that security sector officials should not be disinterested in politics. Janowitz argues on the contrary that the security sector should be politically astute, and acquire some knowledge of broader political affairs. Janowitz's model of a military commander

On *substance*, the consensus holds that SSR must extract the security sector out of politics and put civil–military relations on a democratic footing, while at the same time ensuring that a new civilian authority is not able to manipulate or abuse the security sector for partisan or personal purposes (e.g. financial gain). It also requires reforming the army, police, and intelligence services to serve society through adhering to appropriate laws. Clearly, SSR is an essential element of a new constitutional order. The reason is that security services wield coercive powers that can be used to violate human rights and interfere with democratic processes, and usually performed these roles under authoritarian rule. Democratic constitutionalism requires and is impossible without armed forces, police, and intelligence agencies that are the obedient servants of the state and whose work is fully controlled by the proper executive, judicial, and legislative oversight bodies, all operating under a legal system that adheres to a new democratic constitution. The successful institutionalization of these arrangements in consolidated democracies is held out as a goal to which all transitional democracies should aspire.

The consensus on the appropriate role of security reform in constitutional transitions extends beyond the imperatives of establishing civilian oversight and compliance with the rule of law in the new constitutional order. The consensus also holds that in the *process* for the peaceful transfer of power from authoritarian to democratic rule, the military should stay in its barracks and not participate in the ensuing constitutional transition, except to cede control to new civilian authorities with reasonable dispatch and without making any demands to maintain its status. Indeed, security sector agencies of all kinds—the military, the police, and the intelligence services—should be the passive objects of transformation and transition, but not active participants or actors in the processes of constitutional reform, except as strictly necessary.

It is difficult to dispute that the often arduous transition from authoritarianism to democracy is much easier when there is no *violent* military intervention that would add complexity and great uncertainty to what could already be an extraordinarily difficult process. Fortunately, such peaceful transitions do happen fairly often. For instance, the transition from socialist dictatorships to democracy occurred more or less peacefully, without the interference of the military in the post-communist regimes of Central and Eastern Europe (save for Romania). Most Latin American democratization processes following military rule also transpired without violence (albeit, as this volume attests, with the generals' active political involvement). However, the consensus goes further and extends to proscribe even the peaceful participation of security sector agencies in constitutional transitions. In Myanmar, for example, the military (the Tatmadaw) remains politically involved in the

is thus as a 'politicomilitary' official who remains committed to the primary professional role of maintaining security, but interact with other institutions of government in policy-making, planning, and national security strategy (Morris Janowitz, 'Civic Consciousness and Military Performance' in M. Janowitz and S.D. Westbrook (eds), *The Political Education of Soldiers* (Sage, 1983)). The case studies in this volume, and the lessons we extract from them, build on these challenges to the Huntingtonian consensus.

gradual but halting transition from military rule to democracy and has conducted a brutal campaign of ethnic cleansing against the country's Rohingya Muslim community.[2] The lacking commitment of the Tatmadaw to peaceful change, *and* its heavy and often heavy-handed political involvement, is sobering and a cause for worry, raising concerns about the likely success of Myanmar's democratization.[3]

However, as the case studies in this volume illustrate, the relationship between SSR and constitutional transitions, on both substance and process, is much more complex than the consensus suggests. Consider one issue, often overlooked in the large literature on constitution building: the importance of stability to successful democratic transitions. The main components of stability are basic, street-level, public safety; a broader sense of national security, meaning the protection of the people and the country's borders from external incursions; and the rule of law. Stability allows those states to restructure their political systems and to create an economic environment in which commerce and industry can flourish, and provides an opportunity for a political community to embark upon a process of healing and reconciliation after a variety of different authoritarian experiences. Perhaps more fundamentally, stability is a basic precondition for the emergence, growth, and consolidation of constitutional democracy, which we define as 'the settlement of political disagreement through electoral contestation and political competition, and the operation of constitutional institutions without recourse to force or fraud'. The recent instability, violence, and conflict in Iraq as the security services failed to contain the rise of ISIL, violent uprisings in post-Mubarak Egypt, and ongoing civil war in Libya and Yemen illustrate that the failure to maintain security can itself threaten transitions to democracy.

Security services have an important role to play in ensuring stability and promoting conditions that are conducive to democratization. The difficulty is that in many post-authoritarian environments, the integrity of the police and intelligence agencies, on whom the task of ensuring stability falls, has been compromised by their complicity in the prior regime. The police may be co-opted by political direction about whom they should and should not investigate and charge with the resulting lack of public confidence in their impartiality and commitment to the rule of law. The armed forces, which are frequently needed to guarantee domestic security during the transition period because the regular police lack sufficient capacity to re-establish order, are likewise, in many cases, beholden to the rulers of the *ancien régime*. These realities on the ground—pervasive in constitutional

[2] See e.g. Zoltan Barany, 'Elections and Constitutional Constraints: How the Generals Have Stayed in Power in Myanmar' (2018) 38(1) *SAIS Review of International Affairs* 105–17.

[3] See e.g. Amrita Dey, 'Myanmar's Tryst with Democracy: Lessons from India' (2015) 12 *US-China Law Review* 827; Janelle Saffin and Nathan Wills, 'The Need for Constitutional Settlement to Further the Reform Process in Myanmar (Burma)' (2014) 28 *Temple International and Comparative Law Journal* 253; and Zoltan Barany, 'Where Myanmar Went Wrong: From Democratic Awakening to Ethnic Cleansing' (2018) 97(2) *Foreign Affairs* 141–54.

transitions—raise a genuine dilemma for the prevailing consensus, and suggest the need may arise to compromise with unyielding constitutional democratic principle, *in the service of* the long-term success of a transition to constitutional democracy. Moreover, this is but one dilemma among many.

The major contribution of this volume is to expose and analyse the complexities of the relationship between SSR and constitutional transitions through detailed case studies, and the dilemmas that must be openly wrestled with and resolved. Working up from concrete cases has implications for both the scholarly understanding of these phenomena and the policy question of how countries embarking on the process of constitutional transitions should approach SSR.

The country case studies that comprise the bulk of this volume provide a rich and diverse source of comparative knowledge about the role of security services in constitutional transitions towards democracy. To be sure, there are many differences among the countries under study. The chapters on Spain, Chile, Argentina, and Indonesia focus on transitions from military rule towards democracy, whereas the chapter on Kenya, and to some extent the chapter on the Middle East and North Africa (where Egypt and Tunisia are of special interest), focus more on transitions from police states. The South African case study examines the unique transition from apartheid to democracy and includes the successful integration of opposition paramilitary forces into a national army. Nonetheless, there are cross-cutting themes that enable us to draw more general lessons.

In approaching these broad research and policy questions, it bears emphasis at the very outset that the case studies in our volume also indicate considerable differences among the military, intelligence agencies, and the police. Indeed, each of these security institutions has a distinct culture, occupational norms, and capacities. For that reason, each kind of institution has produced its own academic literature. Thus the literature on constitutional transitions must also differentiate among the functions of the military, intelligence, and the police. Moreover, as the case studies attest, a blurring of these separate functions is often an important strategy employed by an authoritarian state. In particular, the fusion of domestic policing and intelligence in either the military or a specialized police force is often the hallmark of an authoritarian regime. Authoritarian states may also deploy the military to act to maintain internal order, and direct the military and the police to use force against potential security threats as identified through fallible intelligence-gathering. The necessity of a separation of powers among security sector agencies in constitutional democracies is among the chief insights of this volume.

In addition, while this volume has focused on SSR during constitutional transitions, and especially on ways to establish civilian oversight of the security services in post-authoritarian democracies, we do not seek to diminish in any way the need for vigilance in established, consolidated democracies to ensure that the intelligence agencies and police remain subject to transparent democratic control. As the Edward Snowden leaks reveal, established democracies continue to struggle to ensure that intelligence agencies respect democratic norms. With respect to the police, in countries whose fundamentally democratic character is seldom called into question, grave errors are made and old habits die hard. Recent examples include police corruption in Finland—one of the least corrupt societies in the world—and well-publicized police brutality, particularly against black citizens in the United States.[4] Moreover, the war on terror, as we explain later, has blurred the line between threats to external and internal security, creating new possibilities for abuse.

The challenges of minimizing and providing accountability for human rights abuses by those who wield coercive force in the state's name are great in both established and emerging democracies. These challenges continue to evolve with security threats and the state's need to manage both internal and external threats to security. A lesson from consolidated democracies is that the establishment of democratic control and oversight over the police and intelligence agencies is closer to a continual work in progress than something that can be achieved with measurable and permanent success in a finite period of time characterized as a transition to democracy. A key reason for this phenomenon may be that intelligence agencies and especially the police are in far more direct contact with the general public on a daily basis than the armed forces, and thus must respond to at times rapid changes affecting society, in terms of behaviours, customs, and attitudes.

Institutional Legacies, Constitutional Processes and Political Leverage, Economic Interests, and the Separation of Functions

Path-dependency: institutional legacies and post-authoritarian trajectories

Context matters. This may be one of the most important lessons of this volume. Just how different individual settings are becomes abundantly clear when we consider the starting point of democratization. As one of us has argued elsewhere, the kind of state that immediately precedes democratization has a major impact on the democratization process and the impact on SSR. The legacies of the past, in other words, must not be discounted.[5] Different starting points may accordingly require different constitutional remedies.

[4] See e.g. 'Drug Unit Police Chief Arrested on Bribery Charge', *Finland Times*, 13 November 2013; Dan Bilefsky and Mari-Leena Kuosa, 'Finland Unnerved by Trial of Police Detective on Drug Charges', *New York Times*, 2 August 2015; Jill Nelson (ed.), *Police Brutality: An Anthology* (Norton, 2001); and Malcolm D. Holmes and Brad W. Smith (eds), *Race and Police Brutality: Roots of an Urban Dilemma* (SUNY Press, 2008).

[5] On this issue see e.g. Zoltan Barany and Ivan Volgyes (eds), *The Legacies of Communism* (Johns Hopkins University Press, 1995); Klaus Ziemer and Jerzy W. Borejsza, *Totalitarian and Authoritarian*

A *praetorian regime*—that is, one ruled by generals—would have a fundamentally different legacy on its armed forces and coercive apparatus, and its transition to democratic rule, than a *single-party regime*, regardless of whether the hegemonic party was of the communist or socialist variety in Europe (e.g. in Poland or the former Soviet Union), or a sultanistic regime based on the personal power of a single leader, such as in Iran, Haiti, and the Philippines.[6] The key challenges after military rule and after a single-party regime are essentially reversed. Once a military regime comes to an end and the Army leaves power, the chief concern of democratizers is to ensure the military remains outside politics; that is, to terminate the generals' interference in political life. If the military had a role in overseeing the economy or participated in business activities, that issue requires careful attention as well, as part of the process of transition.

In transitions from single-party regimes, by contrast, a hegemonic party's comprehensive control of the armed forces means that the main task is to take politics out of the military; that is, to banish the hegemonic party and its agents (political officers, party organizations, etc.) from the barracks. An additional question to be concerned with after single-party states is professionalism, since under single-party rule the dominant (and often only) factor in promotions and advancement was not merit but fealty to the regime.

With respect to other issues, the character of the challenges in each context differs not in kind, but in degree; for example, with respect to the nature of civilian oversight. After military rule, a whole new institutional architecture must be erected for the democratic functioning of civilian military relations within the framework of constitutional democracy, with special attention to establishing civilian control by *both* the executive and legislative branches, as well as the relationship between systems of executive and legislative control.[7] The case studies of military juntas in this volume where the military was the dominant institution and permeated all aspects of governance—Argentina, Chile, Spain in the Franco era, and Indonesia in the Suharto era—illustrate this issue.

After single-party states, by contrast, where the Army was under close executive control, the more specific job is to bolster the legislative oversight of the armed forces against a backdrop where parliaments were little more than façade institutions and were dominated by executives. Thus, in cases such as Kenya, Ghana, and Tunisia, the problem was not so much the military domination of politics, but rather the abusive practices of Special Branches that fuse policing and intelligence

Regimes in Europe: Legacies and Lessons from the Twentieth Century (Berghahn, 2006); and Teri L. Caraway, Maria Lorena Cook, and Stephen Crowley (eds), *Labor and Authoritarian Legacies in Comparative Perspective* (Cornell University Press, 2015).

[6] See H.E. Chehabi and Juan J. Linz (eds), *Sultanistic Regimes* (John Hopkins University Press, 1998).

[7] On this issue, see Zoltan Barany, 'Exits from Military Rule' (2015) 26(2) *Journal of Democracy* 86–100.

functions, under the control of the executive. The problem in Ben Ali's Tunisia was not the military but the secret police or *mukhabarat*.

Constitutional processes and political leverage

The democratization of a military regime—that is, the process by which a regime where members of the armed forces occupy the offices of government gives way to a system where government is elected in competitive elections—presents a particular set of substantive and procedural challenges. The consensus view holds that members of the armed forces should stay in the barracks during the transition, and should play no part in designing structures of government for the new system. This stance makes both a descriptive claim about successful democratization processes that have occurred, and a normative claim about the legitimate role that security agencies ought to be able to play in shaping the new regime.

In some cases, however, it is unlikely that a transition to democracy would have occurred without the active participation of the armed forces. In Ghana, for example, Air Force Flight Lieutenant Jerry Rawlings seized power in a 1981 *coup d'état* and established the Provisional National Defence Council (PNDC) as Ghana's government. Responding to public opposition to military rule in the early 1990s, Rawlings transformed the PNDC into a civilian government and political party—now called the National Democratic Congress (NDC)—simply by having all its members resign their positions in the military. Although the NDC government effected institutional and structural reforms to the security services, these changes happened gradually and largely followed the military's own agenda. Rawlings remained President until 2001.

Similarly, although the military Junta formally relinquished power in Chile in 1989 after General Pinochet's eight-year term as President came to an end, Pinochet remained Commander-in-Chief of the Armed Forces until 1998. Having entrenched constitutional provisions that safeguarded the privileged position of the military before it gave up political power, and having packed the country's legislative bodies with sympathetic appointees, military leaders retained largely autonomous control over military affairs for two decades after the fall of the Junta. In addition, although Indonesia's military government began to lose popularity during the Asian financial crisis in the late 1990s, the military retained enough influence and credibility to stage-manage the process of democratization and the withdrawal of the armed forces from politics. The civilian who succeeded General Suharto as President, B.J. Habibie, had little choice but to leave the internal reform of the armed forces to the security services themselves, even as Indonesia embarked on a process of broader constitutional reform.

In South Africa, the security sector had less involvement in the process of reform but was able to influence the substantive arrangements for the post-apartheid security services. South Africa's minority apartheid government relied on the security sector to suppress and undermine political opposition, thus hanging onto political power despite massive unpopularity domestically and internationally. The government initiated a negotiated transition in the early 1990s in large part because the security sector informed the government that it could not continue to prop up the regime by force. Indeed, early discussions about a negotiated transition occurred between opposition groups and members of the apartheid intelligence services. The security sector in South Africa was able to leverage its role in providing stability and security during the transition to secure substantive outcomes for the military's future in the new system, such as amnesties and guarantees against lustration.

In other cases, however, the security services had less influence, both procedurally and substantively. In Argentina, the military government began to lose popular support and credibility after the disastrous Malvinas war with the United Kingdom, and was forced from power with little formal opportunity to safeguard its future. The period of democracy immediately after the fall of Argentina's military regime in the 1980s was, however, marred by failed military rebellions spearheaded by military leaders unhappy with their exclusion from the process of transition. Spain's democratic transition provides something of a middle-ground position, where the military held a procedural veto over the constitutional arrangements for a democratic post-Franco Spain agreed by civilian political negotiators. While the armed forces were thus unable to influence the direction or substance of democratic reform directly, they did hold this important blocking power. Although the armed forces did not ever act to impede the process, providing a veto was an important concession to generate buy-in to the process of reform from the security sector.

The larger question this raises is whether security sector interests can or should be represented by political parties or other actors during the transition, or even participate themselves in that process. The idea that the security sector agencies could or even should be completely removed from politics during the process of constitutional transition is complicated by a number of factors. An important issue that has a major bearing on the entire transition process is how much leverage the security sector holds in the negotiations that lead toward democratic transition.[8] This may depend, for example, on how securely the military holds political power immediately before the transition, or how heavily the stability of the transition itself depends on the cooperation of the security services. The more leverage the security sector holds, the more favourable terms it may be able to secure under a new constitutional framework, such as amnesty from prosecution for past misdeeds

[8] An excellent study that closely engages this question is Harold A. Trinkunas, *Crafting Civilian Control of the Military in Venezuela: A Comparative Perspective* (University of North Carolina Press, 2005).

(especially human rights violations), maintenance of some political and financial perquisites, high levels of defence spending, and institutional safeguards against state meddling in defence policy.

An authoritarian government's relative performance along a number of dimensions shapes the leverage it enjoys. For example, in cases of military regimes, some are relatively successful in the economic realm (e.g. Chile), whereas others pursue policies that result in economic malaise or worse (e.g. Argentina). Some military regimes stay out of wars while others enter into foreign adventures or outright wars in an attempt to shore up their flagging legitimacy, although this had the opposite effect in Argentina. It is easy to see why military regimes that were relatively more successful and maintained some legitimacy would enjoy more political leverage during the transitional process.

At the same time, drastic and rapid reform of the security sector following the collapse of an authoritarian regime poses a separate risk to the democratization process. The temptation to follow this route is understandable: the danger posed by a powerful security sector leads to a desire to keep the security sector out of politics and to hold them accountable for past abuses. However, effectively gutting a security sector that has been compromised by its involvement in an oppressive regime may lead to a neglect of the important role that security agencies play in ensuring the basic external and internal security that makes transitions to democracy possible. Iraq stands as an example of where a failure to protect national security from the threat of ISIS (previously called ISIL) undermined the transition, however unsuccessful the transition might have been (or not) on its own terms. In Libya, the absence of disciplined and effective security services in the wake of Gaddafi's fall led to civil war that continues to undermine the prospects of democratic transition.

Reformers cannot simply disband security agencies or make the need to provide security go away. They need to ensure that security agencies perform their basic duties in a competent and accountable way while also reforming those agencies to ensure that they do not interfere in politics or abuse human rights. This requires an approach that is attentive to the effectiveness of security agencies while at the same time ensuring that they act in a proper manner and follow legitimate democratic direction. Military effectiveness—'the process by which armed forces convert resources into fighting power'—is, in fact, one of the most often overlooked issues related to SSR in emerging democracies.[9] So too is the need for the police to maintain minimal levels of peace in societies and to work with intelligence agencies to combat high-profile and potentially destabilizing acts of terrorism.

[9] Allan R. Millett, Williamson Murray, and Kenneth H. Watman, 'The Effectiveness of Military Organizations' (1986) 11(1) *International Security* 37.

Amnesties

Security sector agencies that played a dominant role in a prior regime may focus on the possibility of prosecutions during and after a constitutional transition. A pattern that emerges from a number of the case studies is the ability of the military, and perhaps other security sector agencies, to negotiate amnesties *before* a transition. A constitution may constitutionally entrench an amnesty (e.g. Ghana), frame the composition of the legislature and its decision-rules to make an amnesty enacted by legislation or decree hard to repeal (e.g. Chile), or expressly contemplate an amnesty and protect it from potential legal challenges by victims and their families (e.g. South Africa). From the perspective of constitution-building, such amnesties can help facilitate the process of democratic transition by reducing the incentives of security sector agencies to act as spoilers. Indeed, where the security services hold a great deal of leverage over the transition, some form of amnesty might may be a condition necessary to convince security officials to allow the transition to proceed and to provide security and stability as it proceeds. As a consequence, amnesties should be on the constitutional agenda.

Justice, needless to say, is tremendously important for the health of any society and is arguably necessary for transitions from democratic rule. Military officers who visited great suffering on their compatriots should not get away with their crimes. At the same time, in many regime transitions—particularly in those in which the outgoing generals enjoy significant leverage—the new democratic political elites must make painful choices and set difficult priorities. It is reasonable for them to not endanger the long-term prospects of a democratic future by commencing the transition process by rushing to prosecutions to hold culpable generals accountable, no matter how tempting and popular that measure might be. As Francis Fukuyama recently said, 'if you spend all your time seeking justice, you're not going to accomplish anything else'.[10]

An important point in this regard is that there are numerous ways to seek justice or redress for the wrongs of a defunct authoritarian regime, and amnesty is itself a flexible idea. Whether amnesty should be considered as an element of a democratization process, should be somehow constitutionalized together with the conditions or extent of amnesty, will be informed by the context of the transition and the leverage that security services hold—as perpetrators of abuses and crimes under the previous regime—over the transition process. As Chile's experience demonstrates, even constitutionally protected amnesties may not last forever and may eventually be challenged in court through judicial interpretation, or rolled back through legislation. In Chile, even in a situation in which the military returned

[10] Aung Zaw, 'Francis Fukuyama: "It's Not That Hard to Hold a Free and Fair Election"', *The Irrawaday*, 13 August 2015, <https://www.irrawaddy.com/in-person/interview/francis-fukuyama-its-not-that-hard-to-hold-a-free-and-fair-election.html>.

to the barracks but retained political leverage, and therefore was able to negotiate an amnesty, which was protected against repeal because of the composition of the Senate as well as its decision-rules, the incoming democratic politicians made symbolic but important gestures in the direction of accountability for human rights abuses under military rule. During the administration of the first post-junta government those responsible for human rights violations were protected by law, but in a stroke of political genius President Patricio Aylwin established the Commission on Truth and Reconciliation—the so-called Rettig Commission—to search for the truth, identify victims, and investigate accountability.[11] The government's action provided moral reparations and monetary compensation, although the military, insisting that its 1973 intervention was a 'patriotic mission', refused to apologize.

In contrast to Chile, Argentina took a comparatively hard line in prosecuting past abuses relatively early in its transitional process, but doing so came at the price of four military rebellions in the late 1980s. Even though these rebellions were unsuccessful in overthrowing the democratic government, they did put great pressure on the democratic regime in its early days. Responding to this pressure, and concerned to avoid further military challenges, President Menem issued 10 decrees pardoning over 1,000 people convicted for crimes committed during the military regime. Moreover, a few years after the transition and the initial rush to accountability, Argentina enacted the law of 'Full Stop', which prevented prosecutions of intermediate and inferior security officials, in an attempt to strike a balance between calls for justice for past wrongs and a blanket amnesty. While the 1994 Constitution permitted these amnesties, it also set boundaries to them, through the constitutional status accorded to international conventions that prohibit pardons and amnesties in cases of crimes against humanity. It was on this basis that some of the Menem pardon decrees were subsequently declared unconstitutional by the courts.

A relevant question in each case will be whether the transition both to democracy *and* the reform of the security agencies are stable enough by the time amnesties are reviewed and revisited to prevent the security sector from inappropriately intervening in politics to protect the prior endowment of an amnesty.

In Spain, perhaps counterintuitively, the demand for amnesty came from the democratic reformers, rather than from military officials who had served under Franco. The reason was that many anti-Franco campaigners had themselves been convicted of various crimes in the fight against Francoism, and sought to have their criminal records expunged. Similarly, in South Africa, both the apartheid security forces and the armed wings of the opposition parties agreed in principle on some form of amnesty, as both sides had committed politically motivated crimes during the apartheid years. In Spain and South Africa, there was general consensus that

[11] See Eric Brahm, 'The Chilean Truth and Reconciliation Commission', The Beyond Intractability Knowledge Base Project 6 (2009), <https://www.beyondintractability.org/casestudy/brahm-chilean>.

amnesty would be a feature of the transition to democracy. At the same time, it is unlikely that the transition would have proceeded without a guarantee of amnesty.

The general theme here is that there may be a trade-off between pursuing accountability and justice for past abuses (at least in the short term, and with respect to certain categories of officers), and creating the conditions for a transition to democracy where the military are less likely to interfere with democratic institutions and at least 'stay in the barracks' during the transition. The case studies in this volume illustrate how amnesties or similar concessions may help keep the military out of politics during fragile democratic transitions and thereby increase their likelihood of success, and how a hard line on past abuses, whether justified or not, can result in security agencies becoming political actors during the transition, posing a risk to the rise of democratic constitutionalism.

Economic interests

A failure to provide some guarantee against prosecution after the transition to democracy is not the only issue that may prompt the security services to derail the process of democratization. Armies often have economic stakes ranging from pensions to industries, and can often be very significant participants in the economy. Egypt, Indonesia, and Chile provide examples where armies sought to protect their economic interests during the transition from authoritarian to democratic rule. In fact, in the cases in this volume, most military regimes were involved in their countries' economies to some degree. In regimes under de facto military control, such as Egypt, the armed forces actually own or control entire sectors of the national economy and possess vast land holdings.[12]

Democratizing regimes must address the issue of the Army's economic interests with care if the constitution-building process is to be successful. In some cases, the revenues from military-owned enterprises provide material comforts to the military, which are important perquisites they will seek to protect under a new democratic regime. A difficult choice to make during a democratic transition is whether to allow the security services to continue to enjoy these perquisites—and at the extreme end to condone or ignore out-and-out corruption—in order to convince a powerful security sector to stay in the barracks and let the transition occur, or to risk the transition by cutting off the supply of perquisites and economic benefits to security officials. This choice will be informed by how much leverage the security sector holds, alongside how deeply invested in the country's economy the security sector is, and in turn by how much the country depends on the military's

[12] See e.g. Ayesha Siddiqa, *Military Inc.: Inside Pakistan's Military Economy* (Pluto Press, 2007); and Yezid Sayigh, 'Above the State: The Officers' Republic in Egypt', Carnegie Middle East Papers, <http://carnegie-mec.org/2012/08/01/above-state-officers-republic-in-egypt-pub-48972>.

investment in the economy. Leaving such arrangements in place is rarely provided for in the Constitution. Rather, they should be regarded as tacit understandings or bargains on which the Constitution is silent, but which may be necessary to allow the constitutional process to succeed.

A separate consideration is that military budgets are sometimes so low that militaries ordinarily spend a significant portion of the proceeds from their business enterprises on operational expenses rather than on personal enrichment. Indonesia may well be the best example of the latter situation. For this reason, the country's democratizing President, Susilo Bambang Yudhoyono, had little choice but to give up on the ambition to eliminate or drastically scale down the armed forces' involvement in the country's economy. Forcing this issue would have been counterproductive; it would probably have alienated not just the top brass but also most uniformed military personnel because the conditions of military service would have undoubtedly deteriorated.

In Chile, the cost of ensuring the security sector's cooperation during the democratic transition in 1989 was that SSR did not happen until the mid-2000s. Civilian leaders involved in designing the institutional arrangements for Chile's new democracy were able to ensure the cooperation and political withdrawal of the members of the military Junta by allowing the security service to maintain control over their budgets, benefits, and command structure. In particular, the 1990 Organic Law on the Armed Forces—enacted after the election of President Aylwin but before he took office—indexed the armed forces' budget to inflation, eliminating congressional debate over the size of the military budget, and guaranteeing the military a degree of autonomy. Spain's experience was similar, with the drafters of the 1978 post-Franco Constitution agreeing to entrench the armed forces as institutions of state in the same chapter that established Spain as a constitutional monarchy and provided for regional autonomy within Spain. This provided a guarantee of institutional security and independence to the military, allowing the process of democratization to begin while putting off deeper SSR until the mid-1980s (only in 1986, for example, did the Organic Law of the Security Forces separate the domestic police from the military for the first time).

A lesson we draw from the case studies is that keeping security agencies out of domestic politics and out of the process of transition itself is an important goal, but that achieving it may require different trade-offs in different cases. Providing guarantees of amnesties or establishing some process for conditional amnesty is one such trade-off, while protecting the economic and financial security of the security sector or protecting the institutional autonomy and command structures of the security services are others. Pragmatism and a willingness to compromise could go a long way in assuring that the armed forces stay in their barracks during the transition period, when political stability could not be more important. It may be wise to make concessions to the military and security agencies if the given context so requires. Unyielding fidelity to democratic principles may be admirable, but democratizers should not take their eyes off the ultimate prize, which is the consolidation of democracy. If obtaining that prize requires temporary compromises, however distasteful they might seem at the moment, then strategic democratizers should give the most serious and careful consideration to those compromises and recognize the costs that may occur if they decide to forego them in favour of an uncompromising and immediate commitment to democratic values in their fullest form.

Separation of functions among security sector agencies

One clear theme that emerges from the case studies is the need to remove the military from day-to-day internal governance and to focus it on external threats. Security service members should play no role in non-security public policy, law-making, or civilian governance. At the same time, the military itself should not be used for domestic law enforcement or internal security. Indeed, using the military to respond to internal threats is often associated with human rights abuses, authoritarianism, and political interference. In Argentina, for example, the 1992 Internal Security Law and the 1998 National Defence Law played an important role in confining the scope of the military to external as opposed to internal threats. Spain followed a similar strategy, with organic laws enacted after the constitutional transition more clearly specifying the functions and scope of operation of distinct security agencies. The two key objectives of defining the mission and functions of the security services are to extract the security services from politics, and to clearly distinguish the roles of the military, police, and intelligence services in a new democracy. This is a relatively simple and cross-cutting theme in otherwise disparate circumstances.

The narrowing and reorientation of the mission of the military illustrates a more general point. A central component of democratic constitutionalism is the separation of powers, with one of the central aims being to fragment and disperse authority across institutions that have the incentive to safeguard their own prerogatives to make it more difficult to exercise public power. A parallel strategy is at play in defining the respective roles and responsibilities of security sector agencies. In established democracies, there is a clear separation of the role of the military (to protect the state against external threats), the role of the police (to investigate and prevent crimes), and the intelligence services (to assess external and internal threats to national security). This separation of functions is often rooted in legislation which also places these different security agencies under the control of different ministries, led by different civilian ministers and staffed by distinct civilian bureaucracies, to reinforce this functional distinction.

In South Africa, a military that prided itself on its professionalism and dedication to the mission of providing security against external and international threats had grown weary of being asked by the apartheid government to act against internal political opposition. The apartheid-era South African Defence Force (SADF) was already committed to withdrawing from internal security, and even before the democratic transition in 1994 was insisting that this was the province of the police. Meanwhile, revelations that covert, militarized branches of the South African Police Force (SAPF) had been operating beyond the country's borders drew heavy criticism from both the apartheid government and opposition parties. There was accordingly significant appetite for creating constitutionally based distinct roles of the police and armed forces in the new Constitution.

In a number of transitions, such as Spain's and Chile's, laws codifying such separation of functions were enacted a number of years after the initial transition to democracy. Some of the considerations behind the timing of such a change relative to other elements of democratization are discussed in the section, 'Sequencing'. In many cases, delaying SSR is a necessary compromise to begin the process of democratization. However, the risks of a failure to engage at all in an internal separation of powers between the military and the police are significant. Indonesia provides an example. From the earliest days of Indonesian independence, the military, intelligence, and the police were integrated into and used by the Indonesian government. No distinction was made between internal and external security, in part because the national police was integrated with the armed forces and the main security threat came from inside the vast and diverse country. Civilian control of the military was only achieved after the 1998 transition, but these arrangements are still compromised by the fact that the chief officers in charge of the military and the police report directly to the President, as opposed to the responsible Cabinet minister.

The absence of civilian ministerial control has meant in practice that the police are left to devise their own policies and budget, apparently immune from democratic control. Despite efforts to limit the scope of military action to external threats, however, 'old habits die hard': the Indonesian public is accustomed to and indeed expects the military to respond to internal disorder, and the retention of 'Territorial Command' despite democratic reforms sets out a role for the military in ensuring internal stability and security at the village level. In Argentina too, years after a successful transition and SSR that separated the internal and external functions of the police and military, the military has controversially been brought back into domestic affairs in an attempt to combat drug trafficking.

The legitimate interests of localities in policing also present challenges for the democratic control of the police. While local control is important, it must be borne in mind that federalism or decentralization presents challenges in ensuring optimal controls and oversight at the lowest levels of government, especially if they have limited resources and capacities. In Indonesia, there are concerns that the autonomous nature of the police allows it to escape both national and local control. The South African government has a national minister responsible for policing and one national police force, but nevertheless consults provincial governments before establishing policing priorities and also delegates some policing powers to the provinces. In addition, the police force established for the quasi-independent, apartheid-era region of KwaZulu was allowed to operate until the 1994 elections despite concerns that it, like the South African Police Force, had participated in human rights abuses.

Kenya and Ghana have suffered from the fusing of policing and intelligence functions under authoritarian rule, which had the result of conscripting law enforcement into internal repression. In parallel fashion, military intelligence may identify internal threats to national security, in turn embroiling the military in surveillance, repression or other forms internal action. One promising approach is to remove all intelligence functions from the military and police, and to separate all three functions from one another: law enforcement, military, and intelligence. The intelligence agency can then be subject to special oversight, in recognition of the particular danger that spying and political policing present to both transitional and established democracies, and in recognition of the highly confidential nature of the methods and content of their work.

It is important to recognize, however, that there are some challenges to hiving off the intelligence function from either the police or the military. Both the military and the police will legitimately claim that they need intelligence—secret information about future threats—in order to do their job. Indeed, insecurity caused by external or internal threats will inevitably result in criticism of intelligence failures. This suggests that the intelligence function cannot be strictly hived off from other security sector agencies; rather, those links need to be clearly defined by a legal mandate and subject to oversight. In particular, linkages among intelligence agencies, the police, and the military need to be as transparent as possible. This is a tall order, and a recurring problem, including in established democracies such as Canada and the United States.

Another challenge facing attempts to define the institutional structure and mandates of the military, police, and intelligence agencies, and to separate and differentiate their functions, is that a growing number of security threats place pressure on these distinctions. For example, demands on a country in transition that it play its role in the international battle against terrorism, organized crime, drug trafficking, or human trafficking may challenge divisions among security sector agencies. Established democracies have, especially since 9/11, taken a more whole-of-government approach to security that often blurs distinctions between external and security matters. As will be discussed in the next section, whole-of-government approaches to security challenges traditional agency-based forms of accountability. The point in this section is that external and internal demands that governments as governments provide security also can threaten internal separations of powers among the military, intelligence, and police functions.

The National Security Council (NSC) in the 2010 Kenyan Constitution embraces a whole-of-government approach to security. It is composed of the President, the Deputy President, various ministers responsible for national defence, foreign affairs, and internal security, the Attorney General, as well as the heads of the military, intelligence, and police. The NSC exercises 'supervisory control' over national security. This whole-of-government approach to security can challenge strict ministerial lines but it also recognizes the reality that both domestic publics and the international community expect the government as government to supply security. The NSC allows the sharing of intelligence at the highest level. Such high-level operations, however, need to be subject to adequate oversight. One challenge will be secrecy of the NSC's deliberations. The Constitution directs the NSC to report annually to parliament, and the enabling legislation (NSC Act 2012) states that parliament can call for the NSC to report to it on any issue. In addition, the same act details how the confidentiality of the NSC interacts with the right to access to information in the Constitution. The lesson is that security deliberations will be secret, but it is important that there is legal procedure in place which regulates that domain of confidentiality.

The 2010 Kenyan arrangements are more whole-of-government than those in the 1992 Constitution of Ghana, which contemplate separate councils for the armed forces, police, and intelligence agencies. Ghana's intelligence-focused National Security Council (NSC), however, combines military intelligence with external and internal intelligence in something of a whole-of-government approach. Although the President remains the chair of the NSC, the whole-of-government approach the NSC adopts was augmented in 1996 with the creation of a national security coordinator to act as the professional head of the NSC.

It is not only terrorism that is driving countries towards whole-of-government approaches to security issues. International pressures to respond to organized crime, human trafficking, corruption, illegal migration, and a variety of man-made and natural disasters all put pressures on governments to respond in a coordinated fashion. In a new democracy, this creates a risk that bad habits of the past may resurface in response to these external pressures. Indeed, they could be justified as responses to security pressures similar to those being undertaken by the same consolidated democracies. In other words, established democracies could be pursuing security agendas that are at cross-purposes to the consolidation of democracy in countries in transition towards democracy.

In addition, presidents may have an incentive to fuse intelligence with the police and/or military and justify it as part of the creation of a new, effective, constitutional democracy. A military brought in to respond to a disaster may revert to old practices of policing internal security. The frequent design choice in constitutions to describe the President as 'Commander-in-Chief of the Armed Forces' presents some dangers of partisan political abuse of the armed forces in a manner that blurs the separation between military, intelligence, and police functions. Both Kenya's

2010 Constitution and Indonesia's revised 1945 Constitution include provisions conferring supreme command of the armed forces on the President. In circumstances where the President's role as Commander-in-Chief is carefully spelt out and circumscribed by the Constitution or legislation, the risk of abuse is reduced.

Iraq's recent experience most clearly illustrates the danger of a poorly specified commander-in-chief power. Although the President held the same position under Iraq's 1970 Constitution, a large body of legislation set out in some detail precisely what the President was entitled to do as Commander-in-Chief, and made it clear that the Minister of Defence exercised operational control of the armed forces. Designating the Prime Minister as the Commander-in-Chief of the Armed Forces in the 2005 Constitution, in circumstances where all of the more detailed legislation structuring the armed forces had been repealed, created institutional ambiguities that Prime Minister Al-Maliki was able to exploit. He deployed military counterterrorism and intelligence units to investigate and surveil political opposition groups and in turn to intimidate and undermine them. More generally, the distinction between presidential and prime ministerial political systems has important implications for the question of who is the Commander-in-Chief in war, national emergencies, and in peacetime.[13]

In summary, it is clear that separating the powers and functions of the military, intelligence, and the police is important to democratic transitions. As will be discussed in the third section, there is a variety of mechanisms to separate security functions, ranging from formal constitutional change to organic laws, ordinary statutes, and executive decrees. This section, however, has illustrated some of the common challenges to achieving a better internal separation of powers for security sector agencies.

Civilian and Social Oversight

In modern democracies, a civilian government's relationship with the security sector should be understood as a set of relationships among a set of institutions. The institutions belong to one of the three sides of the government/security sector triangle: state, society, and the security sector agencies themselves. The crucial challenge of civilian control of the armed forces, police, and intelligence is to ensure their unconditional obedience to the institutions of liberal democratic government, while at the same time insulating them from partisan abuse, and allowing them sufficient autonomy to discharge their functions and execute their missions effectively. The Army must be strong enough to prevail in war but conduct its own

[13] On this issue, see Arend Lijphart, *Parliamentary versus Presidential Government* (Oxford University Press, 1992); and Thomas A. Baylis, 'Presidents versus Prime Ministers' (1996) 48(3) *World Politics* 297–323.

affairs so as not to destroy the society it is intended to protect. Intelligence agencies must protect society from internal and external threats, but must do so while respecting liberal democratic norms. Police must be capable of enforcing the law and maintaining public order without becoming an instrument of civil oppression, either at the behest of political actors or in pursuing its own agenda. Moreover, the security sector agencies should use society's resources only to the extent justified by the threat confronting the state, and must not extract state assets merely to increase their own strength.[14]

Civilian and social oversight of security sector agencies is a challenge in established democracies, and can be particularly daunting in transitional democracies. As discussed in the previous section, there is a need for oversight to prevent human rights abuses and provide accountability if they do occur, but there is a fine balance to be struck. Too much political involvement may open the security agencies up to partisan abuse, while too much oversight in the form of onerous reporting or regulatory requirements may undermine the security sector's capacity to provide basic security. Both outcomes can undermine transitions.

Civilian ministries

A relatively simple and effective way to achieve civilian oversight of the security sector, while decentralizing political control over each security agency and separating their functions and mission, is to establish civilian ministries at the apex of each agency's command structure. This helps to ensure that there is a civilian political office-holder who bears political responsibility for each security agency, and to whom each agency reports.

Civilian lines of authority are important in each security agency. Under authoritarian rule, the military may be used to reporting directly to a president; the interposition of a minister or even a prime minister may help curb the abuse of power and help guarantee the separation of powers among intelligence, police, and armed forces (as discussed earlier). Indonesia and Iraq provide examples of post-authoritarian constitutions in which the military has a direct relationship with the head of government (the President or Prime Minister), as 'Commander-in-Chief', with no obligation to report to a minister or political official other than the head of government. Contrast this with the position in South Africa's 1996 Constitution, which provides that the President is Commander-in-Chief of the Armed Forces in his or her capacity as head of the national executive. This requires the President to act as Commander-in-Chief only in consultation with the rest of his or her Cabinet.

[14] Peter D. Feaver, 'The Civil–Military Problematique: Huntington, Janowitz, and the Question of Civilian Control' (1996) 23(2) *Armed Forces & Society* 150.

South Africa's post-authoritarian Constitution builds on the limited political control afforded to the President by firmly locating political responsibility for the security services with distinct members of Cabinet. The Constitution provides that a member of Cabinet shall be responsible for the direction of each the security services—the armed forces, police, and intelligence service. In Argentina, one of the first changes President Alfonsín's democratically elected government made was to wrest administrative management of the armed forces from the military itself and vest it in the civilian bureaucracy under the Ministry of Defence.

Attention should also be paid to the development of a civil service that may have autonomy and neutrality to mediate between security agencies and elected representatives. South Africa's constitutional arrangements for civilian ministries politically responsible for security is bolstered by separate pieces of legislation that, respectively, cement the Department of Defence as a ministry within the executive, establish the national police secretariat as a civilian bureaucracy to oversee police conduct and monitor implementation of police policy, and establish the civilian Office of the Inspector General for Intelligence to monitor intelligence activities.

Kenya's approach has been similar, with the 2010 Constitution defining the national security organs as the Kenya Defence Forces, National Intelligence Service, and National Police Service and providing that each must be subject to civilian authority. Legislation in turn distinguishes between the powers and functions of the Cabinet member responsible for defence and the officer with ultimate military command over the armed forces. Civilian oversight of the police in Kenya has been a challenge, however, as a result of the proliferation of distinct police forces accountable to and taking command from distinct officers.

Chile faced a comparable problem in that under the Junta, political accountability for the police was removed from the Ministry of the Interior and placed under the Ministry of Defence. This facilitated the integration of the domestic police force with the military, and allowed the Junta to use both forces for the suppression of political opposition within Chile. The challenge of re-establishing civilian oversight of the security services was compounded in Chile by the fact that the former members of the Junta remained high-ranking members of the security services. The process of doing so was therefore gradual, with President Alwyin's government first moving administrative management, but not operational control, of the police from the Ministry of Defence to the Ministry of the Interior, and establishing the civilian Directorate of Public Security and Information to coordinate the functions of Chile's disparate police forces. The Ministry of the Interior did not regain full operational control of the police until statutory reform in 2005.

In Spain, the establishment of civilian control over the security sector, and the military in particular, took place over a period of time between Franco's death in 1975, the enactment of the new Constitution in 1978, and the consolidation of democracy by decree-law and statute after the failed 1981 *coup d'état*. The transition illustrates how establishing civilian ministries institutionally capable of exercising effective control over the security services and to which security officers are accountable can take some time, especially if security officers hold leverage in the transition. First, the idea of a single civilian Ministry of Defence was a change for the leaders of the Army, Air Force, and Navy, who had become accustomed under the Franco regime to a distinct ministry for each branch of the armed forces. Establishing a civilian ministry responsible for the armed forces thus required not only the institutional disestablishment of three separate ministries, but more importantly, a change in attitude among military leaders. This unified Ministry of Defence was not established until after the first democratic elections in June 1977.

Second, the military's insistence that it be considered an institution of the Spanish state alongside the government, rather than subject to it, resulted in a 1977 decree-law that provided, on the one hand, that the joint chiefs of the armed forces were subject to the command of the King but, on the other hand, were under the political authority of the government. This created two parallel lines of management for the armed forces: direct military command in the person of the King, with political oversight the function of the government.

This only changed with the 1980s defence statute, which provided that the joint chiefs of the armed forces were accountable to the President, who in turn exercised command through the Ministry of Defence. A further statute in 1984 provided that the joint chiefs of the armed forces serve the President in an advisory capacity only, cementing the executive's command over the armed forces.

Civilian ministries help to ensure that the security services operate transparently, and minimize the opportunities for politically motivated conduct on the part of security officials. Indeed, there may even be a case for each security agency to report to two separate ministries, on the argument that a dual report enhances the detection and prevention of abuse. To be sure, there will often be a need for coordination among all three agencies and other parts of government, but this can be done through the whole-of-government approaches reflected in the national security councils established, for example, in Kenya and Ghana. Needless to say, context matters and there are no guarantees. In Egypt and Tunisia, Interior Ministries separate from the military were renowned for their role in repression.

The process of appointing the chief of each security agency can help define lines of authority. There may be a long tradition of direct presidential appointment, but this may have to be changed to break patterns of presidential interference in day-to-day security matters. One way is to involve legislative committees, either *ex ante* in preparing a short list of candidates, or *ex post* in terms of ratification of the appointment. Where possible, appointments should be made by the minister who will be responsible for the agency, and not by the President. Recent amendments to Kenya's statutory provisions for the appointment and dismissal of Police Inspector General have, unfortunately, concentrated power in the hands of the President and raised fears that the Inspector General will become a partisan political actor.

Legislative and executive oversight

Legislative committees can be an effective means of exerting control over the security sector, both because they carry the weight of an electoral mandate and because their proceedings are generally open and transparent. On the other hand, legislative committees may lack expertise that would enable them to ask the right questions of the military, intelligence, and police. The Indonesian experience suggests that legislators may not only lack expertise but also be prone to corruption and that they may 'politicize' military and police matters. Another factor, common to established democracies as well as emerging ones, is that the electoral cycle and the lack of institutional memory in a constantly rotating institution may prevent the legislature from developing expertise on security matters. As with oversight in established democracies, developing democracies often face trade-offs between expertise and transparency.

One of the important takeaways of this volume is the close relationship between vigorous parliamentary participation in security sector affairs and democratic civil–security sector relations. Enhancing the legislature's clout—by increasing the authority of its committee(s) with carriage of security sector issues, and encouraging its substantive contribution to procedures and deliberations pertaining to the armed forces, intelligence agencies, and the police—should be a priority for democracy activists. In fact, the legislature's robust involvement in defence issues is usually a reliable predictor of democratic civil–military relations.

Comparative experience, however, counsels caution. We know the most about the role of legislative committees in overseeing the military: only in a few countries do legislatures play the kind of role necessary for properly balanced civilian control of the armed forces. This role comprises not just debating and passing of defence-related bills but, of crucial importance, taking an active part in three aspects of the armed forces' fiscal affairs: determining the process of how defence budgets are devised and by what institutions; participating in the formulation of the actual defence budget; and overseeing the disbursement and implementation of defence outlays, especially with respect to procurement. In our case studies, the two countries with a long-term record of active and vigorous parliamentary oversight are Spain and South Africa.

Legislative committees may have a greater incentive than executive watchdog bodies to conduct public hearings and they may be more responsive to civil society and media demands. The Chilean case study highlights that where legislative committees have access to secret information and are capable of initiating investigations at their own behest, they can effectively engage in focused review of security agencies. This flexibility is especially valuable given the frequency in which security sector oversight focusses on particular aspects of alleged abuse. For example, in Chile, the legislature formed an ad hoc committee to investigate a scandal regarding illegal surveillance of political leaders by military intelligence, ultimately making recommendations as to how to avoid such scandals in the future. Legislative committees, including ad hoc committees, able to investigate scandals of their own motion will be able to act on the information brought to light by civil society and the press. This establishes linkages between civil society and the legislature, and may help to encourage and foster an active and vigilant media and non-governmental organization (NGO) sector.

An important criterion of democratic governance—as we flagged at the outset—is that civilian control over the armed forces incorporates both the executive and legislative branches of government. More precisely, as Robert Dahl wrote, 'the civilians who control the military [and police] must themselves be subject to the democratic process'.[15] The legislature debates foreign policy and defence issues and ought to have the power to call on members of the executive branch, as well as the armed forces, to testify before it in open or closed hearings. An oversight committee's terms of reference may include a broad spectrum of matters, ranging from reporting progress made in a war, the acquisition of weapons systems, the expansion or reduction of periods of conscription, to appropriate levels of defence burden sharing within an international alliance. In democracies, parliamentarians enjoy the opportunity to advise or otherwise convey their opinions to the executive branch. The legislature's comparative advantage over the armed forces is with respect to its power to debate, vote, and monitor the implementation of the defence budget, and its deliberation and adoption of laws regulating civil–military relations.

However, there is an important role for executive institutions standing apart from civilian ministries as well, in the form of specialized watchdogs. Therefore, there is no necessity for emerging democracies to make a choice between either legislative or executive oversight. New democracies—as well as established ones—ought to pursue an institutional arrangement in which civilian oversight of security sector agencies is shared by these two branches of government.[16] For example, South Africa provides for both an executive watchdog and legislative oversight of its intelligence agency. An Inspector General is a civilian monitor who is nominated by the President but whose appointment must be confirmed by two-thirds of the National Assembly. This appointment process provides some safeguard against partisan abuse of the intelligence function. Requiring opposition leaders or parties to agree to the nomination could also address such concerns at the appointment stage. The role of the Inspector General is also supplemented by a fifteen-member standing legislative committee, which must reflect party representation in Parliament. Concerns have been raised in South Africa that secrecy

[15] Robert A. Dahl, *Democracy and Its Critics* (Yale University Press, 1989), 245.

[16] On the allocation of war powers between the executive and legislative branches, see Mariah Zeisberg, *War Powers: The Politics of Constitutional Authority* (Princeton University Press, 2015).

creates a barrier to oversight. As will be seen, secrecy is a dilemma that cannot easily be resolved.

Regardless of whether oversight is situated in legislative committees, in the watchdog arm of the executive, or in some combination of the two, access to secret and sensitive information is important to developing effective oversight. Yet access to such information carries with it many dilemmas, also seen in established democracies. Overseers who have access to secret information will almost always lack the authority to release that information over the government's objections. Indeed, the unilateral release of sensitive information has the potential to undermine the legitimacy of the entire security sector oversight structure, especially if it prevents security sector agencies from doing their job by exposing confidential sources, and methods and information shared in confidence with them, by other domestic or foreign agencies. At the same time, an overseer may lose credibility in civil society and the media if it is perceived to have sat on secret information of inappropriate conduct by a security agency. This suggests that thought needs to be given to having a legislated framework that sets out the competing interests in disclosure and non-disclosure of information and how they are to balanced, and then assigns this task to a credible mechanism for deciding whether the overseers can make secret information public in cases where the security agency or the government will not agree to disclosure. One candidate here is the judiciary, but there may also be alternative mechanisms within the executive that can engage in this assessment.

The goals of oversight should be clear. Most people associate oversight with a concern about the propriety of security sector conduct, especially in relation to human rights. This will continue to be an important goal of oversight, especially if the former regime was characterized by human rights abuses. At the same time, oversight can be aimed at monitoring the efficacy of security sector performance, including whether value for money is achieved and whether performance is hindered by a lack of training, equipment, or factors such as corruption and demoralization. Oversight for efficacy should not be ignored, given the importance of security for transitions, as well as the substantial budgets of security agencies for governments.

For any form of civilian oversight careful thought needs to be given to who the civilians that review various security agencies should be. In some contexts, the civilians will be chosen because they can help create public confidence in a perhaps discredited security agency. In other contexts, particular expertise, for example, in human rights or in the particular security sector agency being reviewed, may be required. In divided societies, and particularly in those where there is a history of security sector abuse of a certain segment of the population, it may be important to have representatives of that segment of the population represented in the oversight mechanism. Candidates for such representation will depend on the particular context, but could include women, and various racial, tribal, and religious minorities. Such representation may be especially important in transitional societies where the security sector agencies have gained a full or partial amnesty for their past deeds. Indeed, the establishment and operation of oversight mechanisms might be a continuation of ongoing process of transformative or restorative justice.

Oversight mechanisms should also be attentive to the treatment of political minorities.[17] The concern that security agencies, particularly the police and intelligence agencies, can be used against political dissenters will be a real concern in many transitional democracies. Thought should be given as to how parliamentary and even extra-parliamentary opposition parties will be represented in oversight mechanisms. In parliamentary systems, it may be possible to require consultation and even agreement of the opposition parties to key appointments within security sector agencies. Sectorial representation of salient groups, including the bar and the media, might also be appropriate in some contexts. Careful attention to who sits on oversight mechanisms can help create links between government and civil society, and such links may be vital to ensure a sustainable culture of oversight and accountability.

Societal oversight

The societal side is an indispensable component of the civil–security sector relations triangle that often falls beyond the scope of constitutional analysis because it lives outside a formal legal framework. In emerging democracies, the media must be free to investigate and report on the armed forces and security agencies, thereby acting as society's overseer. NGOs also fulfil an essential function in civil–military relations. Independent defence experts, who may work at think tanks, research institutes, or universities, produce policy-relevant research on military and security issues. Along with the media, it is their job to raise 'fire alarms' if they discover anti-democratic activities in the security establishment—such as corruption, political interference, human rights abuses, etc. In many newly democratizing states—especially in countries emerging from military rule where all defence-related expertise was monopolized by active duty military and security professionals—there is a shortage of independent defence expertise. Filling this vacuum quickly is a necessary task of the democratizing state.

The Kenyan case study reveals how in the vacuum of effective oversight by formal oversight institutions, civil society watchdogs, and NGOs have exposed police abuse. Indeed, the 2010 Constitution tries to bring societal oversight into institutional structures—for example, the police commission has 'three persons who have served the public with distinction' appointed by the President. Argentina, Chile, and Indonesia have been quite successful in fostering NGO sectors where

[17] See e.g. Zoltan Barany, 'Building National Armies after Civil War: Lessons from Bosnia, El Salvador, and Lebanon' (2014) 129(2) *Political Science Quarterly* 211–38.

more and more organizations have focused on international relations and security issues, producing important research and generating societal discussion. Of course, without formal processes for discipline and accountability, the revelations of civil society investigations may produce little change in the conduct and practice of errant security agencies. Legislative, executive, and independent oversight bodies may be necessary to ensure political consequences follow from civil society's scrutiny of the security sector.

Self-regulation by the security sector

One approach to regulating the conduct of the security sector in established democracies is to authorize the security sector agencies to exercise primary control over their own internal functions, with external command and control regulation as a secondary mechanism at best, and mostly as a last resort. Much will depend on context, and whether a particular security sector agency has effective internal disciplinary mechanisms. Although the use of military justice against civilians may often be repressive, military justice may have some advantages in dealing with misconduct within the military, including corruption. There is a strong international norm against military justice systems having jurisdiction over civilians.[18] In the new democratic systems in Chile, Argentina, and Indonesia it was important to circumscribe carefully the jurisdiction of military courts accustomed to reaching far into the realm of the civil courts to protect the position of the military rulers.[19]

Occupational norms—that is, more or less formal rules of conduct, discipline, and professionalism—may be weaker in the police and intelligence agencies than in the military, but should not be ignored when structuring oversight mechanisms. Even if these internal norms are not a resource that can be used as part of the oversight process, norms that encourage poor behaviour may be a barrier to oversight, and as such should be factored into the design of the oversight process. Respect for good internal norms of security sector agencies, and the cultivation of better internal norms through regional and other alliances (e.g. Spain's membership in NATO), can help build internal capital in the accountability process. It can also be a hedge against a demoralized and perhaps underpaid security agency simply giving up on its core mandate. Indeed, international and regional partners can strengthen both security agencies and their accountability and oversight structures.

[18] See Commission on Human Rights, United Nations Economic and Social Council, 'International Standard: Principles Governing the Administration of Justice through Military Tribunals' (2012), Principle 5.

[19] See e.g. Anthony W. Pereira, 'Virtual Legality Authoritarian Legacies and the Reform of Military Justice in Brazil, the Southern Cone, and Mexico' (2001) 34(5) *Comparative Political Studies* 555–74.

Constitutional and Legal Issues: Choice of Law and Sequencing

A critical issue that runs through all the case studies is which kind of legal instrument is best to implement the reforms discussed here in relation to internal separation of security sector agency functions and civilian oversight. Although it might be thought that provisions for the political control, structure, and oversight of the security sector are best entrenched in a new constitution, this may serve only to preserve the privilege of a security elite who wield great leverage over the transition process. The architects of transition must decide what role a constitution will play in SSR. There is a spectrum of options. A constitution may itself set out the structural and institutional details for the security sector, entrenching those details and making sure they cannot be changed except by following onerous amendment provisions. An intermediate position is for a constitution to play more of an agenda-setting role without entrenching the details of the new security sector; that is, the constitution sets out the normative and institutional baselines for security sector control and oversight, but leaves it to subsequent legislation to fill in the details. Yet another option is for a constitution to say nothing at all about the security sector, thus leaving the door open to further discussion as the transition to democracy proceeds. Of course, constitutional negotiators may choose among these options with respect to different aspects of the security sector, blending different choices in a single set of arrangements. Similarly, a country in transition may rely on one option at the time of the transition and move to a different option at a later date.

Choice of law: constitution, organic law, statute

The arrangements made during South Africa's and Kenya's constitutional transitions are examples of a hybrid approach to SSR. Many of the details of SSR in these countries have been entrenched in constitutions that are meant to serve as a driver of social and political transformation.[20] For example, these constitutions expressly require that commanding officers of the security services be accountable to a civilian member of Cabinet.

But both the South African and Kenyan Constitutions leave some important institutional details to be worked out later. Section 204 of the South African Constitution, for example, provides that national legislation for a civilian secretariat for the national defence force be enacted, but says nothing directly about the structure of the secretariat. However, the Constitution does set out the general principles and norms with which future institutional arrangements must be

[20] Karl Klare, 'Legal Culture and Transformative Constitutionalism' (1998) 14 *South African Journal on Human Rights* 146.

consistent. Both the Kenyan and South African Constitutions set normative baselines or foundations on which legislation structuring the security services in more detail must build, thus setting the agenda for subsequent legislative action.

Both the Kenyan and South Africa Constitutions aim for as much detail, comparatively speaking, as one sees in constitutional texts, but there will always be gaps that leave open the risk of abuse. Amendments to Kenya's police laws reduced the independence of the Inspector General of Police, and although these amendments were challenged as inconsistent with the 2010 Constitution, the Kenyan High Court held, reluctantly, that they were not. The adoption of legislation after the enactment of a new constitution could also be a vehicle for some degree of backsliding towards old habits. For example, there is a danger that security sector immunities that were left on the cutting-room floor in Tunisia may resurface in organic laws that will be enacted for various security agencies. On the other hand, it could also be argued that the enactment of laws that backslide after transitions, to accommodate concerns within the security agencies, can be preferable to the sort of military rebellions that occurred in Argentina and which lead to the enactment of amnesties for some security officials after the transition to democracy.

A constitution may also, in contrast, close the door to progressive SSR. Indonesia and Egypt stand as examples where constitutional provisions present a barrier to goals of SSR. In Egypt, the 2014 Constitution guarantees that the military will retain the power to control its own budget and demands that Cabinet members responsible for the military be drawn from the ranks of the military. These provisions limit the degree of civilian control over the military and ensure that the situation will last until the relevant constitutional provisions are amended. In Indonesia, constitutional provisions relating to the security sector did not effectively distinguish between the functions of the armed forces, police, and intelligence services, perpetuating one of the structural features that has facilitated security sector abuse in Indonesia. Early drafts of the 2014 Tunisian Constitution would have constitutionally entrenched broad immunities for security agencies, which could have served as a barrier to democracy. In Spain, proposals to entrench the police as part of the armed forces and to entrench a joint military council as an alternative to civilian control were made but, fortunately for the separation of functions and the assertion of civilian control, rejected by those drafting the Spanish Constitution of 1978. Entrenchment of such proposals would have made subsequent statutory reforms asserting civilian control impossible without constitutional amendments.

Formalizing arrangements in a constitution reduces the opportunities for future legislative restructuring of the security sector and can entrench the privileged position of a military or political elite even as it loosens its grip on power. Robust constitutional arrangements surrounding the security sector may be a component of a transition to democracy, but may conversely reflect the entrenched power of security agencies in the previous non-democratic regime.

If the security sector exerts a great deal of leverage over the transition, however, it may be difficult to avoid entrenching these arrangements in a constitution. At the same time, a security sector with slightly less leverage may reject the constitutionalization of provisions that tend to promote civilian control and oversight, meaning that SSR cannot take place through purely constitutional means. An alternative to constitutionalization is to allow the institutional arrangements for the security sector to be worked out in ordinary legislation or executive decrees. With no constitutional provisions requiring this legislation or setting baseline content for this legislation, the agenda for these changes will be set by the government of the day. This agenda may change with governments, and ordinary legislation can be easy to repeal or amend.

An intermediate option is to enact organic statutes constituting and regulating the security sector. In both Spain and Chile, organic laws require higher legislative thresholds to pass into law, and are accordingly more difficult to enact and amend than ordinary statutes (although less difficult to enact and amend than constitutional provisions). The more gradual transitions in Spain and Chile illustrate that even though the compromises necessary to begin the transition to democracy might make it impossible to entrench civilian control and oversight of the security sector in the Constitution, fundamental reforms can be achieved years later, and effectively consolidated, in the form of organic laws.

The enactment of organic or other laws pertaining to security agencies and their oversight, after a transitional constitution, provides an opportunity for solidifying and enriching the transition. It could help ensure that civil society takes an active interest in security sectors, and that the security agencies themselves are involved in ongoing processes of professionalization and adhering to democratic norms. This is, admittedly, an optimistic scenario.

There is a danger that constitutions may be lopsided if they make reference to either various forms of security coordination or civil oversight to the exclusion of the other. The entrenchment of elaborate forms of whole-of-government security coordination, such as security councils, without corresponding accountability mechanisms in the legislature or executive branches, can entrench an accountability gap,[21] if oversight never catches up to whole-of-government security coordination. Conversely, a constitution that is top heavy with oversight mechanisms and does not outline the functions of security agencies and provide for their coordination, may also be unbalanced and lead to extra-legal resistance ranging from coups to withdrawal of services by security agencies. As suggested earlier, whole-of-government approaches to security are now part of international best practice, and new constitutions and new democracies have a good opportunity to reflect this

[21] See e.g. Kent Roach, 'Review and Oversight of Intelligence in Canada: Expanding Accountability Gaps' in Zachary K. Goldman and Samuel J. Rascoff (eds), *Global Intellligence Oversight Governing Security in the Twenty-First Century* (Oxford University Press, 2016).

new reality by including whole-of-government security integration and oversight in new constitutions or statutes.

As a final note, it is worth mentioning that even in countries that take a minimalist approach to embedding security arrangements within a constitution, there may be a case for writing the powers that an executive can exercise into a constitution, and in particular doing so regarding the uses to which the security services can be put during a state of emergency. Emergency provisions can govern domestic uses of the military to respond to natural or man-made disasters or extreme threats to national security. Emergency provisions may impose increased accountability obligations on the executive and strict oversight responsibilities on the legislature. Consistent with the general principle that oversight and review should expand as the activities of security sector agencies do, there is also a case for imposing extraordinary oversight and reviews to match any emergency powers. While there is always a risk that emergency powers will be abused and provide a vehicle for the revival of the bad habits of the past, the invocation of emergency powers also has the important effect of signalling to both domestic and international civil society that a country is about to enter a period in which increased scrutiny of the security sector and executive's actions will be required.

Sequencing

Questions of timing also influence the choice among constitutions, organic laws, statutes, or executive decrees. The cases collected in this volume represent three broad scenarios of sequencing SSR and constitutional transition. In Argentina and Indonesia, the military loosened or lost its grip on political power and the transition from military rule to democracy—including some key elements of SSR—happened prior to constitutional change. In Chile, Ghana, and Spain, the constitutional transition preceded any meaningful SSR. The South African and Kenyan cases represent a third scenario, where significant SSR occurred simultaneously with the constitutional transition, through the provisions of the new constitutions themselves.

To a great extent, these variations in sequencing reflect the leverage of security sector agencies. In Argentina, the fall of the military Junta was swift, following defeat in the Malvinas. The changeover from military rule to democracy in 1983 was effected in part by executive decrees that were only later codified in legislation, and later reflected in constitutional reforms in 1994. In Argentina, a law limiting the military to responding to external threats was not enacted until 1988, five years after democracy was restored. This law was also subsequently endorsed and expanded in a 1992 Internal Security Act. Military and intelligence restructuring came even later, in 1998 and 2001, respectively.

By contrast, in Chile, the military had greater leverage and was able to enact many self-protective laws immediately before it left power, following its unexpected loss in a referendum on its continued rule. Despite its electoral loss, that military was still able to manage its exit from politics, and protected its position by securing budgets and pensions before it ever left power. These laws ultimately presented a challenge to SSR, and even though the constitutional transition in Chile was quick, it was not until decades later that SSR could be said to have occurred. Chile only saw the reform of its security council with the 2010 enactment of a new defence law, and the shifting of civilian control over the police from the Ministry of Defence to a Ministry of the Interior in 2011, many years after the transition.

Spain, too, is an example of a slow-burning transition with full democratization and the enactment of laws governing the security sector taking decades. The initial focus in post-Franco Spain was on preventing military interference in politics, which came at the cost of accepting military autonomy; a second consolidation period focused on democratic control of the military. Ghana, also a case where the constitutional transition preceded SSR—and was initiated by the military government—adopted a new constitution in 1992, but only reformed its intelligence function in 1996, through legislation that included both parliamentary and judicial oversight and the centralization of intelligence functions. That leverage has been the overriding factor is illustrated by Indonesia, where the military initiated and undertook SSR prior to, and in anticipation of, democratic reform, but did so in order to protect its own institutional prerogatives and withdraw from politics.

South Africa and Kenya are examples of countries where SSR and the constitutional transition happened more or less in parallel, with both countries deciding to have relatively elaborate provisions for security sector agencies in their constitutions. We view these cases as examples where security sector agencies had an intermediate degree of leverage, which led to SSR being part of the constitutional agenda where it could be negotiated along with other issues. We would argue that just as important, if not more so, is that South Africa may also have marked out a new way of looking at the relationship between security sector and constitutional reform, which recognized the intrinsic link between the abuse of the security sector and authoritarian control, and therefore regarded the Constitution as playing what we referred to earlier as an agenda-setting role in setting out some fundamental details, with the rest to be worked out through legislation.

The very notion of a transition implies distinct periods before and after a watershed moment, and a change in political regime, with radically differing governing arrangements under both. Framed this way, the idea of a transition may be misleading not only because of the complex range of choices regarding sequencing and instrument choice, but also if it discounts the need for continual fine-tuning and consolidation. Fine-tuning may be necessary both with respect to security sector function and organization, and oversight. Security threats will continue to evolve. Even if the external functions of the military and the internal functions of the police are accepted, the relative importance of each institution will vary with the nature of the prime security threat facing the country. The nature of security threats will also affect the contours of whole-of-government responses to security and the role of intelligence. The democratic governance challenges and processes of a country facing low and manageable security threats will be different from those of a country facing high security threats. A country focused on an external threat will face different challenges with its security sector agencies than a country focused on an internal threat. The importance of regional and other transnational alliances will also play a role with respect to all three main types of security sector agencies, and such alliances may place new and unexpected demands on security agencies.

Oversight no less than security will evolve with the times. The practice of established democracies suggests that oversight of security sector agencies will often focus on the latest revelations of wrongdoing. Although this may not be optimal, it is natural given the secrecy that pervades much security work, and the dramatic impact of particular security sector activities on human rights. Thought needs to be given to how different oversight structures will interact and what sort of work they will prioritize. For example, Kenya's Independent Policing Oversight Authority has a wide-ranging jurisdiction to hear complaints, propose administrative reforms to the police, and investigate and recommend prosecution for individual acts of misconduct. Oversight bodies will have to resolve the tensions between the emphasis they place on responding to individual acts of abuse and addressing systemic issues that have the potential to reduce similar acts of abuse in the future. Kenya also has a national police service commission which carries out vetting in part in an attempt to combat corruption. There is a danger that corruption and improper training within security agencies may negate oversight and reform efforts.

Even if oversight structures in the executive and legislature remain constant, they will need to engage with different segments of civil society and obtain different forms of technical assistance, depending on the current focus of limited oversight energies. A committee that is examining a spying scandal with threats to privacy may have a different composition or at least engage with different actors and experts than a committee examining allegations of disappearances or extrajudicial killings by the police, or one examining alleged human rights violation by the military.

Questions of the need to differentiate among security sector functions examined in the first part of this chapter may resurface at the oversight stage. The legal implication is that oversight mechanisms must be supple and flexible and have sufficient powers to enable them to follow the trail within government and to engage with appropriate persons both within and outside government to perform their vital functions.

Conclusion

This conclusion identifies overarching themes, and must of necessity attempt to abstract from the particular case studies while at the same time drawing on their rich contextual lessons. Although context matters, the case studies examined in this volume underline the recurring importance of a few themes.

First, there is a need to separate security functions and define them through transparent and durable means. Laws (or understandings) that the military will confine itself to national defence from external threats are a fundamental feature of successful transitions from military regimes. At the same time, however, a neat and stable distinction between external and internal threats is becoming more difficult to define accurately and apply firmly, given the globalization of security threats ranging from organized crime and terrorism to natural and man-made disasters and epidemics. This suggests that thought should be given to governing the legitimate circumstances in which the military can be used for internal purposes. Constitutional or statutory provisions governing emergencies may be a promising means of governance. When they are used, there is a case for matching the use of such extraordinary security powers with extraordinary oversight measures.

For the same reason, there is also a need to separate intelligence and policing functions. The combination of these functions has presented a threat to democracy in Ghana and Kenya. The separation of policing and intelligence provides an opportunity to subject the intelligence function to special oversight mechanisms commensurate to the threat that secret intelligence-gathering can pose to democracy and the rule of law. That being said, it is difficult and perhaps impossible to cabin the intelligence function, which can legitimately be used to inform the activities of not only the police and the military, but also other parts of government such as finance (i.e. money laundering, terrorism financing, cyber-crime, etc.), border control, transportation, and the like.

Second, one of the main challenges facing new and old democracies alike is the need to ensure that oversight keeps pace with the evolving character of security threats, and growing need for whole-of-government responses to them. A failure of government to provide security will erode the conditions of democracy. At the same time, democracy and the rule of law will be challenged by whole-of-government security responses that overtake and outmatch oversight both within government and civil society. The trick is to ensure that the democratic direction of security functions and oversight is designed to reflect and accommodate the evolving nature of whole-of-government responses to evolving and perhaps growing security threats.

Third, the case studies collectively warn against constitutional quick fixes. Early constitutionalization of SSR may simply reflect and reproduce the power of those forces under authoritarian regimes. For example, the constitutionalization of the idea that the police are part of the armed forces in Indonesia presents a barrier to reform, and to assert civilian control over, the police. Such a result was narrowly avoided during the negotiation of Spain's 1978 Constitution. Early drafts of the new Tunisian Constitution contained problematic immunity provisions for security officials, which were fortunately deleted from the final draft. Egypt's 2014 Constitution entrenches military power and frustrates attempts to subject such power to civilian control including on budgetary issues. South Africa and Kenya provide more promising examples of entrenching security sectors into the Constitution but even so, there is need for ongoing work that builds on constitutional foundations. Civilian control and accountability of the military, intelligence, and the police is a work-in-progress even in established democracies. Premature constitutionalization can entrench barriers to these difficult goals.

Fourth, just as there are no quick constitutional fixes, the case studies also illustrate that prosecuting those in the security sector for their past abuses may often have to be delayed or forgone in successful transitions to democracy. Many of the case studies have seen amnesties and/or the appointment of truth and reconciliation commissions. One exception is Argentina, but prosecutions in that country resulted in military rebellions and legislation restricting the prosecution of middle-ranking or senior officers.

Fifth, steps need to be taken in transitions to ensure that security agencies do not interfere in politics and do not violate human rights. Militaries, police, and intelligence agencies that accept democratic control and respect human rights are important hallmarks of democracy. However, reformers need to be careful not to kill their security sector patient with their remedies. Iraq stands as the most dramatic example of the need to ensure that security agencies fulfil their basic functions of protecting people from external and internal threats during a transitional process in which the fate of the security sector is a major issue. Egypt also underlines the danger that such threats can present to transitions. If security is lacking during a transition, the public will often demand security, even to the point of reconsidering or withdrawing their support for democratization. Even in countries with successful transitions, such as South Africa, Kenya, and Chile, there is a danger if the most advantaged in society attempt to opt out of the public security system by relying on private security. Democratic transitions cannot succeed without basic security, and it will be important to give public security agencies the funds, training, and motivation that they need to perform their basic functions. In the end, competent and accountable militaries, police, and intelligence agencies subject to continual democratic debate and control are essential features of a healthy democracy.

In closing, let us reiterate two key general themes that underpin this volume. First, although we can certainly identify best practices and optimal scenarios, there is no escaping the fact that a great deal depends on local conditions. As much as it would be convenient, there is no blueprint that can be adapted or used for every situation. So, for instance, while allowing the South Korean armed forces to continue their business activities would have been a serious mistake, it was an acceptable compromise in Indonesia. Organizing army units by ethnic group or religion generally impedes societal integration (e.g. in Ghana) but doing so in post-civil war settings (e.g. in Bosnia-Herzegovina) for a limited period of time may be the price to pay for stability and democratic consolidation. In other words, what makes eminent sense in one context may be a recipe for disaster in another. Good leadership helps as do good laws, well-crafted and long-lasting constitutions, sensible defence reforms, active parliamentary involvement, societal and media participation, and so on. And, as always, sheer luck plays a large role. At the end of the day, we must recognize that, as disappointing as it is, there is no sure-fire road map to democratization.

Second, it is worth remembering that there is no perfect democracy, there are no perfect civil–military relations, and the perfect constitution has yet to be written. True democracies are perennially engaged in the process of democratization. It is a continuous undertaking; as times change, new circumstances develop producing new challenges that require constant rethinking, adjustment, and improvement.[22] The most important objective for all countries, no matter where they are located on the imaginary 'emerging to consolidated democracies scale', is to keep advancing toward more democracy, more fairness, more equity, and more equal representation.

[22] See e.g. Larry Diamond, Marc F. Plattner, and Philip J. Costopoulos (eds), *Debates on Democratization* (Johns Hopkins University Press, 2010); and Zoltan Barany and Robert G. Moser (eds), *Is Democracy Exportable?* (Cambridge University Press, 2009).

Index

Note: For the benefit of digital users, indexed terms that span two pages (e.g., 52–53) may, on occasion, appear on only one of those pages.

The manufacturer's authorised representative in the EU for product safety is Oxford University Press España S.A. of el Parque Empresarial San Fernando de Henares, Avenida de Castilla, 2 – 28830 Madrid (www.oup.es/en or product.safety@oup.com). OUP España S.A. also acts as importer into Spain of products made by the manufacturer.

www.ingramcontent.com/pod-product-compliance
Lightning Source LLC
Chambersburg PA
CBHW051109160626
46752CB00004B/99

* 9 7 8 0 1 9 8 8 4 8 9 4 3 *